Goal to Goal

100 Seasons of Football at William and Mary

Fullback Jack Cloud (50) and quarterback Tom Mikula (36) lead William and Mary tailback Jack Bruce (33) around end for a gain against VMI on November 8, 1947 in Williamsburg. Photo by the Richmond Newspapers, Inc; courtesy of the W&M Sports Information Department.

Goal to Goal

100 Seasons of Football at William and Mary

By Wilford Kale,
Bob Moskowitz,
and Charles M. Holloway

Foreword by Dr. Davis Y. Paschall

The Botetourt Press
Williamsburg, Virginia
1997

For the late John Randolph, class of 1964,
William and Mary Athletic Director, 1985–95

and for all the William and Mary football players and coaches since 1893

© 1997, The William and Mary Athletic Educational Foundation
All rights reserved
Printed in the United States of America

William and Mary Athletic Educational Foundation
P.O. Box 399
Williamsburg, VA 23187-0399

Library of Congress Catalog Number 97-075139
ISBN 0-9660815-0-1

Contents

Part 1—The Players ... The Coaches ... The Seasons

Part 2—The Games ... The Statistics ... The Honors

Foreword

Goal to Goal is an informative saga of a hundred years of football that knits the generations each-to-each in spirit for William and Mary. The old familiar grid iron echoes the yell: "We will fight, fight, fight for the Indians!" And the nostalgic remembrance of hard-fought contests by teammates and supporters still makes the adrenaline flow faster for the "Green and Gold."

Wilford Kale conceived this publication during his student days working in the Athletic Department and as a reporter covering sports assignments for the College newspaper, *The Flat Hat,* and later when he served many years as Williamsburg bureau chief for the *Richmond Times-Dispatch.* The final inspiration stemmed from his authorship of the College's only illustrated history, *Hark Upon the Gale,* a cherished table-top treasure for so many alumni and friends of the College.

Charles M. Holloway, former director of university relations at William and Mary, and now a distinctive free-lance writer, along with Bob Moskowitz, a popular sports writer for the *Daily Press,* now retired, who covered William and Mary football for many years, assisted Kale in preparing several sections, and are to be commended. Dean Olson, longtime direc-

On the evening of October 21, 1967, following the Indians' 26-17 victory over Navy, several thousand W&M students gathered outside Blow Memorial Gymnasium to welcome the team home. Coach Marv Levy holds the game ball high above his head during the celebration. W&M President Dr. Davis Y. Paschall (upper left) holds a microphone after greeting the squad. Photo by Thomas L. Williams; courtesy of the W&M Sports Information Department.

Thirty years later, members of the 1967 team, gathered back on campus as Marv Levy, now head coach of the NFL's Buffalo Bills, was inducted into the W&M Athletic Hall of Fame. Left to right are Ted Zychowski, Terry Morton (seated), Ralph Beatty, Steve Slotnick, Eddie Herring, Levy, Mike Madden, Bob Shea, and Chip Young. Photo by C. James Gleason; courtesy of the Office of University Publications.

tor of publications, served ably in coordinating editing, photography, format, printing, and in "officiating" issues!

Extensive research detail reflects an objective effort for fairness to those "who played the game" as well as to the memorable "wins and losses." Above all, this book reinforces the belief that a strong sports program at William and Mary contributes to the classical concept of a sound mind in a sound body; it aids clear thought and heroic feeling; it is a revealer of character under pressure; it encourages the competitive spirit while respecting the values of teamwork; it provides a needed and wholesome release from tension emanating from classroom pressures; it builds a camaraderie from which lifetime friendships emerge; and it gives vitality and spirit to the campus.

As this exciting story grips the reader, the challenging admonition of Theodore Roosevelt comes to mind:

> It is not the critic who counts, not the man who points out how the strong man stumbles, or where the doers of deeds could have done better, the credit belongs to the man who was actually in the arena; whose face is marred by the dust, the sweat and the blood; who strives valiantly; who errs and comes short again and again; who knows the great enthusiasm, the great devotion and spends himself in a worthy cause; who at the best knows in the end the triumph of high achievement and who at the worst, if he fails, at least fails while daring greatly, so that his place shall never be with those cold and timid souls who know neither victory or defeat.

Davis Y. Paschall '32
President
The College of William and Mary
1960–71

Acknowledgments

Grateful appreciation to Douglas Morton, president, Morton Publishing Co., Englewood, Colorado for financially underwriting the publication of this book on behalf of the William and Mary Athletic Educational Foundation, which will receive all the proceeds from its sale.

Many people are due much credit for suppling material and information. Thanks to all the past William and Mary football players who offered their own "most memorable" football moment. Thanks to the dozens of persons who have encouraged this effort over the past six or seven years as the project was planned and developed.

S. Dean Olson, William and Mary's Director of Publications, has been the "bulldog" of this effort. We thank him sincerely for steering the book to its completion, for managing the day-to-day effort, for scanning hundreds of photographs, and for ensuring this would be a top quality product. Without Dean, *Goal to Goal* would never have been published.

The excellent layout of the book is the work of Mary Ann Williamson who took ideas and suggestions and wove them into this very fine format. She also served as principal copy editor, cleaning up poor phrases, keeping out redundancies, and helping ensure that the writing styles of authors did not get in the way of the reader. Thanks also to Louise Lambert Kale who helped with the editing of three chapters.

A special thanks and congratulations to C. James Gleason for his copy photography work, which in many cases enhanced the quality of existing photos and brought others from the depths to highly usable caliber.

Important recognition and thanks to Bob Jeffrey, Jr., who initially was one of the writers on this project. Unfortunately, he had to step aside after spending many hours researching and writing. Much of his work has been incorporated into Chapter 2. His research was thorough and strong, and we thank him for later reading the text and offering much needed suggestions.

We are also grateful to Bob Sheeran, Joe Agee, and Dudley Jensen for reading the text and providing help. Teri Edmundson's thorough proofreading helped eliminate many typographical errors.

Jean Elliott, W&M's aggressive and active Sports Information Director, also must be high on the list of those persons who pushed to get this book completed, along with Bobby Dwyer, executive director, W&M Athletic Educational Foundation (AEF). Jean was also there to help find photographs, to make telephone calls, to provide materials, and to do some last-minute proofreading.

Each of the authors wishes to thank a group of people for their special help.

Wilford Kale: Gratitude and love to my wife, Kelly, for all her patience, understanding, and perseverance, even through the birth of two children. A special thanks to Jackie Freeman, former W&M player and head coach, who provided a veritable encyclopedia of W&M football history from 1939 through 1956. Coach Freeman's numerous telephone conversations and portions of his own scrapbook helped provide much of the material used in Chapter 3. He gladly offered help whenever asked. Others also graciously loaned us scrapbooks to use: Al Vandeweghe, Jacqueline Phillips Allen, and James Kirkpatrick.

Thanks to William H. Millsaps, executive editor, *Richmond Times-Dispatch,* for allowing use of the paper's archives and photographs and some of the stories written by Kale. Thanks also to Kathy Albers of the paper's library staff for her dedicated and sometimes relentless archival work. Special appreciation goes to Kay Domine, university archivist at W&M's Swem Library, for her frequent extra help; to Will Molineux, editor of the Editorial Page, Newport News *Daily Press,* for arranging use of the paper's photographic library; and Frank Soden of Richmond, longtime broadcaster, for his help in compiling various lists.

We should not forget Heather Chesock, public relations director, Southern Conference, for her help, along with Brenda D. Sloan, special collections librarian at Mary Washington College; Virginia J. Renner, reader services librarian, The Huntington Library; Constance Novak, supervising librarian, New York Public Library Picture Collection; James H. Parkerson, Jr., general chairman, Khedive Temple in Norfolk; John Brinkley, clerk of the faculty, Hampden-Sydney College; and George Rudd, curator, Joyce Sports Collection, Hesburgh Library, University of Notre Dame.

Bob Moskowitz: Thanks to the Newport News *Daily Press;* the *Richmond Times-Dispatch;* and *The* (Norfolk) *Virginian-Pilot.*

Two individuals should be cited. Marv Levy's spirit of cooperation near the end of preseason training camp for the Buffalo Bills of the National Football League was far beyond the call of duty. He actually telephoned the writer three times in between a relentless crush of meetings. The word *gracious* hardly does him justice.

"Friend wife," JoAn, doesn't really understand football. She has been a high school English teacher and put her past to good use while asking probing questions that no one else in history could dream up. They helped whittle away words and clarify, at least to a goodly degree, the structure in Chapters 5 and 6.

Charles M. Holloway: Sincere thanks to Jean Elliott and all the W&M Sports Information staff for their personal help and the use of various publications, newsletters, and films. Special thanks to Bob Jeffrey for all his background notes and meticulous research.

Introduction

Oh Hail Indian Warrior Team,
Down the Field march on to Victory.
Hail, Brave, Old Indian Team
On the Warpath fight to Victory.
Swing Down the Field Today,
Goal to Goal for Indian Jubilee
And Raise the Silver, Green and Gold Today
William and Mary, V-I-C-T-O-R-Y.

Those are the words of the William and Mary Victory March written in 1949 by the late Rolfe Kennard '24. His great claim to W&M fame, one for which he was extremely proud, was the fact that he attended every William and Mary Homecoming from 1924 to 1995. His return in the fall of 1924 with several friends was, in fact, two years prior to the first official Homecoming program by the Society of the Alumni in 1926.

The Victory March tune, rarely heard now at William and Mary football games except at Homecoming, was written by Oliver C. Zinmeister, a member of the U.S. Marine Corps Band, who collaborated with Kennard. The first performance was in the spring of 1949 by the William and Mary Band under the direction of Professor Alan Stewart. The Victory March was played after every touchdown from 1949 until the early 1980s. It was very much part of the repertoire of W&M Marching Band

Tommy Korczowski (14) scoots down the field with Virginia Tech players in pursuit. Knox Ramsey (22) and teammate clear away the last defender in the 1946 touchdown dash. *Colonial Echo* photo; from the collection of Knox Ramsey.

directed from 1953 to 1984 by Charles R. Varner. When band directors changed, however, another William and Mary "tradition" was lost to the years.

"Goal to goal" is a term often used by commentators during football games, but its use as the title of this century look at William and Mary football comes from a line in the Victory March—"Goal to Goal for Indian Jubilee"—which seems fitting. Goal to goal is 100 yards, the size of a football field and the 100th season of William and Mary football was in 1994.

Michael Clemons takes off on a long run against VMI in 1986. Courtesy of the W&M Sports Information Department.

An introduction to William and Mary football came for me in the fall of 1962 after arriving on campus as a freshman. Part-time work was available in the Athletic Department, and Pappy Gooch, longtime business manager, would spin yarns about the lengendary William and Mary players, especially those from the era of the 1940s and 1950s. About twenty-five years later when Jean Elliott became the new Sports Information Director at the College, she asked me to provide historical vignettes for the home football programs. After six years or so, about twenty-five had been written and the idea for this book began to develop, again with her encouragement.

In this account we have tried to hit the high spots and the low ones. We have tried, with every opportunity, to discuss the major football years and the major participants in those years. We will, of course, leave some things and persons out. We apologize for that. It was our intention to be inclusive wherever possible. For those omitted, we have regrets.

William and Mary's football history is rich. The 100 plus seasons of football have been very exciting and eventful and many years, within their own context, have been legendary. Names have come down through the years: Driver, Matsu, Davis, "Buster," Lou, "Flyin'" Jack, the Iron Indians, Christie, and Green. We have attempted in this narrative to give a comprehensive overview of William and Mary football from its rag-tail beginnings to the "Big Time" and to its current Division I-AA successes.

—Wilford Kale
September 1997

Part I

The Players
The Coaches
The Seasons

The will to prepare is equally as important
as the will to win. ...
Thorough preparation is the gateway
to building confidence. ...
When you hit the basement,
don't give up, get up!

—Marv Levy, 1967

1

In the Beginning—It Was Football?
1893 to 1918

Wilford Kale

Football did not come easily to The College of William and Mary. Many colleges throughout Virginia and in other parts of the country had already fielded teams for years, and strong intercollegiate rivalries had developed by the time students at William and Mary began to talk about starting a football team in the early 1890s.

The reasons for the delay, however, were understandable. The little town of Williamsburg—Virginia's former colonial capital—and its small college were in a sad state of disrepair in the years following the Civil War. The conflict had raged near the community and in the surrounding woods and fields; battles were fought within sight of the College, and Union troops later encamped in the front yard.

Buildings at the school were severely damaged during the conflict, but the College struggled and reopened just months after the surrender at Appomattox of Gen. Robert E. Lee's Army of Northern Virginia. Later, William and Mary was forced to suspend classes for the 1868–69 term while the Main Building was rebuilt after being burned during the war and other facilities were repaired. It took time for both the institution and the town to recover.

Robert Morton Hughes, a 16-year-old Norfolk lad, described the scene in 1870 after he arrived for his freshman year at the College:

> Everything betokened poverty and paralysis. Some of the houses on Woodpecker [now Waller] Street still showed holes made by cannon in the battle of Williamsburg [fought in May 1862]. Houses were unpainted and dilapidated. The sidewalks and driveways were unpaved, the street unlighted, and the feeble lights from the new houses scattered along the street only made darkness visible. The

A rare early photograph of a Dartmouth College team practice in 1893, the year it won the Ivy League championship and football began at William and Mary. Note the "gridiron" effect of marking every five yards with a chalk line. Courtesy of the Dartmouth College Library.

Hair-pulling and head-knocking were part of football in 1887. Courtesy of the New York Public Library Picture Collection.

Harry Gass Humphreys

William and Mary's first football captain was Harry Gass (H. G.) Humphreys, who joined with C. L. Hepburn to help organize the College's initial team in 1893. Born in New York, Humphreys apparently learned about the game while living in the Washington, D.C., area.

Humphreys came to know the College while his father was stationed at nearby Fort Monroe and enrolled in 1891. Little is known of his College career, except his involvement with football in 1893. He played fullback and starred in the first game and scored touchdowns in the next two games—W&M's first football victories.

Humphreys, a member of Kappa Sigma, left the College in 1894. Later, he received his M.D. at the University of Pennsylvania and went on to a career in the U.S. Army, following his family's custom. His grandfather, Gen. Andrew Atkinson Humphreys, came to the College in May 1862, during the Peninsula Campaign, as chief engineer of the Army of the Potomac. Humphreys's great-great-grandfather was Joshua Humphreys, Philadelphia shipbuilder and architect of the frigate, *U.S. Constitution* ("*Old Ironsides*"). (—WK)

only "tapers to light the vale and hospitable ray" were the lights from the numerous bar rooms which lined Duke of Gloucester Street.

The nation's second-oldest institution of higher education had just a handful of male students. President Benjamin Stoddert Ewell, who with the entire student body had gone off to war in 1861, returned in 1865 and reopened its doors, but the glory of the antebellum South was gone forever, and so were the College's finances, lost in the ruins of the Confederate States of America.

Elsewhere in the nation's North and Northeast, colleges and universities flourished, unhampered by postwar problems. Academics were at a high level, and young men amused themselves with various sports, including a new game called "foot-ball"—a sport that had developed in the secondary schools of Europe and the United States in the 1860s.

Hughes reported that, in the early 1870s, the boys of the College "enjoyed long tramps in the country, hunting, fishing, skating, and a crude football at which any number could play."

Dr. William Glover Stannard, author and antiquarian in the 1920s, recalled his freshman year at William and Mary in 1875–76, and described college life in much the same fashion as Hughes. He wrote, however, in more detail about football:

> The Court House Green was the chief ball ground, and we once hung Mr. Montague Thompson in effigy from a tree in front of his house, for trying to get the city government to stop foot-ball playing on the green. His reason was that a mob, followed [*sic*] the ball, so frequently deluged his front yard.
>
> One of the two proudest moments in my life was in connection with the game of ball here. Archie Brooks was one of the most powerful, and at the same time, most active men I had ever seen. As an athlete he led the College. Once I happened to be in front of my side [in a football game].

The ball was rolling towards me with Archie following full tilt. I knew he would probably knock me so far that I would be out of the game for the day, and I would have given something handsome to be out of the way; but I was ashamed to carry out my desires and crouched low so that I would be hurt as little as possible.

Brooks was coming so fast and properly regarding me as a triangle to be brushed aside, could not check his pace and fell a cropper over my back. There I was, with the ball, and the great Archie Brooks on the ground with the breath knocked out of him. I kicked it, feeling as David must when he hit Goliath.

Thus, in the fall of 1875, a full eighteen years before a collegiate football team was fielded at William and Mary, students from the College enjoyed playing the game. Courthouse Green or the nearby Palace Green—the main cleared grounds near the school—were probably where students gathered to play.

Six years earlier, on a field in New Jersey, intercollegiate football marked its birth at three o'clock on November 6, 1869, when the team from the College of New Jersey (which in 1896 became Princeton University) accepted a challenge from a similar group of football-minded men at another of the nation's colonial schools, Rutgers College. The event, held in New Brunswick, New Jersey, on the Rutgers campus, was the nation's first intercollegiate football game.

What was the nature of football in those years?

According to Melissa Larson in her volume, *The Pictorial History of College Football,* there were few rules and no organization of the game in America in those early years; an inflated balloon-like ball, looking more like a soccer ball than anything else, was used.

The 1869 game in New Brunswick bore more resemblance to soccer, we are told, than to present-day football, because running with the ball was strictly prohibited and there were twenty-five players to a side. (There was another version of football being played in the Northeast. Termed the "Boston game," it was more akin to rugby, where the ball could be picked up and carried by a player until someone tackled him.)

A description of that first intercollegiate game noted that

To describe the varying fortunes of the match [play by play], would be a waste of labor, for every [play] was like the one before. There was the same headlong

A Winslow Homer engraving shows a soccer-style football match between "sophs and freshmen" at Harvard about 1857. Courtesy of Corbis-Bettmann.

This drawing depicts the first intercollegiate football game, played November 6, 1869, between Rutgers and Princeton. Courtesy of Rutgers, the State University of New Jersey.

running, wild shouting, and frantic kicking. In every [play] the cool goaltenders saved the Rutgers goal half a dozen times; in every [play] the heavy charger of the Princeton side overthrew everything he came in contact with; and in every action, just when the interest in one of those delightful rushes at the fence was culminating, the persecuted ball would fly for refuge into the next lot, and produce a cessation of hostilities until, after the invariable 'foul,' it was put in straight again.

So proclaimed the *Targum*, the Rutgers student newspaper.

Rutgers won the game, 6-4. Each goal counted as one point, and six points were needed for a win.

The sport caught on, and four years later on October 19, 1873, representatives of Princeton, Yale, Rutgers, and Columbia—all but Rutgers would ultimately form the heart of the Ivy League—met in New York City to establish formal rules to govern the new game:

- Scores could be made by kicking or butting the ball with the head across the opponent's goal line and under the crossbar.
- Players could not run with the ball.
- Passes could only be made laterally or backward.
- Tackling below the waist was prohibited.
- The field of play was to be 140 yards long and 70 yards wide.
- There were to be two forty-five-minute periods of play.

The first game played under the new rules was a 3-0 victory by Princeton over Yale.

Also in 1873, intercollegiate football moved south. The first intercollegiate game below the Mason-Dixon line was played in Lexington, Virginia, between the Virginia Military Institute and neighboring Washington College (now Washington and Lee University). Each squad consisted of some fifty players.

The game began to evolve in 1874 when the "Rugby Union" football rules gained popularity. These rules allowed running with the ball and permitted an oblong rather than a round ball. Touchdowns gained more points, and an extra-point kick for a goal after a touchdown was

Before the turn of the century, football was a brutal game as shown in this Frederic Remington woodcut. Courtesy of the Brompton Picture Library.

added. Distinctive team clothing first appeared in the Harvard game against McGill University in 1874. The Intercollegiate Football Association was formed in 1876. The first Midwestern collegiate game was played in 1879 between the University of Michigan and Racine (Wisconsin) College at a baseball park in Chicago.

All this was happening before an official football program appeared at William and Mary. The College faced major problems and did not have time for the luxury of intercollegiate athletics. Its finances had been ruined by the war, and the lack of funds made it difficult to attract distinguished faculty scholars who would, in turn, attract the numbers of students needed for the College to operate efficiently. This vicious cycle continued, and enrollment declined until there were only twelve students in July 1881.

Again, while many other colleges and universities across the nation flourished, William and Mary languished. During the "silent years" between 1881 and 1888, there were no students in the halls, although the College's Board of Visitors continued to function and faculty members were hired and fired.

"The old gray-haired President [Ewell] as each October comes around, goes to the college and has the college bell rung, as a formality to still retain the [royal] charter," the *Boston Christian Register* newspaper reported in 1886. The bell did ring again for students in the fall of 1888. The Virginia General Assembly had enacted legislation providing $10,000 annually to the College to establish a normal school for the education of male school teachers.

These new funds enabled the College to hire a much-needed faculty, a group later known as the Seven Wise Men. These professors attracted young men wanting to go to college in Williamsburg, and 104 students were registered by 1890.

Although football had been played by students at the College before the cessation of classes in the 1880s, no formal athletic programs appeared when the students returned. Efforts were spent to increase the academic prowess of the school. Students, it was felt, should spend their extra time on studies and other pursuits, such as literary societies.

Student editors of the *William and Mary College Monthly*, the literary journal published by the Philomathean and Phoenix literary societies, first raised the question of a football team for the College in the April 1891 issue. In an editorial, Harris L. Moss, editor-in-chief, wrote that "foot-ball

An early football game illustrates a French advertisement. Courtesy of Corbis-Bettmann.

MANUFACTURE FRANÇAISE D'ARMES ET CYCLES
LOIRE · ST ETIENNE · LOIRE

SPORTS ET JEUX

In 1892 the idea of a football team at William and Mary was first being discussed, but Princeton (in striped sweaters) had been playing intercollegiate football for twenty-four years. Courtesy of the University of Pennsylvania Sports Information Department.

Terrible injuries were normal in the game in the 1890s as depicted in this drawing titled, "Out of the Game, 1891." A number of players died during this era, when there was virtually no protective equipment. Courtesy of the New York Public Library Picture Collection.

seems to be all the rage" on other campuses and urged that the College organize football and baseball teams.

> We believe heartily in gymnasium work, but at this season of the year out-door exercise is much more preferable, and more conducive to good health. Although we have no gymnasium, we can easily come to the front in field sports. … We certainly have material with which we can break the records of many of our sister colleges.

Some intramural football teams appeared at William and Mary during the 1891–92 school year. In December 1892, the faculty received a petition "on behalf of certain members of the foot-ball club who wished to play a match game on Wednesday, Dec. 21, and asked for a suspension of lectures on that day." The faculty acceded, "with the understanding that like requests not be made too frequently." But it was still a game among students, not with a team outside of the College.

A year later, in 1893, the bicentennial of the College's chartering, the game of football achieved a new status. As the fall term opened in October, the Athletic Association, a student organization that was to govern athletics during the early years, set out to organize a football team.

Although the students apparently took the lead, the College administration voiced its approval. The *Virginia Gazette,* Williamsburg's weekly newspaper, reported:

> The Executive Committee of the Board of Visitors has showed their progressive ideas by encouraging our [football] team. Their encouragement did not consist of words alone, but it was of a more material nature—having made arrangements to have trees removed from a part of the rear campus, and the grounds leveled for a permanent football field.

This photograph of the first William and Mary team in 1893 is a prized archive possession. The members were: left to right, upper row—John W. Smith, substitute; Allan Campbell Tyson, substitute; Charles L. Hepburn, manager. Second row—Richard Haynes, halfback; Herbert Larrick, substitute; Robertson, center; John Campbell, left guard; Wade Hampton Brinkley, right guard. Third Row—P. F. Parker, end; R. Wesley Williams, substitute; Harry Gass Humphreys, fullback (captain); Oscar Lane, tackle. Bottom—Jack Brown, left tackle; Ben Rowe, right guard; Henry W. Lamb, quarterback; Lloyd P. Hepburn, halfback; and J. Jenkyn Davies, substitute. Courtesy of the University Archives, College of William and Mary.

This first campus field was located behind Old Main (today the Wren Building) parallel to Richmond Road in the area where Monroe Hall is now located. Contests in football, baseball, and later tennis were held in this area until the first Cary Field was constructed in 1907–08 farther down the road where the Bryan Complex was later built.

William and Mary College Monthly editor Jonathan Weymouth wrote an editorial in the November 1893 edition:

> It is with pleasure that we note the first athletic spirit in our college. For the past four or five years we have had no athletics worth speaking of, and no foot-ball team at all; but this team, under skillful management … was started and met with phenomenal success in the athletic arena.

> While we do not countenance the carrying of athletics to excess to the detriment of class work; yet a healthy athletic spirit shows to the world that the school or college is not the place of physical degeneration, but rather of the highest physical development, as well as mental, and that there is brawn as well as brain in our college.

Those student editorial words of the 1890s would play well among many segments of the William and Mary family today. Concerns among academics regarding the College's athletic role appear not to have changed much in the succeeding century. Students and the fabled Seven Wise Men faculty of the 1890s also were concerned, as faculty minutes attest, that football not detract from academic endeavors.

William and Mary played three games during its initial season, but none against collegiate opponents. The first contest was against a YMCA team from Norfolk; a second game was played on campus against a team called the Old Dominion Club, also from Norfolk; and the final game on Thanksgiving Day in Richmond was against Capitol City, a local athletic club.

It is important to note that the William and Mary faculty had to approve all these early football games, and, in fact, required that every request for the team to play outside Williamsburg be formally approved by a faculty vote.

John Lesslie Hall, faculty secretary, reported in faculty minutes in late October 1893 that a request had been received from the Athletic Association seeking permission for the football team to travel to Richmond to play the Richmond College team on November 11. Permission was granted, "provided each of the students engaged

Ivy League football was already under way when this drawing depicted the 1889 Princeton-Harvard game. Courtesy of Princeton University Office of Athletic Communication.

Charles L. Hepburn

Charles L. Hepburn should be considered the founder of William and Mary football. In the fall of 1893, this student from an extraordinary family brought together the College's first organized athletic team and helped establish the fledgling Athletic Association, the student-run organization that governed athletics in the days before the creation of the athletic department.

As the manager of the Athletic Association and an editor of one of the College's literary magazines, *The Phoenix,* he also was instrumental in lobbying for the first baseball team and for the development of later athletic policy.

Eldest son of the Rev. Sewell Hepburn and Selina Lloyd Powell Hepburn, Charles had already been teaching school for several years when he entered William and Mary in 1893. Having graduated from Episcopal High School in Alexandria in 1889, he possessed the credentials to become an instructor in the budding public school system there. However, with his family's support and blessing, he enrolled at the College, along with his younger brother Lloyd, to further his education.

The Powell family was prominent in Virginia educational and political circles. Hepburn's maternal grandfather, Charles Leven Powell, and his aunt, Rebecca Powell, taught school in Northern Virginia. Hepburn's letters to them provide a fascinating source of material on the life of the College in the 1890s.

Unlike most of the other students at W&M, Hepburn had prior experience in playing football, a new and developing game. He was one of the featured players at Episcopal High School.

"I have been playing football several times last week," he wrote to his "Aunt Beck" in November 1888. "I have been promoted [to] 3rd [team] from the 4th eleven. The boys say I play very well. I am going to get a football jacket ... if I can bring it within my means.

Other evidence of Hepburn's athletic and competitive nature is a story from his years at Episcopal. After his younger brother Sewell had been bullied by an older boy, Charles challenged the older foe to a bare knuckles boxing match, which went on for some fifteen to eighteen rounds before the bully lost.

By the time Hepburn arrived on campus, students had been pressing the College administration since 1891 for the establishment of a football team. The groundwork had been laid, and, under his leadership, progress was rapid. In October 1893, the *Virginia Gazette* reported, "The Athletic Club has been reorganized, the football teams have begun to play and a baseball nine will be organized shortly."

As manager of the Athletic Association, Hepburn not only recruited the students to play and trained those unfamiliar with the

Artwork from the
1901 *Colonial Echo.*

game of football, but also performed the duties of coach, business manager, trainer, equipment manager, and groundskeeper.

Initially, the team needed a place to practice and play. Informal games had been held on Court House Green for years, but Hepburn had other ideas. The *College Monthly* noted, "The grounds ... are in very bad condition. The cost [to repair them] ... should be nominal and not above what the association is able to pay."

Hepburn petitioned the Executive Committee of the Board of Visitors to defray expenses incurred in creating the College's first athletic grounds. The site along the Richmond Road side of campus where Monroe Hall now stands, was used until another field was constructed in 1907–08. He was reimbursed $17.60 for "improvement of the College campus."

William and Mary played three games during its first football season. After losing its first game, the team played Old Dominion (a club from Norfolk) in the second game, which the

Richmond Times-Dispatch called "the first game ever played on the [William and Mary] campus." Hepburn was at quarterback with his brother Lloyd playing end. The College won, 14-4. A crowd of 250 students and townspeople attended the contest and reportedly "yelled themselves hoarse."

The last game on Thanksgiving Day saw Hepburn providing the winning score in William and Mary's 8-6 victory over Capitol City. "Hepburn took it through the centre, got loose from the crowd, and scored again after a 50-yard run." It was his first and last touchdown for William and Mary.

A scrimmage between the University of Pennsylvania and Harvard in 1890 was captured in this chromoprint. Courtesy of Corbis-Bettmann.

After the season, Hepburn turned his considerable talents to shaping public opinion about athletics. *The Phoenix,* one of the literary society publications [along with *The Philomathean*], published the editorials. Although unsigned, his touch was evident in the March 1894 edition when *The Phoenix* promoted the establishment of a baseball team.

What is the matter with baseball? Here we have in college several men who would do well on the diamond, and yet we have no team. It is not that there is a lack of funds to start one. Through the kindness of the Board we have money ready for our athletic needs.

The College, in fact, organized its first regular baseball team that same spring. The writer ended with a visionary plea to those student-athletes who would follow:

But a great deal may yet be done. Organize the Association on a permanent basis; make its offices posts of honor; make it an influential institution. Let it work for a gymnasium; let it fix up the athletic field on the College grounds. We might ask for a field day after a while. The Faculty has given us encouragement, and we think they will do so in the future.

Hepburn did not see those wishes come true. Because of financial hardship, he and his brother left the College after the 1893–94 term.   (—WK)

An early photograph of Court House Green. Boys from town and the College are known to have played football here as early as 1875. From the 1906 *Colonial Echo*.

have written permission from home in a letter addressed to the authorities of the college." The Richmond game never took place.

At a faculty meeting on November 2, C. L. Hepburn and H. G. Humphreys petitioned on behalf of the football team "that lectures be suspended Monday, Nov. 6 at three p.m. to permit their team and its friends to enjoy a game with the Randolph-Macon team." Faculty approval again was given, but, again, no game materialized.

Finally, on November 9 the faculty approved a November 11 game in Norfolk, "provided they have permission from home." Apparently, some team members lacked permission, for some did not make the trip.

Two accounts of that first game against the YMCA team have been found. The *William and Mary College Monthly*, in its November 1893 edition, carried a detailed report:

> We can point with pride to the excellent record of our team during the season just closing, and we sincerely hope the good work will continue next year. We began with material entirely raw, but under the management of Mr. Hepburn and captainship of Mr. Humphreys, the team attained a high state of proficiency, which bore its fruit on the hard fought fields.
>
> The first game of the season was played November 11 in Norfolk with the YMCA team of that place. Our team was badly in need of practice, and the team was necessarily much disorganized on account of the absence of several of its members, who were unable to leave college.

The article continued:

> Considering these disadvantages, we think they did remarkably well to hold the score down to 16-4 in Norfolk's favor. The Williamsburg boys took the ball and started with a wedge, but gained very little. On three downs the Norfolks took the fall. Then by good running and interferences on their part, it was slowly worked down to the Williamsburg goal, and a touchdown was scored. Tunis failed to kick goal. The game went on in this way until YMCA scored three touchdowns. Time was then called for the first half with the score of 12-0 in Norfolk's favor. [A touchdown was four points and kicking a goal after the touchdown—today one extra point—was then two points.]

Early in the second half the YMCA team scored again, and soon after was made the prettiest play of the game. The Norfolks had the ball, and the quarter-back pitched it to Taylor, who fumbled it. [R. C.] Haynes, by a play for which he has since become famous, grappled it, and carried it past the home team's goal fifty yards away. Time was soon after called, the score standing, 16-4, in favor of the Norfolk boys.

The stars for W&M were Humphreys, Haynes, Robertson, and Brown.

The *Virginia Gazette* reported the results in its November 18, 1893, edition under the headline, "Norfolk Wins a Game. Team from the William and Mary College the Victims."

"About 250 people, many of whom were ladies, stood in the mud and shivered from the northeast wind Saturday afternoon to witness the game of foot-ball between the YMCA team and an eleven from William and Mary College at the YMCA park," the *Gazette* reported. "The condition of the grounds, more resembling, in some places, a marsh than a park, prevented any brilliant playing by either side, but did not prevent some hard work being done."

The paper noted that the W&M players lacked a "thorough knowledge of the game and on account of being too light, were not 'foemen worthy of steel,' yet it gave an opportunity for them to show their ability in team work."

The feature of the game was a sixty-yard run made by Haynes [W&M]. Taylor, [YMCA] quarter-back, fumbled in receiving it. Quickly as a flash Haynes secured [the ball] and dashing from among the players who were trying to find it, started off down the field. He had secured a start of about fifteen yards before the Norfolk boys had found out where the ball was. It was then a case of "the hare and the hounds" until the "hare" made a touch-down, which did not result in a goal.

William and Mary's team for that first game was composed of Haynes at right end, Brown at right tackle, Campbell at right guard, Robertson at center, Rowe at left guard, Sullivan at left tackle, Lane at left end, Lamb at quarterback, Davies at right halfback, Hepburn at left halfback, and Humphreys at fullback.

The next weekend, on November 18, W&M played its first football game on campus on the field carved out along Richmond Road by Hepburn and probably some other team players.

The *Richmond Dispatch* reported in a small headline, among some other sports items: "William and Mary's Defeat Old Dominion's."

The 1894 team played the College's first intercollegiate game against Hampden-Sydney College. Courtesy of the University Archives, College of William and Mary.

W&M football player is illustrated in 1903 *Colonial Echo*.

About 250 people gathered this evening to witness a very exciting and interesting game of football between the William and Mary College and Old Dominion (of Norfolk) teams. The score was 14 to 4 in favor of the college boys. This was the first game ever played on the campus. The weather was all that could be desired and the crowd, which was in sympathy with the home-players, yelled themselves hoarse.

William and Mary's touchdowns were made by Humphreys and Haynes, who scored twice. Humphreys also had one goal.

In the *College Monthly* account, W&M found itself down, 4-0, after the first five minutes against Old Dominion. Then the W&M team took over "by a good gain on the V, and with the help of fine end interference, the ball was carried to Norfolk's twenty-five yard line, when Humphreys took it around the right for a beautiful run and touch-down. He then kicked goal. Both teams worked hard after this, but the ball stayed near the middle until Norfolk's got twenty-five yards on a throttle, and pushed it by good center work to within ten yards of Williamsburg's line. Here Haynes got the sphere by his sleight of hand trick and scored four more points. Humphreys failed on goal and time was called." Haynes scored again for the second half's only score.

Players recounted that P. F. "Silent" Parker, W&M end, distinguished himself by throwing an opposing end over the fence that encircled the field "to the delight of the crowd."

The victory, the first ever for the College, paved the way for another victory in Richmond on Thanksgiving Day, when W&M defeated the Capitol City Athletic Club, 8-6, in an early morning contest. "Captain Humphreys was in luck with the coin once more, and chose the west goal with a favoring slope in the ground," the *College Monthly* magazine reported.

> Time was called at 11:30 a.m. as the Universities of Virginia and North Carolina were to play on the same ground in the evening. The ball was fumbled a great deal by both sides during the first half; so that very little pretty playing was done, and neither side scored.

First Touchdown

One curiosity of the inaugural William and Mary football game on November 11, 1893, was the story of the first touchdown scored by a College gridder.

It was described thirty-three years later by John Weymouth '94, in a letter to *The Flat Hat*, the student newspaper. Weymouth, who saw the College lose to Norfolk YMCA, 16-4 in Norfolk, wrote:

The hidden ball trick was invented by Dick Haynes, halfback, who plunged headfirst in a scrimmage, and in some way to possession of the ball, though no one knew it. When he had succeeded in disentangling himself, he started running toward the goal of the opposing team and everyone wondered why, as he did not appear to be chasing anyone and there was no one near him.

When he passed the crowd, a hump was discovered on his back, and we then saw that he had tucked the ball under the back of his blue jersey and was carrying it in that way, making a touchdown before any of the players really knew where the ball was. (—WK)

Early in the second the ball was carried to within 10 yards of William and Mary's goal by a beautiful run by Richardson, around his left end. Then Wibon carried it across for a score, and afterwards kicked goal. Soon after it was put into play again, on a fumble by Richmond, Williams got hold of it and ran forty yards for a touch-down. Humphreys missed the goal. Capitol City put the ball in play in a V, but William and Mary got it on downs. Hepburn then took it through the center, got loose from the crowd, and scored again after a fifty yard run. No goal kicked. Neither side made much after this, and time was soon called. Score, William and Mary, 8; Capitol City, 6.

"Both teams played badly, and showed sad lack of team work," the report concluded. Nevertheless, W&M's first football season was a winning one.

W. C. Johnson, editor and publisher of the *Virginia Gazette,* lauded the first year's football effort:

> The football team at William and Mary is doing a good job for so young an organization. … The pigskin is now resting … they will not play another game this season, having played three with two scores in their favor. This is simply remarkable. … They were wholly unacquainted with the game the first of last October, not a single man had been trained in athletics.

By the time W&M began playing football, the rules had begun to resemble those of today's game. Teams were allowed eleven men per side, instead of the original fifteen; the scrimmage of rugby was replaced by a scrimmage line; and teams were required to give up the ball if they failed to gain five yards (now ten) in four tries. The field, therefore, had to be marked in five-yard increments, a pattern which looked like a grate or a "gridiron."

The 1897 team posed next to the Wren Building for this picture. Team members are: standing, left to right— John Elliott, "Mary" Wilson, William Rickard, Alfred Anderson, and J. B. Hackley. Middle row—Roderick Triplett, Arthur Parker, Bill Shawen, John Woods, and John Counselman. Front row—Paul Garrow, Tom Brown, Phil Jones, John Tyler (mascot), and Paul Palmer. Courtesy of William and Mary Athletic Department.

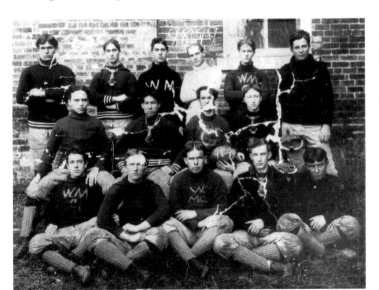

There was such a good feeling about athletics on the campus after the first football season that efforts began in March 1894 to establish a baseball team and other athletic programs.

In 1898, when this team photograph was taken, William and Mary played its first game against Richmond College (later the University of Richmond), beginning the longest football rivalry in the South and the fourth longest in the nation. From the 1899 *Colonial Echo.*

Yale developed the famed "flying wedge" in the early 1880s as a weapon to use against rival Princeton. The wedge was created by guards and tackles surrounding the ball carrier after the snap. Courtesy of Corbis-Bettmann.

The College's only game of 1894 was the program's first intercollegiate contest. In those early days of athletics, there was little formal organization, and games were often scheduled by the players, but more frequently by coaches or team captains. Unfortunately, games "scheduled" in that manner rarely took place, primarily because the W&M faculty still required permission letters from parents for team members to leave campus.

This apparently was the case on November 10, 1894. The *Richmond Daily Times* newspaper reported an item with the headline, "A Game That Was Not Played." Dateline Norfolk: "The foot-ball game scheduled for to-day between William & Mary and the Norfolk team did not come off this afternoon. William and Mary did not come to time and Norfolk was disappointed."

Two days later, however, the W&M team did travel to Southside Virginia to play Hampden-Sydney College (the name was often spelled "Hampden-Sidney" until 1927). The *Richmond Dispatch* reported in its November 13, 1894, edition: "Nearly the whole village turned out en masse Saturday evening to see Hampden-Sidney down William & Mary in a well-played game of foot-ball. The teams lined up at 3:30 p.m. sharp, William & Mary having the ball."

Hampden-Sydney scored three touchdowns, but W&M was at least on its opponent's 2-yard line when the first half ended. "After ten minute's intermission the game was called for the second half, Hampden-Sidney having the ball. The first touchdown in this half was made by Hampden-Sidney in two minutes. Three touchdowns were made in this half, all of them by Hampden-Sidney." The final score was 28-0. "William & Mary played a good up-hill game, but showed lack of training and practice, especially in the matter of tackling," the Richmond paper concluded.

An exceptionally charitable account of this first intercollegiate contest appeared in the December 1894 issue of the *Hampden-Sidney Magazine:*

The game was of great interest to the home boys, but we hear that the visitors were disappointingly surprised. However, when men have spent the night traveling and slept only a few hours in the morning, they are not supposed to be in good condition to play ball.

This photograph may be a posed shot for the yearbook. If not, it is the earliest known photograph of a W&M football game. From the 1899 *Colonial Echo.*

The Rev. W. J. King, the Presbyterian Church's minister, served as coach of W&M's teams in 1897, 1898, and 1900. He also served for several years as "director of physical culture." From the 1905 *Colonial Echo*.

This was the case with the Williamsburg boys, and though they played on with desperate determination, doing all that eleven good men could do, yet when time was called, Hampden-Sidney had scored 28, while William & Mary held a clean card. ... The boys from Williamsburg seemed to lack practice. Especially was their teamwork open to criticism. Then, too, many of their men tackled too high, and only one or two could "drop" for mass plays. But there were others who tackled well, especially Parker, Davies and Booker who went at the thing the right way, according to our idea.

Others rendering valuable service in tackling, but they were not sure [tacklers]. It is very seldom that one meets more perfect gentlemen, consequently the game lacked the unnecessary roughness which too often characterizes such contests.

The W&M team members for that first intercollegiate contest were: P. F. Parker (left end), J. A. Hardy (left tackle), G. B. Spidle (left guard), J. G. Campbell (center), E. C. S. Taliaferro (right guard), G. B. Nichol (right tackle), Scott Triplett (right end), J. J. Davies (quarterback), G. S. Booker (right half), F. Shawen (left half), and R. K. Slaughter (fullback), who also was team captain.

There is no record of a team coach during W&M's first two years of organized football.

There apparently were no games in 1895, possibly due to the students' lack of interest. Early in the year, the Athletic Association was organized with Ralph Leigh elected team captain and G. B. Nichol, who played right tackle on the 1894 team, named the team manager. "Arrangements have been made to secure Harry Holt of Hampton as trainer [coach?], and he is expected up in a few days, and if satisfactory arrangements can be made, will at once take charge of the team," the *Virginia Gazette* reported on October 18, 1895. Holt's name is not mentioned again.

Notice some of the members of the 1900 team are wearing shin guards, and their sweaters are decorated with a CWM cipher. From the 1901 *Colonial Echo*.

The *William and Mary College Monthly* reported in its November 1895 edition that athletic "interest manifested on the part of the students is encouraging and membership [in the Athletic Association] is good. Every afternoon the rear campus is alive with students, some getting in a few games of base-ball, before the cold weather closes the season; others practicing foot-ball, eager for promotion to our 'first team.' The manager of our [football] team has received a good many letters, but he has not been justified in making arrangement for our first game."

The *Virginia Gazette* also reported the organization of the Athletic Association, but there is no mention in its editions of a game being played against an outside opponent.

The tone of the *William and Mary College Monthly* had changed dramatically a month later in the December 1895 edition. The editor's note read:

> We wish to put before you this letter of appeal. It was signed "Athletics," who left us recently for worlds unknown. We feared lest we might never learn his where-abouts; but he has written us of his sad condition, and we commend his appeal to your consideration, hoping that someone will be found zealous enough to bring back our old friend.

This series of photographs was taken of the 1901 contest against Richmond College. The game was played on the first athletic field where Monroe Hall now stands. The homes in the background are along Richmond Road. From the 1902 *Colonial Echo*.

SNAPSHOTS TAKEN FROM GAME WITH RICHMOND COLLEGE. WILLIAM AND MARY DEFENDING EASTERN GOAL.

The letter lamented:

> It is true I have been weak and poorly developed, but I did what I could. Is my weakness a reason for your desertion? I should by this time be patronized largely by your students, and your cheeks should be aglow from my subtle influence. And had you given me the opportunity, I should have met my kindred spirits and rejoiced to contest with them. Why, you didn't even present me to the Board of Visitors this fall, and you turned your back on me now. … Will you not pity me in my forlorn condition?

Team players of 1899 proudly wear their athletic sweaters; team captain F. S. McCandlish is holding the football. Courtesy of the University Archives, College of William and Mary.

By March 1896, student attitude toward football and other athletic endeavors had shifted again. A *College Monthly* editorial declared:

> It is with a great deal of pleasure that we can say that an interest in ATHLETICS has been revived. The Athletic Association at a recent meeting elected as president Mr. H. C. Hughes and as secretary and treasurer Mr. W. C. Rickard. It is very gratifying to know that active steps are being taken toward training a base-ball team.

> The officers should bear in mind that our students have committed to them our interest in the field of athletics. To-day no college is complete without a well organized Athletic Association; and it is no small thing to have in charge the direct interests of so important a thing as a college. We need serious, earnest men in Athletics as in every-thing else we would have prosper and now in the name of the College at large, we congratulate you for the active preparations so far made, and so earnestly hope that the interest along this line may be not only maintained but increased, until William & Mary shall take her rightful place in this field among the colleges of the Old Dominion.

This enthusiasm carried over into the fall. The Athletic Association was organized with fifty-three members, and the *College Monthly* reported in its November 1896 edition: "The spirit of athletics is by no means wanting in our college this fall. … The principal feature just now is foot-ball, and the lovers of the pigskin have a practice game every evening when the weather permits."

The *College Monthly*'s next edition reported:

> The all-pervading subject that absorbs the student's mind has for some time been foot-ball. Attention has been called to the growing interest in this subject, and now it is talked about as nothing else. It is on everybody's tongue, and is a never-failing subject of mutual interest in all conversations.

The student who approaches another with an axe to grind, leads off on foot-ball as being something sure to awaken interest in the conversation. Friends make an easy exchange of greeting by reference to foot-ball. The technical terms of the game, happily used, lend telling force to what would ordinarily be hardly observed. On the campus, little knots soon come to discuss foot-ball; in the drawing-room and parlor, an awkward silence is easily broken up by a reference to the last game, or by a discussion of comparative merits of players.

Certain it is that foot-ball stands far ahead of what it has been for two or three years. There are several reasons for this. In the first place we have splendid material. Our team averages a good weight, and we have some men who are hard to handle. In the second place we have had a stronger and better organized effort to build up a team than ever before. Our team work is by no means perfect, but shows steady improvement. We have had two games with Randolph-Macon, with scores showing marked improvement.

The *College Monthly*'s "spin" on the 1896 season was optimistic in the extreme: these glowing words followed shutout defeats in the only two games of the season. Randolph-Macon won both, 10-0 and 4-0. W. P. Cole was W&M's captain, and for the first time the squad was called "the Orange and White," the school's first colors.

Robert G. Robb

Dr. Robert Gilchrist Robb, a W&M student in the 1890s and later Professor of Chemistry at the College, offered an unusual football claim. In one of his notebooks saved by his daughter Frances, the following notation is found:

I feel like I was the grandfather of football at William and Mary.

When I came to William and Mary in the Gay Nineties—the fall of ninety-three to be exact, I contributed a whole month's allowance—fifteen cents—towards the purchase of the first foot-ball ever used by the students of William and Mary. We weren't handicapped by any referee or umpire, but just chose-up sides and played on the Court House Green every afternoon till we wore that football to a frazzle.

Then the football season closed. It had to close—we couldn't finance two footballs in one season! (—WK)

The team's appearance and the fact that it held strong, good practices should be credited to the fact that there was a coach for the first time, a Mr. R. Armstrong, "so well known in the athletic world that the mere mention of his name is sufficient to identify him as the recent star player on the Varsity team of Yale where he graduated," reported the *College Monthly*.

As in many colleges of that era, debates were held at William and Mary on the merits of football and its relationship to academics. While the College faculty initially had very little interest in football or even athletics in general, they abided by the students' desires.

Thomas Jefferson Stubbs, one of the Seven Wise Men, eventually became a supporter of student athletics and later a patron of the baseball team. He also acted as chairman of the faculty committee entrusted with oversight of athletics. Rules were set to provide a structure for the developing athletic program, which also included baseball. Stubbs insisted on strict enforcement of the "Rules for Government of Athletics" established in 1896, especially those provisions for monthly progress reports on the academic status of each athlete, with immediate suspension from the team the penalty for anyone found neglecting his studies.

The *College Monthly,* in an 1896 edition, presented the football-versus-academics debate on the campus:

> Foot-ball establishes a point to be worked for, something to aim at. A great many men work for positions on the first team, and there is a spirit of emulation that pervades almost the whole school.
>
> The influence of foot-ball on a man's class standing has been discussed from beginning to end. There was a great outcry in the Yale faculty about this matter recently, and all manner of statistics were taken. The result was that every man on the Yale team stood above the average. The better physical condition of a ball player enables him to buckle down to work after the season, and make headway right along. In great measure the position of the faculty towards the team depends on the men that compose it, and if the fellows work conscientiously, make the game serve them, and not serve the game, their standing will not be injured. The most important point for the authorities to consider in this connection is that a good team, especially a winning team, draws students.

The 1901 team poses on the front steps of the "Old Main" (now the Sir Christopher Wren Building). Team coach, the Rev. Dr. W. J. King is left rear in suit. Henry "Doc" Billups, the College bellringer from 1888 until 1955 also poses with the team. From the 1902 *Colonial Echo.*

Football was becoming a routine part of the College's fall activities, but experienced coaches were lacking before 1897. The Presbyterian Church's new minister, the Rev. W. J. King, became W&M's coach in 1897 and apparently headed the team for three of the next four seasons. Described as a "clever athlete" in the *College Monthly,* he had impressive records at Hampden-Sydney College and later at Princeton University, where he had attended seminary.

The faculty agreed to encourage the Athletic Association's efforts to pursue greater athletic success by granting its petition that afternoon lectures begin at 2:30 so they would be complete earlier, allowing more time for football practice games before dark.

While intercollegiate football games were few—only one game was played in 1897—football activity on the campus "permeated the whole" school. "Indeed, for breakfast, for dinner and for supper, we have football," the *College Monthly* reported. "Each man has his opinion as to who did the most scientific playing, and whose fault it was that the touch-down was not made. Indeed, you find fellows who are packed with football lore, who would even apply for the instructorship, if that department were established in college, and who set at naught such unpopular trash as English, Math, or Greek."

There was such a rivalry between the first and second College teams, evening after evening, that injuries proliferated. Teams were also organized for the Brafferton and Taliaferro dormitories and among the various boarding houses in town.

The lone collegiate game of 1897 took place November 6 between the College and Columbian (later George Washington) University, which won, 26-0. William and Mary's poor playing was attributed to a lack of practice because of the late opening of the College.

The Reverend King had another chance to improve the College's football lot the next year, which also marked the beginning of the rivalry with "the college up the road" in Richmond. The W&M and Richmond College games would eventually become the longest football series in the South and the fourth longest in U.S. intercollegiate football.

Traditionally, William and Mary began classes later than most other colleges in Virginia, and games scheduled in October afforded the men little time for practice. Thus, the two 1898 games against Randolph-Macon and Richmond College were played in November.

Accounts of the games were different and lacked the color of today's narratives. For example, on the Randolph-Macon game, the *College Monthly* reported: "On the third down, W&M lost the ball, but by hard work soon captured it again; and using her backs and ends to the greatest advantage, carried it steadily down the field to R-M's five-yard line, where by a mass play, [W. M.] Hackley, our doughty left-end, was pushed across the touch-line, scoring 5 points for W&M. O. Barron, on account of the strong wind blowing, failed to kick goal." (Touchdowns now counted for five points, and goals, or extra points, were two points.)

On November 30, the College team traveled to the capital city to play Richmond at Broad Street Park. The *Richmond Dispatch* reported that the 15-0 triumph by Richmond was a case of "triumph of skill over matter for though the home team was outweighed by 99 pounds, they pressed their opponents from whistle to whistle and whitewashed them."

Although W&M lost its first game against Richmond College, a strong rivalry began to develop almost immediately and would increase in intensity through at least the next hundred or so games. Many a time, a successful season for W&M would be decided, not by a winning season, but by a victory over Richmond.

There was an official schedule of games for the first time in 1899, with five contests arranged. W. H. Burke

Captain Oscar L. Shewmake (middle with football on his knee) poses with colleagues of the 1902 team. Shewmake also was captain of the 1901 team and was involved with W&M football for the next fifty years. From the 1903 *Colonial Echo.*

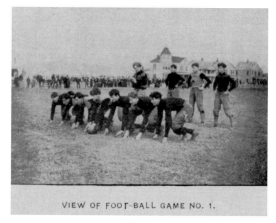

VIEW OF FOOT-BALL GAME NO. 1.

VIEW OF GAME NO. 2.

Photographs of the 1904 home games. Game one opponent was Norfolk High School followed by the Portsmouth Athletic Club, Richmond College, and Randolph-Macon College. From the 1905 *Colonial Echo.*

VIEW OF GAME NO. 3.

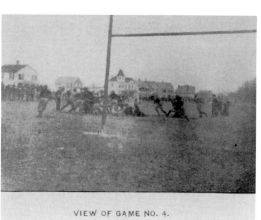

VIEW OF GAME NO. 4.

of Hampton apparently served as the "trainer"/coach. The Reverend King's ministry had evidently caused him to give up coaching, although he remained "director of physical culture" at the College. The *College Monthly* reported a high degree of student interest in athletics, "for now no college is up-to-date without a good football and baseball team. We have one of the best football teams this year that we have had for some years, and it is hoped that the boys will win a good reputation before the season closes."

Richmond won the opening game, 14-0, perhaps because W&M's team had been in training only ten days, and several of the players had never been in a game before. Richmond's team consisted entirely of experienced players and had already played two games.

Hampden-Sydney handed the College its second shutout, 6-0. The *College Monthly* praised the team for a scoreless first half, noting: "After hammering our line for sometime, they had the ball within three yards of a touchdown. Here is where William and Mary did good line work." Hampden-Sydney scored early in the second half while the clubs played stand-off ball the rest of the game.

Portsmouth Athletic Club gave the College its third straight loss of the season, before the team turned things around with a 41-0 victory over the Hampton Athletic Club. William and Mary scored within four minutes of the Hampton kickoff, and touchdowns and goals mounted up. R. E. Phillips kicked six goals of the seven he attempted and was one of the game's stars, along with L. H. B. McCandlish.

The season's last game was against Baltimore City Club on the Soldier's Home gridiron in Newport News and was seen by about four thousand persons, the largest crowd to witness an early W&M game. "There were many ladies present who wore long streamers of ribbon, signifying their choice of the two schools," the *College Monthly* reported. "The contest was a battle royal, and was interspersed with a number of brilliant plays made by each eleven. Every point in the game was contested in a manly and fearless manner." Baltimore scored in the last two seconds of the half on a 40-yard place kick, scoring 5 points. Later, halfback McCandlish raced 35 yards around end, setting up a touchdown for halfback Curtis. Phillips kicked for 2 points in the College's 6-5 win.

At the turn of the century, there were no helmets or pads. Teams wore jerseys or shorts with snug-fitting canvas jackets over them. Football was fast becoming a brutal game, and serious injuries were common. Games

This rear view of the Wren Building in the late 1890s shows a portion of the new athletic field. Notice what appear to be blocking dummies in front of the Great Hall wing. Courtesy of the University Archives, College of William and Mary.

were hair-pulling, shin-cracking affairs, and the "flying wedge"—with its principle of mass momentum—became a common play. Football was raw and untamed, but that would change in 1905.

The 1900 season began with gloomy prospects as only two members from the 1899 team returned, although the Reverend King was back as coach. Because of the continuing late start of classes, the entire season was played in November. The lone victory came against Newport News Athletic Club, with shutout losses in intercollegiate contests to Hampden-Sydney and Randolph-Macon.

After its initial winning season in 1893, the College team did not have another winning season until 1901. In fact, the school won only one game against another college during that time, defeating Randolph-Macon 5-0 in 1898.

The 1901 season was distinguished by the fact that two of

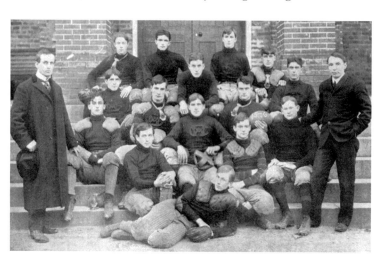

The 1904 football team posted a 3-3 season. Note the rudimentary shoulder pads some players were wearing. From the 1905 *Colonial Echo*.

J. Merrill Blanchard coached College teams in 1904, 1905, and 1910. From the 1906 *Colonial Echo.*

the four games were never finished. After an opening 11-6 victory against Old Point Comfort College, W&M played Randolph-Macon to a scoreless tie, with the Ashland team finally leaving the field because W&M refused to continue playing.

The *College Monthly* reported: "We could stand being penalized in the first half for an offense which could be conceived only by the most fertile imagination, and thus kept from scoring, but when, in the last half, our boys by a supreme effort held the visitors for three downs right under the goal posts, and then were not permitted to take the ball, it was just a little too much."

After losing to Richmond, 27-11, W&M tried to play Fredericksburg College, but after seventeen minutes of play, Fredericksburg protested a referee's decision and finally left the field, forfeiting the game. The Reverend King reported to the faculty that an overzealous student, J. H. Harnsberger, had attacked the opposing Fredericksburg team.

"Without any provocation Mr. Harnsberger broke through the lines and struck one of the visiting team over the head with a stick, and came near to precipitating a riot. Afterwards he came back a second time and I took him by the collar and carried him from the field," King said.

Another scheduled game with Richmond was cancelled by Richmond "much to the disappointment of our boys who were anxious for a chance to redeem in Richmond the game they had lost here," the *College Monthly* reported.

In addition to the play of the "regular" College football team, each class fielded an intramural team. In 1901, since no team players could participate in intramurals, there were no senior or junior class teams, but the sophomores and freshman "ducs" played, with the victorious sophomores getting their team photograph in the 1902 *Colonial Echo,* the College yearbook.

At this time, the College was building its first gymnasium, touted as "one of the finest in the South," with up-to-date equipment. This facility and the efforts of the Reverend King caused a resurgence in many other sports, especially those associated with a gymnasium, such as basketball and gymnastic-type events.

There is no record of a coach for the 1901 team, although the Reverend King continued as physical education director. The season was only the school's second winning campaign (2-1-1) since 1893. But the year's loss was to Richmond, the team that was quickly becoming W&M's biggest rival.

1905 football captain C. E. Johnson and team business manager J. A. Carson are surrounded by team members in this photographic montage in the 1906 *Colonial Echo.*

Unfortunately, schedules were still being developed by the team's managers and were haphazard at best. The season, however, was composed completely of college-team opposition—Randolph-Macon College, Richmond College, Fredericksburg College, and Old Point Comfort College. The latter two institutions have long-since vanished.

The College's Athletic Association, which continued to be run by students, held a mass meeting in October 1902 in support of its football program. The Reverend King "did much to show what is necessary for the success of our football team this season. Especially did he emphasize the absolute necessity of enthusiasm and financial support on the part of the whole student body," the *College Monthly* reported.

The Association's officers lamented the fact that there were no funds available to hire a coach from "outside" the College, and the team that fall had little training. "This to use an undignified expression is indeed hard luck, for William and Mary has as good material for football as is to be found in any college in the state. We hope that our team may yet succeed in overcoming all of its many disadvantages, and in the end give a good account of itself," the magazine explained.

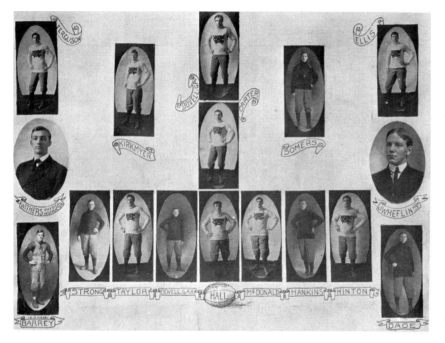

An elaborate representation of the 1906 football team. Team captain, G. G. Hankins is third from lower right. From the 1907 *Colonial Echo*.

The opener against Old Point Comfort College was against a team comprised not of students, but rather of soldiers, sailors, laborers, and ex-collegemen from nearby Fort Monroe. Nevertheless, W&M triumphed, 6-0.

Hampden-Sydney trounced the Orange and White, 42-0, in W&M's second encounter of the season. "The only comment to be made is that our team, made up partly of substitutes and having had no coaching and little practice, was no match for their well-trained opponents," the *College Monthly* noted.

A game with Hoge Military Academy in Blackstone was cancelled by W&M's captain, Oscar L. Shewmake, because the Academy did not send students to play, but rather fielded a team consisting of railroad men, businessmen, and Hampden-Sydney substitutes.

Coach H. W. Withers, who headed the 1906 team, was joined in mid-season by James H. Berry. Withers served for several years as W&M's "Physical Director." From the 1907 *Colonial Echo*.

The 1907 team compiled the most wins—six—of any squad in the College's history. Coach James H. Berry (extreme right, under post) was well liked and successful, but was not retained. From the 1908 *Colonial Echo.*

The game against St. Vincent's Academy of Newport News ended in a scoreless tie and unexpectedly became the last game of the season. During the first half, Shewmake suffered a broken leg, which seriously weakened the team's offense. As a result, the remainder of the season's games were cancelled and the team disbanded.

Shewmake's name was associated with the College and its sports programs for some fifty years. He served as a member of the Board of Visitors from 1919 to 1921 prior to becoming dean of economics and law and professor of constitutional history from 1921 to 1923. While dean, he was involved with the athletic program. He returned as a Board member from 1940 to 1952 and served on the Board's Athletic Committee.

The *College Monthly* called for the football players to get ready for the 1903 season and "to never again enter the intercollegiate arena with a football team until our advantages are equal to those of the other colleges in our State which are in our class."

The Athletic Association's organizational meeting of 1903 established regulations governing the winning and wearing of the College monogram (athletic letter), and retained orange and white as the official colors for the College's athletic teams.

Yearbook art had not improved much in this representation of the 1908 football team in the 1909 *Colonial Echo.*

Unlike the other athletic teams featured in the 1910 *Colonial Echo,* the 1909 football team picture was a composite of head shots rather than a group photograph.

"The Foot-ball Man"

A letter from *The William and Mary College Monthly*, Vol. 9, No. 2 (December 1899).

Dear Billie: The foot ball season is now on and I am in it. Caesar, Cicero, Pestalozzi and other kindred fossils occupy a back seat at present. The Binomial Theorem has to be dusted every time I use it, which is seldom, quite seldom. The following is the day's programme: In the morning I get up at five and take a cool bath in sausage gravy. Immediately after this I run four miles; then comes a hearty breakfast of rubber balls and mushrooms. At nine I go to the Chemistry Class and "cork" on every question. At ten we have a delightful luncheon of paper collars and garlic, washed down with a jorum of ale. Eleven o'clock is the hour for "skipping" Math. and skipping rope ten minutes.

From twelve to one we hop around the campus on one foot; from one to two we hop around on the other foot; then we use both in rushing to dinner, which dinner, by the way, usually consists of huckleberry quadrants and Saratoga chips. Our first afternoon lecture is German; two days in the week I jump this altogether; the remaining four my toothache pulls me through. Four o'clock is the time set for afternoon practice. In order to be on time for this I must "skip" Literature. Julius Caesar is on the "Boards" at present, but he isn't as lively as foot ball. For supper we are allowed by our trainer a spoonful of beef tea and a Uneeda Jinger Wayfer. From seven until nine thirty we study our signals, which are very fine this year. I give you some of them,

"2—4—6—8—Boom," which being interpreted means, "Right guard break through Tackle and reduce the eye teeth of the Left Halfback."

"X—Y—Z, Turnips," "Centre, rush butt Left Guard in pit of stomach and dislocate right Half-back's jaw."

"Unus, duo, tres, hit 'em;" "kill the right end and send for the undertaker;" and there are several others fully as good as those I have given you.

We haven't been beaten this year. We have our first game with B&G on Thursday, at which time we are expecting a walk-over.

Miss Fluffy Bangs is working some exceedingly handsome colors for us. She is not handsome, but quite stylish.

My hair is eighteen inches long. "Bump" Thompkins, however, has the finest head on the team. He is the envy of the whole aggregation. His bangs are five feet long, and when the season is over he will donate the cutting to the faculty to make cushions for the Chapel chairs.

Good Bye, Yours all the time, Bob—Nat Prune."   (—WK)

James G. Driver was the College's first great athletic star. He was a four-letter man in football, baseball, basketball, and track and captained the 1909 gridiron team. From the 1910 *Colonial Echo*.

After two years without an official coach, the team secured H. J. Duvall of Cornell, who had coached one year at his alma mater and one year at the University of West Virginia. Some members of the 1902 team did not return, but the College tried to mount a competitive squad, just as the students had requested. Unfortunately, the game against Norfolk High School produced the only victory of the season; there were three shutout losses to other Virginia college teams.

Old Point Comfort College took revenge for two earlier defeats to trounce the College, 23-0, while Richmond and Randolph-Macon "out-played and out-weighed" the College team, 24-0 and 39-0, respectively. Again, the students lamented their defeats, but they did not deride Coach Duvall, calling him "the finest coach available."

An editorial in the student magazine by James Southall Wilson, who later wrote the College's "Alma Mater," called for a change in the opening date of school and the rearrangement of lecture schedules as ways of making it easier for the school to field a competitive team. If these changes were made, Wilson wrote, "if the powers-that-be in college interest themselves in what the boys are interested in, and thus increase that interest … only then shall it be possible for Victory to deck herself in the good old colors of orange and white."

In 1904 William and Mary became a member of the Eastern Division of the Virginia Collegiate Athletic Association, along with Richmond and Randolph-Macon. The first year of "conference" competition resulted in a better football season.

The 1910 team had a poor record, the first of a decade-long series of losing seasons that plagued W&M football. Captain W. B. Lee, Jr., who was also captain in 1911, holds the football. Notice the crutches carried by one team member. From the 1911 *Colonial Echo*.

Captain W. B. Lee, Jr., holds the football as the 1911 team poses for photo. The ball, like others of the era was numbered for easy identification. W&M won only once, scored only 14 points, and was shut out in five of its seven games. From the 1912 *Colonial Echo*.

Dr. William J. Young was the first full-time coach and physical director employed. He coached football in 1911 and 1912. Notice his "P" letter sweater from the University of Pennsylvania, where he received his M.D. From the 1912 *Colonial Echo*.

The increased prestige of membership in a conference notwithstanding, the team was prohibited by town ordinance from practicing on the Court House Green. The *Virginia Gazette* reported on October 14, 1904: "Does an hour's practice on the precious green when the ground is firm hurt it as much as twenty or thirty cows walking over it miring up to their knees when the ground is soft and miry? But the cows belong to Williamsburg, so does the green." This action later helped push the College toward developing a new athletic field.

The 1904 season also saw what was described as one of W&M's "brightest victories" in the school's short gridiron history. It was the first win over Richmond, 15-6. Played at the campus field, the game featured two W&M touchdowns in the first half. "The time between the halves was spent by the student body in marching around the field and singing as they marched, 'Hike along William and Mary.' They gathered in the center of the field and gave cheer after cheer for the team," the *College Monthly* reported.

Richmond scored early in the second half and later tried an unsuccessful field goal. The Orange and White's last score came late in the game. "Amid wild enthusiasm the victors were borne off the field on the shoulders of admiring fellow-students," the student literary magazine reported.

The last game of the season, a 6-0 loss to Randolph-Macon, prompted a protest to the new football league because William and Mary felt it should have claimed victory. A place-kick (field goal) was attempted, but officials ruled that William and Mary touched the missed kick before Randolph-Macon. Therefore, it was not ruled an Orange and White score. "The game was contested hotly over every inch

The 1912 W&M team, depicted on these two yearbook pages are easily the "best dressed" team in the first twenty years of W&M football. From the 1913 *Colonial Echo*.

A photograph of action during a 1914 game. From the 1915 *Colonial Echo.*

of ground," the *Richmond Times-Dispatch* reported on November 20. "The sensational plays of [William and Mary] were features that elicited a delirium of applause from the sightseers. From start to finish the game was a battle royal, and it was only by heroic efforts and endurance that the visitors were able to score in the second half. Three times did William and Mary come within an ace of making a touchdown."

Another mediocre football year came in 1905, but W&M did defeat Richmond College again, 4-0, in one of three games played against the Richmond team that year. The College also entertained its first out-of-state team, Maryland Agriculture College (later the University of Maryland), losing to the visiting team on the campus field.

The year marked the beginning of a fuller football schedule with seven games played. Eight games were played in 1906, including the College's first out-of-state trip. The team traveled to Raleigh, North Carolina, to play North Carolina Agriculture and Mechanical (A&M) College (later North Carolina State University). The game, which State won 40-0, was part

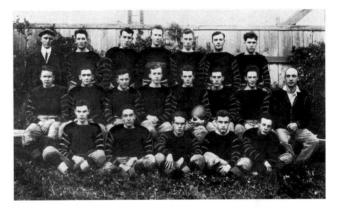

The 1913 team poses in new uniforms with orange-and-black striped sleeves. The school colors had changed in 1909 from orange and white to orange and black. From the 1914 *Colonial Echo.*

of the 1906 opening of the North Carolina State Fair and was played at the fairgrounds. W&M's two victories came against an athletic club and a high school, while the team lost to its six collegiate opponents.

The 1906 season also saw the advent of the forward pass, although it was not executed very well by the College team, according to reports. Among other rule changes, a neutral zone was created at the line of scrimmage; yardage required for a first down increased from 5 to 10; and the game was reduced from two thirty-five-minute to two thirty-minute periods.

During the 1906–07 academic year, the first Cary Field was built, thanks to a donation by T. Archibald Cary of Richmond. The facility included bleachers and was located just west of the original football field along Richmond Road, where the Bryan Complex now stands. It was a rough field surrounded by a wood fence.

Dr. Dexter Wright Draper succeeded Dr. William J. Young in 1913 and coached for three years. Another Pennsylvania man, he was chosen for Walter Camp's All-American football team four times. From the 1914 *Colonial Echo.*

The 1914 team poses in front of the ivy-covered walls of the main College building. Coach Draper wears a bowler, while team captain S. L. Bertschley (middle) holds the football. From the 1915 *Colonial Echo*.

The College's third winning season came in 1907 as Captain G. Ashton Dovell, a fullback and halfback in two earlier seasons, headed a more experienced squad. Although the team was overwhelmed 58-0 by Virginia Military Institute in the second encounter between the two schools and lost to the University of North Carolina in its second out-of-state trip, William and Mary triumphed in six of nine games, losing the season finale—the Thanksgiving Day game—to Richmond, 48-0.

Victories over Randolph-Macon and Hampden-Sydney gave the school a 2-1 record and a tie for first place in the Eastern Division, which had expanded to four teams by adding Hampden-Sydney. Games against division opponents were called "championship" games, while games against non-division opponents were frequently called "exhibition" games, although they were still considered part of the official season. William and Mary's coach was James H. Berry, a former University of Virginia star, who had joined Coach H. W. Withers with the 1906 team in mid-season. Berry brought some coaching skills that apparently had been lacking for years. Unfortunately, he was not retained, and the College continued to suffer from coaching changes almost every year until 1913.

Physical Director F. M. Crawford reported to the Board of Visitors and the faculty that football expenditures for the 1907 season were $1,470.72—quite a contrast to the hundreds of thousands spent on football ninety years later. The receipts were $1,494.99, including $479 in gate receipts with the remainder coming from fund-raising. The profit for the season was $24.27.

The 1908 season had eleven games, the most played in one year until 1925; there were eight intercollegiate games, including another intersectional clash with North Carolina State and the beginning of a rivalry with Mr. Jefferson's other school, the University of Virginia. W&M was shut out by State, 24-0, and Virginia, 14-0. The team compiled a 4-6-1 record.

This 1911 football game in Ashland, Virginia, was won by Randolph-Macon, 14-11. Courtesy of the 1912 *Yellow Jacket,* Randolph-Macon College.

In 1915, College athletic teams adopted the nickname "The Indians." This was the first logo depicting an Indian. From the 1916 *Colonial Echo.*

The next year was important for the team. In 1909 G. E. O'Hearn returned for his second year as football coach. A winning 6-4 season record was achieved, but three of the wins came against non-college teams, including two high schools. Nevertheless, the College closed the season with three wins, defeating Norfolk High School, Hampden-Sydney, and Richmond in a "glorious" victory.

A newspaper account revealed that few followers of the Orange and Black came to Richmond "because odds, even in Williamsburg were at 2 to 1 against the team." The William and Mary team colors by now had been changed from orange and white to orange and black, because white got dirty too quickly, one College publication explained.

The winning season, unfortunately, would be the last for William and Mary for the next eleven years, until 1921 when the College entered its first era of truly competitive football.

What is thought to be the first all-star team for the Virginia College Athletic Association's Eastern Division was published following the 1909 season, with William and Mary captain James G. Driver, right halfback, leading the squad. Three other College players made the all-star team: Joseph E. Healy, left guard; L. A. Peatross, right tackle; and Daniel Barnard, quarterback.

Driver of Hardenburg in Spotsylvania County came into his athletic glory in football in 1909. A four-letter man at the College, he was described in the all-star team selections as "probably one of the best ground gainers who ever played on a team in the Eastern Division." Quarterback Barnard "handled punts with alarming accuracy and ran them back with a degree of satisfaction that stamps him as an aggressive player, and a great open field runner."

Driver's name continued to be associated with the College and its athletics for the next fifty years. In an oral history interview on June 12, 1975, Driver recalled that when he was at the College some of the faculty "disapproved of an athletic association" run by the students. Athletes not only had to make up missed work, which was expected, he said, but also some faculty members, like Dr. John Lesslie Hall, gave athletes extra work. Driver said Hall changed his tune, however, after his two sons enrolled at the College and "became William and Mary sports stars."

Some of the College's competitors gave scholarships to athletes, but not William and Mary. "Teams were small. The boys came to College, and if they were interested tried out for one of the teams," Driver explained. In the early 1900s, baseball was more popular than football, primarily because "the baseball team was better than the football team," he added.

The 1917 team poses on steps of a campus building. From the 1918 *Colonial Echo*.

Football equipment was not sophisticated, Driver said. Often the football team had to use uniforms from other sports. Padding was not used at William and Mary. When Driver later played at the University of Virginia, he wore small shoulder pads, he said, adding that at W&M he also played without a helmet. Athletes, Driver continued, were required to sign a pledge "not to smoke, drink or carouse with women. They were held to this by the honor system which was like gospel to us."

Driver said he agreed with a statement in the 1907 *Colonial Echo:* "We read about evils and abuses in athletics … we are not a training school for professions, nor do we harbor any." He suggested that the reference to "evils and abuses" was occasioned by a W&M alumnus trying to pay a student athlete, and "the College wouldn't have anything to do with it."

By then, however, football was considered a "dangerous" and "deadly" sport. College presidents across the country continued to express alarm at the brutality of the sport. In 1909, there were reportedly thirty deaths and 216 injuries attributed to football.

Before the beginning of the 1910 season, the National Collegiate Athletic Association (NCAA) was established, and strict new rules were designed to reduce injuries. The flying tackle was outlawed, and interlocking interference—linemen locking arms to form a single block—was banned. The two thirty-minute periods were replaced by four fifteen-minute periods; seven men were required on the line of scrimmage; and only backs and ends were eligible to receive passes. (Earlier, any player could be considered a receiver if he lined up behind the line of scrimmage.)

William and Mary football in the 1910s was abysmal. In fact, between 1910 and 1918, the record was 8-52-7. The best season record was 3-5, in 1917; the worst records were 0-7, in 1912; and 0-9-1, in 1915. The 1912 team failed to score at all during the entire season and lost to Virginia, 60-0, and to the Medical College of Virginia, 66-0.

Changes in the organization of the College's athletic program in the fall of 1911 laid the foundation for a new approach both financially and athletically. From 1893 until that season, athletics—intramural and intercollegiate—were controlled by the student-organized Athletic Association. In 1911, athletic governance was placed in the hands of an Athletic Council composed of the officers of the Athletic Association, team managers, coaches, the physical [education] director, and faculty and student representatives. Finances for all athletics were placed under the control of the council, and gone were the days when college spirit, according to some students, was permitted to be "killed" by the transfer of home games to other places for financial reasons.

With approval of the Board of Visitors, the College also employed a permanent physical director and coach, Dr. W. J. Young, who was also listed in the *Colonial Echo* for the first time as "athletic director." Even with the new Athletic Council, the College's football performance did not improve immediately.

As enrollment at the College grew, student participation in athletic teams likewise increased, and conflicts arose. *The Flat Hat*, the student newspaper, reported on October 21, 1913: "Coach D. W. Draper stressed that 'hot-water baths after daily practice are an essential factor in conditioning an athlete.' There is sufficient water for everyone, but 'there are men here who make a practice of using up the hot water before the football men return to the gymnasium every afternoon.'"

The student paper appealed to students "to take their baths at night and reserve the hot water for the use of football men in the afternoon." If the appeal failed, the paper said, Coach Draper would close the gymnasium every afternoon from 4:30 to 6:00 to save the water for the football players. Hot water did not, however, help the team, which had a 0-5-1 season that year followed by a 1-7 season in 1914.

William Mumford Tuck, a W&M student in the mid-1910s and later governor of Virginia, recalled in an April 1976 interview that the College lost twice to Richmond in 1913 with both scores, 20 to 13. At one of these games, Jack Wright made an eighty-yard run for a touchdown "and the students in the William and Mary section," Tuck said, "went wild." But the referee ruled that Wright had stepped out of bounds. The referee was Willis Robertson, later U.S. senator from Virginia and a Richmond College man. Tuck explained, "I know he did what he thought was right; he declared him outside and, of course, that made us feel bad. The R.C. man brought his banner down in front of us and our cheerleaders hit the banner and knocked it down. When that happened bedlam broke loose. … It broke up the game."

Yearbook art shows 1915 football leaders, Robert P. Wallace (top), the team's top player; Coach Draper (left); and "Doc" Marrow, W&M's first assistant coach. Although selected as captain for 1916, Wallace did not play because he left school to enter the Army. From the 1916 Colonial Echo.

The 1915 team poses on the gymnasium steps. This team included a number of "hometown boys": Robert P. Wallace, later a well-known businessman; H. M. "Polly" Stryker, later town dentist and mayor from 1948 until 1968; and Vernon M. Geddy, later an attorney and local counsel for Williamsburg Restoration, Inc. From the 1916 Colonial Echo.

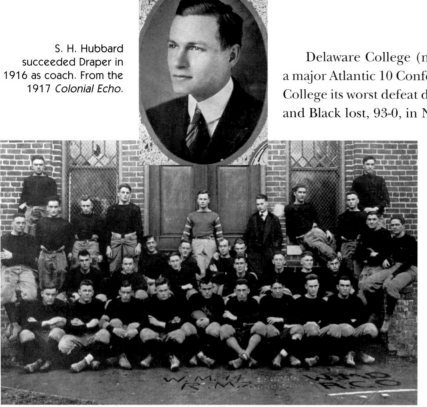

S. H. Hubbard succeeded Draper in 1916 as coach. From the 1917 *Colonial Echo.*

The 1916 team was one of the largest teams in W&M's early football history. Notice that the scores of that year's two victories over Richmond (RC) and Randolph-Macon (RM) are painted on the sidewalk in front of the team. From the 1917 *Colonial Echo.*

Delaware College (now the University of Delaware and a major Atlantic 10 Conference opponent of W&M) gave the College its worst defeat during the 1915 season. The Orange and Black lost, 93-0, in Newark, Delaware, on Thanksgiving Day. An account of the game found in the *Delaware College Register,* a student newspaper, noted that Delaware scored 67 of its points in the first half. The "scrubs" played the second half, adding 26 points. "Although [Delaware] tried hard to make the total reach the century mark," the paper reported, perhaps with tongue in cheek, "William and Mary was a little too much for them."

Henry Morrison Stryker, who later became a dentist and was longtime mayor of Williamsburg, played left tackle, and Vernon M. Geddy was a substitute quarterback on the 1915 team. Vernon M. Geddy, Jr., recalled a favorite story his father used to tell about "Polly" Stryker and that Delaware game: "My father said that the W&M line had been beat-up so much that afternoon that, toward the end of the game, Polly Stryker just stayed on the ground for several plays instead of getting up. He just didn't want to get knocked down again."

Opponents racked up 307 points, while the College team scored a measly 20 points during the 1915 season. The 1915–16 school year also brought a new nickname. The College's athletic teams, especially the football, picked up their longtime nickname, "Indians," according to E. Ralph James '18 of Hampton.

For years, the William and Mary teams had been called first the Orange and White and later the Orange and Black, after the school's athletic colors. In the 1910s the rivalry between the College and Richmond College intensified. By then, the Richmond team was known as the Spiders.

> There was a great Black Baptist preacher by the name of John Jasper and he had a great sermon entitled, "The Sun Do Move." As a result of Jasper and Richmond College being a Baptist school, William and Mary students began calling the Richmond College team the Jaspers. They didn't like it and retaliated, calling the W&M team the "Loonies" because of the nearby Eastern State [Mental] Hospital.

In 1915–16 James's roommate, William Durham Harris from Virgilina, "a very literary person," according to James, was editor of the literary magazine and *The Flat Hat.* Harris came up with the idea to call the athletic teams the "Indians" after the Indian School which was housed in the Brafferton in colonial times. Harris at that time was also a member of the Brafferton Club on campus. A short article with its simple headline, "Dubbed Indians," in the *Richmond Times-Dispatch* early in the 1916 season made the nickname official.

Unfortunately, World War I—"the war that would end all wars"—involved the United States and W&M students in 1917. A Student Army Training Corps (SATC) was formed on the campus, while many other students were drafted and went off to war. The football team suffered greatly, and the season record was 3-5, with all losses being shutouts.

There was no football team until late in the 1918 season when young men returned from military service. The coach then was a volunteer, Vernon M. Geddy, a 1915 W&M graduate and former football player, who was stationed at nearby Fort Monroe when the war ended. Geddy served a brief stint in early 1919 as acting athletic director, while coaching basketball and baseball.

For many years William and Mary's football media guide listed no games for the 1918 season. It was not until William and Mary and University of Richmond athletic officials began planning for the 100th meeting of the rivals in 1990 that a game in 1918 was discovered. Richmond won, 7-0. This long-lost game was a hard-fought defensive struggle, with William and Mary threatening only once in the contest.

Research has uncovered a second 1918 game; it was played November 16 in Lynchburg against Lynchburg College. There is no account of the game beyond a single paragraph in the *Richmond Times-Dispatch* listing the score, 13-0, with Lynchburg the victor.

The end of the war ushered in a new era in athletics at William and Mary. Run on a shoestring and managed out of various hip pockets, the football program was ripe for changes in management and organization.

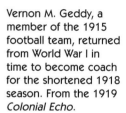

Vernon M. Geddy, a member of the 1915 football team, returned from World War I in time to become coach for the shortened 1918 season. From the 1919 *Colonial Echo.*

The 1918 football team was put together quickly as young men returned to college following the November armistice. Courtesy of the University Archives, College of William and Mary.

THE COLLEGE SHOP
for THE STUDENTS
On the Corner

POCAHONTAS TEA ROOM
FACING THE CAMPUS

The ideal place for students to board. When visiting
Williamsburg, the best place to have lunch
with friends.

FOR EVERYBODY

"Zulu" Mawson, Cheerleader

Est. Price 1.81
Fed. Tax .19
TOTAL
$2.00

NOV. 7, 1936
EAST SIDE
SEC. F
ROW J
SEAT 18

WILLIAM & MARY
VERSUS
V·M·I·
HOMECOMING ·:· SATURDAY, NOV. 7, 1936

2
Moving onto the National Scene
Football Between the Wars
1918 to 1938

Charles M. Holloway

The war years had been lean and somber for the College. By 1918, enrollment had dropped precariously to 131 students, but the appointment of Dr. Julian Alvin Carroll Chandler as the College president in 1919 seemed to energize the whole campus. Two dozen women students entered the all-male sanctuary and helped to vitiate the gloom. Within a few years, women would have their own intramural and intercollegiate sports competition.

While Chandler shrewdly recognized the appeal and drawing power of athletics in recruiting students, in fund-raising, and in building vital alumni support, he moved cautiously early in his tenure, promising to maintain the College's traditionally rigorous academic standards.

His dynamic presence was perhaps best summed up by the 1921 *Colonial Echo* when it reflected on the 1919–20 year. With returning veterans and improved finan-

Players gather in front of the gymnasium to pose for 1919 football team photograph. From the 1920 *Colonial Echo*.

cial resources through Chandler's work, the College community witnessed an immediate and welcome upsurge in athletic activity. The football players returned older and stronger. "[These were] men who had waded through fire and mud in Europe. They brought to college a spirit of renewed determination."

In March, the Board of Visitors had selected the 46-year-old Chandler to be the next College president. Chandler was a native Virginian who had graduated from William and Mary in 1891 and received his Ph.D. in history from Johns Hopkins University. As an experienced teacher and administrator, Chandler was given a princely salary of $5,000 a year, somewhat less than he had been earning as superintendent of schools in Richmond, but nearly double that of his predecessor, Lyon G. Tyler.

This June 1920 view of campus shows the original football field cleared by the students (1); old Cary Field established in 1906–07 (2); and, further west on campus, in the foreground, is the site of the current Zable Stadium at Cary Field opened in 1935 (3). Courtesy of the Office of University Publications, College of William and Mary.

Tyler, an energetic scholar, able fund-raiser and diplomat, had guided a small and moribund institution through two critical decades, skillfully engineering William and Mary out of a twilight zone and into state ownership in 1906, and then toward the admission of women in 1918. Together, these major changes assured a degree of permanence and financial security and laid the groundwork for a period of physical and institutional growth.

As incoming president, "Jack" Chandler was prepared by nature and background to transform the College into a modern liberal arts college with an expanding campus and a reputation far beyond its region. Athletics, particularly football, would play no small role in Chandler's mission. While assuring the faculty of his concern for the College's traditional liberal arts, the new president also began talking about something he called "the Sphere of the Modern College," which meant expanding courses into vocational areas—applied science, business, and home economics. He also laid plans for advertising and canvassing and proposed a staff position responsible for securing students for the College.

Clearly, he was the right man at the right time—the beginning of a decade that would soon become known as the Roaring Twenties—and he helped move W&M and its football team onto a much broader stage.

Dr. Chandler began to lay the groundwork for a new and successful football program almost as soon as he took office. A strong on-the-job leader was needed, and Chandler knew the ideal man for the job. James Glenn Driver had become a legendary sports figure during his four years at the College, 1905–09. He had excelled in football, basketball, baseball, and track, and became the only person in the College's athletic history to captain all four sports in a single academic year.

During 1919, Driver, known as "Jimmie," neared the end of his Army service in Utah, and it took the president a while to get him back to Williamsburg to rebuild the men's athletic programs. Once on campus, the popular and versatile Driver quickly took charge, coaching all sports, arranging schedules, and handling business affairs. He named as football assistants Bobby Gooch, a former Virginia quarterback, and John S. Counselman, who had been a star at Virginia Tech and assistant to John Heisman at Georgia Tech.

Driver, encouraged by Chandler, invested in the town by starting several entrepreneurial activities, including a bookstore and soda fountain (later known as The College Shop) at the edge of the campus at South Boundary and Duke of Gloucester Streets, as well as an adjacent pool room.

The football renaissance started slowly. During 1919, the team lost six of nine games and tied one. The rare schedule had W&M playing only five different opponents—Randolph-Macon and Hampden-Sydney were faced twice, and Richmond was a three-game foe. The tie was a scoreless one played in October against a larger Lynchburg team in which the slightly prejudiced College paper noted that the Indians were losing fumbles and "getting no breaks."

Later in the month, William and Mary was outweighed 30 pounds a man and lost to VMI, 21-3. One of the stars, Robert Copeland, who had just returned from military service, said he came back "first to play football; second, to get a degree." He did both admirably well and became a school superintendent.

Decorative page in the yearbook shows football action during the 1919 season. From the 1920 *Colonial Echo.*

James Glenn Driver

During 1908–09, his last year at William and Mary, James G. "Jimmie" Driver captained the football, basketball, baseball, and track teams and lettered in all four sports. The following year, his first of two at the University of Virginia, he repeated his feat—lettering in and captaining all four sports. In 1911, he took a course in physical training at Columbia University. With these singular credentials in hand, he became athletic and physical director at the University of South Carolina.

With the onset of World War I Driver became an infantry captain, "directing physical training and athletics in camps." At war's end, he was stationed in Utah when W&M President J. A. C. Chandler called and invited him to come to Williamsburg to preside over the rebuilding of the men's athletic program. During 1919 and 1920, Driver coached all the sports, ran the business aspects as well, and carried faculty rank.

His versatility extended beyond the campus, and with Dr. Chandler's encouragement, he also became a small business entrepreneur in town, creating a combination bookstore–soda fountain called The College Shop on the corner of South Boundary and Duke of Gloucester Streets. Robert Wallace, an assistant coach, helped him run the place, which became a student hangout. They even rented upstairs rooms to about ten students. Eventually, the two expanded into the Pocahontas Tea Room nearby, and then opened a pool room. According to an oral history, Driver said he had Dr. Chandler's blessing "because he knew if I were in charge it would be run properly."

But apparently Driver was overextended and fell victim to campus and alumni forces who aspired to greater (and prompter) athletic glory for the College. In 1923, when he was obliged to resign, *The Flat Hat* reported that "a great injustice was done to the College and to Mr. Driver."

Jimmie Driver went on to become Athletic Director at the University of Virginia and then at the University of South Carolina. After a long and successful business career, he returned to live in Williamsburg. At his death in 1975, at age 86, he left a business venture, Fine Virginia Foods, to the W&M Society of the Alumni. (—CMH)

Also on the squad was Julian A. "Judy" Brooks, a three-sport letterman, of whom the yearbook said, "Though small in stature, he is a Hercules in every branch of athletics." Another teammate was lineman Robert Perry Wallace from Hampton, called "Fats" and "Stonewall." He returned after serving with the Army's 29th Division and later became owner of Driver's College Shop, which became a student hangout.

An almost palpable new sense of pride and confidence spread through the College. As the 1920 yearbook noted, there was a feeling of school unity and vitality, and, though "the Indians won only two of six games … they took the scalp of the Richmond College Spiders for the first time in eight years. Everyone drank deep of this cup of nectar."

Other aspects of college life began to revive. *The Flat Hat* reported there were "delightful dances … held in the dining hall decorated with orange and black streamers [the team colors of the time], … many guests and alums crowded the floor and 'Gippy' Smith's orchestra furnished music—all discreetly supervised by an appropriate number of chaperones."

Williamsburg in the early 1920s remained a small, sleepy southern town, still untouched by the Rockefeller Restoration. There was a strip of grass down the middle of the Duke of Gloucester Street. Casey's store, the Norfolk Cafe, the

THE COLLEGE SHOP
for THE STUDENTS
On the Corner

POCAHONTAS TEA ROOM
FACING THE CAMPUS

The ideal place for students to board. When visiting Williamsburg, the best place to have lunch with friends.

FOR EVERYBODY

The College Shop and the Pocahontas Tea Room were originally owned and operated by Coach James Driver and later by former player and Assistant Coach Robert Wallace. From the 1921 *Colonial Echo*.

Kandy Kitchen, the Palace Theatre, and the Pocahontas Tea Room were commercial landmarks.

In 1920, the team's 4-5 record did not represent marked improvement, but new talent and the skilled coaching contributed to the growth of the athletic program. Performances by outstanding players, such as Fairmont R. "Monk" White and Stanley "Bake" Jones, sparked the team to victories over Gallaudet, Lynchburg, the Union Theological Seminary, and Randolph-Macon. Unfortunately, the team fell to Richmond and Virginia, and took a terrible 81-0 drubbing from North Carolina A&E (formerly A&M and ultimately North Carolina State).

The 1920 football team poses on the campus field. Coach James Driver, who also was W&M's first athletic director is on the far left, back row. From the 1921 *Colonial Echo*.

One of White's singular contributions was not on the field, but in print; he wrote a "duc's [freshman's] letter" that was clearly a precursor of Andy Griffith's classic comedy routine, "What it Was Was Football." White's letter began,

> Pa, we have croquet and horseshoe pitching at Montross, but here they have the peculiarest game I ever seen. They put twenty-two men in a pig pasture marked off with white lines. … Then a fellow blows a whistle and one side kicks a bag full of nothing wrapped up in a hog hide to the other side and they rush together and fight.

On-field "fights" or not, Driver remained in control of all sports at the College, aided by an "Athletic Council" composed of officers and managers of various teams and one faculty member. In 1920, he named William E. Fincher, another former assistant to Heisman at Georgia Tech, to take over duties as head football coach. At the time, William and Mary belonged to the old Virginia Intercollegiate Athletic Association, which expanded in 1922 to become the Virginia–North Carolina Association with the addition of Wake Forest, Trinity (later Duke), Elon, Guilford, and Davidson.

This photograph is apparently from the 1921 game against Trinity (later Duke University) in Durham. The Indians won, 12-0. Note the style of helmets. From the 1922 *Colonial Echo*.

This advertisement is for the Kandy Kitchen, one of the student hangouts in the 1920s. From the 1928 *Colonial Echo*.

Though the College began to schedule additional games with northern teams, it remained in this association until it joined the Southern Conference in the 1935–36 school year. This resulted in more regular games with the state's "Big Four"—Virginia, Virginia Tech, VMI, and Washington and Lee.

In 1921, the Indians produced a 4-3-1 record, their first winning season since the 6-4 campaign in 1909. They rolled up 171 points to opponents' 79, beating Wake Forest and Randolph-Macon, but losing to Richmond in the year's final game.

Despite the winning ledger, some influential alumni apparently were dissatisfied with the progress and grew restless. Driver began to feel the pressure. After the 1921 season, Dr. Chandler contacted Heisman, the former highly successful Georgia Tech Coach by then at the University of Pennsylvania. Chandler offered him the jobs of athletic director and football coach. The proposed starting salary was reported to be an astronomical $10,000 a year.

Action shots of games were still rare in the early 1920s. This one comes from the game in 1921 against Richmond. Notice the ball in the air following a punt. The Spiders won, 17-7, in the Thanksgiving Day game. From the 1922 *Colonial Echo*.

Heisman, a notably successful coach and an early exponent of the forward pass, was receptive, but a brouhaha erupted, possibly abetted by Driver, when it became known how the $10,000 would be raised. Half was to have come from student fees and half from alumni in a separate contract. The salary was at least twice as much as the president, or any of the faculty, earned.

A special faculty committee was convened and quickly advised the president it opposed the hiring; Chandler withdrew the offer. After a distinguished career, Heisman eventually gave his name to the national trophy now awarded annually to college football's outstanding player.

But the seeds of conflict between academics and athletics had been planted. They would germinate, persist, and proliferate, sometimes resulting in bitterness and even scandal. Increasingly, Chandler faced the complications of dealing with a more diversified student body, growing budgetary needs, and his Board of Visitors. Meanwhile, the new popularity of football was superimposed on the scene. In Williamsburg, as around the country, public interest in the sport seemed to spread like wildfire. With a diversified and increasingly wide-open, crowd-pleasing style, the game grew quickly and audiences expanded rapidly, even before the advent of radio broadcasts starting later in the decade. Within a decade its popularity challenged that of baseball as a national pastime.

Football at William and Mary began to generate a whole series of activities that enriched and enlivened campus life— cheers, school songs, bonfires, pep rallies, mascots, bands, and dances. And the players' team unity seemed to produce cohesion within the still small student body and stirred excitement among Williamsburg residents and state alumni.

Although his authority diminished, Driver remained as College athletic director through 1922, while new Coach Bill Ingram, a former All-American at Navy, directed the Tribe to a 6-3 record, winning six in a row, but losing the finale to Richmond, 13-3.

Driver resigned the next spring and was succeeded by J. Wilder Tasker, who had been the head coach at Connecticut Agricultural College (University of Connecticut). Tasker took advantage of the solid foundation Driver had built and directed a series of winning seasons that extended through 1926. In all, starting with that 4-3-1 ledger in 1921, the Tribe would mount six successive winning campaigns, ending in 1927, when the 4-5-1 record would be the only losing one in a span covering 1921 through 1933.

When the *Colonial Echo* looked back on the 1922 season and Driver's tenure, it observed that

> William and Mary had risen to its present high standing in intercollegiate sports circles, meeting teams like Penn State, the U.S. Naval Academy, and Syracuse on the gridiron ... and besides his athletic victories [Driver] has instilled an excellent spirit of sportsmanship and gentlemanly conduct that will leave its impression long after his victories on Cary Field have been forgotten.

Driver became director of athletics at the University of Virginia and later at the University of South Carolina before retiring in Williamsburg. Upon his death in 1975, his estate provided for the endowment of a special James H. Driver Award for Excellence in Athletics to be awarded yearly to a scholar-athlete at William and Mary.

By 1923, football at Cary Field had taken on many aspects of the modern game, though it remained basically simple. The foundation was in place: size of the field, scoring, uniforms, shape and approximate size of the ball. Players wore slightly padded jerseys; high-waisted, belted canvas pants;

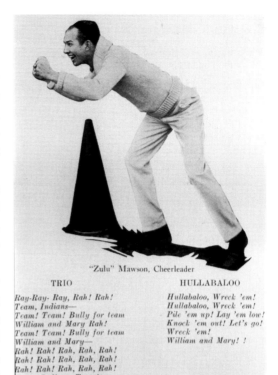

"Zulu" Mawson, Cheerleader

TRIO	HULLABALOO
Ray-Ray- Ray, Rah! Rah!	*Hullabaloo, Wreck 'em!*
Team, Indians—	*Hullabaloo, Wreck 'em!*
Team! Team! Bully for team	*Pile 'em up! Lay 'em low!*
William and Mary Rah!	*Knock 'em out! Let's go!*
Team! Team! Bully for team	*Wreck 'em!*
William and Mary—	*William and Mary! !*
Rah! Rah! Rah, Rah, Rah!	
Rah! Rah! Rah, Rah, Rah!	
Rah! Rah! Rah, Rah, Rah!	
Team, Indians, Team!	

Winning teams in the early 1920s increased school spirit. Emblematic of the new excitement was Thatcher H. "Zulu" Mawson of Norfolk, one of the cheerleaders in 1922 and 1923 when the team won six and seven games, respectively. Two of the cheers are printed above. From the 1924 *Colonial Echo.*

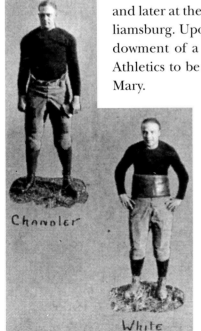

Chandler

White

Team captain Ferdie Chandler was a tackle on the 1922 team and is shown here with "Monk" White, star halfback. The duo especially excelled in the games with Virginia Tech and Hampden-Sydney. From the 1923 *Colonial Echo.*

Matsu

Art Matsu

If nothing else, this "little field general" born in Scotland was blessed with a flair to be noticed. It was that way before he wowed 'em at Cary Field and for long, colorful, productive years after that.

Art Matsu developed into a great athlete and coach, not simply because of the records he set, but because of his depth and understanding of football. He perceived elements of the game and preached them, confident that even his most controversial ideas would prove out.

As an infant, he immigrated with his Japanese-born father and his Scottish mother, first to Canada and then to Cleveland, Ohio, where he became a national high school diving champion.

Matsu credited his football skills, at least indirectly, to World War I. He once wrote that to support the war effort, the nation indulged in "autoless weekends" to conserve gasoline. The result was that "all up and down Carnegie Street" in Cleveland, youngsters busied themselves in all kinds of sports, including "football played on the host of vacant lots along that stretch, with whatever would pass as a ball, no matter what its shape or size."

At William and Mary, he jumped into football fame, excelling as a scrambling, adventurous quarterback at only 5'7" tall and weighing 150 pounds. He and Lee Todd were the only freshmen to make the varsity squad in 1923, and Matsu began to demonstrate his punting and kicking skills. His 38-yard drop-kicked field goal against Syracuse kept the Indians from being shutout by the Eastern powerhouse.

In 1924, Meb Davis, a freshman end, joined the team and the Matsu-to-Davis "passing combination" was created. The combination "completely dazzled the Navy eleven with nine of 13 passes completed," the yearbook said. In W&M's 21-3 victory over Duke, Matsu to Davis passes accounted for two of the three touchdowns.

The 1925 and 1926 W&M seasons brought the Matsu legend into focus. Along with his passing expertise, he also displayed brilliant punting and drop kicked extra points and field goals. In fact, his 47-yard field goal against Chattanooga at the end of the 1926 season provided the margin in the Indians 9-6 first postseason game win. His 75-yard punt is still one of W&M's longest.

Matsu became W&M's first alumnus to play in the National Football League as a 1928 halfback with the Dayton Triangles.

Moving to Rutgers University in 1930, he became an associate professor of physical education, while simultaneously carving out a reputation as a football coach—first with the freshman team and later in various capacities as assistant coach with the varsity Scarlet Knights. He enjoyed a quarter-century of success there, partly because he studied his subject and reflected on it. During his Rutgers tenure, which ended in 1955, Matsu penned the following thoughts on football offense:

A metronome set at 120 beats per minute is the standard meter, regulating all plays, running or passing. This tempo is the regular marching cadence every male knows from the time of watching his first parade. So it is very simple to install and make into a disciplined teamwork mechanism, from "down set" to whistle.

With that precise operation preceding the snap, likened to the rifle drill team which, on just one starting command goes through a series of maneuvers in total silence but with varying moves, it adds quandaries facing defenses.

But the warehouse of likewise covert plays it can develop, all tried and proved, resulting from scouting or game developments, add dilemmas for oppositions.

It is no wonder that coaches like Rutgers gridiron boss Frank Burns called the little man "one of the best football minds I've ever met, an excellent teacher."

The happy irony is that Matsu nearly went to Princeton, not W&M. Promises that he could play immediately lured him to the Reservation, where he helped write football history.

Later, he was selected into the National Football Foundation's Hall of Fame. Following his era at Rutgers, he helped Frank Kush coach at Arizona State in Tempe. Matsu lived there until his death in 1987 at age 83.

(—RM)

In addition to his passing skills, Art Matsu was an excellent punter and kicker. Courtesy of the W&M Sports Information Department.

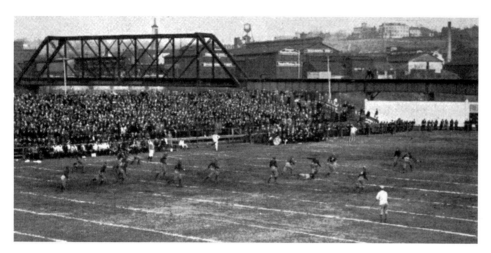

William and Mary often played in Richmond on the Mayo Island Field in the James River. Note the railroad trestle spanning the James in the background. The Thanksgiving Day defeat of Richmond, 20-6 in 1924, produced both state and conference championships. From the 1925 *Colonial Echo*.

and cleated shoes. Helmets were made of thin, close-fitting leather; the heavy ball was larger and fatter than current models. Squads were relatively small, barely numbering over two dozen, and everyone played both offense and defense. There were infrequent substitutions and few specialists. Arthur "Art" Matsu, for example, who became one of the state's preeminent players between 1923 and 1925 not only ran and passed, but also drop-kicked field goals and extra points.

The 1923 season produced a 6-3 record, and the Indians began to play more consistently against traditional opponents like Richmond, which they beat, 27-6; Randolph-Macon; and Hampden-Sydney. Tasker, a graduate of Syracuse, was able to arrange games with his alma mater and Navy, both national football powers. Even though W&M was walloped in both games, the news was that the College was playing them.

Almost the entire student body traveled to Mayo Island on a special train for late-season action at Richmond.

> A crowd of eight thousand was given a treat when the Indians took the field clad in new uniforms which revived the ancient colors of the college ... gold jerseys with green numerals, and green stockings with silver and gold stripes.

The uniforms went back to orange and black with gold helmets in 1935.

Earlier in the 1923 season, the multitalented Matsu, a wiry 5'7", 145-pounder, began to direct the offense as quarterback. The Tribe "completely outclassed and defeated the Trinity (Duke) Blue Devils at Rocky Mount [North Carolina] 21-10, and Matsu led a dazzling aerial attack," the *Colonial Echo* reported.

On November 10, the College played what yearbook writers called "the best football game that Williamsburg has witnessed in many a year," beating Delaware, 14-0. Matsu again excelled as a field general, working behind

J. Wilder Tasker (bottom) became coach in 1923 and produced four consecutive winning seasons, 1923–26. John B. Todd played for Tasker and became assistant coach following graduation in 1925. From the 1927 *Colonial Echo*.

Knute Rockne, Notre Dame's celebrated coach, liked his experience at W&M in 1924 so much that he returned for a second two-week clinic at W&M in 1925. Courtesy of the University of Notre Dame.

a solid line. By mid-season, papers were suggesting that he would receive All-American mention.

Matsu, of Scottish and Japanese ancestry, was regularly referred to in the press as "The Jap." The label was not intended to be derogatory, as he was a much admired individual off and on the field.

While Matsu made many headlines, he was ably supported by a range of other colorful standouts, such as key receiver Melvin "Meb" Davis, tackle Francis "Snook" Elliott, and John and Lee Todd, brothers who anchored the line at center and end, respectively. Davis was one of the best all-around W&M athletes, also excelling in basketball and track. The W&M yearbook proclaimed him "the greatest receiver of forward passes that ever donned an Indian uniform."

A mainstay of College teams in the early 1920s, John Todd also starred in three other sports and plunged into every aspect of life on campus. He and his brother Lee were lauded by many, including a Navy Coach, who reportedly said "I'd swap my whole line for the two Todds." John Todd graduated in 1925 and spent the next three years as an assistant football coach and freshman basketball and baseball coach at W&M. He was honored for his sports talent and his professional service as a leading dentist on the Peninsula when Todd Stadium in Newport News, Virginia, was named for him.

It is interesting to note the size of players in this period. Only George "Tiny" Grove, weighed more than 200 pounds, while Matsu at 145 and Andre Goetz at 138, the two listed quarterbacks in 1925, were the lightest. The average for running backs was 154, for the line it was 184, and for the team it was 173.

While the only losses in the 6-2-1 season of 1924 were to Syracuse and Navy, the highlight may have come before play began, when Knute Rockne brought his two-week coaching clinic to the campus, attracting national press, coaches from near and far, and, of course, the William and Mary team and staff.

Head coach at the University of Notre Dame, Rockne was at the peak of his fame and generally regarded as the best and most innovative football coach in his field during an era that dealt in superlatives. His Irish

Meb Davis (at the top), on an end-around play, scores W&M's lone touchdown against Harvard in 1925 in Cambridge, Massachusetts. It was the first time the nation's two oldest schools had met on the gridiron. From the 1926 *Colonial Echo.*

The Palace Theater was the scene of recreated W&M football games. Courtesy of the John D. Rockefeller Jr. Library, Colonial Williamsburg Foundation.

teams were undefeated five times, won 105 games and lost only 12. In choosing William and Mary as one of his few clinic sites, Rockne brought prestige and attention to the developing program.

Rockne delivered a no-nonsense presentation that included morning lectures (chalk talks) on strategy and psychology and afternoon sessions of training on-the-field with drills demonstrated by members of the William and Mary team.

Richmond Times-Dispatch reporter James Selvage, in Williamsburg to cover Rockne's summer camp, described the coach as

> a mass of nerves and color. His every move on the field is fiery and although past middle age [he was then 36 years old], he is powerfully built … [and] more agile than the majority of those he's training. … [He stresses] a powerhouse offense is the best defense—He's a great believer in psychology of the game and endeavors to have his team strike where a blow is least expected. A team has everything to gain and nothing to lose most of the time by an unorthodox move.

An Associated Press story reported that Rockne put on a uniform and regularly mixed it up with players in practice sessions. While he stressed details and fundamentals, he also brought a cutting sense of humor to the drills.

Following the clinic, Rockne told Selvage that Coach Tasker had "the makings of a great team … one that could hold its own with any of the northern colleges of comparative size." The following year, Rockne cut back his summer camp schedule and appeared only at Notre Dame and Williamsburg. Tasker corresponded with the coach until Rockne died in 1931.

Throughout the country, football prospered at the college level. Riding the wave of interest and popularity during the decade, William and Mary began to schedule bigger and better-known northern teams such as Syracuse and Navy in 1923, Harvard in 1924, and Princeton in 1927.

Alumni began to follow the Indians avidly as the teams compiled six straight winning seasons from 1921 to 1926. Here, cheerleaders, in 1925, urge them on. From the 1926 *Colonial Echo*.

The first such meeting with Syracuse turned into a 63-0 disaster for the Tribe, but the next year W&M earned the nickname "Fighting Virginians" from the "Northern Press," the *Colonial Echo* reported, as a result of its effort in a 24-7 loss to the Orangemen.

Since it was impractical for students and others to follow the team to distant points such as New York, a hundred or more of them gathered on autumn afternoons at the Palace Theater downtown to hear and see re-creations of away games.

There were no radio broadcasts yet, but wire services sent out play-by-play accounts, which were received in Williamsburg at the old telegraph office. The College arranged for a bicycle messenger to pick up these dispatches, perhaps ten plays at a time, and deliver them to the theater. There, crowd members paid a quarter each to hear a narrator describe the progress of the game and illustrate it by moving a pasted-up football on a large gridiron superimposed on the movie screen.

Officials in the 1920s and 1930s were dressed in white. Here a game official watches the line of scrimmage as a W&M play begins during the 1926 season. From the 1927 *Colonial Echo.*

Surely, there were agonizing and suspenseful lulls between the deliveries of ticker tape, but William and Mary's number one sports fan for decades, Leonard (Lenny) Graves '35, recalled with delight his participation as a 12-year-old. "There were lots of cheers and groans," the former proprietor of Frazier-Graves clothing store in Merchants Square, said, "depending on the course of the game. We all brought our own snacks and had a great time." Graves bought one of the first season tickets when the new Cary Field opened in 1935 and missed very few home games, rain or shine. He died in October 1996, just a few days after watching William and Mary beat New Hampshire, 31-7.

During most of the 1920s there was considerable controversy over the use of freshman players. Most Virginia colleges did not allow them to play on the varsity, but William and Mary did, with no apparent anxieties about the unlikely possibility that an occasional vagabond would enroll in the fall, play football, and then leave. The issue complicated life for Coach Tasker and progressive alumni who sought stiffer competition. However, the problem pretty much disappeared after the College was accepted into the Southern Conference in 1936.

Coach Tasker's winning ways continued into 1925 as Matsu and Davis led the way to a 6-4 season, running up a scoring advantage of 217 points to 86. One highlight

E. Carlton "Five-Yard" Macon

E Carlton Macon sounds a little like a name belonging to a corporate lawyer, but when he played on William and Mary's hard-scrabble teams of the mid-1920s, he was as tough as anyone on the field. It was this toughness that helped him earn the "five-yard" sobriquet from sports writers.

In 1926 and 1927 W&M began playing northern powerhouses like Syracuse, Harvard, and Columbia. While the Tribe lost more than it won on the road, Macon once noted that "it's all right to play those games; it's a thrill for the players and it shows that William and Mary is on the map. Don't worry if we don't win them."

"We had men on the team like Russell 'Iron Hands' House, 'Pea Head' Walker, and of course, 'Tiny' Grove," Macon recalled. "Tiny" was about 6 feet tall and weighed around 240 pounds.

We all played 60 minutes. I played fullback on offense and linebacker on defense. ... I broke my nose in the Chattanooga game; a doctor put it back in place, stopped the bleeding, taped it up, and back I went into the lineup. We didn't have very good equipment then, soft leather helmets, no face masks. My nose got broken four times during my career.

In 1926, such rugged play, and his five-yards-per-carry average, prompted sports writers to dub him "Five-Yard" Macon. It was the same squad, quarterbacked by Art Matsu, that beat Chattanooga, 9-6, in a postseason bowl game. While Matsu had drop-kicked 47 yards for the winning points, Macon had plunged over the goal line for the Fighting Virginians' only touchdown.

Off the football field, Macon was an outstanding student and missed election to Phi Beta Kappa by one-tenth of a percent. He was also active in several social and professional fraternities and vice president of the Men's Athletic Council. Macon majored in business administration and commerce and later became a successful finance officer and real estate broker in Virginia.

(—CMH)

came on Halloween when the Indians traveled to Cambridge, Massachusetts, for their first match against highly favored Harvard. After leading, 7-0, at the half, W&M lost, 14-7. A *New York Times* headline said, "Harvard is surprised by William and Mary, and wins 14-7, only by a late rally." The story singled out Matsu for special praise, "besides punting in fine fashion and making some steady advances when he carried the ball, the tall [*sic!*], thin player saved his team many times when he called the plays so that the Crimson defense was baffled."

The 1926 season supplied at least two unprecedented events. One took place on October 23, when the Alumni Association staged the first Homecoming Day in the College's 233 years of existence. More than 2,000 invitations were sent out to help celebrate remarkable campus changes, including, "a colonial wall that now surrounds the campus, colonial walks, a handsome dormitory, and one of the best gymnasiums in the southland [Blow Memorial], ... a new auditorium, athletic field, two other dorms, and a huge science hall."

The second was the Tribe's first postseason appearance. Representing the Virginia–North Carolina Association, the Tribe (a member since 1922) brought a 6-3 record against the University of Chattanooga in Tennessee (4-0-2) on December 4. Chattanooga was co-champion of the Southern Intercollegiate Athletic Association. Put together by the teams, rather than the respective associations, the December 4 contest was devised to improve the reputation of both teams.

The Virginians triumphed in a thriller—a 9-6 upset, won on Matsu's 47-yard drop-kicked field goal with six minutes remaining—"thereby establishing a good claim to the Southern Title," the *Colonial Echo* said. As the *Richmond Times-Dispatch*

The 1926 team poses on the top of Lookout Mountain prior to the December 4, 1926, game against the University of Chattanooga. W&M won, 9-6, on a touchdown by Carlton "Five-Yard" Macon and a 47-yard drop-kicked field goal by team captain Art Matsu. The victory gave the "Fighting Virginians" (as they were called by the northern press) "a good claim to the Southern title." Courtesy of the W&M Sports Information Department.

noted, "Saturday's victory was more than a win for William and Mary, it was the means of establishing a name in the South that will match that won on northern fields the past three years."

Quarterback Matsu, center Lee Todd, tackle Grove, and guard Pete Williams were the lone seniors on the twenty-four man squad. One other 1926 standout was E. Carlton Macon, a rugged and reliable back who was nicknamed "Five-Yard" Macon by sports writers. In 1990, when he was 83, Macon's comments on the Chattanooga triumph credited Matsu with playing flawlessly. "It gave a great finish to the little general's gridiron career," he said. He failed to mention that, according to the Newport News (Virginia) *Daily Press*, fullback Macon was removed from the game after "he smashed his nose in the first quarter." He wasn't removed until the next period.

The *Daily Press* ran an Associated Press story that said a third-period Chattanooga field goal attempt was blocked by Eason. That would be James M. "Suey" Eason, who became a short-term W&M coach in 1952. Following that block, the story said, "the Indians hammered to a touchdown." Later a 75-yard Matsu punt "put the attack in Chattanooga territory and Matsu's drop kick for the victory came a few moments later." Matsu's punt has been superseded only by 77-yard efforts by Jackie Freeman (1940), Russ Brown (1972), and Joe Agee (1975). His game-winning field goal also was a W&M mark until 1986.

On December 12, a *Daily Press* article by the Associated Press, revealed an all-SIAA football team, without divulging that SIAA was the Southern Intercollegiate Athletic Association. The story said, "It must have been organized teamwork and not individual playing that marked the season for William and Mary, for none of the eleven men who composed the team that brought the Old Dominion an

The 1926 starting varsity eleven propelled W&M to its first postseason game. They are (from left to right on the line) "Meb" Davis, end; William Carmichael, tackle; Leland Walker, guard; Lee Todd, center (with ball); Alfred Williams, guard; George "Tiny" Grove, tackle; and Suey Eason (end) while the backfield was Clare Wallick, left halfback; Carlton Macon, fullback; Welton "Bud" Bloxsom, right halfback; and Art Matsu, quarterback. From the 1927 *Colonial Echo*.

The first night football in the East was played on September 24, 1927, under the new lights at Cary Field. The photograph shows the lights and the College's freshmen huddling on the field prior to the game. From the 1928 *Colonial Echo*.

enviable record in football for 1926 were awarded places on the mythical All-State eleven selected recently." The story said that end Meb Davis had been named to the South Atlantic team and "was regarded in Tennessee as the greatest wingman seen in action there."

By 1927, college football was very much a part of what many have called the Golden Age of Sports in the United States, and thirty million spectators paid more than fifty million dollars to watch many games in huge, new stadiums, like those in California and Michigan. At William and Mary, there were nearly 1,200 students on the expanding Williamsburg campus and another 477 taking extension courses. During the decade, numerous major dormitory and classroom buildings were completed, including Jefferson, Monroe, Rogers, Old Dominion, Barrett, and Phi Beta Kappa Memorial (later Ewell) Halls.

During his 1927 senior season, Davis captained a team that included a number of students from states such as Massachusetts, South Carolina, and California. Davis had also starred in basketball and track and some called him the greatest athlete to attend William and Mary. He was included in *Who's Who in American Sport* and played well despite the 4-5-1 season's record.

The largest crowd to date—more than 6,000—flocked to Cary Field on September 24 to see the first night game played in this region of the country. A battery of lights strung on twelve tall poles bathed Cary Field in 40,000 watts of incandescence.

Macon, a W&M fullback then, recalled that "They weren't the best lights ... a few bulbs and big metal reflectors ... but they worked." Frequent night games continued until the construction of a new stadium in 1935.

Unfortunately, as the *Colonial Echo* remarked, "this hard-fought game ... saw Catholic University hammer its way down field twice for touchdowns" and win, 12-0. In one of two other night games that season, William and Mary beat Lenoir-Rhyne, 19-0, in a drenching rainstorm. Also that year, an "all-star" team of Quantico Marines beat W&M, 20-14, in what was boldly proclaimed in the yearbook as "the hardest and best fought game of the season."

By the end of 1927, the College's athletic department had expanded considerably, and there were full-time coaches for major sports. In September 1928, the new position of athletic manager was created, and President Chandler appointed William S. Gooch to fill the job, which he held until becoming business manager in 1936.

At the same time, the president named James Branch Bocock, a graduate of Georgetown University, to be head football coach and replace J. W. Tasker. Bocock, a respected and experienced coach who had worked at the University of North Carolina, Virginia Tech, and Louisiana State University, also held a law degree. While at W&M, he ran a state agricultural research farm in Brunswick County.

In 1928, Bocock produced a 6-3-2 record and the first of what would become six successive W&M winning years. Still, it was a season that would disappoint fans because of the two scoreless ties and two close calls among the losses. So, what should have been a pleasant time became a complicated, frustrating one for Coach Bocock.

Early on, Bocock knew he had lost graduating veterans Davis, Eason, Elliott, and James Cook, among others and he also had to field a team with no freshmen. Nevertheless, he started with a 41-0 mauling of Lynchburg and held Marshall to a scoreless deadlock. Then Syracuse romped, 32-0, and the Indians were in the midst of a slump in which they were held scoreless for three games and lost four out of five.

The Bocock approach was dealt with by John W. Tuthill '32, a distinguished American diplomat and former ambassador to the European Economic Community and Brazil. He wrote about those days in the summer 1986 issue of the *William and Mary Magazine*. "Branch Bocock was a 'mensch,'" Tuthill recalled. "His concern was for the boys on the squad. He brought out the best in us."

Tuthill modestly characterized himself as a small, slow and myopic quarterback, but he credited the coach for working patiently with him and others to develop whatever talents they had. "During my undergraduate years, Bocock was certainly the most important influence in my life," he wrote.

Much later, *Sports Illustrated* selected Tuthill as an end on its "Silver Anniversary" team of All-Americans, along with Dan Edmondson '36, Walt Zable '37, and Col. Seymour Schwiller '40.

Among the 1928 team members were Ted Bauserman, who scored 59 points and became captain of the 1929 squad; William Fields; Powell Rogers; and William Scott, who scored 27 points in a season when the team amassed 219 points to their opponents' 54. This is a reproduction of a partial page from the 1929 *Colonial Echo*.

Melvin C. "Meb" Davis

"**M**eb" Davis will forever be linked with quarterback Art Matsu in W&M football history. The Matsu-to-Davis passing combination was legendary, thrilling W&M fans for three years in the mid-1920s, an era when the College's football finally came into its own.

The Flat Hat in 1926 heralded the combo as "the greatest scoring factor that W&M has ever placed on the gridiron and [their] names will go down in football history as the Indians' greatest."

Details of many of Davis's personal gridiron feats have been lost, but excerpts have survived like his 90-yard sprint for a touchdown after he picked up a fumble during the Columbia game in 1926 or a daring run around end that resulted in a touchdown during the 1924 Richmond game. He also holds the distinction of being the only W&M player to score a touchdown against every Ivy League team played during his varsity years.

A rangy 180-pound left end, Davis showed not only his versatility but also durability by also playing baseball and track. He lettered in all three sports and was captain of the three squads, including football, in 1927. He later returned to coach the three sports.

After the 1925 Harvard game, *The Flat Hat* reported Davis "played a wonderful game, making several end runs. On several of his punts, one of which went over sixty yards, Meb went down the field and made tackles."

In 1927, when Davis made the *Richmond Times-Dispatch*'s first-team All-State for the second consecutive year, sports editor Robert Harper wrote:

Davis is a valuable all-round performer. He is a splendid receiver of passes, a punter and a passer, as well as ball carrier. The W&M captain made a great receiver during his four years of play scoring touchdowns against Harvard, Princeton, Columbia, Navy and Syracuse, in addition to state rivals. Fast in getting down under punts. A hard tackler and a great fighter, Davis is given a place for the second year in succession. There was no deterioration this season in the standard of play which made Davis a much-talked about man in 1926.

He also was named to the all–South Atlantic first team in 1925 and 1926.

Davis graduated with a science and physical education major and later became athletic director at Fork Union Military Academy, returning to coach at his alma mater in 1929. He lived for many years in Richmond and was a real estate agent. Davis always maintained his close ties with the College and was a major donor to the W&M Athletic Educational Foundation.

In 1984, then athletic director James Copeland said, "Meb was an athletic institution at William and Mary. Through his astute character, good graces, and generosity, he remains in highest regard here . . . and symbolizes all the values and dignity the College stands for."

Davis died in 1989 at the age of 86. (—WK)

"Meb" Davis grabbed a Matsu pass and scrambled around end for a long touchdown in the 1924 game against Richmond. Courtesy of the *Richmond Times-Dispatch*.

Clarence "Red" Maxey led the Indians in scoring in 1929 with 96 points and continued to lead the offense through the 1931 season. In those three years, W&M's record was 20-6-3. From the 1930 *Colonial Echo.*

Bocock's 1929 team went 8-2, producing the best record at the College until the 1941 club went 8-2 and the 1942 Tribe posted a 9-1-1 season. The lone losses in 1929 were to Navy and Virginia Tech as the Indians ran up 250 points to 77 by the opposition. Solid wins over Richmond and Hampden-Sydney helped earn the Virginia Conference championship.

Sophomore Clarence "Red" Maxey led the team in scoring with a state-high 96 points. Paul "Rosy" Ryan was a triple-threat quarterback, who, with fullback and team captain Teddy Bauserman, helped provide a strong and versatile Tribe backfield.

One writer rhapsodized over Maxey's skills in a 36-13 win over Catholic University, "A football dynamo in the person of 'Red' Maxey twisted, squirmed and bolted his way up and down the field last night to furnish the fireworks."

Although the runners and passers usually captured the headlines and public fancy, it was a solid and determined line that helped build Bocock's record between 1929 and 1931. Otis Douglas, the legendary "Reedville Strong Boy," dominated the line of scrimmage as both offensive and defensive tackle. Standing 6'2" and weighing a massive—for that era—240 pounds, Douglas dominated the line while those teams ran up a 20-6-3 combined record. He also found time to wrestle, never losing a match, and participated in track and swimming. After graduation, Douglas returned as an assistant coach in football and track, before moving on to a long and varied career as pro-

Game action during the 1929 season, when the "Fighting Virginians" averaged 25 points per game. From the 1930 *Colonial Echo.*

fessional player and then college coach. His strength and durability caused one writer to describe him as "a Paul Bunyan sort of guy."

In the course of the 1929 season, not long after W&M's 59-0 thrashing of Bridgewater, the dramatic crash of the stock market in New York set off a financial panic that quickly deepened into a worldwide economic depression, lasting almost a full decade. The long shadows of unemployment and despair crept closer to the campus, and fringe effects gradually began to touch every aspect of college life, including enrollment, faculty pay, athletic recruitment, and fund-raising.

Otis Douglas

In the spring of 1989, a 77-year-old man died in Kilmarnock (Virginia) General Hospital after what was described as a long illness. Actually, his iron constitution had kept him alive for two full years after being shot in the heart by a burglar. It was a sadly ironic ending for an unusually strong man who had taken much delight in competition and in turn contributed much of himself to sports and to society.

His obituary began, "Otis Douglas dies; NFL oldest rookie and W & M star." True enough, but the story of the legendary football player from the 1920s involved much more than his physical achievements. Through the years, his friends, students, and family remembered his kindness and compassion most. Throughout his lifetime, he loved working with children, strong and weak. He helped establish, and worked at, schools for the handicapped in Georgia and later served on school and church boards in Westmoreland County.

Sports fans and writers marveled at Douglas's physique. The "Reedville Strong Boy" was 6'2" tall, weighed 240 pounds, possessed extraordinary muscle structure, partly congenital, partly developed through hard work and sports.

Opponents from Virginia to Massachusetts felt his punishing blocks as he led the way for runners like "Red" Maxey and Billy Palese. During his three years at the College, he anchored the line on a team that won 20 games and lost only 6.

After graduating in 1932, Douglas coached football, swimming, track, and wrestling at W&M. He played some semi-pro football before trying out for the Philadelphia Eagles of the National Football League in 1946. He was 35, then, which made him the oldest NFL rookie ever. He played regularly at tackle for the Eagles for four years and also coached at Drexel Institute in Philadelphia.

Along the way, he also found time to earn a master's degree from the University of Michigan.

In the 1950s, Douglas became head football coach at the University of Arkansas and later coached the Canadian Football League's Calgary team. In 1961, he was a trainer and consultant to the Cincinnati Reds baseball team when it won the National League pennant.

Ten years before his death, Douglas was inducted into the Virginia Sports Hall of Fame.   (—CMH)

Douglas's Philadelphia Eagles jersey hangs in the Virginia Sports Hall of Fame.

Nevertheless, the 1930 season opened on schedule at old Cary Field with an easy 24-0 victory over Guilford. The inimitable Maxey, Douglas, Bauserman, and Edward Meade were among all but four lettermen who returned for the impressive 7-2-1 season that included a 13-13 tie with Harvard. That game in Cambridge, Massachusetts, proved to be the most dramatic of the season, with Harvard scoring early and W&M fighting back to take a 13-6 halftime lead. Thomas "Happy" Halligan intercepted a Harvard lateral and ran 35 yards for the Tribe score. As the Associated Press reported, "the gallant little football band from ancient William and Mary outfought and outsmarted all of Harvard's mighty army here today … though outweighed from five to thirty-five pounds in every position."

The two losses came against Navy (19-6) and Virginia Tech (7-6), and the Tribe blanked its final four opponents, including Richmond, while scoring 98 points.

Halligan and Maxey were All-Conference selections, and Halligan received honorable mention as an All-American. As 1930 quarterback, Mitchell Mozeleski played well all season and combined with Maxey in nearly upsetting favored Virginia Tech before 9,000 at Richmond Stadium.

Paul "Rosy" Ryan, senior quarterback, was the field general for the 1929 team that ran up 250 points to the opponents' 77. He was dependable either in passing, running, or kicking. From the 1930 *Colonial Echo*.

By the spring of 1931, Governor John Garland Pollard warned that the prospect for salaries was bleak and urged the College to exercise "utmost economy." President Chandler responded by cutting expenditures to the bone, noting that "the College is in a terrible fix."

Despite the spreading effect of the Depression, Williamsburg and the College experienced something of a renaissance as the Rockefellers moved ahead with their major efforts to restore the colonial grandeur of the area. More than a third of the town was revived, including the Wren Building, the Brafferton, and the President's House. Several churches and businesses opened their doors, among them restaurants such as the Corner and Middle Greeks.

During 1931, Bocock resigned to work at the Colonial Williamsburg restoration, and his assistant, John Kellison, took over as head coach, directing the team for the next four years. Kellison's first year was successful but not outstanding, with five wins, two loses and two ties. One of the heroes of the Harvard game, Halligan, returned, along with Douglas, in his last year.

In the season's first game against Guilford, Maxey continued his skillful play, scoring three of the team's touchdowns despite a torrential rain. There was a touch of showmanship before the Homecoming Day game against Roanoke College when a low-flying College biplane dropped a football into the arms of Indian captain Douglas. Later, William Joseph "Billy" Palese scored twice as the Indians won 13-6.

Against Bridgewater in mid-season, the Indians ran up 95 points to none and established a single-game scoring record that still stands. There were disappointments, too, including "an unexpected and heartbreaking" 6-2 loss to Richmond on Thanksgiving Day. Writers described the crowd of 15,500 at Richmond Stadium as "the largest ever to witness a game in Virginia."

At year's end, three William and Mary players—Maxey, Halligan, and Douglas—were named to the All-State team.

Halligan, who returned to Williamsburg later in life and managed the Williamsburg Theatre on Duke of Gloucester Street, was known

The 1929 football team, pictured here on the bleachers of old Cary Field, posted an 8-2 record, the best in the school's gridiron history to that date. Losses to Navy and Virginia Tech kept them out of postseason play. From the 1930 *Colonial Echo*.

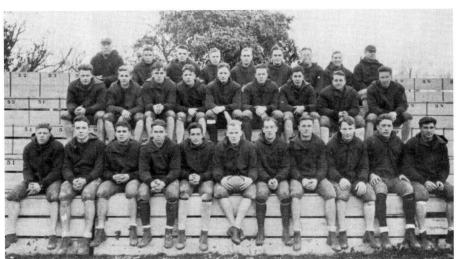

for his booming punts. He once recalled that by 1932 some players received $37.50 each semester as a scholarship toward tuition. "It was called a state scholarship," he explained.

During 1932, Kellison coached the Indians to a strong 8-4 season, beating Navy and VMI, but losing narrowly to Virginia Tech, and 18-7 to Richmond. In winning the Navy game, 6-0, at Farragut Field in Annapolis, the Indians scored what was then called "one of the most sensational victories in its history," with the only score resulting from a 17-yard touchdown run by Palese. A native of Camden, New Jersey, Palese was easily one of the best players to return from the previous year. Halligan and other teammates called him "the outstanding player on the team—strong and rugged, a very good runner." At 5'9" and 165 pounds, Palese played tailback in the single-wing system.

Harvard University was considered "big-time" football in 1930, and W&M's 13-13 tie in Cambridge, Massachusetts, was national sports news. These three shots of action during that historic game are from the 1931 *Colonial Echo*. The program is courtesy of the W&M Sports Information Department.

Halfback Billy Palese starred on the Indian teams for three seasons, 1931–33. During the 1931 game with Bridgewater, he scored six touchdowns for 36 points, still the standard for W&M players. From the 1933 *Colonial Echo.*

Against Randolph-Macon, Palese put on "one of the greatest exhibitions of broken-field running ever witnessed at Cary Field ... electrifying the crowd time after time," according to one reporter. William and Mary won 27-13 before some 6,000 fans.

In 1933, Palese was the high scorer and got the Indians off to a good start in a nighttime home opener against Roanoke, passing for W&M's sole touchdown in a 7-6 victory. Then, in a 12-0 triumph over Randolph-Macon, he gained 206 yards and scored twice. Reality set in against Navy, however, and though Palese made several long runs before the Annapolis crowd of 17,000, the Indians fell, 12-0.

The next week in Richmond, with Palese and other key players injured, William and Mary lost to Virginia Tech, 13-7, but nearly pulled off a miracle in the final minute. With the ball on his 5-yard line, Dale Worrell "twisted his way through the entire Gobbler team, but tripped over one of his own teammates after he had run 50 yards," the W&M yearbook recorded. The spectacular effort failed. After successive losses to Emory and Henry and Davidson, the Indians went into the Thanksgiving Day game against Richmond as distinct underdogs, but "playing aggressive, heads-up ball," they

A W&M ball carrier is tackled during a 1931 game. The W&M uniforms had become very up-to-date with vertical stripes on the W&M jerseys and cross-stripes on the helmets. From the 1932 *Colonial Echo.*

upset the Spiders, 6-0, in what one writer called "a day that will go down in football history at William and Mary and a team that will take its place with the greatest of all time at the college."

As the nation searched desperately for solutions to the Depression in the early 1930s, college athletics in general, and football in particular, was an anachronism. Scholarly groups called for reform and de-emphasis in sports, but football remained immensely popular with the fans, who were perhaps seeking escape from the gloom of the times. Even though money was tight everywhere, bowl games proliferated, and the professional league expanded its audiences. The day of separate offensive and defensive squads had not yet come—players still went both ways. The single-wing remained a primary offensive style, and the repertoire of plays was small.

The Miami Non-Game

W&M's gridiron success, especially in 1929 and 1930, apparently attracted the attention of athletic officials in Florida at the University of Miami. They were seeking new intersectional opponents and decided to invite W&M to play a game in Miami during the 1932 season. Unfortunately for the Indians, the invitation went astray.

According to school records, the invitation was mistakenly mailed to the William and Mary Norfolk Division. The division opened in 1930 and began playing football that fall under the nickname "The Braves" to distinguish them from the Indians on the main campus and the Papooses, the W&M freshman team. In 1930 and 1931 their opponents had been high school teams, small-college teams, like Atlantic College and Atlantic Christian College, and squads of college freshmen.

With the invitation from Miami, came a contract already signed by the athletic officials there. The W&M team in Norfolk was elated to have an opportunity to play a varsity squad from a big, "name" university and quickly accepted. It was not until later that anyone noticed that the letter had been misaddressed.

The night game, played Friday, October 14, 1932, before a Miami crowd of 10,000, was the first game of the season for Miami, which won a squeaker, 6-0. A newspaper account said, "The William and Mary air offense brought great applause from the stands." On one drive, the Braves threw five straight completions before an interception ended the threat at the Miami 10-yard line.

It would be another fourteen years before W&M in Williamsburg played the first of two games against the University of Miami. The Indians traveled to Florida and lost in 1946 and 1970. (—WK)

For William and Mary, however, the 1934 season provided little to cheer about. Playing in Annapolis against a tough Navy, led by All-American Buzz Borries, the Indians lost their opener, 20-7. They rebounded to trounce Emory and Henry, 20-8. The second, and last, victory didn't emerge for a month. Then the Tribe stopped Roanoke, 15-0, as Melville "Stumpy" Bryant led the way with booming punts and clever running.

In the season's last game on Thanksgiving Day against Richmond, rain created "a sea of mud," as the Spiders sloshed to a 6-0 victory in Kellison's coaching finale. He was replaced by Tommy Dowler for a single year, after which the College would turn again to Bocock in an attempt to revive the unsuccessful program.

Support and/or subsidization of athletics increasingly became a sore subject on campus. New President John Stewart Bryan, who preferred a traditional amateurism in sports, was nonetheless a realist and began to support the prevailing sentiment among the Board of Visitors that the College must seek parity with their rival teams. "Let's go after good players," he once told his deputy, Charles Duke. Later, on a visit to New York, he told a friend only half in jest that he wasn't searching for faculty, but "looking for a halfback."

In this same period, the Southern Conference, which the College joined in 1936, adopted modest proposals regulating financial aid to athletes. William and Mary added its own caveats, specifying that scholarship regulations would be the same for participation in all other College activities as were required for those in athletics.

Thomas "Happy" Halligan was a stalwart on the 1930, 1931, and 1932 W&M teams. He was an honorable mention All-American in 1930, led the team that rolled up a 95-0 score against hapless Bridgewater in 1931, and was team captain in 1932. From the 1933 *Colonial Echo*.

A favorite W&M coach was "Honest" John Kellison (seated) with team manager William Henry Savage (in jacket), team captain Joe Bridgers (left), and assistant coach Tommy Dowler (right). Kellison served as assistant coach before and after his four years as head coach, 1931–34. Courtesy of the W&M Sports Information Department.

Although this issue would slowly simmer toward a boil during the 1930s, the most significant event of the time was the completion of a state-of-the-art football stadium at Cary Field. It was inaugurated with a game against the University of Virginia on a steaming September day in 1935. Built in large part with Public Works Administration funds, the stadium included a quarter-mile track and a practice field.

The cost was calculated at about $170,000, and the original seating was closer to 8,500 than the expected 10,000, something like $21 per seat. Additional end-zone bleachers and modifications eventually expanded capacity to about 13,000. Subsequently, the College repaid 70 percent of the loan.

Other major buildings—Taliaferro Hall and the Marshall-Wythe Building—were part of the grant and loan package for construction. PWA regulations had prohibited the use of funds for stadiums, per se, but W&M officials proposed that such an amphitheater could be used for concerts, convocations, and other unspecified open-air events.

As early as January 1934, various publications, including the *Alumni Gazette*, had openly referred to "our new Athletic Stadium," which, it said, "will have an outdoor stage at the end for College and community performances." A unique configuration of the east-side stands included unusually wide iron grille entrance gates that eliminated some 500 choice mid-field seats below the press box (the gates were still operating in 1996).

This special architectural styling soon led to rumors that it was all part of a deal to get PWA approval of the project, and that "the feds" had

"Hap" Halligan gets off one of his trademark punts against Washington and Lee in a 1932 game the Indians won, 7-0. Notice the new, very modern W&M football uniform. From the 1933 *Colonial Echo.*

Mr. Cary's Field

At first it was called Mr. Cary's Field. It was the ground upon which a stadium and football history were built.

It is understandable that the stadium, now named for Walter Zable '37, was designed to blend with the adjacent academic campus. Its Flemish bond brickwork, Georgian moldings and trim are like the other buildings on the main campus across Stadium Drive. The architecture blends so well, in fact, that people passing often do not realize it is a football stadium.

But why, when it was constructed in 1935, were about 500 50-yard line seats eliminated?

This incongruous feature has given credence to the curious tale about the stadium: that it was originally built to accommodate livestock expositions and auctions in the manner of a state or county fair. A search of the College archives, minutes of the Board of Visitors and official papers of College President Dr. J. A. C. Chandler reveals no written verification of the story. Many alumni, nevertheless, corroborate the tale.

"That's how William and Mary got the stadium," the late Leonard L. Graves, Sr. '35, a Williamsburg native and longtime resident explained in a 1993 interview. "The Roosevelt administration offered to help with capital improvements. President Chandler tried to get the PWA [Public Works Administration] to build a stadium, but they couldn't build a football stadium at taxpayers' expense."

Ashton Dovell of Williamsburg, a member of the Virginia House of Delegates and later its speaker, suggested that Dr. Chandler propose to the PWA that an agriculture exposition center be constructed at the College. According to Graves, the stadium has never been used for a livestock show.

Dr. Davis Y. Paschall, W&M president emeritus, agreed with Graves to some degree and carries the story a step further. He recalled from his student days, when he waited on the private table of Dr. Chandler, that the president "was quite keen on sports."

It was one of the reasons why he encouraged giving prospective athletes jobs in the dining hall. They didn't have athletic scholarships back then.

President Chandler wanted to have good football, not big, but good football. He wanted to play competitively. So, when the PWA came along, if you thought up a good idea, you could get wheelbarrows and shovels paid for. Chandler conceived the idea of a PWA project to build a stadium.

I never heard Dr. Chandler use the word rodeo about the facility, but basically I always thought it was a noble idea. They would have it for agriculture and they could eventually play football in there. Football in those days was not a great big attraction.

The first football game played in the stadium was held September 21, 1935, between W&M and the University of Virginia. The stadium had not been completed, and the graceful arcade at the north end, called the most pleasing aspect of the design, was not finished until near the season's end.

Before the kickoff, W&M President John Stewart Bryan addressed the crowd from the president's box, which has now been returned to its original usage. Bryan, in a joking vein, said the stadium site "was once the playground of Indians who scalped the original Cavaliers of Virginia." There was no scalping that day; the game ended in a scoreless tie.

Since then, nearly 250 W&M football games have been played at Cary Field. In the early 1990s, several games attracted more than 15,000 people. The W&M game against the University of North Carolina in 1949 attracted an estimated 19,000-plus fans and one of the largest crowds in the stadium's history. It was certainly one of the major games. UNC won, 20-14, with famed Tar Heel back, Charlie "Choo Choo" Justice, scoring once. In 1985, an official 18,054 fans packed the stadium for W&M's 28-17 Homecoming victory over Richmond. Perhaps, the largest crowd ever at Cary was the 20,000 attending a Jimmy Buffett concert in the summer of 1988.

The "new" Cary Field opened in 1935 with a 0-0 tie against the University of Virginia. This photograph, taken during a game that year, shows the unfinished portico at the north end. Courtesy of the *Richmond Times-Dispatch*.

The architectural firm of John W. Wilson Co. of Richmond designed the facility. A newspaper account reported that "the huge sum of $170,000 went into the construction of the stadium, with 30 percent of the cost coming as a grant from PWA." The College had to pay the remainder. In 1979, a $1 million renovation project replaced wooden seats, repaired the masonry, renovated the team dressing rooms, and finally provided an enclosed press box.

Mr. Cary's Field became known as such through the years in reference to its origins as part of a farm owned by Archibald Cary. The land was donated by Cary's family during the administration of W&M President Lyon G. Tyler. Mr. Cary is believed to be a descendant of another Archibald Cary, who was a W&M student in 1740.

Another ancestor, Henry Cary, the younger, also was associated with the College in the eighteenth century. That Cary, who took over construction of the Governor's Palace in 1720, was probably the builder of The Brafferton in 1723. He also built the house for President James Blair on the campus in 1732.

The football stadium was built in 1935 near the site of old Cary Field, an athletic field with old baseball-style bleachers seating about 500 persons. The first Cary Field, built in 1906–07, was located where Blow Gymnasium (now Blow Memorial Hall) sits. The field, primarily a baseball field, was also used for football and other intercollegiate sports in the late 1910s and 1920s.

As the College began to grow in the late 1920s, Cary Field was moved westward to approximately where the Bryan residence complex is currently located, across the road from the field's current site. Because of the difficulties in reaching Williamsburg during the 1920s and 1930s, many home football games were played either in Richmond or Norfolk.

W&M made football history at Cary Field on September 24, 1927, when the first night football game in the East was played under newly installed light towers.

The College's first effort to raise money for an athletic stadium came in 1924 when the College embarked upon its first fund-raising effort. In an elaborately illustrated booklet titled, "The Romance and Renaissance of the College of William and Mary in Virginia," the lack of athletic facilities was described.

The College had no adequate athletic fields, the booklet said, noting that there was "ample room for the layout of thoroughly fields" to the west of the campus, accessible to Blow Gymnasium, then under construction. The estimated cost of the field and new stadium was $275,000.

The drive, directed by Dr. W. A. R. Goodwin, later of Colonial Williamsburg restoration fame, did raise funds for a number of campus buildings, but no new football field was built until the Depression hit and the PWA came through with the needed finances. (—WK)

This football program is from the away game against the University of Richmond on Thanksgiving Day 1933, which W&M won, 6-0. W&M's first football program for its home games also was produced in 1933 by editor Tom McCaskey '31. Courtesy of the University Archives, College of William and Mary.

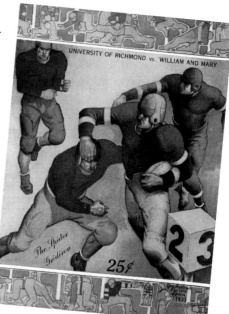

been told the special openings would accommodate livestock for exhibitions. The fact that William and Mary had neither the credentials nor the slightest interest in being an agricultural college seemed irrelevant. Through the years, the story was embellished and eventually took on a folkloric credibility. Lenny Graves, among others, regarded it as gospel.

With nineteen lettermen on hand in 1935, new Head Coach Dowler entered the season with high hopes. Dowler had been a Colgate star under Coach Andy Kerr and played two years of professional ball after his 1930 graduation.

His first game attracted a record home crowd of more than 10,000 and saw the Indians and Virginia battle to a scoreless deadlock. Coming into the conflict, Dowler predicted, "I'll say this—barring unforeseen breaks, we should be able to hold our own with any team in the state." He promised a new and more open style of play, and said he "planned to complete the Williamsburg restoration."

Although W&M went scoreless in its first four games, contests with U.Va. and Virginia Tech were ties. Navy won, 30-0, and Army, 14-0. However, the Tech game was costly because Bryant broke his ankle and missed the rest of the season. Still, the Tribe seemed to regroup by beating Guilford, 44-0, and then Roanoke, 14-7, before only 2,500 at Cary Field. The passing of Otis "Pete" Bunch to Zable provided the margin of victory in a furious last-quarter Indian rally.

A crushing setback came on Homecoming Day, when the Tribe, seeking its third straight win, faced Virginia Military Institute. Instead, the Tribe fell, 19-0, but the *Alumni Gazette* called the general celebration "an outstanding event, one of the most successful in years."

The 1933 team compiled a record of 8 wins and 4 defeats, playing the most regular season games in the school's history. W&M played thirteen games in 1990 and 1996 but that number includes two playoff games each year. From the 1934 *Colonial Echo*.

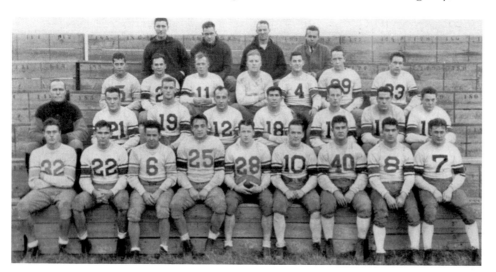

More than fifty organizations took part in a colorful parade down Duke of Gloucester Street in a tradition that began in 1929. Venerable Henry Billups was presented with a gold watch and Bible, honoring his forty-seven years of service at the College, where his tasks included indefatigable ringing of the Wren Building bell.

Two weeks later, the Indians knocked Emory and Henry out of the state championship with a 22-0 victory as six of the Wasp regulars were benched by the coach following a dispute over their eligibility. The victors were paced by Johnny Trueheart and Zable, who scored three times, twice on passes from Arthur Blaker and once by recovering a fumble in the end zone.

The always crucial contest against Richmond ended in a frustrating 6-6 tie in a game played Thanksgiving Day at City Stadium in a chilling rain. Though the Indians scored in the last minute on what the *Colonial Echo* called "a freak" play, this was also described as "an inspired game … their best of the season as they outmaneuvered Richmond." Zable excelled again, along with Bunch and "the Old Dominion's best line," but in the last sixty seconds, a tipped pass fell into Johnny Coiner's hands, and he stumbled 2 yards into the end zone. Edmondson's kick of a slippery, soggy ball for the game-winning point failed to clear the bar. So, in the descending gloom of a late November afternoon, the difficult season ended with a 3-4-3 record.

Despite the Indians' disappointing season, Zable, a track star and talented pass receiver, was named an end on the All-State team. A physics major, he received many more honors later in his life. He was named to the 1962 *Sports Illustrated* Silver Anniversary All-American Team and was the first recipient of the Distinguished American Award conferred by the National Football Foundation and Hall of Fame, which in 1980 also honored him with the Gold Medallion Award. In 1981, the College Football Hall of Fame in King's Island, Ohio, inducted him into its Hall of Fame. In addition, Zable received the NCAA's highest honor, the Theodore Roosevelt Award in 1987, an honor which has gone to such distinguished Americans as Dwight D. Eisenhower, Gerald Ford, George Bush, and Bill Cosby. An eminently successful businessman who founded the Cubic Corporation, a multimillion dollar electronics firm in San Diego,

By the mid-1930s a rivalry of sorts had already developed between W&M and the U. S. Naval Academy. Although the series was one-sided with Navy winning 35 of the 42 games through 1996, the match always posed a good challenge for the Indians. W&M won its first game, 6-0, against the Middies in 1932. This photo is of the 30-0 Navy victory in 1935. Notice the buildings of the Academy in the background. From the 1936 *Colonial Echo*.

Walter Zable (right) was named to the All-State squad in 1935 despite the team's disappointing season. He scored 19 points in his career-closing game against Richmond. Pictured here with Coach Branch Bocock. Courtesy of the W&M Sports Information Department.

This complimentary pass was given to W&M President John Stewart Bryan and is signed by William S. Gooch, Jr., athletic director and later longtime business manager of athletics. Courtesy of the University Archives, College of William and Mary.

California, Zable has been honored by William and Mary with induction into its Athletic Hall of Fame and the naming of the stadium at Cary Field for him in 1990.

At the end of the 1935 season, Coach Dowler resigned, but remained as an assistant coach until leaving the College in the spring of 1937. Late in the 1936 season, Bocock returned as head football and basketball coach, but proved unable to bring about any magic during a dismal 1-8 season. It was the school's worst record since 1915.

As events would prove, the Indians were trapped in a changing of the guard, something that L. McCarthy Downs, the College auditor of public accounts first signaled in early 1934. He released the results of a two-year study of W&M finances that he and his staff made. The report was quite critical of Dr. Chandler's fiscal practices, suggesting that some of them "disregarded the statutes relating to the control of the Commonwealth over the financial affairs of the College."

There were allegations that some loans had been made to as many as two dozen athletes, either from alumni or unspecified sources. The *Alumni Gazette* called these stories unfortunate, "creating the impression that athletics at William and Mary are subsidized. ... We state emphatically that such is not the case." The same denial had been issued two years earlier when Business Manager Gooch stated unequivocally that William and Mary "did not subsidize its athletes. We have no such thing as athletic scholarships; nor do we have influential graduates who pay the tuition."

Well into the decade, the College continued to take pride in the purity of its athletic program, but, by 1936, after two losing seasons, the climate had begun to change perceptibly. *The Flat Hat*, for example, argued, "If we want good teams in the future, we've got to go out and get them."

The Downs report recommended that managers of state institutions be placed under supervision of the state comptroller as well as the College president, and that the state treasurer become custodian of all endowment and donation funds.

The *Alumni Gazette* said "the report is full of mole hills," and Chandler's staff said there was no wrongdoing, only some possible technical violations of minor state rules. Chandler's illness prevented him from responding personally. He died within a few months.

Action in a game during the 1935 season. Notice that the president's box is completed above the stadium entrance, but the press box at the rear has not yet been constructed. From the 1936 *Colonial Echo*.

Although from the 1936 season, this is the new-style ticket for W&M home games, first issued when the stadium at Cary Field opened in 1935. Notice the portraits of King William III and Queen Mary II. From the collection of Bob Sheeran.

However, the Board of Visitors agreed to new accounting procedures, and, within a year, Downs reported that "the records of the College are in excellent order."

Nevertheless, late in 1936, Bocock warned a faculty athletic committee that "the better organized schools with superior facilities ... scholarships and jobs ... usually get the cream of the lot." That clearly meant subsidies loomed ahead, and it meant entering a new era for the ancient College.

Bocock cogently described a problem that would endlessly face colleges and universities and become further complicated by commercialization and the lure of television revenues. "Practically all desirable athletes seek to capitalize on their athletic ability to defray a portion, if not all, of their college expenses," he told the faculty. "Their presence on campus is justified because they possess the capacity to give the College something it wants."

Increasingly organized and militant alumni offered to advise the College on its athletic policy and to provide financial aid to athletes.

On November 30, 1936, the *Alumni Gazette* published a prescient editorial focusing on the emerging problem: "Why does the football player of today expect financial aid?" The editorial, which represented the views of the Society of the Alumni board, said:

> This commercialization begins when the football fan walks up to the ticket office of a stadium and is required to put up several dollars to see two football teams play sixty minutes. ... Any educational institution that wants to de-commercialize its athletic system can do so if it is willing to forego the large and alluring income from football.

W&M and University of Virginia players fight for the ball in the 1937 game in Charlottesville. From the 1938 *Colonial Echo*.

President Bryan responded in part to such pressures by saying that "in the long run the history and prestige of the College depend not upon its athletics, but upon its scholastic achievements." But he welcomed alumni ideas and involvement. The conflict was only beginning.

The 1936 season generated discontent from both students and alumni and found William and Mary defeating only one team—Guilford, 38-0—in nine games. The

W&M's 45-0 victory over Guilford College was one of the few bright spots during the 1938 season. Courtesy of the University Archives, College of William and Mary.

The ___en Gridiron

William and Mary vs. Guilf___
W. & M. STADIUM
FRIDAY, OCTOBER 14th, 193_

Alumni Gazette had predicted an outstanding year, noting that along with the return of Coach Bocock, William and Mary would have "the greatest array of coaching talent ever assembled at the College." The list included Kellison, Dowler, and Douglas, all of whom had been Tribe varsity coaches.

Unfortunately, the playing talent came up far short, despite Zable's return for his senior season in which he continued making impossible catches, blocking punts (two against Guilford) and reaffirming his All-Conference status.

Quarterback Trueheart and halfback Bunch joined Zable as seasoned veterans, but a surprising newcomer, fifth-year student Joe Flickinger, quickly stole some of the early headlines. In the 18-6 season-opening loss to Navy, the 140-pound scatback ran 50 yards for the Tribe's only score. Though he had excelled in other sports (basketball, track, and swimming—some said he was the best diver in school) during his first four years at the College, this was Flickinger's first effort to play varsity football. His exciting open-field running soon earned him a regular spot on the team.

Right after the Navy game, Flickinger received a telegram that read: "Great work. Atta boy and cheers for Big Joe, Little Joe, Branch Bocock, Billy Gooch, Kellison, Dowler, Scott, and all the Tribe." The wire was signed, "Stewart Bryan, President of William and Mary."

In the fourth game, the Tribe romped past Guilford, 38-0, for what would be its only victory of the campaign. The Quakers were one of two schools that W&M truly overwhelmed during its football history. The Indians won all ten games played between 1923 and 1939, outscoring Guilford, 409-13. As dominant as that rivalry was, the one with Bridgewater was even greater. In five games

Left halfback Pete Bunch scoots around end in a 1937 game. From the 1938 *Colonial Echo*.

between 1928 and 1932, the Tribe relinquished no points, while running up 380—an average of 76 points per contest! They unfolded this way: 68, 59, 81, 95, and 77.

The season deteriorated after the Guilford romp, and William and Mary scored only 7 more points in the final five games. Those came in a 13-7 loss to Washington

Tommy Della Torre (21) swings around end on a quarterback keeper against Guilford in the opening home game of 1937. W&M won 37-0. Later in the game a razzle-dazzle play put the icing on the cake: Della Torre passed to end Frank Cuseo, who lateraled to trailing center Rudolph Tucker who finally lateraled to trailing tackle John Dillard for a 55-yard gain. From the 1938 *Colonial Echo.*

and Lee at Foreman Field in Norfolk when W&L scored on a blocked kick. Despite the slump, Flickinger and others showed flashes of brilliance. However, by then Bunch was lost for the year with a fractured collarbone suffered during the fifth game of the year, a 13-0 loss to Roanoke.

The *Alumni Gazette* reported that, while the Richmond Spiders had been favorites on Thanksgiving Day and finally won, 7-0, "those who saw the game will never forget the gallant battle of the Indians. … Otis Bunch stood out above every player on the field … and gave the most brilliant performance seen here this winter."

The fall of 1937 opened inauspiciously with a crushing 45-0 loss at Navy. Bunch had returned, but with only five other lettermen, the Tribe was no match for the Midshipmen's depth and skill. During spring practice that March, Coach Bocock had revealed some anxieties about the forthcoming season. "Relatively few boys at William and Mary possess the required talent," he said, "and too few of them seem disposed to make the sacrifices necessary to attain superior athletic capacity."

After another "respectable" loss to VMI in Lexington, 20-9, the Indians gained some confidence with a major upset of Virginia Tech, 12-0, the next week, and then went on to waltz past Guilford, 37-0, and American University, 38-0. Against Tech, Bocock used a new play to fool the secondary and score the first touchdown: Stan Kamen took Clarence Twiddy's pass on the 12 and ran it in. W&M marched 40 yards for the second score, with Twiddy and Bunch alternating carries. Bunch plunged over from the 1 to put the final count at 12-0.

The November 13 Homecoming game was played under soggy conditions. Washington and Lee won, 14-12, in a game the *Alumni Gazette* said was "one of the hardest-fought in the series." William and Mary led, 12-7, at the half, but W&L pushed across the game-winning score in the fourth quarter.

OFFICIAL PROGRAM

William and Mary vs. Washington and Lee
W. & M. STADIUM NOVEMBER 13, 1937

This is a game-day program from the 1937 Homecoming game against Washington and Lee University. Courtesy of the University Archives, College of William and Mary.

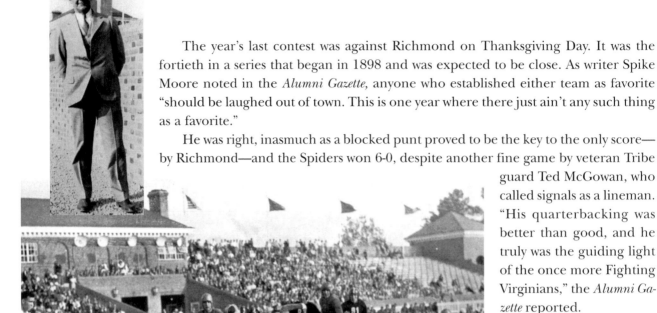

The year's last contest was against Richmond on Thanksgiving Day. It was the fortieth in a series that began in 1898 and was expected to be close. As writer Spike Moore noted in the *Alumni Gazette,* anyone who established either team as favorite "should be laughed out of town. This is one year where there just ain't any such thing as a favorite."

He was right, inasmuch as a blocked punt proved to be the key to the only score—by Richmond—and the Spiders won 6-0, despite another fine game by veteran Tribe guard Ted McGowan, who called signals as a lineman. "His quarterbacking was better than good, and he truly was the guiding light of the once more Fighting Virginians," the *Alumni Gazette* reported.

While some considered 1937's 4-5, a success, if only by comparison with the previous year, it was part of a mostly dreary era in which one of the most popular features was the

The W&M loss to The Apprentice School of Newport News Shipbuilding in 1938 was the final blow to the coaching career of Branch Bocock. He served as head coach for three winning seasons, 1928–30. He returned in 1936 for three more seasons, but he had not kept up with the changes in football. He was fired at the close of the 1938 season. From the 1939 *Colonial Echo.*

team mascot. It was an Indian pinto pony named Wampo, who appeared regularly on the sideline with bareback riders aboard in full Indian attire. Earlier, a 17-foot alligator named Cal had served as a mascot in 1927.

The pony didn't help much in 1938, either, and the only wins in nine games came against Guilford and Hampden-Sydney. The finale was a 10-7 loss to Richmond.

At the season's outset, added reserve strength and thirteen returning lettermen, including captain and center Herb Krueger, end Stan Kamen, and quarterback Twiddy, gave the appearance that W&M had the potential to improve. But five shutouts revealed weaknesses and gave rise to growing dissatisfaction with the coaching situation.

Following the team's opening 26-0 loss to Navy before 20,000, one reporter said the lighter, shallower Indians "were trampled, to no one's surprise." Several members of the team report that after they returned home, some of the players asked to meet with Charles J. "Charlie" Duke, President Bryan's assistant, to protest Bocock's coaching. According to Carter Holbrook '41, a sophomore guard, "the team felt we had to have a change. Duke agreed, and Bocock was "replaced" by freshman Coach

Douglas. He and Flickinger, by then an assistant, coached the rest of the season, but Bocock was still on the sidelines at the games and was still officially head coach.

Sophomore end Al Chestnut '41 recalled that after the Navy game Douglas handled all the details of practice "and was our game coach. We all felt we could play better than we had under Coach Bocock. We just needed some coaching to help us."

There were a couple of good wins, over Hampden-Sydney, the College's oldest intercollegiate rival, and Guilford, but many injuries contributed to several defeats.

Another loss came as something of a surprise. The Apprentice School, substituting for St. John's of Annapolis, won, 9-8. According to the *Colonial Echo*, The Apprentice School brought "a smartly coached" eleven and "some 1,500 enthusiastic supporters" to the game, which they won. One of Twiddy's punts was returned 50 yards for a touchdown, and a safety proved to be the difference. The confused Indian defense was described as "a jig-saw puzzle trying to solve itself."

The next week against VPI, the Tribe again could do little right and gained only 34 yards rushing. Quarterback Twiddy did not play, no doubt one explanation for the feeble offense in Tech's 27-0 victory.

After giving Guilford its usual drubbing, 45-0, the Indians faced a different problem in the Homecoming game against the VMI Keydets. Despite excellent play by the W&M line, the hard-hitting visitors spoiled the day for W&M with a 14-0 victory behind the passing of Paul Shue to Rob Shelby. VMI scored early in the second half on an interception of a Twiddy pass that VMI returned 74 yards to the end zone.

Virginia Military Institute was W&M's Homecoming opponent in 1938; the Indians lost, 14-0. Notice the game program cover and the "W&M Stadium" reference. The field was always called Cary, but the stadium did not receive an official name until 1990. The game photograph is from the 1939 Colonial Echo; *program is courtesy of the University Archives, College of William and Mary.*

After a 34-0 loss to the University of Virginia Charlottesville, Moore reported that "evidently the Cavaliers were in an ugly mood." Four Tribe regulars were hurt on the third play of the game and things went downhill from there. Virginia's romp extended the hosts' record of remaining unscored on by a W&M team.

As the College yearbook put it, "this team fought its heart out and played to the best of its ability ... but was literally buried in defeats." Bocock would leave as coach, and the president began his search for new leadership, an undertaking that would bear surprisingly rewarding results in a surprisingly short span of time.

3
"Big-Time" Football and Bowl Games
The Golden Era
1939 to 1951

Wilford Kale

B y 1939, W&M President John Stewart Bryan, a Richmond newspaper executive, had made a significant impact on the College by strengthening the liberal arts through hiring several Harvard University–trained professors.

With the help of E. Gordon Bell, dean of the faculty at Dartmouth College, Bryan also restructured the curriculum and defined a liberal arts college model that he felt was best suited for William and Mary. But he was still faced with the athletic problem, specifically football, which had haunted him from the first days of his presidency in 1934.

Bryan solved his problem with the selection of Carl Marvin Voyles as W&M's new football coach and athletic director. The College's search committee, following Bryan's admonition, went after a "big-time" coach to turn the program around. Since 1931, Voyles had been an assistant coach at Duke University, a major college football power in 1938. That year, the Blue Devils, under head coach Wallace Wade, were undefeated, untied, unscored upon, and destined to play Southern California in the Rose Bowl game.

Without reservation, Wade heaped praise upon his assistant, who, at 39 years of age, had been coaching for nearly twenty years. Voyles, a former five-letter athlete at Oklahoma A&M (now Oklahoma State), was a native of McLaud, Oklahoma, although his family hailed from Wytheville, Virginia.

Voyles was selected by the College's athletic committee on November 28, 1938. Committee head Judge H. Lester Hooker of Richmond had urged W&M to develop a stronger football program, which he knew the alumni would help finance.

President Bryan, in his annual report to the Board of Visitors, wrote on May 27, 1939:

Carl Voyles came to the campus ready to teach and coach football. During his first spring practice at W&M, in 1939, he demonstrated how he wanted blocking handled. From the 1940 *Colonial Echo*.

The 1939 team, Voyles's first, was composed primarily of players recruited by previous coach, Branch Bocock. Voyles also recruited several junior college players from Tennessee, who helped the squad win six games, four more than in 1938. This team began W&M's "Golden Era" of football. From the 1940 *Colonial Echo*.

The problem of athletics, as the Board well knows, has given us a great deal of concern for many years. As has been abundantly shown, this problem is not solely one of amusement or gratification for the alumni, but involves the deeper and more extensive consideration of attracting young men, both those who are athletes and those who are not.

I can say to the Board without the slightest hesitation that the choice of Carl M. Voyles gives the best assurance we could have of a satisfactory solution of this matter. In the employment of Mr. Carl Voyles as athletic director, I may say here that never has anyone come to William and Mary with more lamentation from the place he left, and with more praise from everyone with whom he has been previously associated. I believe that we have in Mr. Voyles not only a coach of extraordinary ability, but a powerful influence for good on this campus.

Those were powerful words from a college president, especially when applied to an athletic director and a football coach.

Tom Wiley, writing in the *Richmond Times-Dispatch* on February 13, 1939, reported that Voyles already had made a big hit with the approximately 1,300 students and athletes on campus: "Concrete evidence of Voyles's popularity with the boys and girls at the Williamsburg school was given Saturday night in the Blow Memorial Gymnasium just before the William and Mary–University of Richmond basketball game got underway." Voyles was greeted by a boisterous ovation noticeably louder than the one given Bryan, the College's popular president.

Bryan and many W&M alumni wanted to bring "big time" football to the Reservation with all its accouterments—heavy recruitment, many assistant coaches, tougher schedules, and better players. Voyles, however, downplayed the notion when he told *The Flat Hat* in the spring of 1939: "We are not out for 'big time' football in the sense

Members of the 1939 team enjoyed being part of Carl Voyles's football program. Left to right, top row: John Dillard, Jimmy Howard, George McComb, and Mervyn Simpson; (second row) Clyde Ramsay, Frank Stephens, Jim Hickey, and Al Chestnut. From the 1940 *Colonial Echo*.

that we want Rose Bowl teams or that we want to play schools that have only football reputations. We want to play games with our natural rivals and hope to break even with them over a 10-year period."

Voyles and R. N. "Rube" McCray accomplished this goal. Between 1939 and 1950, W&M's record against Richmond was 11-0; 9-0-1 against Virginia Tech; 5-0 against Hampden-Sydney; and 4-0 against Randolph-Macon. In the mid-1940s, those small in-state teams, along with Washington and Lee, were replaced on the schedule by N.C. State, University of North Carolina, Maryland, Oklahoma, Michigan State, and Boston University.

But there was definitely one "big time" element to Voyles—the salary he commanded. Although there is no mention of what Voyles was paid when he arrived in 1939, he made $8,000 in 1941, compared with $5,000 for James W. Miller, professor and dean of the faculty, who was the highest paid faculty member. W&M President Dr. John Pomfret, who came to the College in 1942, made $10,000.

Even before Voyles arrived on campus, he named his first assistant at the College: R. N. McCray, who would become the varsity backfield coach and eventually succeed Voyles after the war. Among those added later were Albert Henry "Pop" Werner, varsity line coach, and Eric Tipton, backfield coach, who would remain at W&M for eighteen years.

W&M's football mascot "Wampo," appeared first at the Guilford game in October 1937. The pony, with Tim Hanson and Jimmy Keillor riding tandem bareback, would gallop around the track to celebrate each score. The pony began to make more touchdown gallops in 1939, when W&M football took a decided upswing. From the 1938 *Colonial Echo*.

Voyles's first year at William and Mary produced a 6-2-1 season, a major turnaround from Coach Branch Bocock's 3-7 in 1938. Following the 1939 introduction of Metro-Goldwyn-Meyer's hit movie, *The Wizard of Oz*, it was not surprising that Voyles was proclaimed, "The Wizard of Ourz." Not only did Voyles transform a varsity team into an overnight winner, but he also recruited a talented squad that would forever be called, "The Fabulous Freshmen." Landing those high school graduates was an amazing saga, and each player had a different story to tell.

McCray, head coach of Tennessee Wesleyan College, knew of the talents of Garrard "Buster" Ramsey of Maryville, Tennessee, and other East Tennessee athletes. When Ramsey decided to come to William and Mary, he recalled McCray "took a station wagon full of East Tennessee boys with him to Williamsburg."

> I was working out at the University of Tennessee when he drove up in that station wagon, right on campus, and picked us up and took us to Williamsburg. I'd never heard of William and Mary. He just said, "Let's go and look the place over." He had Red Irwin and Glen Knox, a few others and me when he headed out. They hid us out in Virginia Beach for a week and then took us to Gloucester Point.

Carl Voyles

They called him the "silver tongue" because of his persuasive speech. His tenure at W&M began what has gone down in history as the "Golden Era." He has the best winning percentage in William and Mary football, and his 1942 team, with the exception of one tie, won all of its intercollegiate games.

Carl M. Voyles was a legend to the students and players during his 1939–44 coaching stint. One example of what elevated him to such high esteem can be found in the way he responded in 1944 to Hank Wolfe, sports writer for *The Richmond News Leader* about his William and Mary experience. Surprisingly, Voyles did not discuss his championship 1942 team, but instead reflected on his first one.

One of the biggest thrills occurred when the 1939 team came from behind and beat Washington and Lee. We were leading by five points with three-and-a-half minutes to play and had the ball on our own 10-yard line.

Waldo Matthews threw a pass to Harley Masters and the ball was advanced to the middle of the field. It looked like it was our game then, but one of our linemen was across the line of scrimmage on the play and we were penalized five yards.

On the next play we elected to punt, and the tackle, who was offside, let a W&L lineman come through and block the punt. This put W&L ahead 13-12 with two minutes to go.

We received and ran with the ball twice. Then Matthews switched to the wingback position and went down the field and caught a long pass on the sideline surrounded by W&L players. He jerked loose and ran 54 yards for a touchdown to give us a 18-14 win.

Each of our Homecoming games since that time has been a thrill to me, for we promised the boys if they beat W&L that day, every William and Mary team on Homecoming Day under me would make a special attempt to give the old grads a good day.

Players remember Voyles as "the type of coach who made us play game by game. I don't think we realized that the team was as good as it was until many years later," explained William J. "Bill" Goodlow, captain in 1941.

Voyles came to Williamsburg in November 1938 after serving for eight years as the first assistant to Duke University's football coaching legend Wallace Wade. In appointing Voyles, W&M President John Stewart Bryan said of his previous experience: "Under these dynamic and brilliant generals, Carl Voyles studied the wide field of college athletics in all of its major phases . . . this training, coupled with his own force and attractiveness, won him the deep affection and fullest confidence of his former associates."

During his years at W&M, he compiled a 29-7-3 record before football was halted by World War II in 1943. His teams outscored opponents 851 to 274 and compiled a winning percentage of .806. He had seventeen first-team All-State players, seven second-team players, and three named to the third team. They included eleven all–Southern Conference team members and 1942 All-American guard Garrard "Buster" Ramsey.

Ramsey recalled that Voyles was steeped in fundamentals and got plenty out of each player. Another of the "Fab Frosh," Jim Hickey, who went on to be head coach at the University of North Carolina, called Voyles "one of the great coaches. He was a hard, tough man." Some others did not like his "professional" approach, which sometimes included keeping them in games at the risk of injury.

Players also mentioned that Voyles was a strong supporter of academics and wouldn't tolerate players missing classes. Voyles was so concerned that players finish their schoolwork before practice that he had lights installed on the practice field, so they could drill on into the night.

In the spring of 1944, W&M President John E. Pomfret said Voyles was a "free agent" to talk with Auburn officials. When Volyes finally accepted a six-year contract at the Alabama school, Dr. Pomfret said Voyles had developed a "splendid team from mediocre material. He [was] a strict disciplinarian and [did] not permit the boys he worked with to fall into bad scholastic habits."

Unfortunately, Voyles did not attain similar success at Auburn. His 1944 team finished 4-4, but his center, Tex Warrington, who followed him from Williamsburg to Auburn, was named an All-American. With only a 15-12 record and winning only four Southeastern Conference games, he was released by Auburn in 1947 with two years remaining on his contract.

After Auburn, Volyes became head coach of the Brooklyn Dodgers professional football team of the All-American Conference, then rival of the National Football League. He later coached the Hamilton Tiger-Cats of the Canadian Football League and won the Grey Cup in 1953.

His collegiate coaching record was 63-34-5 over twelve seasons at Southwestern Oklahoma State College (1922–24), W&M (1939–42), and Auburn (1944–47), and his overall record was 128-82-6, including 9-0 high school credentials in Altus, Oklahoma.

Voyles retired to his home in Florida to manage his real estate holdings, including an automobile agency and a tomato farm he owned in Vero Beach. In 1969 he was named to the William and Mary Athletic Hall of Fame in the first group of inductees. He died January 11, 1982, at the age of 82.   (—WK)

Coach Voyles poses on Cary Field with his 1942 All-American guard Garrard "Buster" Ramsey. Courtesy of the W&M Sports Information Department.

Fullback Harvey Johnson (50) with the ball was one of several players from the "Fabulous Freshman" team of 1939 who made the starting eleven on 1940s state championship W&M team. From the 1941 *Colonial Echo*.

While we were in Gloucester, they entered all of us in school at William and Mary. That was the way to keep us from going to any other college. I know it sounds unusual, but that's the way things were done back then.

Still others, like Johnny Korczowski, were literally "footballnaped" away from other schools. Korczowski was enrolled at Georgetown, but wound up at William and Mary, taken out of his dormitory and brought to Williamsburg to play for the Indians. He was a freshman and had been on the Georgetown campus about a week before he suddenly disappeared, recalled another 1939 Georgetown freshman, Edmund Derringe, who later became a W&M coach under Milt Drewer and business manager of athletics in the 1970s and 1980s.

Other 1939 W&M freshmen included, Al Helslander, Harvey Johnson, John Torma, Jack McAfee, Lane Phillips, Marvin Bass, Pat "Pappy" Fields, William Wade, Robert Templeton, Al Vandeweghe, Baxter Jerrell, and Bob Longacre. That freshman squad compiled a 4-1 record.

Players arrived early in September when, according to the *Colonial Echo*, "they first banded together as a unit. Since that time they have lived as a group, studied in unison, and, greatest of all, they became a highly successful football team."

The baby Spiders from Richmond cast the only dark shadow of the season with a 20-19 victory. Papoose triumphs were recorded over the Norfolk Naval Base, Fork Union Military Academy, Wake Forest, and the College's Norfolk Division team.

With co-captains John Dillard and Lloyd Phillips taking charge, the Indians' 1939 varsity put together its best season since 1932, starting with a season-opening 31-6 demolition of Guilford College.

William and Mary faithful did not expect much from the 1939 Indians and neither did an outgoing coach, according to the December *Alumni Gazette* magazine.

The Indian Gridiron

William and Mary   vs.   Guilford College

SPIRIT OF FALL

W. & M. STADIUM
Saturday, September 23, 1939

That unidentified departing coach reportedly said, "there isn't a man on this squad who could make any of the other five teams in the [Virginia Big Six—Richmond, U.Va., VMI, Virginia Tech, Washington and Lee, and William and Mary]. Our freshman team last fall was the worst in ten years and you already know the record of last year's varsity [3-7]."

W&M football became fun quickly in 1939 as evidenced by this program cover. Courtesy of the University Archives, College of William and Mary.

But Voyles and his coaching crew did turn the football program around. "The Wizard of Ourz" used no magic. "Hard work and tenacity turned the tide—a tenacity that revealed itself in his regard for fine detail," wrote Spike Moore, a co-director of athletic publicity, in the *Alumni Gazette*.

> The writer of this piece is of the opinion that most credit for this year's football team must go to Coach Voyles, the drillmaster. And yet credit also must be given the squad which accepted and cooperated in the regimentation necessary for the production of any winning football team.

William and Mary's 7-0 triumph over a previously unbeaten Richmond University eleven on Thanksgiving Day, the first Indian victory over the Spiders since 1933, is ample proof of Voyles coaching wizardry. The Indian mentor had exactly three days to get his boys ready for an unbeaten Richmond team that needed only one more victory to claim the state championship.

In its nine games, W&M was behind only once at halftime. That showed, Moore added, "that only a lack of reserve strength kept the Indians from being perhaps THE top team in this state." The Indians also were hampered by an unusually high number of end-of-season injuries to key personnel. Talented full-back Howard Hollingsworth missed the last four games, and fleet-footed sophomore halfback Harlie Masters the last six. Ben Simpson, hard-nosed blocking back and the team's most valuable player, missed the season's last two games.

The cheerleader squad of 1940 was typical of the era. The members were: (front row, left to right) Dorothy Jean Ross, Etta Louise Wallace, Alice Black, and Helen Jerry; (back row) Lawrence Goldsmith, Charles M. Sullivan, and Joseph Harold Markowitz. From the 1941 *Colonial Echo*.

With victories over Guilford, The Apprentice School, Hampden-Sydney, and Randolph-Macon; losses to Navy and Virginia; and a tie with Virginia Tech, the Indians came to Homecoming with a chance to ensure a winning season. Voyles made Homecoming a very important game for his team, telling players that not only would many former football team members be there to watch, but thousands of alumni expected them to win. Voyles said it was the most important game of the season; they might lose other games, but *not* Homecoming. Voyles's teams won all four of their Homecoming games, and his successor, Rube McCray, added five more victories to the string.

The 1939 Homecoming game, an 18-14 victory over a highly favored Washington and Lee team, was played before some 9,000 people at Cary Field. The Generals struck first in the opening period, but the Indians came back. Waldo Matthews kicked a field goal and threw a touchdown pass to end Charlie Gondak to take a 9-7 halftime lead.

Another Matthews field goal put the score at 12-7, but the Generals blocked a W&M punt in the end zone for a touchdown to lead 14-12 in the fourth quarter. With four minutes remaining, Harold Burchfield passed to Matthews, who ran the remaining 30 yards for the winning touchdown.

The season-ending, 7-0 win over Richmond was just as rewarding. Although the Spiders had a heavier line, W&M simply outplayed them. The game's lone touchdown came in the third quarter on a line plunge by Jimmy Howard. The game-winner was set up by a pass from Howard to Matthews, who made a spectacular catch on the 2-yard line. Richmond was within the Indians' 4-yard line twice during the game and was stopped once a foot from the goal.

In reflecting on the 1939 season, Voyles wrote in a *Flat Hat* article:

> Throughout the season the team has shown continual improvement. At times we faced, due to numerous injuries among key men of both the defense and offense, almost impossible odds, but those who filled-in at these crucial times had the ability to fight, the love of conflict and the general willingness to play sixty-minute football if necessary. We emerged with three candidates for All-State honors, captain-elect Chuck Gondak, lineman Hank Whitehouse and back Waldo Matthews.

Coach Carl Voyles (third from left) and Assistant Coach "Pop" Werner (second from left) cheer the 1940 team from the bench. To the left of the coaches is Bill Goodlow and at the far right are Jimmy Howard and Al Vandeweghe. The player beside Voyles is unidentified. From the collection of Al Vandeweghe.

Although the 1940 season brought the same results as 1939, 6-2-1, those "Fabulous Freshmen" had become varsity players and were maturing. Four of the "frosh" —Bass, Johnson, Ramsey, and Fields— were starters. The team scored about 25 more offensive points than in 1939, while the defense held the opponents to 35 fewer points.

Expectations on campus were high for the team, but the so-called sophomore jinx apparently hit in the season's opening game when highly favored W&M lost to N.C. State, 16-0, in Norfolk. The game was only four minutes old when State scored. According to *Richmond Times-Dispatch* Sports Editor Chauncey Durden, "the Indians were never in the ball game after that. State's country boys "conned the green Indians, who appeared to have buck fever as the season opened under the lights," Durden wrote. "The Wolfpack isn't a ranking power in North Caro-

lina, but it was too good last night for what we had thought to be one of the Old Dominion's better teams."

A second-week loss to Navy put Voyles in a corner, but then his team won four straight. The comeback featured a 13-6 Homecoming victory over Virginia, the first ever for W&M in a series that began in 1908 and included ten defeats and one tie. Underdog W&M surprised the Homecoming crowd by scoring 13 points against the Cavalier team led by famous back Bill Dudley, the most ever against a Virginia team. W&M's attack, offensively and defensively, was awesome, the *Richmond Times-Dispatch* reported. After a scoreless first half, fullback Harvey Johnson led the Indians, which struck quickly to score all their points in the third period. Dudley tossed a 25-yard pass for Virginia's only score, and the game ended with W&M on the Cavalier's 3-yard line.

With the exception of that year's 0-0 tie with VMI, W&M defeated every Virginia college it played between 1940 and 1949. Ironically, a VMI victory in the opening game of 1950 ended the incredible string.

The season-ending, Thanksgiving Day 16-0 triumph over Richmond before a crowd of 18,000 at Richmond's Mayo Island Park brought W&M

In 1941, following W&M's two consecutive winning seasons under Voyles (in middle of field with reporter in jacket), Press Day attracted much attention. Some players are posing at far right while others wait their turn at the left. Photo by the Newport News *Daily Press;* courtesy of George F. Wright (the reporter on the field with Voyles) and the W&M Sports Information Department.

Pile-driving runner John Korczowski carries the ball past two defenders. Courtesy of the W&M Sports Information Department.

This montage of photographs shows the Indian team in action during four games in 1941 when W&M won eight games losing only to Navy and North Carolina State. From the 1942 *Colonial Echo.*

its first state championship. It was a game in which superiority was evident from the start. The *Times-Dispatch* reported William and Mary's tackling and defensive play was not as vicious as it was in the earlier victory over Virginia, but it was just as convincing. Offensively, Harvey "The Stud" Johnson, junior Jimmy Howard, and Harlie Masters, and most of the "Fabulous Freshmen" of 1939 dominated.

It was a tight defensive struggle through the first half, with the Indians leading 2-0 on a safety scored when the ball was snapped over the Richmond punter's head and out of the end zone. In the third quarter, according to Durden, "Johnson, 210-pound fullback, went berserk and shattered the Richmond line as he led a 50-yard drive" for the first touchdown. "Johnson smashed over the Spiders' last white line from three yards out." The Tribe's second touchdown and final score came in the fourth quarter, Durden wrote, "and followed a 32-yard run by Masters on a naked reverse. The touchdown came on a pass from Waldo Matthews to sophomore end Newell Irwin, the only pass the Indians completed in seven attempts."

Last-ditch goal-line stands saved the Spiders on two other attempts, one each in the second and third quarters. Voyles played a six-man defensive line in the first half and switched to seven men in the second half, stopping Richmond's fantastic runner Art Jones for a net minus 14 yards on seven carries. Meanwhile, Johnson netted 114 yards running on twenty-nine attempts and Howard had 87 on eighteen attempts.

There was a special sweetness in the Richmond victory because the Spiders had already upset a powerful University of North Carolina team that had whipped Duke's mighty Blue Devils and the University of Virginia Cavaliers.

Voyles's third W&M team began 1941 with a 53-0 trouncing of The Apprentice School at Newport News Shipbuilding. Ironically, it was a 9-8 loss to The Apprentice School in 1938 that some people say pushed President Bryan toward "big-time" football and, ultimately, to hiring Voyles. Using just a few plays in its offensive arsenal, W&M scored seven touchdowns with seven conversions and two safeties.

Facing its first major opponent of the campaign, the Indians fell, 34-0, to a strong U.S. Naval Academy. Severe heat and the loss of All-State tackle Marvin Bass for most of the game did not help. Navy triumphed behind a hard-charging line that was three-deep in most positions.

Voyles and his Indians now needed a good win. They got it by smothering Randolph-Macon, 51-7, in Williamsburg before only 2,000 on an October day with temperatures in the mid-90s. Randolph-Macon ran up two first downs early in the first quarter and never got another. W&M scored first on a 9-yard Harvey Johnson run and later on a 7-yard pass from Jackie Freeman to end Al Vandeweghe. Freeman scored again before the end of the first period on a 48-yard broken-field dash. The Tribe led 26-0 at the half, and W&M's Jimmy Howard received the kick-off and raced 90 yards for a touchdown.

Senior Jimmy Howard was featured in this yearbook pose surrounded by adoring coeds. The fleet-footed back could run, pass, and kick extra points. He also excited the crowd with kickoff returns, especially the 90-yard touchdown in 1941 against Randolph-Macon and a 58-yarder in 1940 against North Carolina State. From the 1942 *Colonial Echo*.

The Indians did not let up the next week in a 16-7 defeat of Virginia Tech with Harvey Johnson, once again leading the way, followed closely by the sensational running of Freeman and Howard. When Freeman wasn't returning punts and kickoffs (he accumulated 130 yards for the day), he intercepted two passes that led to two scores.

W&M continued its winning ways with lopsided victories over Hampden-Sydney and George Washington in its first appearance in Southern Conference play.

What really made 1941 a great football year for the Tribe was its 3-0 defeat of Dartmouth, a major Eastern football power. The win at Hanover, New Hampshire, played on a cold, rain-drenched field, turned on two third-quarter plays. W&M tackle Harold "Pappy" Fields finally came into his own. After a long punt by Freeman, Dartmouth started on its own 35-yard line, but Fields crashed through the line on successive plays to throw the Dartmouth ball carriers for 6- and 9-yard losses, respectively. Then Fields came through the line on a third-down punt play to block the kick. W&M had the ball on the Ivy League squad's 21-yard line. But Dartmouth held, and a 25-yard field goal by Johnson accounted for the game's lone score.

After the game, Coach Voyles praised Johnson and Fields and gave much credit to Freeman, whose consistent punting of the water-soaked ball, which in those days

became heavier when wet, kept Dartmouth backed up for most of the game, although the New Hampshire school dominated game

This game football from 1941 was saved by William S. "Pappy" Gooch. It is in his collection at the Virginia Sports Hall of Fame. Photo by C. James Gleason/VISCOM.

1941 team captain Bill Goodlow. From the collection of Jack Freeman.

statistics. Dartmouth led the Indians ten to five in first downs; 165 to 117 in yards rushing; 34 to 10 in passing yardage, and 199 to 127 yards in total offense.

W&M's Masters-and-Johnson act shut down VMI, 21-0, the next week for the sixth shutout of the season—the most for the Tribe since 1930, when all seven victories were shutouts. Harlie Masters, a 165-pound back, combined with 200-pound senior fullback Johnson to roll over the Keydets. In all, Indian runners pounded VMI for 356 yards against 32 for the Lexington crew. Johnson scored a touchdown and tallied three extra points, while Masters also scored and made a 49-yard kickoff return to open the game.

The *Times-Dispatch,* in its Thanksgiving morning edition, questioned whether there would be murder that afternoon at Richmond's City Stadium. Durden wrote:

> The Spiders will fight. You may be sure of that. But spirit ain't gonna make up for the big difference in squad personnel. This W&M team has the power. Far too much for Richmond. The Indians, who have come a long way since the shellacking by Navy, have everything it takes except passing. They'll spot the Spiders the passing and draw away breezing.

And that's exactly what happened. W&M won 33-3 in the traditional game, earning a tie with U.Va. for the state championship. The Indians even passed. In fact, they scored on a touchdown pass from Howard to end Vandeweghe. But it was the running by Johnson—113 yards of it—and fine kicking by Freeman that put the Tribe way out in front.

A last-game victory over North Carolina State would have given W&M its first Southern Conference title, albeit a tie. Uncharacteristically, the team was not up. The Tribe threatened only once, and failed on an 18-yard field goal attempt. While the line did well against State runners, W&M could not cope with the pinpoint passing of N.C. State's Art Faircloth and lost, 13-0.

Harvey "Stud" Johnson (50) gets nailed by a North Carolina State player after a short gain. W&M lost the 1941 game, 13-0, to end an otherwise good 8-2 season. Courtesy of the W&M Sports Information Department.

The 1941 team's 8-2 record boasted the most victories since 1932 and matched the 1929 record as the best in school history. The best, however, was yet to come.

Following the 1942 spring game, rave reviews were being tossed William and Mary's way for the first time. Coach Voyles was cautious. "We're going to be a very good team this year," he told the *Richmond Times-Dispatch*, "but it very definitely won't be a great one." The schedule was perhaps the toughest in the College's history, he acknowledged. After what would be a 27-0 season opening romp over Hampden-Sydney, the last of a 39-game series that began in 1894, the Indians would face Navy in a game that Voyles believed his team had little chance of winning:

> We're being overrated this year, and Navy is being underrated. If we played them later in the season, we might have a chance, but they're too far ahead of us now, and, with our morning practices messed up by summer school, we can't possibly get in enough work by the 26th to give them an even battle.

Ten of William and Mary's leading players attended 1942 summer school in an accelerated wartime program to speed graduation. Those classes, running through September 12, prevented the players from attending morning football practice. Fifteen lettermen returned, but lost to the squad were Howard, Masters, and Jim Hickey from 1941. Voyles lamented:

> All three of these boys could get up and go. But as things are now, we simply don't have the speed. Our passing game may be better with Buddy Hubbard (now a sophomore) throwing, along with Jackie Freeman and Bob Longacre, and our kicking—when Freeman is in—should be as good. Unfortunately, we don't have a second kicker who was as good as Hickey was last year.
>
> Nope, we're being overrated. The speed in the backfield just isn't there, and our sophomores aren't good enough to compensate for it. But, I'll say this: we have two mighty fine football players in Harvey Johnson, our fullback, and Garrard Ramsey, our left guard. These boys are as good as any college players in the country today.

Glenn Knox, end, takes the ball away from a Virginia Tech defender and subsequently scores a touchdown as Al Vandeweghe (17) the other W&M end watches. The victory was W&M's first consecutive win over Tech in the schools' rivalry. From the 1943 *Colonial Echo*.

This page is from an early 1942 W&M football program. Some of these men did not play during the season because they had already entered military service. Tackle "Pappy" Fields (center) joined the Army later and died early in the war. From the collection of Wilford Kale.

Garrard "Buster" Ramsey

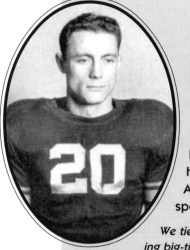

In the era of "big-time" football William and Mary had only one true Associated Press First-Team All-America football player: Garrard "Buster" Ramsey of Maryville, Tennessee.

He was part of the 1942 William and Mary team that finished 9-1-1. At guard, Ramsey was a standout both offensively and defensively. Although he believes his best all-around season was probably his junior year (1941), he knows his play in 1942 against Harvard and Dartmouth made him an All-American, "because I had good games and was playing before the Eastern sportswriters. They had never seen me play before."

We tied a very good Harvard team and beat Dartmouth at a time when both were play-ing big-time football. [At the Harvard game] I played against [Endicott] "Chub" Peabody [later governor of Massachusetts] who was supposed to be the best in the East and the hottest football player around. He also played guard and I beat him real bad. It was then that I knew I had a chance to make it—to be All-American. … The day before we played Oklahoma, the Associated Press sent [Coach Voyles] a telegram saying that I had made first team. He brought it out before the whole squad. I still have it in my old scrapbook. I was overwhelmed; it was hard to believe. My teammates were jubilant and congratulated me warmly.

W&M, with Ramsey leading the way, went out the next day and beat Oklahoma, 14-7. A few weeks later Ramsey played in the Blue-Gray All-Star Football game, and the next summer played in the 1943 College All-Star football game. Ironically, Ramsey played his second All-Star game in 1946. After three years in the Navy, "I was still considered a collegian, and we played the Los Angeles Rams and defeated them, 16-0." Ramsey is one of only three people to play in two College All-Star games.

Ramsey's Knoxville, Tennessee, high school team won the mythical national championship in 1937 by defeating a Miami, Florida, team, 25-0. Although the 1938 Knoxville team was not as good, Ramsey's play drew the attention of many college coaches. Herman Hickman wanted him at North Carolina State, "but I didn't have good math grades," Ramsey admitted. He came to W&M as a member of the "Fabulous Freshmen" of 1939.

Accounts of the 1942 season focus most of the attention on the Indians' offense, but the defense in many cases created opportunities for W&M to win. Jackie Freeman, the team's punter and later a W&M coach said, "Ramsey was phenomenal."

We played a six-man line in those days, and he had such great speed. He could just cover that field from sideline to sideline. I've seen him more than once chasing people down from the back. He was fast. He wasn't too big weight-wise, but he could move and was quick as a darn cat. … His opposition might beat him the first yard, but not the second. He was a great football player.

Coach Freeman said the best thing about Ramsey "was his determination. He felt nobody could play it better than he could—and he was right."

In a 1992 interview, Ramsey recalled,

In those days, we played the single-wing. It was single-wing right and single-wing left and that was just about it. … And, of course, everybody played both ways. It was not unusual for players to play 60 minutes a game. I'm crippled up now because of all that ball. … [Football in 1942] was basic knocking. I'm not even sure you can throw a side body-block anymore. Then, as now, if you didn't have a line you were up the creek."

For his gridiron prowess, Ramsey received All-State honors, was named all–Southern Con-ference, and, in 1978, was inducted into the National Football Foundation College Football Hall of Fame.

Ramsey needed one or two class credits to graduate in 1943 when he entered the Navy. "But they didn't need me right away and sent me back to school. I got my degree in the summer."

While in the Navy (1943–45), Ramsey played two seasons of football at Bainbridge (Maryland) Naval Training Station with fellow W&M players Al Vandeweghe and Harvey Johnson and one season in Hawaii with another naval outfit. During those Navy years, he broke his neck and got his right knee torn up.

After being discharged from the service in 1946, he went down to Auburn to coach with Carl Voyles, who had become head coach of the Tigers in 1944. "But late in the summer I got a call from the [College] All-Stars and played in another All-Star game," he explained, and later signed to play pro ball for the Chicago Cardinals (now the Phoenix Cardinals) for $6,000 a year. He played six seasons and earned only $8,000 his last year.

In 1946, the Cardinals, the oldest club in pro football in continuous operation, won its first NFL championship since 1925. Ramsey had torn up his right knee during the season, but still played in the championship game in 1947 against the Philadelphia Eagles and another former Indian, Otis Douglas. The Cardinals won, 28-21.

Ramsey said one of the "nicest things that ever happened to me was when Johnny Counselman, who later started the Pro Football Hall of Fame, was a coach with the Cardinals." Counselman, who was an assistant W&M coach in 1920–21, came up to Ramsey in Chicago and asked what he was doing. Ramsey explained:

I had come in with my little notebook. Now every player has a playbook, but I had my own notebook and was taking notes on what Counselman was saying. He looked at me and said, "I've been in this business twenty years and you're the first player to take notes at a meeting." Pretty soon, everybody had a notebook and was taking notes.

In a 1969 retrospective of the first fifty years of the National Football League (NFL), the Pro Football Hall of Fame selected one all-NFL squad for each decade of the league's history. Ramsey was selected as one of five outstanding 1940s guards. Only he and Charles Trippi, the great fullback, were selected from the Cardinal teams during that ten-year span.

In all, Ramsey participated in six NFL championship contests, two as a player and four as a coach. He was defensive coach for the Detroit Lions from 1952 through 1959 when another Indian, Lou Creekmur played and the Lions won the NFL "World Championship" in 1952, 1953, and 1957. With the Cardinals' earlier win, Ramsey earned four NFL world championship rings.

In 1960, Ramsey became the first head coach hired in the new rival American Football League, when Ralph Wilson tapped him to coach the Buffalo Bills. Ramsey's teams won about half their games in the two years he stayed with the club before leaving in a disagreement with Wilson. Ramsey was immediately "re-hired" by Buddy Parker, who had moved from Detroit to the Pittsburgh Steelers. "Buddy talked me into going to Pittsburgh as defensive coach. I had just about decided to come back to Tennessee and farm. I finally did it after the 1964 season," Ramsey explained. He retired to a 160-acre Charolais cattle farm outside of Maryville, Tennessee, just west of the Smoky Mountains.

You will not find football jersey No. 20 on the W&M field today, because, for Coach Jimmye Laycock and other W&M followers, No. 20 *means* Garrard "Buster" Ramsey, and No. 20 is simply retired. (—WK)

| Glenn Knox | Harold Fields | Garrard Ramsey | Tex Warrington | Doc Holloway | Captain Marvin Bass | Al Vandeweghe |

W&M's "award winning" 1942 line was (from left to right) Glenn Knox, Harold Fields, Garrard Ramsey, Tex Warrington, Doc Holloway, Captain Marvin Bass, and Al Vandeweghe. Photo by Richmond Newspapers, Inc.; from the collection of Jacqueline Phillips Allen.

But W&M in 1942 was not overrated. Indeed, it would become historic.

In Annapolis, Maryland, against the Navy team Voyles had said the Indians "had little chance" of defeating, success was sweet indeed. The *New York Times* said it simply, "Harvey Johnson's accurate field goal from the Navy 20-yard line six minutes after the opening whistle provided the margin by which a veteran William and Mary team turned back the Midshipmen [3-0]."

Scoring was as simple as that. Although Johnson's kick was from a very difficult angle, the victory was not. The score came on the Indians' only offensive threat of the game, while the team was forced to repulse the Navy advances—twice at the Tribe 26, twice at the 18, and once at the 14. Navy's offense tried everything—runs, passes, and quick-kicks. But the stellar play of the Tribe's line—Vandeweghe, "Buster" Ramsey, and Glenn Knox playing like rocks of Gibraltar—helped turn back the tide. The defense chalked up four pass interceptions. Navy recorded fourteen first downs against five for W&M and racked up 142 total offense yards against 70 for the Tribe, but could not get into the end zone. The victory marked only the second win for W&M over Navy, after nine consecutive losses. The only other Tribe win was in 1932.

W&M grabbed its third straight victory that season with a third consecutive win over Virginia Tech, 21-7. A crowd of 8,000, the largest up to then in Blacksburg, saw Carl Voyles's powerful grid machine, *The Roanoke Times* reported.

The Indians' initial tally came in the opening quarter on a 5-yard-line "buck" by tailback Bob Longacre after a 58-yard sustained drive headed by Johnson. The *Times* called Johnson a "200-pound battering ram at fullback." The other two W&M scores came on a 23-yard pass from Longacre to Glenn Knox and an 11-yard end-around play by Vande-weghe.

End Al Vandeweghe breaks loose for a big gain against Virginia Tech early in the 1942 season. From the 1943 *Colonial Echo*.

W&M's next game proved a big hurdle. The Tribe faced the Crimson of Harvard for the first time since the 13-13 tie in 1930. Meanwhile, Harvard had become one of the nation's gridiron elite. The teams played to another tie, 7-7, before a large crowd at historic Harvard Stadium. Following a first-half stalemate, W&M recovered a third-quarter Harvard fumble and scored on a 26-yard drive. Veteran back Johnny Korczowski, supplying much of the Tribe's offensive spark and punch, scored on a 3-yard plunge.

The *Colonial Echo* noted that although "completely outplayed by the Indians for the first three quarters, the Harvard combine found themselves in the last period." After the game, Coach Voyles said, "Two penalties—one for holding and one for off-side—cost us the ball game. The forward wall played superb ball, and Buster Ramsey was outstanding for his fine all-around play. Marvin Bass played one of the greatest games of his career."

Massachusetts sports writer Ben Wahrman challenged Arthur Sampson of the *Boston Herald* in his implication that "all of this football renaissance at William and Mary was pointed to this one game with Harvard," and that the two-game series

Harvey Johnson, nicknamed "Stud," scampers through the George Washington line en route to a big gain. Teammates Jackie Freeman (55), Nick Forkovitch (44), and Marvin Bass (40) react to the play. From the 1943 *Colonial Echo*.

"would add a little prestige to the anniversary [W&M's 250th] that would be celebrated." Wahrman responded:

To say [W&M] didn't do their best to reach the goal they had been shooting at for a college generation would be tampering with the truth. They not only went all out, but they gave one of the best exhibitions of old-fashioned football we had seen in many a day. That this application of real power didn't produce the desired victory was due to a miracle as much as anything else.

It apparently wasn't in the cards for William and Mary to win that game. It didn't take an experienced eye to see that they had a more powerful and more experienced operative in every position than did Harvard. The fiercely charging William and Mary line outplayed Harvard's inexperienced frontier from the opening whistle to the final gun. In fact, it is difficult to recall when a Harvard line has been outclassed so definitely.

The 1942 W&M team compiled the best percentage record ever—9 wins, 1 loss, and 1 tie—but missed out on a bowl bid because the College's football program was not nationally known. From the W&M Sports Information Department.

Wahrman concluded that, when Coach Dick Harlow said, "'Harvard got out of this game all that it deserved,' he wasn't making either a psychological gesture or a diplomatic statement. He was speaking from the heart."

In the 1942 Homecoming game, the George Washington Colonials faced the Indian machine and got smashed, 61-0, the most one-sided W&M victory since the 77-0 bashing of Bridgewater a decade earlier. Six W&M players scored touchdowns, including two by defensive tackles Bass and Fields. Bass recovered a blocked punt in the end zone, and Fields picked up a fumble and raced 25 yards for a score.

In another romp, Voyles used only three regular linemen and two regular backs during the first half of a 40-0 victory over Randolph-Macon. And third-stringers saw action in much of the second half. This game, like the one with Hampden-Sydney, ended the series against Randolph-Macon, which had begun with two games in 1896.

Still undefeated, W&M journeyed the next week to Hanover, New Hampshire, for another encounter with Dartmouth. Although Coach Voyles was concerned that his squad was not keyed up, Longacre, showing his versatility, scored three times, with Korczowski and Freeman adding one each in a 35-14 Tribe win.

As the season progressed, it was clear that, if W&M was going to lose the state football title to anyone in 1942, it would be VMI. The game, played in Norfolk before

some 17,500, turned quickly in favor of the Keydets, who scored first on a series that included a 30-yard pass and a 20-yard run. Down 6-0, the Indians came from behind and scored four touchdowns in the next 20 minutes to seal the 27-6 triumph. Longacre scored first, followed by Korczowski. The final scores came on two Longacre passes—30 and 46 yards—to Knox at end. This was the first back-to-back triumph for the Indians over VMI in the rivalry that dated from 1905. The twenty-game series included only one other W&M win—in 1933.

Halfback John Korczowski made an impact on the Indians' offense from his first game as one of the "Fabulous Freshmen" and continued top performances throughout his varsity career. From the 1942 *Colonial Echo.*

With a 7-0-1 record, W&M ranked among the top twenty teams in the nation, apparently for the first time in the school's history. The next game was against North Carolina Pre-Flight School, a Navy team consisting of former college and professional football stars. Voyles was the first Southern Conference coach to schedule games against military teams.

Coming against W&M, the Pre-Flight Cloudbusters had lost only to Boston College. More than 10,000, the largest crowd in the school's history, packed into Cary Field, with hundreds standing between the famed white-picket fence and the brick stadium. W&M would have had at least a tie, but the Indians were simply overwhelmed in the final three minutes, as Pre-Flight won 14-0.

The Tribe's sturdy line took hit after hit from the bigger and faster Pre-Flight team, and the battering took its toll as linemen Vandeweghe, Holloway, and Warrington were all injured. Pre-Flight was still unable to penetrate inside W&M's 22-yard line in the first three quarters. With the game winding down, the military squad started on its own 21-yard line and pounded 79 yards in ten plays, scoring on a double reverse. The final touchdown came seconds later, after Longacre's pass was intercepted.

"We played a fine game. Their reserve strength was too great for us. They had a world of backs and they were all good—in fact they were excellent," Voyles told *The Flat Hat*. "Had we had the opportunity to rest a few of our key men, it may have been a different story."

The Flat Hat reported an unusual situation. Members of the North Carolina Pre-Flight team acknowledged that W&M probably would have won the game had it not been for a W&M fan offering to bet all the money the Cloudbusters could raise that the Indians would win. Most of the Pre-Flighters had played pro ball, and it was still in their blood. They raised $400, and the William and Mary man took their bets. Well, *The Flat Hat* said, when the chips were down the Pre-Flighters didn't quit but kept on fighting because their money was at stake. "We sincerely believe and the squad believes that had it not been for this one man antagonizing the Pre-Flighters, W&M would have won the ball game

Halfback Bob Longacre (middle running toward the camera) tries to outmaneuver North Carolina Pre-Flight defenders in hot pursuit. The Cloudbusters' win was the only Indian loss of the season. From the 1943 *Colonial Echo;* ticket, courtesy of University Archives, College of William and Mary.

"Tex" Warrington

"What ifs" are great to talk about, and there is an interesting one related to a player on W&M's 1942 team: center Caleb Van Warrington, better known to his teammates as "Tex."

Virtually every newspaper account of that 9-1-1 team has something good to say about Warrington. His teammates all talk about his prowess and his innate athletic ability.

After that great 1942 season, like many of his fellow team members, Tex found himself in the U.S. armed forces—in the Marines. In 1944 he was able to return to college, but not at William and Mary. He followed his coach—Carl Voyles—to Auburn University, where "Tex" was their 6'2", 205-pound All-American center.

What if Tex had stayed at William and Mary? Would the College have had its second All-American, in three years, following "Buster" Ramsey's accomplishment on that 1942 team?

Although he did not graduate from William and Mary, Tex is very loyal to those teams and his W&M teammates. Newspaper articles about Warrington virtually always include comments about his William and Mary days and the 1942 team and its players.

Warrington also played in two major postseason games: the 1944 Blue-Gray All-Star Football Classic and the 1945 NFL-College All-Star Football game.

After Auburn, Tex played professional football for three years with the Brooklyn Dodgers of the All-American Football Conference. During that time he also was a scout for the National League Brooklyn Dodgers baseball team. Later he became athletic director, football and baseball coach, and teacher at Vero Beach High School in Vero Beach, Florida.

During those Florida years, Warrington became involved in helping troubled young people as a county juvenile and adult probation officer and family court investigator. This work ultimately led him to the position of superintendent at Ferris School for Boys, a correctional institution in Wilmington, Delaware. Later he was named executive director of the Youth Service Commission of Delaware.

In 1969, he moved to Miami, Florida, as dean of students and football and baseball coach at Ransom Everglades School. The following year, he became headmaster at Palmer School in Miami, where he remained until retiring in 1980.

During retirement, he spent three years as a pro football scout for the National Football Scouting Combine. Tex also has been involved for twenty years with VisionQuest, a private rehabilitative organization designed to help troubled teenagers and juvenile offenders.   (—WK)

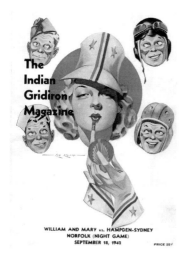

U.S. involvement in World War II was well under way by the 1942 football season. Many team members went into the service just before and during the season. The military flavor of the times was evident by this opening-game program, September 15, 1942. From the collection of Wilford Kale.

and in all probability be making preparations for a New Year's Day game," the paper said editorially. Old-timers recalled the incident a half-century later.

The Pre-Flight victory would be the lone W&M loss of the season. The Indians defeated old-time Thanksgiving rival Richmond again and added the game against the University of Oklahoma.

Against Richmond, W&M sought its first Southern Conference championship and its second State Big Six crown. The team had only four days' rest between Pre-Flight and Richmond, but Voyles challenged his team, which rose to the occasion, beating stubborn Richmond, 10-0. Tired, but fighting, W&M finally scored in the third period after charging into Richmond territory all afternoon. John Korczowski recorded the team's lone touchdown on an 11-yard jaunt. Johnson, who hit most of the placement conversions during the season, added another and also hit on a 12-yard field goal.

The season's finale, December 5, was in Norman, Oklahoma, against the University of Oklahoma. W&M scored in the second and third periods and held the Sooners off at the end to preserve a 14-7 win. Statistically, however, Oklahoma won. It had the most yards for rushing, passing, kicking, and punt returns. The Sooners repeatedly hit the W&M line with a unique A-formation, but were unable to break down the Tribe's front seven.

The last game of the 1942 season was against the University of Oklahoma in Norman. W&M won in an upset, 14-7. The team poses on the steps of the Main Street Station in Richmond, Virginia, after returning. Notice many of the players wearing cowboy hats and Coach Carl Voyles in his Indian chief's headdress. The Medallion was used in the coin-toss prior to the game. The coin is from the Marvin Bass display at the Virginia Sports Hall of Fame; photo courtesy of the Associated Press.

Indian back Dave Busher (8) goes on a big carry during W&M's 61-0 mauling of George Washington University at Cary Field in 1942. Photo by the *Richmond Times-Dispatch*, from the collection of Jacqueline Phillips Allen.

Although Oklahoma successfully stymied Ramsey on many plays, it couldn't get past players like Bass and Knox. Korczowski scored on an 8-yard sprint, and Knox tallied on a 15-yard pass from Buddy Hubbard, W&M's substitute quarterback.

At the end of the season W&M was ranked fifteenth in the country by the Associated Press.

In 1942, there were only four major bowl games—the Rose, Cotton, Sugar, and Orange—and the Associated Press reported that William and Mary was definitely a candidate for the Orange Bowl. When Alabama and Boston College were chosen from a field that also included Tulsa and Missouri, some alumni and media criticized Voyles for not lobbying hard enough for a bowl invitation. Nevertheless, the 1942 team's 9-1-1 record is still the best W&M season mark. Despite one loss, the 1942 Indians were never defeated by a collegiate team. No one on that varsity W&M squad realized that the victory over Oklahoma would be the last game they would play under Voyles.

The strong season helped many team members win All-State and All-Conference honors. Ramsey and Johnson became the first W&M players to play in the famous Blue-Gray All-Star Football Classic in Montgomery, Alabama, and, in August 1943, the duo also represented W&M in the College-NFL All-Star game at Soldier's Field in Chicago. Ramsey became the first player from any Virginia school to start in the game. His play was described by coaches as "outstanding," and he threw two down-field blocks on a single 95-yard run by Otto Graham in the College All-Stars' victory.

The ultimate honor for W&M came when "Buster" Ramsey, the tall and scrawny lad from Maryville, Tennessee, was named an Associated Press First-Team All-American. Ramsey also received an honor unusual for a football player. He was named to the "Virginia Honor Roll of 1942" by the *Richmond Times-Dispatch*. Other recipients included Admiral William F. Halsey, U.S. Senator Harry F. Byrd, and Bishop Henry St. George Tucker. Ramsey was cited not only for the glory he brought to himself, college, and state, but also for his constant fair play and clean sportsmanship in his chosen "field of combat."

By the close of the 1942 season, the football budget had increased to $45,000, up more than $10,000 since Voyles arrived. The men's athletic department deficit had also grown, reaching $78,600 before the 1942 season. Much of that resulted from spending on football scholarships. In 1942, for example, $35,000 in scholarships were awarded with initially only $12,000 available through fund-raising. A $12,000-plus profit during 1942, reduced the deficit to about $65,000.

As World War II continued, more of W&M's young men were called into active service. Dr. Pomfret wrote to the Board of Visitors in March 1943, that "the war will certainly curtail big-time football." With enrollment shrinking, it soon became obvious that it would be difficult, if not

W&M placed an amazing seven players on the eleven-member Associated Press 1942 Virginia All-State team. The miniature gold footballs (top) were collected by Glenn Knox for the team's state and conference titles. Photograph courtesy of the Associated Press; footballs from the Glenn Knox display at the Virginia Sports Hall of Fame.

The 1943 Football Team

There was no varsity football team in 1943. The reason: World War II. But for William and Mary players like Tom Mikula '48, Austin Wright '49, Ed Dunbar '48, Paul Reynolds '47, Jesse Jackson '45, and Harvey Chappell, Jr. '48, that was not the case.

For eight Saturdays during the fall of 1943, William and Mary's "informal" freshman team, which included some sophomores, or about ten freshmen joined by fourteen men from the Army Special Training Program (ASTP) on campus, took the field. They kept the gridiron battles alive, producing a 4-4 season overall that included three consecutive wins by the combined team. Rube McCray coached during the games, although W&M head coach Carl Voyles, Arnold "Swede" Umback, and Dwight Steussy assisted during practices. No team or individual statistics were kept.

Several members of that team gathered during 1993 Homecoming festivities to recall the team that few people remember. For them, it was the best of times.

Mikula, a guard on that team and the group's unofficial historian, recalled:

The College had just come off the high of that fabulous 1942 football team [with its 9-1-1 record and its season-ending, 14-7 victory over Oklahoma]. We had every reason to believe that returning players would continue the highly successful Voyles era in 1943. World War II, however, called all those men into service. … The College was left with 17-year-old boys, who were waiting to be called to duty.

The W&M gang keenly remembers the first game of the season against the Navy Plebe team in Annapolis. The *Richmond Times-Dispatch* reported that W&M was outclassed by the Navy freshmen who were looking for their fifth straight undefeated season. That game was played in a driving rain storm, which tailback and sometime punter Jackson said was so hard, "you couldn't see some of the defense secondary players on either team."

Some people even said the coach left the field one time because it was raining so hard. During the game we probably had the shortest kick in W&M history. This young man, Preston McIlwaine [punted] into a high wind that carried the ball backward. It ended as a minus-10-yard punt.

According to the newspaper accounts, the punt ended in the Indians' end zone for an automatic safety and two points for Navy.

Reynolds also remembered playing in the Navy mud when center Ed Dunbar snapped the ball over the punter's head and completely out of the end zone. Dunbar acknowledged he must have snapped the ball 40 yards with the wind. "After it happened Rube [McCray] wanted to get me out of the game," Dunbar explained, "but we had a substitution rule, and he couldn't get me out. I think he almost croaked when we had to punt again, but the second time was a good center, and we got the punt off."

Dunbar had never played football before, even in high school. I went out there to practice one day and said I can do as well as these guys. ... Daily practice was another. We were all volunteers and practiced from 3 p.m. until 6 p.m. when we had to wait tables in the dining hall.

Chappell recalled that Ben Raimondi, out of Erasmus High School in Brooklyn, New York, was an excellent passer. Raimondi, who left W&M and went to the University of Indiana where he later became an All-American, "was probably the best player on our team," according to Mikula.

Chappell also recalled that the ASTP guys were "much bigger and older" than the college boys. Although many first names have been forgotten, ASTP football players included Kress, Ocque, Boone, Bardsley, Caruso, Allison, Fair, Sullivan, Kidder, Lipinsky, and Golden. Wright added that it is important that those Army players be remembered.

They were great guys. I remember "Foots" Holland, who was co-captain of the Hampden-Sydney team and made Phi Beta Kappa. Another great ASTP player was Ed Holle, who was captain of our basketball team that year. These guys were all thrown into the Battle of the Bulge. Holle got killed, and Holland was listed as killed in action, but later turned up alive. The point I'm making is that we were lucky to be associated with these guys, and a lot of credit has not been given to them. Because of regulations, they couldn't play in our away games, but they played with us at home.

After the Navy defeat, the College freshmen played Newport News Shipbuilding's Apprentice School in Newport News and lost 24-6, then defeated Randolph-Macon College in Williamsburg, 38-6. Two more games were played against Apprentice School—a 19-6 defeat in Newport News and a 24-13 defeat in Williamsburg. When the combined William and Mary team faced Apprentice School on November 13, 1943, W&M was victorious, 15-0.

The next weekend W&M defeated Richmond Army Air Base, 14-6, with Raimondi, the triple-threat Indian back, accounting for both of the Tribe's scores on passes to Joe Och and running his string of touchdown passes to twelve in six games.

The final contest of the season on Thanksgiving Day was a 72-0 route of the Norfolk Fleet Marine team. Highlights of the game were four

W&M freshmen attempt to bat down a pass by the Richmond Airbase quarterback (far left) in a 1943 Cary Field game. Approximately 500 soldiers from nearby Fort Eustis attended. Courtesy of the *Richmond Times-Dispatch.*

touchdown passes by Raimondi, interception returns of 30 and 60 yards by ASTP's Everett, and a punt return of 65 yards by ASTP's Derisi.

"Those 72 points were the most ever scored by a William and Mary team on Cary Field," Mikula said proudly.

I also played in '44, '46, and '47, but none of those times were as memorable as the '43 team. This was a group of guys who were volunteers. None of us were professionals. When we came out, we came out because we enjoyed the idea that we were going to play football. We were kids—16, 17, and 18 years old—and we enjoyed being together. I think that's what football is about, and that team symbolized it for me.   (—WK)

impossible to field a varsity football squad in 1943. Unlike other colleges and universities, where military programs had been established and teams were expected to be fielded, W&M's military effort was limited to a Navy Chaplain's School and an Army training unit that did not allow its members to participate in intercollegiate athletics. Dr. Pomfret told the Board of Visitors at its June 4, 1943, meeting that a varsity football team could not be fielded with an anticipated male student body of only 150.

After studying the situation for several months, Voyles announced that none of the 1942 freshman and varsity football team members were expected to return to school. Of the sixteen or seventeen students who could probably play, only three or four were age 18 or older. Football would not, however, be absent from the campus, Voyles said. He hoped to field either a freshman team or a 150-pound team, but not a varsity squad.

The *Alumni Gazette* reported that many of W&M's 1942 freshmen and varsity players would see action on the gridirons of

The "D-Day" landing in Europe in June 1944 helped W&M and other schools to renew their football programs as young men rotated back to the States after their war service. W&M cheerleaders watch the Indians against the University of Richmond in City Stadium. From the 1945 *Colonial Echo*.

other institutions in 1943. W&M players were in V-12 military programs at the University of Pennsylvania, Richmond, Duke, North Carolina, South Carolina, Georgia Tech, and Hampden-Sydney. Some ninety-five students from W&M were at Richmond, among them, fourteen members of the 1942 freshman and varsity teams. These included Marvin Bass, captain of the 1942 champions; Bob Longacre, W&M's 1943 captain-elect; Jackie Freeman; and Lou Hoitsma. Harvey Johnson, All-American "Buster" Ramsey, and Al Vandeweghe played for the Bainbridge (Maryland) Physical Training School.

Since there was no varsity team in 1943, the freshman team took center stage. Under the coaching of R. N. "Rube" McCray, Voyles's assistant varsity coach 1939–42, the team compiled a 4-4 record, defeating The Apprentice School of Newport News Shipbuilding, 15-0; Richmond Army Air Base, 14-6; Randolph-Macon College Frosh, 38-6; and ending the season on Thanksgiving Day with a 72-0 victory over the Norfolk Fleet Marine team. The Frosh lost to the Navy Plebes, 28-0, and three times to Apprentice School, 19-6, 24-6, and 24-13.

Tom Mikula was a freshman in 1943 and part of that junior varsity team, including some on-campus military personnel, that kept football alive on campus when there was no varsity team. As a lineman, he went on to distinguish himself on the 1944, 1946, and 1947 varsity squads. From the 1945 *Colonial Echo*.

Coach Dwight Stussey who helped McCray coach the 1943 junior varsity team after varsity football had been scrapped for the year. From the 1944 *Colonial Echo.*

It was unusual to see McCray on the field with a W&M football team and Voyles in the stands watching the game. Little did anyone know that by the time the 1944 football season rolled around, Voyles would be coaching at Auburn Polytechnic Institute (Auburn University) and McCray would be the new W&M head coach.

In January 1944, rumors began to circulate that Voyles was being considered for several other head coaching positions, including the University of North Carolina. But suddenly, in early March, discussions with Auburn became public. When Auburn President Luther N. Duncan contacted W&M, President Pomfret told him: "Coach Voyles is a free agent. He has an indefinite contract that goes on year after year and as long as he likes. The College will not stand in his way if he wishes to accept another position."

About this time there were some accusations on campus against Voyles, involving personal misconduct, a charge that was never explained or formally investigated by the Board of Visitors. However, when the Board offered Voyles a new contract on March 23, 1944, during the Auburn overture, the draft suggested that Voyles "should make his decision in the light of the several rumors regarding his conduct, and in the full knowledge that the Board of Visitors might be compelled to take cognizance of such rumors."

President John F. Pomfret and his wife, Sarah, always enjoyed a good football game. They are shown here at an away game in Norfolk. From the 1945 *Colonial Echo.*

The Auburn offer—a six-year contract—came quickly; Voyles accepted. It did not take President Pomfret and other College officials long to name McCray as Voyles's replacement. On April 4, 1944, Pomfret told reporters that McCray had accepted a three-year contract at $5,000 per year to be head football coach and athletic director. He also held an assistant professorship in the College's physical education department, but did not become department head, another position Voyles had held.

McCray was 38 when he took over the W&M helm. His background included taking Tennessee Wesleyan to six football championships in eight years, winning twenty-three straight games during the run. During his early W&M years, McCray

Halfback Chet Mackiewicz played as a freshman in 1944 and became a backfield stalwart, providing important reserve strength in 1945, 1946, and 1948. From the 1945 *Colonial Echo*.

had also coached basketball and baseball, piloting the Indians to the State "Big Six" baseball championship in 1941 when Vic Raschi, who went on to become a famed New York Yankee, was the star pitcher.

"I am fully cognizant of the fact that it will be extremely difficult to fill adequately the shoes of such an eminently successful man as Carl Voyles," McCray said. "It will be my hope to carry out efficiently a good program of intercollegiate athletics as outlined by President Pomfret and the Board of Visitors of the College."

The Indians resumed varsity practice about seven weeks after the D-day invasion of Normandy, planning for the 1944 season. But like many other small colleges throughout the nation, fielding a football team was difficult because there were still very few men on campus. Athletic Director and Football Coach McCray faced the unenviable task of rebuilding a team to continue the Voyles legacy as a Southern Conference power.

With the assistance of veteran coach Eric Tipton and new coaches Glenn Knox and Marvin Bass, two heroes of W&M's 1942 championship season, McCray worked with the many freshmen and a few upperclassmen. Only captain Johnny Clowes, the *Alumni Gazette* reported, had any previous varsity experience. Joining him was Henry Shook, who played for the 1942 freshmen. At the beginning of the season, many of the key prospects, indeed, turned out to be the team leaders: Clowes, guard and tackle; Shook, a guard; Tom Mikula, guard, who played on the Freshman/Army Student Training Program (ASTP) team in 1943 and moved to the backfield; Jack Bruce, tailback; Stanley Magdziak, fullback; and Chester Mackiewicz, back. Joining this group were center Tommy Thompson, tackles Knox Ramsey and Louis Creekmur, and end Denver Mills.

The 1944 record of 5-2-1 was somewhat misleading, but it also enabled W&M to continue what would be an unequalled stretch of 10 successive winning seasons, not counting 1943, of course. Victories came against smaller and less competitive clubs—Hampden-Sydney, Fort Monroe, Richmond Army Airbase, VMI, and the University of Richmond—while the losses were against major powers like N.C. State and the University of Pennsylvania with its squad led by military trainees. Playing one of its better games, W&M held the talented University of North Carolina to a 0-0 tie, blunting two Tar Heel drives and pushing 80 yards in the waning minutes to reach the North Carolina 3-yard line as the game ended.

Nick Forkovitch, who played on the 1942 Southern Conference championship team, returned to the Indians in 1945 after the war, joining a host of other veterans who gave much needed depth to the squad. From the 1943 *Colonial Echo*.

When the 1945 football season began, the war had just ended, but there was precious little time for most veterans to return to campus. Therefore, thoughts of the prewar halcyon days when Tribe gridiron glory blossomed were not on students' minds. Several vets, however, did return. Doc Holloway, Dave Bucher, Nick Forkovich, Mel Wright, and Bill Klein joined ten returning 1944 lettermen to offer bright potential. Bucher, however, was injured and did not play. Freshman halfback Tommy Korczowski made an impression in his first game that continued throughout his four-year college career. He scored all three of the team's touchdowns against Catawba College in the opener on runs of 25, 36, and 42 yards. Korczowski—either by running or passing—accounted for eight more touchdowns in the next eight games. Chet Mackiewicz and back Stan Magdziak, also the team's place kicker, contributed with outstanding running and pass receiving, adding to the Indians' formidable scoring punch. Defensively, the team was led by tackle Knox Ramsey, "Buster's" younger brother. Ramsey was the team's lone first-team all–Southern Conference member.

The Indians rolled up a 6-3 record, but again, the losses were against major football powers—the Universities of Tennessee and North Carolina and N.C. State—while two of the victories came against Catawba and the Merchant Marine Academy. There were also state wins over VMI, Virginia Tech, and Richmond as well as one over the University of Maryland.

The season showed the continued results of Coach McCray's ability to recruit talented young men to the Williamsburg campus. Much of the success on the field could be credited to three of McCray's coaches. Marvin Bass, considered by many as one of the finest linemen ever to play the game, returned as line coach, and Eric Tipton, Duke University's great All-American and splendid back, continued his backfield teaching. They were joined for the year by S. B. "Frosty" Holt, on a leave of

Drewery "Doc" Holloway returned for his senior year in 1945 after playing on the 1941 and 1942 Indian teams. His impressive guard play put him on the All–Southern Conference first team in 1945. From the 1946 *Colonial Echo*.

Indian defenders, John Pellack (49), Knox Ramsey (22), and Sonny Davis (28) rush to stop North Carolina runner in a 1945 game at Foreman Field on the campus of W&M's Norfolk Division. UNC won, 6-0. From the 1946 *Colonial Echo*.

Reuben N. "Rube" McCray

In 1992, twenty years after he died and forty-one years after he left William and Mary, the community of Lake Waccamaw, North Carolina, still felt so strongly about Reuben Noe McCray that it named the new public library in his memory. Such was his legend in the Tar Heel State.

Known to everyone simply as "Rube," he came to Williamsburg with Carl Voyles in 1939, and the two coaches created "The Golden Era" of W&M football. McCray succeeded Voyles as head coach in 1944, remaining until his resignation in 1951. Many observers of the W&M football scene believe that Voyles would not have been as successful without McCray because McCray was *the* recruiter.

McCray recruited most of the members of the "Fabulous Freshmen" of 1939 and continued to bring top talent to W&M for the next twelve years. In his oral history of the College, J. Wilfred Lambert, longtime W&M dean of students, said that McCray "was probably a better recruiter than a coach" and that's saying something, since McCray's record also shows he was quite a successful coach.

Before coming to W&M, he coached eight years at Tennessee Wesleyan, where his teams won six championships and once had a streak of twenty-three straight victories. His 1936 team won the national junior college football championship. At W&M, McCray compiled a 45-22-3 record, leading the College to its first two bowl games.

McCray was highly regarded by players and alumni supporters, and, on October 18, 1969, was inducted into the W&M Athletic Hall of Fame as part of the first class. With him on that day were four players he had coached who achieved national recognition: Tommy Thompson, center; Jack Cloud, back; Vito Ragazzo, end; and Knox Ramsey, guard.

McCray resigned as head coach and athletic director in 1951 and moved to nearby West Point, Virginia, where he became president and general manager of his own automobile agency—West Point Motor Co. In September 1955, McCray was appointed to fill an unexpired term on the town council, serving until 1958.

In 1958, the Tennessee native was drawn to Lake Waccamaw, a community in the eastern North Carolina sandhills, where the state's Civitan organization was building Boys' Home of North Carolina and looking for a director. What they found in McCray was more than an administrator. They found a father-figure and leader, whose efforts would mold the lives of many young boys who passed through the Home during the next fourteen years.

Boys' Home was designed to provide help for homeless or neglected youths from ages 10 to 19. McCray had rules for the young boys, just like he had rules for his football team, but everything was geared to instill confidence and self-worth in each boy. "Our biggest reward at Boys' Home is the boy himself," McCray told a reporter. "Boys can be taught, boys can be worked with, but you've got to treat them like people. You've got to let them know they are not 'anybody.'"

Celebrating Boys' Home's tenth anniversary in 1968, Kays Gary, nationally known columnist for the *Charlotte* (N.C.) *Observer* devoted a column to McCray. At the beginning, the Boys' Home Directors "made their biggest score" in hiring McCray as executive director, Gary wrote.

The big, ham-handed former football coach at William and Mary ... has been charging hard ever since [1958] just as he'd taught his Indians at W&M.

He charged up and down the state laying some hard facts and challenges on the line and steadily but surely that single cottage with its 16 boys expanded into a terrific campus as more civic clubs statewide built cottages to care for 100 boys from all sections of North Carolina. That was the goal. Rube and his wife, Hester, made it in 10 years.

The big man can tick off one name after another of "his" boys who were walking that path of delinquency (most come recommended from the state's domestic courts or State Welfare Department) when somebody plucked them off it and into Boys' Home. And there are grown men, now, college graduates among them, who give the alumni list prestige.

In May 1972, just six months before his death, McCray received the highest recognition of his life. North Carolina Civitans gave him its "Outstanding Citizen of the Year" Award and he joined a distinguished list of recipients including Luther H. Hodges, former North Carolina Governor. The award recognized McCray's "outstanding service to youth, his years of coaching and developing character of young men, and his civic and religious activities."

During his Boys' Home tenure, McCray served as president of the National Association of Homes for Boys (two terms) and president of the North Carolina Child Care Association. He was named Tar Heel of the Week in 1971 by the Raleigh *News and Observer* newspaper.

McCray, however, did not seek honors for himself. The High Point *Enterprise* newspaper, in an editorial following McCray's death on November 19, 1972, said this of the former coach:

McCray stands in front of the fireplace mantle in old Blow Gym. Numerous trophies and awards are pictured, including the Delta Bowl trophy of January 1949 (tall one with football) and the photograph of "Buster" Ramsey, W&M's first team Associated Press All-American. From the 1950 *Colonial Echo*.

Few men have gotten more from their lives—gotten more by giving more—than did Rube McCray. Largely because of his personal and indefatigable efforts, Boys' Home is today a solid institution, doing a great work in reclaiming youngsters once headed in wrong directions. Not only was R.N. McCray the great father figure so important to such ventures, but his was the untiring voice that enlisted so many civic organizations around the state to its financial undergirding. ... The state will miss the man, his dedication and his selflessness.

McCray's legacy grew after his death. In Huntersville, North Carolina, near Charlotte, at a second Boys' Home campus, founded by McCray's organization in 1968, the R.N. McCray Memorial Activities Building was dedicated in 1977.

McCray loved coaching, but his friends said his real love "was working with 'his' boys. Following McCray's death, one of those boys, UNC graduate Ron Faircloth, said, "I thought he would live to be 100. He worked 24 hours a day—I think he even worked in his sleep—and I think now that there just aren't too many men like him around these days." (—WK)

Coach McCray found himself in a strong backfield situation in 1946. Stan Magdziak (left) returned for his junior year, and Jackie Freeman (center) returned from the service after playing on the 1941–42 teams. Freshman Buddy Lex was ready to demonstrate his talent. *Richmond Times-Dispatch* photo from the collection of Jack Freeman.

absence from Carson-Newman, where he was head coach and athletic director. Bass continued coaching with McCray every year except 1949, and Tipton remained on the staff through 1956.

Only selection committee members know why W&M's 1946 team with its 8-2 record did not go to a postseason bowl game. The squad of seasoned veterans easily rivaled the 8-2 seasons of Coach Voyles in 1941 and of Coach Bocock in 1929. McCray enjoyed the return of twenty-five lettermen for 1946, but most of them were not veterans of the 1944 or 1945 teams. Rather, they were standouts in 1942, and some went back as far as 1940.

Those returning from military service included Bob Steckroth, end, and 1942 great; Ralph Sazio, another 1942 player; end Bob Longacre and triple-threat Jackie Freeman from W&M's 1941 and 1942 teams; blocking back Tom Mikula, 1943; and halfback "Jumping Jack" Bruce, returning from the 1944 team. End Lou Hoitsma and tackle Harry "Red" Caughron were 1942 freshmen. The 1945 re-

Griffith Stadium, home of the pro football Washington Redskins (note the tepees on top of the stands) was the scene of the Indians' 20-0 victory on November 16, 1946, over George Washington University. From the collection of Mel Wright.

turnees were Knox Ramsey, guard; Tommy Korczowski, versatile halfback; Mel Wright, tackle; and team captain Denver "Denny" Mills at end. Freshmen who were touted by the coaching staff during the preseason included "Buddy" Lex, back; George Hughes, flanker; Jim McDowell, guard; and a fullback Jack Cloud, boasting the nickname, "Flyin'."

Laurence Leonard, who in 1946 was W&M's director of public relations and later became sports editor of the *Richmond News Leader,* described the 1946 season as "sensational, not only did [the Indians] enjoy the

Mel Wright spent two football seasons—1943 and 1944—in the military. He returned to play in 1945 and 1946 and brought with him still more experience from the Indians' 1942 championship squad. From the 1943 *Colonial Echo.*

fruits of victory, but they reaped national recognition."

Ramsey, who won first- and second-team All-American honors, despite missing the last game-and-a-half with a broken arm, spearheaded a great line. Steckroth, Korczowski, and Cloud also received Associated Press All-American honorable mention.

Except for some injuries and a few bad breaks, the season might have been more successful. A second-game loss to the University of Miami (Florida), 13-3, and a 21-7 defeat at the hands of the University of North Carolina were the only blemishes. For the ten-game season, however, W&M outscored its opponents, 347 to 71. The team closed the season with back-to-back shutouts, bringing the total to four among its eight wins.

The team gained initial conference recognition in the Virginia Tech game, which pregame predictors considered a toss-up, since Tech had earlier tied UNC and U.Va. From the opening whistle, however, the outcome was not in doubt, thanks mostly to Korczowski. He returned the opening kickoff 40 yards; one play later he scooted around his end for 50 yards and a touchdown; minutes later he negotiated an 80-yard pass play to Steckroth; and five plays later Korczowski scored again on a 46-yard run. The Indians' 49-0 rout was under way.

Magdziak was the star of the 41-0 win over VMI, throwing three touchdown passes and kicking four extra points. In the 41-7 victory over Maryland, Magdziak and Korczowski threw two touchdown passes each.

The 1946 W&M team with its 8-2 record should have gone to a bowl game. Captain Denver Mills poses in this montage. From the 1947 *Colonial Echo*.

Tommy Korczowski (14, far right) uncorks at least a 15-yard pass that was hauled in by Bob Steckroth (30, at left) during the North Carolina game. From the 1947 *Colonial Echo*.

Season-ending shutouts over George Washington and Richmond again featured a strong defensive show and a multitalented offense. Longacre ran back the opening kickoff against GW 93 yards for a touchdown, while Cloud added the other two scores. The Richmond game on Thanksgiving Day featured Magdziak throwing for three touchdowns and adding four extra points. Cloud and Longacre also scored.

During the year, fullback Cloud rushed for 536 yards in 121 carries or 4.4 yards per carry, while injury-plagued Korczowski still was able, through running, passing, and receiving, to average 16.6 yards per play.

Statistically, the team fared well nationally. According to the NCAA, the Tribe ranked eleventh in total offense, averaging 338.3 yards per game, and fourteenth in rushing with 211.8 yards per game. In total defense, the Indians were fifteenth, allowing 181.6 yards per game and eighth in rushing defense, allowing only 89.5 yards per game. The team led the nation in kickoff returns, totaling 665 yards in twenty-one tries for 31.7 yards per return. Longacre was second best nationally with 375 yards in nine carries. The team was third nationally in running back intercepted passes, with 444 yards. All-State and all–Southern Conference laurels went to a dozen players, and the team grabbed second place in the conference behind league leader UNC.

Although W&M was good enough in 1946 to go to a postseason bowl, it did not; it still lacked a major football reputation. Some sports writers speculated that the Indians "were likely" to receive an invitation to the Gator Bowl in Jacksonville, Florida, but that bid

Tommy Korczowski (14) takes off on a 50-yard scoring sprint against Virginia Tech in the 49-0 romp over the Gobblers. From the 1947 *Colonial Echo*.

As center, Tommy Thompson anchored the W&M line for most of the games during the 1946, 1947, and 1948 seasons. This sports cartoon in 1948 was drawn by *Flat Hat* staffer Hugh Haynie '50, who later became an award winning editorial cartoonist for the Louisville *Courier-Journal* newspaper. He drew a series of these depictions during the football and basketball seasons.

Guard Knox Ramsey shows his dare-devil techniques in a publicity shot used during the 1947 season. From the 1947 *Colonial Echo*.

went to N.C. State, which finished just one win below W&M in the conference race. Southern Conference champion North Carolina played in the Sugar Bowl.

Sponsors seeking to establish a new postseason contest—the Dixie Bowl—in Birmingham, Alabama, formally asked W&M to play, but the faculty athletic committee turned down the invitation because of the tentative status of the event. (Ultimately, the College agreed the following year to play in the inaugural Dixie Bowl game.) Therefore, in 1946, W&M suddenly found itself not being considered for any bowl game, while mediocre Virginia Tech, walloped by the Indians 40-0, played in the Sun Bowl.

McCray's 1947 contingent was probably just as good as Voyles's fabled 1942 team. While much of the country was beginning to move toward the newly introduced T-formation, McCray stayed with the tried and tested "single-wing" because he was returning a stable full of stars. The Indians were at least four deep at every position, and 72 players were available to open practice.

Francis Wallace, in his preseason prognostications in the *Saturday Evening Post*, listed five Indians on his first-team All-Southern squad: Bob Steckroth, Knox Ramsey, Tommy Thompson, "Flyin'" Jack Cloud, and Tommy Korczowski. He also identified Ralph Sazio as a "darkhorse."

Except for a 13-7 loss to a Charlie "Choo Choo" Justice–led North Carolina, W&M ruled the eastern seaboard. The team took the Southern Conference championship—its second.

The Indians opened with a win over Davidson, 21-0, behind a strong second-half surge, in which Cloud scored twice and Magdziak passed for the other touchdown.

The fast-striking, pass-throwing, T-formation Bulldogs from The Citadel were expected to give the Indians a game, but did not deliver. W&M won, 56-7, with Magdziak passing for one touchdown and kicking seven extra points. Tommy "The Kid" Korczowski had two touchdowns, while Cloud,

End Bob Longacre grabs an Indian pass in the end zone against the University of Richmond. From the 1947 *Colonial Echo*.

"Flyin'" Jack Cloud

Through his career he made many All-America, All-Conference, and All-State teams, and, until recently, some of his numerous school records still stood as challenges to today's gridiron heroes.

For almost forty-five years Cloud held the records for most touchdowns in a season, seventeen (1947); most points scored in a season, 102 (1947); most points scored in a career, 270 (1946-1949). He still holds the mark for the most touchdowns in a career, forty-five (1946–49) and ranks ninth among W&M's all-time rushing leaders with 2,058 career yards.

Grantland Rice, America's dean of sports writers in the 1920s through early 1950s, wrote in 1948: "William and Mary has a well-equipped squad, led by Jack Cloud, a terrific fullback." Shirley Povich, long-time sports writer of *The Washington Post,* also lauded the W&M back that same year: "In Cloud's hands and feet, the Indians' running game has been something super. ... He's classed as a spinner, but bouncing off tacklers is only part of his virtue. What he doesn't bounce off, he runs over."

Four decades after he last played on the turf at Cary Field, "Flyin'" Jack Cloud was inducted into the National Football Foundation's College Football Hall of Fame. Only Cloud was surprised.

I can't believe it. I'm just very, very happy that this has happened to me, but I know that without that team there would be very little chance of me being in the hall of anything. When I think of Knox Ramsey, George Hughes, Jim McDowell, Buddy Lex, Henry Blanc, Joe Mark, Tom Mikula, and look at those guys today, they're just outstanding to me and they were then. ... There are so many other people that probably should be there from W&M, including some of those men on teams with me. I was the final point man. Cloud made the touchdown, but they didn't realize how we got down there.

How good was "Flyin'" Jack? "As good as the offensive linemen would let me be," Cloud said.

I was a good size for my position and had good balance and quickness. When the line gave me a crease or a seam, I had the ability to hit it. And because God made my legs short, nobody got a good shot at my legs. They had to tackle me high.

Cloud came to W&M in 1946 and had a good season, compiled 539 yards rushing and scored eleven touchdowns, but it was in 1947 that he attracted national attention with 558 yards rushing and seventeen touchdowns. Preseason publications touted Cloud and W&M as capable of ending the University of North Carolina's dominance of the old Southern Conference. In fact, *Street & Smith*'s 1948 college football preview had a color photograph of Cloud on its cover, no small honor considering that this was the same year that talents like Doak Walker of Southern Methodist University, Charlie "Choo Choo" Justice of North Carolina, Notre Dame's Terry Brennan, and Michigan State's Lynn Chandnois played.

Cloud was named an Associated Press All-America honorable mention in 1946; *New York Sun* first-team All-America in 1947; NEA All-America in 1948, and the *Police Gazette* All-America in 1949.

Cloud, co-captain of the 1949 team, commented on the camaraderie of the 1946–49 teams:

Almost every school that you could think of had good teams then because they had players back from the war. They were older, had more maturity and were back in school for things more than just football. ...

We also had some tremendous leadership from our team captains. ... Without such good leadership, you're not going to be a good team. We became a real good team because we had great individuals who were more concerned about the team than they were about themselves.

On defense, Cloud played behind Tommy Thompson as a defensive halfback and learned a lot from Coach Eric Tipton.

Tipton was probably the best coach I've ever been associated with, period. He was extremely talented himself and had a great rapport with the players. Tipton was respected, and he could do just about everything that he expected you to do.

After Tipton left W&M in 1957, he became lightweight (150-pound) football coach at the U.S. Military Academy at West Point. During many of those years, his teams competed against Cloud's at the U.S. Naval Academy. "We had a good rivalry," Cloud said. "We played 14 games and each one of us won seven. I think we always won at home."

Cloud bulls his way through the line against VMI in the 1948 Oyster Bowl in Norfolk. From the 1949 *Colonial Echo*.

Coach Rube McCray also "was great," Cloud said. "He used to tell us he was dumb. I would sure like to be that dumb. Coach McCray was pretty slick." Another W&M coach ranked high on Cloud's list was Marvin Bass, who "had the same kind of respect from our line as Coach Tipton had from the backs. They loved him and he was great. Marvin is still everybody's favorite."

A native of Oklahoma, "Flyin'" Jack was one-quarter Cherokee Indian. "I've always been proud of my Indian heritage," Cloud said. "In my days, there weren't a lot of Indians to compare to Jim Thorpe. He was always one of my idols as a kid." Cloud acknowledged that his nickname came, "probably because I was part Indian, I'm really not sure. It seems to me that I got the name from a local newspaper reporter in Norfolk."

He came east during his high school days, and graduated in 1943 from Maury High School in Norfolk. After the war, he made a conscious decision to attend William and Mary.

Because of the service I was thinking pretty much about going to Duke [University]. They had talked to my Mother and Dad, but when I came back, and was older and wiser, I started traveling around in the South looking at other schools. William and Mary was nearby and Coach McCray was a pretty good seller. I went over and visited W&M; they had a couple of players off my old Maury team. I guess they were responsible for me going to William and Mary.

Cloud's favorite W&M game—the Dixie Bowl—was good for him, but not for the team.

It was one game where I thought I played pretty well, yet we lost. I also got injured, and it was sort of a downer for everybody at the end. They were pretty physical. [Red] Caughron got knocked out; [Buddy] Lex broke his nose; I had a knee injury; and [Bob] Steckroth also got knocked out. Arkansas defeated W&M, 21 to 20.

After W&M graduation, Cloud played with the Green Bay Packers and the Washington Redskins in the National Football League, where he suffered major knee and back injuries.

I didn't have the blinding 40-yard speed to play the corner [on defense]. I would have been mismatched out on the corners, so I played linebacker, but spent most of my time in the hospital. At Green Bay, I made the all-hospital team a couple of years in a row.

Cloud became coach at the U.S. Navy Academy in 1958, retiring in 1989 after thirty-two years—about twenty-eight of those as a coach. Cloud was as revered at Navy because of his coaching as he was at W&M because of his playing. In fact, for many years, he was in the radio booth as color commentator for the Navy team.   (—WK)

End Bob Steckroth was co-captain of the 1947 Dixie Bowl team, having played on the 1942 and 1946 squads. He was All–Southern Conference and an Associated Press All-American honorable mention also in 1947. From the 1943 *Colonial Echo*.

Buddy Lex, Steckroth, Mikula, and Don Howren each contributed six-pointers.

Virginia Tech came ready to play. They led the Big Green until late in the third quarter, when Henry Blanc broke away for a touchdown and Magdziak converted for a 7-7 tie. The Tribe scored twice in the fourth quarter for the 21-7 come-from-behind win. The victory, however, was costly. Korczowski fractured a bone in his ankle and was out for the rest of the regular season, missing the next week's long-expected showdown between "The Kid" and the "Choo Choo."

UNC and W&M were ready when they met in Williamsburg, but fumbles at two strategic points gave the Tar Heels a 13-7 victory. Fullback Cloud sparked the losers.

But W&M was not disheartened. The team went on a six-game winning streak, including three shutouts, which propelled it into postseason play. Boston University, Wake Forest, VMI, Washington and Lee, Bowling Green, and Richmond tumbled in order.

"Jumpin' Jack" Bruce demonstrates his passing form for this publicity photo, but it was his pass defense—his 10 interceptions during the 1947 season that put him into the W&M record books. From the 1948 *Colonial Echo*.

Vito Ragazzo, end, breaks away for a long run during a 28-0 Homecoming victory in 1947 over VMI. From the 1948 *Colonial Echo*.

Pep rallies were commonplace in the 1947 and 1948 seasons as the success of the team skyrocketed. The rallies often concluded with a giant bonfire, such as this one for the home game in 1947 against the University of North Carolina. From the 1948 *Colonial Echo*.

Cheerleaders' support was important in 1947 as the team gained a Dixie Bowl invitation. Members of the squad included Eddie King, Tom Athey, Billy Hux, Carol Achenbach, Shirley Green, Sue Hines, and Eleanor Grant. From the 1948 *Colonial Echo*.

The Keydets of VMI almost upset the Big Green, and the somewhat overconfident Indians were forced to scratch out a 28-20 victory. W&M led 28-0 in the second half, when VMI bounced back, grabbed the momentum, and scored three quick touchdowns. After the VMI scare, W&M outscored its opponents 100 to 6 in the last three games.

Individual player honors began to flow in for the Indians. Five starters were on All-American teams. Cloud was selected to the *New York Sun*'s first team All-American squad and the Associated Press's second team; guard Ramsey was on the United Press's second team and syndicated writer Deke Houlgate's first team; Harry Caughron, Steckroth, and Thompson were listed as Associated Press All-American honorable

Fullback "Flyin'" Jack Cloud (50) shows one of his trademark moves as he begins a cutback against VMI. Cloud later scored on a line plunge. From the 1948 *Colonial Echo*.

Dixie Bowl

William and Mary finally received its first postseason bowl bid in 1947 with an invitation to the inaugural Dixie Bowl in Birmingham, Alabama.

The Indians probably should have gotten bowl bids in 1942 and in 1946, but the lack of both national media attention and aggressive action by the College's athletic department kept them out in 1942, and a 1946 bowl bid—by the same Dixie Bowl organization—was rejected by the W&M faculty athletic committee. Later, the Dixie Bowl group decided to wait a year to hold their first game.

Although not one of the four major bowls—Rose, Orange, Cotton, or Sugar—the game still offered William and Mary an opportunity to showcase its football talent, especially against the Arkansas Razorbacks of the prominent Southwest Conference.

The final score was 21-19 in favor of Arkansas, but the Razorbacks knew they had been in a game in fabled Legion Stadium.

Coach McCray's "Big Green Indians," as one sports writer said, using both favorite nicknames, had several opportunities to win, and the statistics of the game were as close as the score. Led by a backfield of tailback Buddy Lex, fullback "Flyin'" Jack Cloud and halfback Herb Poplinger the team rolled up 242 yards rushing, compared to 108 yards by Arkansas. Total yardage was 269 for W&M and 242 for Arkansas.

Injuries and a 97-yard late fourth-quarter march made the difference. Indian players down and out were "Red" Caughron, tackle, who had re-injured his bad knee; Tommy "The Kid" Korczowski, tailback, whose weak ankle did not hold up; co-captain Bob Steckroth, end, who left with a leg injury; Knox Ramsey, guard, who was injured; and Cloud, who was hurt after more than twenty rushes into the Arkansas line.

Prior to Arkansas's lengthy late fourth-quarter drive, W&M had played strong and consistent defense. The Razorbacks two earlier scores came on "big" plays: a 70-yard pass interception and a 59-yard pass and run.

W&M's three scores came after long drives, highlighted by its talented backfield. The Indians scored three minutes and five seconds after the opening kickoff. Lex's quick kick was fumbled when the receiver was hit by Ralph Sazio, and Tommy Thompson recovered at the Arkansas 6. Two rushes later and Cloud scored. Stan Magdziak kicked the extra point with Jack Bruce holding.

A W&M score by Cloud midway in the first period was nullified by an offsides penalty, but the Indians finally scored before the end of the period with a 78-yard drive. The scoring march was capped by four Cloud runs. With the ball on the Arkansas 15, he broke away for 13 yards

Guard Knox Ramsey (22) gives an elbow to Arkansas defender, opening a hole for "Flyin'" Jack Cloud (50) in the Dixie Bowl. Photo by *Look Magazine*. From the collection of Knox Ramsey.

to the 2, but it took three more punches at a nine-man Razorback line before Cloud finally scored.

The Big Green's only touchdown of the second half came with three minutes and fifteen seconds remaining in the third period. A 28-yard run by Lex set up the touchdown, but once again inside the Arkansas 10-yard line the going got rough. Cloud got 2 yards up the middle, but was hurt on the play. He got up and gained 2 more yards before a third-down pass fell incomplete. On fourth down, Lex ran to his left and threw to Blanc on the run in the end zone. Again Magdziak's extra-point attempt was wide, and W&M led 19-14, but it would not hold up.

After the Razorback 97-yard drive to score, with just a few minutes remaining in the game, W&M took the kickoff and moved down to the Arkansas 15-yard line, where a fumble ended the Indians' hopes of a win. (—WK)

mentions. All five, along with tackle Sazio, were named to the All–Southern Conference first team. Coach McCray was selected "Coach of the Year" in the Southern Conference.

Cloud also set a school record with fifteen touchdowns in a single season and led the conference and state in scoring with 90 points. According to the NCAA, he was second nationally in points scored, behind Lou Gambino of Maryland. Magdziak was second in team scoring with two touchdowns and thirty-six of forty-one points after touchdown; his points after touchdown placed him second in the nation behind Michigan's Jim Brieske. Another record-setter was defensive back "Jumping Jack" Bruce, whose ten interceptions for the season were not only a W&M record, but also ranked him first in the country. Bruce's four thefts against Richmond also set a W&M single-game interception record that stood through 1996, along with his season record.

The team, however, still waited for a bowl invitation. The Rose Bowl became a closed affair in 1946 when the Pacific Coast Conference (later the Pacific 10) and the Big Nine (later the Big Ten) signed contracts to send their champions to the Tournament of Roses classic. The Cotton, Sugar, and Orange Bowls secured larger and better-known schools, but W&M still had an opportunity for the Gator Bowl, Sun Bowl, or one of the new bowls being established as interest in college football swelled in the postwar United States.

The 1947 team won W&M's second Southern Conference championship, represented by the miniature gold football. Photograph from the 1948 *Colonial Echo*; football from the Buddy Lex display at the Virginia Sports Hall of Fame.

W&M finally accepted the invitation to play in the first Dixie Bowl Classic in Birmingham, Alabama, on January 1, 1948. The University of Mississippi, with its talented quarterback Charlie Connerly was expected to be the Indians opponent, but arrangements could not be made, and the University of Arkansas finally was chosen. A 93-yard scoring drive by Arkansas in the final stages of the fourth quarter gave the Razorbacks a 21-19 victory.

The 1948 season was just eight months away, and returning lettermen were ready. Coach McCray said the team would not "be as strong as last year." He had to rebuild his line and find someone to fill the shoes of Knox Ramsey, but he still had "Flyin'" Jack Cloud, wingback Blanc, and tailback Korczowski.

Dignitaries from Birmingham, Alabama, welcome team players upon their arrival for the bowl game. From the collection of Linda McCray Thomas.

There was one stumbling block: a suicide schedule. In addition to conference opponents, the Indians faced intersectional competition in St. Bonaventure, Boston College, and a repeat encounter with Dixie Bowl champ Arkansas.

The season record of 6-2-2 was not close to the 9-1 of 1947, but *Times-Dispatch* headlines bellowed, "William and Mary football has come of age." For the second straight year the Big Green found itself bowl bound, "a fact which places Tribe grid activities on a 'big-time' basis in the eyes of the colorful and glamorous bowl promotions," the *Alumni Gazette* proclaimed. In fact, the bowl bid was offered even before the Indians played their last game, against Arkansas.

The team suffered two early season defeats, a 21-12 loss to Wake Forest in the second game and a 7-6 loss several weeks later to St. Bonaventure. Thus at the midpoint, the Indians were only 3-2, but significant conference victories and ties against two talented teams helped create an impressive end-of-the-season show.

To shore up the front wall, McCray decided to move George Hughes from tackle to guard, replacing Ramsey. He also moved Lou Creekmur to Hughes's starting tackle position. The arrangement was a stroke of genius. The duo combined with tackle Harry Caughron, center Tommy Thompson, guard Jack McDowell, and ends Lou Hoitsma and Vito Ragazzo for a powerful line-up.

The 14-6 victory over Davidson was fashioned on two passes from Korczowski, one to Hoitsma and the other to Blanc. Davidson's lone tally came on the last play of the game. The contest, however, gave McCray a chance to play reserves, giving them experience that would help later in the season.

Korczowski and Lex passed to Jack Bruce and George Heflin, respectively, in the Indians' only scores against Wake Forest. VMI was next, and

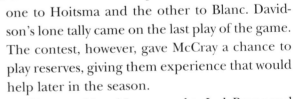

Tackle Ralph Sazio was co-captain his senior year in 1947 and made All–Southern Conference first team. His brother Jerry played in the early 1950s and also made All–Southern Conference in 1951 as linebacker. From the 1943 *Colonial Echo*.

Following W&M's very successful 1947 season and "Flyin'" Jack Cloud's personal gridiron success, Street and Smith selected Cloud to be the "cover-boy" for the *1948 Football Yearbook*. Courtesy of the W&M Sports Information Department.

the Big Green turned up the heat, winning 31-0. Lex tossed two more touchdowns, while Cloud scored another.

Korczowski was the star of W&M's 30-0 triumph over Virginia Tech, scoring on a 56-yard punt return and passing for touchdowns to Vito Ragazzo and Blanc. Cloud also scored. Jim McDowell was named lineman of the week in Virginia for his outstanding play.

Cloud also scored the lone touchdown against St. Bonaventure. In fact, so impressed were the students of the New York school that they wrote Cloud a letter of congratulations. Cloud and Blanc rushed for scores against Richmond, setting the stage for probably the Indians' best performance of the season against North Carolina.

The Tar Heels, with All-American "Choo Choo" Justice, were ranked third in the nation and were undefeated and untied when the Indians, four-touchdown underdogs, played in Chapel Hill before a capacity crowd of 43,000. The game ended in a 7-7 tie after a 22-yard pass from Korczowski to Hoitsma, who made "the catch of the season" for the touchdown. Buddy Lex kicked the tying extra point. McCray's spread defense kept Justice bottled up, and the coach kept his troops fresh, playing his first string on defense and his second string on offense. The game ended with the Indians on the UNC eight, after blocking back Joe Mark intercepted a Carolina pass. While UNC was able to gain a statistical advantage, it could not score the winning points. W&M defensive laurels went to Creekmur, Hoitsma, and Thompson.

The next week's 14-14 tie at Boston College was played on a muddy, rainy field that hampered both teams. Blanc's 41-yard return of an intercepted pass gave W&M

Players pose for the 1948 team photograph. The squad went to the College's second straight bowl game and defeated Oklahoma A&M (Oklahoma State), becoming the first Virginia team to win a bowl game. From the 1949 *Colonial Echo*.

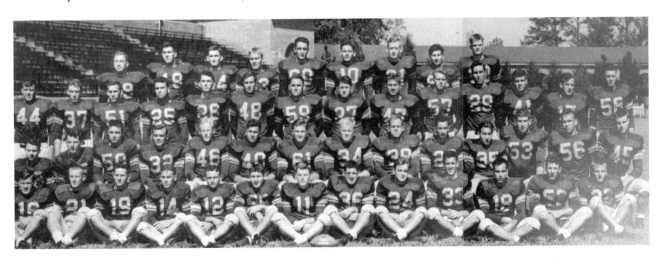

Quarterback Buddy Lex, who really liked to pass, runs off-tackle against VMI in the 1948 Oyster Bowl game in Norfolk. From the 1949 *Colonial Echo*.

a first-quarter score. Jack Bruce went off tackle and, with the help of Thompson's nifty down-field block, scampered 82 yards for the second score.

A 26-6 triumph over N.C. State at Cary Field gave W&M its second bowl invitation. Korczowski was in near-perfect form, tossing two touchdown passes to Bruce and Hoitsma. He was on the receiving end of a pass from Bruce and scampered 74 yards down the sidelines for a touchdown. Bruce's 41-yard punt return ended the scoring.

Sweet revenge came in Arkansas where the Indians defeated their earlier Dixie Bowl nemesis, 9-0. Korczowski, the *Colonial Echo* said, "continued his scintillating performance of the previous week" by contributing to both touchdowns. A 32-yard Korczowski pass to Bruce set up 6 points by Cloud. Minutes later a Korczowski punt went out of bounds on the Arkansas 1-yard line. The Razorbacks went nowhere in three attempts, and Pat Haggerty's blocked punt went out of the end zone for a safety.

Bill Greer, *The Flat Hat*'s exceptional sports columnist of the era, fashioned a singularly observant piece in December to sum up the 1948 season. The team has "done much to put themselves on the football map," he wrote, praising it for execution on the field and the coaches for off-the-field work. "Without the type of scouting and coaching the Braves received they probably would have finished the season deep in the red because of their rough schedule. But the midnight oil burned in the Athletic office many nights during the campaign."

Alumni enjoyed plenty of publicity, beginning with Cloud's photograph on the cover of *Street & Smith's Football* annual and his naming to the preseason All-American team by Grantland Rice. The list of top plays began with Hoitsma's pass

W&M end Lou Hoitsma (dark jersey) makes the "play-of-the-year" catch of a pass from Tommy Korczowski. He eluded two UNC defenders to score the 7-7 game-tying touchdown. From the 1949 *Colonial Echo*.

reception against UNC, continued with Cloud's line plunge and last touchdown against Wake Forest, Korczowski's runbacks against Virginia Tech and N.C. State, and concluded with Bruce's 80-yard reverse against Boston College.

Once again, the Indians gained national attention on an individual basis. Five players were on All-American teams: Cloud, Newspaper Enterprise Association first team as well as second- and third-team selections on three other All-American squads; Thompson, Associated Press third team; Caughron, Hoitsma, and McDowell, Associated Press honorable mention. Creekmur joined these five teammates for All-Conference honors.

W&M capped the season with the first bowl win for any Virginia school in the Delta Bowl, played in Memphis, Tennessee, against Oklahoma A&M (now Oklahoma State).

After back-to-back bowl appearances by the 1947 and 1948 W&M teams, the 1949 season

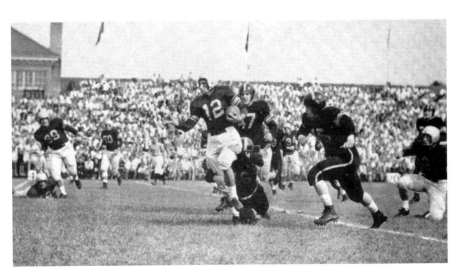

might be considered a letdown in terms of wins, but not in terms of talented players, such as Ragazzo, whose adroit end play netted him a position on the United Press's second team All-American squad.

Henry Blanc rips off yardage against Wake Forest in the 1948 game at Cary Field. From the 1949 *Colonial Echo*.

The schedule in 1949 was one of the strongest of the decade, featuring games against Midwest giants Pittsburgh and Michigan State, bowl rival Arkansas, and Southern Conference giants North Carolina and Wake Forest. W&M faced these teams with only 46 players, the conference's smallest squad. McCray, however, got some new coaching help from three former W&M standouts—Caughron, Hoitsma, and Mikula—who came back to work with their former teammates.

Fullback Cloud, tackle Creekmur, guard Hughes, and tailback Lex concluded their collegiate careers in fine style, while junior end Ragazzo also appeared among the team's all-stars.

W&M's single-wing offense was led by triple-threat Lex, who not only was an excellent passer and runner,

Versatile halfback Tommy Korczowski could run, pass, catch, and block and played an instrumental role in W&M's success during his four varsity years. From the 1947 *Colonial Echo*.

W&M's defensive safety Jack Bruce knocks the ball away from an Aggie receiver. Each player received a seventeen-jewel, fourteen-karat gold watch, with the inscription, "Delta Bowl—1949" (inset) for participating in the bowl game. Photograph from the 1949 *Colonial Echo;* watch from the Jack Cloud display in the Virginia Sports Hall of Fame.

Delta Bowl

The University of Utah was originally scheduled to be the Indians' opponent in the second annual Delta Bowl. W&M quickly accepted the invitation following the N.C. State game, after the College's faculty committee on athletics gave its approval for a postseason appearance.

Utah promised a scrappy contest, having a record of 7-1-1 and a healthy scoring advantage of 180-89 en route to the Big Six or Mountain States Conference title. The Utah team, however, decided to wait a week before answering and, at the last minute, voted to decline the invitation.

The Delta Bowl committee then turned to another champion, Oklahoma A&M of the Missouri Valley Conference. A&M finished the regular season with a 6-3 record, losing to Oklahoma, Texas Christian, and Kansas, while defeating Wichita, Denver, San Francisco, Temple, Tulsa, and Kansas State. They seemed to be a team similar to the Indians.

W&M won the game, 20-0, played before some 15,000 persons at Crump Stadium in Memphis, Tennessee. The contest quickly became a showcase for W&M talent. The first half highlighted the defensive squad as the Cowboys, with a much heavier line, pushed into Big Green territory three times, only to be challenged inside the 10-yard line. They seemed to have everything but the scoring punch, reported Shelley Rolfe who traveled to Memphis to cover the game for the *Richmond Times-Dispatch.*

The Indians struck for two touchdowns in 41 seconds at the end of the third quarter and the beginning of the fourth with Tommy "The Kid" Korczowski tossing up the scores. A pass interception by Lou Creekmur in the final seconds of the game sealed the victory.

At the beginning, however, it looked nothing like a W&M victory day. Oklahoma A&M took the opening kickoff and moved 85 yards from its own 10-yard line only to be thwarted at the Indians' 5-yard line. Twice more during the first half, the Cowboys pushed inside the Tribe's 10-yard line, stopped once at the 1-foot line by the defensive talents of massive Lou Creekmur, Tommy Thompson, "Red" Caughron, and Lou Hoitsma.

Four fumbles kept the W&M attack bottled up, but finally, late in the third quarter, the Indians fashioned their first successful drive. It was then that Korczowski and "Flyin'" Jack Cloud combined their talents in an offensive display moving the ball 75 yards in five plays. Cloud's 29-yard run pushed the ball into Oklahoma territory. "The Kid" then passed to Hoitsma for seven yards and to Vito Ragazzo for another 13. Cloud then went off tackle for 12 more yards. Korczowski capped the drive with an 11-yard pass to Hoitsma at the 1-yard line, and the team's co-captain stepped over for the game's first score. Buddy Lex, whose injured leg prevented him from punting that day, missed his point after touchdown.

The Cowboys fumbled the kickoff, and Creekmur recovered on the Oklahoma 23-yard line. Three plays later, W&M had its second score on a 22-yard looping pass from Korczowski to Jack Bruce. Lex hit the extra point this time.

Oklahoma vainly tried twice in the final period, pushing drives deep into W&M territory. The final drive ended at the Indians' 30-yard line, when Creekmur picked a pass out of the air and raced 70 yards untouched for the score. It was the first touchdown for a W&M interior lineman all season. Lex converted again for the bowl game—ending, 20-0 score in favor of the Indians.

Coach McCray, who was carried off the field by his team, gave victory laurels to the line. "The line was great, wasn't it?" McCray told reporters. "And don't forget the defensive play of Henry Blanc and Jack Cloud in the backfield. This one was a team win."

One of the players yelled, "Hey, Tailback" at Creekmur in the dressing room, referring to his 70-yard pass-interception gallop. Rolfe reported in a *Times-Dispatch* story that McCray yelled back, "I guess I've been playing Creekmur in the wrong position all season."

The ball used for the kickoff was special, having been autographed by General Dwight D. Eisenhower. It was used for just one play, and then became part of the trophy room of the Memphis AMVETS, who sponsored and organized the bowl. The game also was televised by a Memphis station and marked the first television appearance by a W&M football team.   (—WK)

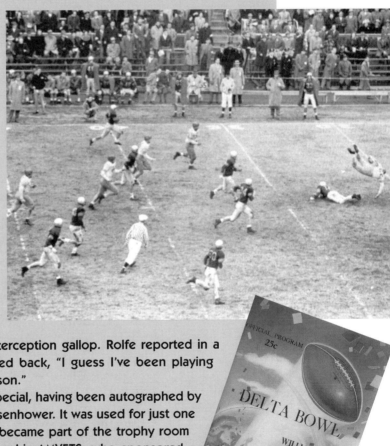

Tommy Korczowski (at right) upends an Aggie runner to thwart another Oklahoma A&M drive in the Delta Bowl. From the 1949 *Colonial Echo*; program from the collection of George R. Heflin.

but averaged nearly 40 yards per punt during his W&M career. Like Freeman and Korczowski before him, Lex had learned the "art of punting" from the Indians' famed backfield coach Tipton, probably the finest collegiate punter of his time.

Offensively, Lex teamed with Ragazzo in a passing combination that rivaled the mid-1920s Indian duo of Matsu and Davis. Lex passed for a record-setting 1,325 yards and eighteen

The starting line-up for the Delta Bowl game pose before boarding a Capitol Airlines plane to take them with the rest of the team to Memphis, Tennessee. Players are, front row, left to right: Lou Hoitsma, Red Caughron, George Hughes, Lou Creekmur, Tommy Thompson, Jim McDowell, and Vito Ragazzo. Second row: Henry Blanc, Frank O'Pella, Jack Cloud, Tommy Korczowski, and Coach McCray. From the collection of Lynda McCray Thomas.

touchdowns and scored three himself. Counting his twenty-seven points after touchdown, he was responsible for 153 of the 256 points the team scored. Lex's total offensive effort (passing and rushing) for the season was 1,736 yards, ranking him second in the nation.

Ragazzo made fifteen touchdown receptions, fourteen of them thrown by Lex. Ragazzo led the nation with 793 pass-receiving yards, a national record, and was the highest scoring lineman in college football history at that time.

The jinx against the University of North Carolina continued when the Tar Heels visited Cary Field. W&M, amid all its 1940s success, could not get a win over UNC, but the 7-7 tie in 1948 had ruined Carolina's bid for an undefeated, untied season. UNC's talented tailback "Choo Choo" Justice, bottled up during most of the two previous W&M games, was also held in 1949, except for one telling play. A crowd, estimated by some at more than 19,000, the largest gathering in Williamsburg since the Yankee invasion of 1862, saw the teams battle head-to-head most of the way. Carolina did not gain any advantage until the final period when Justice

End Vito Ragazzo (right) glances at a defender before catching a pass from Buddy Lex in a 1949 game. Courtesy of the W&M Sports Information Department.

handled a routine punt, faked a handoff, and turned it into a 75-yard touchdown gallop with three minutes remaining. But it was not enough to overcome W&M's lead. The final score was 20-14, with the Big Green scoring on Lex passes to Ragazzo and Ed Magdziak.

W&M had opened the 1949 season with a squeaky 14-13 win over the University of Houston, a developing power in the Southwest Conference. The Indians, however, lost to Pittsburgh, 13-7, scoring only on a Lex-to-Ragazzo pass play; Michigan State, 42-13; and Wake Forest, 55-28.

On the bright side, the victory string against state opponents during the 1940s continued with impressive wins over Virginia Tech, VMI, and Richmond. The Tribe also scored victories over N.C. State, an earlier nemesis, and Dixie Bowl winner Arkansas.

The Lex-to-Ragazzo combination accounted for two touchdowns against Virginia Tech, a couple more against VMI, and three against Richmond. Cloud also exploded for an 87-yard touchdown run against the Spiders.

The W&M–University of North Carolina game in November 1949 attracted some 19,000 persons, the largest crowd in the history of Cary Field. Notice the ribbon of small bleachers between the permanent stands and the field; these were in place until the late 1960s. Courtesy of the *Richmond Times-Dispatch.*

Buddy Lex, a great W&M punter and a pupil of Assistant Coach Eric Tipton, was an equally good passer. The Lex-to-Ragazzo combination worked for the 1948–49 teams in the same way as Matsu-to-Davis in 1925 and 1926. Courtesy of the W&M Sports Information Department.

Lou Creekmur

On July 17, 1996, legendary William and Mary football tackle Lou Creekmur '49 became the first of the Green, Gold, and Silver to become a member of the Professional Football Hall of Fame. For Creekmur, it was the culmination of years of effort. After failing to selection during the regular process, he began to lobby the "seniors" selection committee, sending letters detailing his accomplishments and individual achievements—including All-Pro six of his ten years with the Detroit Lions and eight straight appearances in the Pro Bowl game.

His line play, especially on offense protecting the Lions' great quarterback Bobby Layne and providing holes for halfback Doak Walker, helped Detroit win three world championships.

I guess you could say I played in William and Mary's and Detroit's glory years. I also played in the 1950 College All-Star game against the World Champion Philadelphia Eagles, and there were two W&M football players on the team with me—George Hughes and Jack Cloud. For a little school like William and Mary, three team members on the All-Stars didn't happen often.

Creekmur enjoyed playing pro ball. "For the amount we were making, you had to enjoy it," he said in a 1989 interview, noting that salaries in the 1950s were "no comparison [with] today in money. As a rookie, I was paid a $500 bonus by the Lions and signed a $5,000 contract for the season. I wasn't paid anything for the two months of training camp."

Detroit Lions teammate Walker presented Creekmur at the Hall's induction ceremony. "Back then [in the 1950s] we played the [pro] game because we genuinely loved football," he said.

Creekmur feels strongly that pro teams today have none of the camaraderie that he experienced. "Our Detroit Lions team was as close to a college team for camaraderie and loyalty as you could get. ... That's changed now, I think," he said.

Creekmur was thankful for his academic and athletic experience at William and Mary because "of the values we learned and developed from attending a school like William and Mary. We were also exposed to some of the best coaches you would find. ... I believe most of my success in the pros could be attributed to Marvin Bass. He would take the time to give you individual instruction and tell you the 'whys' of the game."

As for his W&M teammates, such as Cloud, Hughes, and Lou Hoitsma, "they showed you what it meant to be a man and that there were things more important than winning. But believe you me, we sure did win." His College teams of 1944–49 compiled a record of 27-10-3 and received invitations to W&M's first two bowl games on New Year's Day 1948 and 1949.

Creekmur, who completed his football eligibility at W&M while attending graduate school, was a second-round draft pick by Detroit in 1950. For the next eight years he played in every exhibition, regular season, and postseason game—165 straight games. He retired after the 1958 season, but returned four games into the 1959 season to complete a ninth season.

His favorite pro experience was with the Detroit team of 1957, "the last championship the Lions ever won," he said.

We started off with a ragged crew and were talked down by [coach] Buddy Parker. He later left and George Wilson took over. We had so much pride, there was no way we were going to let Parker's opinion of us destroy the team. We made the playoffs against the San Francisco 49ers, but at halftime were behind by 21 points. Wilson didn't holler at us, he just said listen to what was going on next door in the 49ers locker room. We just sat there; they were yelling and laughing. You talk about drawing together as a group. Those 30-some guys did it, and we beat them by three points. We had so much going for us then that in the World Championship game, we beat Cleveland, 59-14.   (—WK)

Dickie Lewis (15) picks up nine yards for the Indians on an end sweep as Jack Cloud takes out UNC's Skeet Hesmer. Photo by the *Richmond Times-Dispatch.*

W&M traveled to Houston, Texas, to play the Cougars on September 17, 1949. The Indians edged Houston, 14-13, in the night game. Courtesy of the University Archives, College of William and Mary.

The yearbook entry for 1949 probably put it best: "Although the backfield of the Indians team gained many honors through the season, it cannot be denied that their glory was in part made possible because of the fine line play produced by men who were big and experienced gridders. It was as heavy and as fast as any in the Southern Conference." Heading that line were stalwarts like guards Hughes and Jim McDowell and tackles Creekmur and Ragazzo.

W&M players also saw postseason all-star play. Lex, Hughes, and Creekmur played in the Blue-Gray Classic. Cloud and Creekmur played in the Senior Bowl in Mobile, Alabama, and in the late-summer NFL-College All-Star game, the last Indian players to be so honored. Earlier Tommy Thompson played with the 1949 College All-Stars, Knox Ramsey with the 1948 All-Stars, and Harvey Johnson with the 1943 All-Stars. By a quirk of the war, "Buster" Ramsey played in College All-Star games in 1943 and 1946.

Members of the 1949 team also embarked on professional football careers. Cloud enjoyed a four-year National Football League career and a long, illustrious stint on the Navy coaching staff. In 1990 he joined "Buster" Ramsey as a member of the College Football Hall of Fame. Creekmur went on to a successful NFL career with the

It was a bit of Indian razzle-dazzle against Pittsburgh, but it gained only four yards on a first quarter pass from Jack Cloud (50) to end Vito Ragazzo, who then lateraled to halfback Ed Weber (17) who was trailing the play. The Panthers won, 13-7. Photo by the *Pittsburgh Post Gazette.*

Detroit Lions and, in the summer of 1996, became the first W&M football player to be inducted into the Pro Football Hall of Fame. Hughes played five years for the Pittsburgh Steelers.

In the middle of the 1949 season, McCray received a five-year contract to coach the Indians through 1954. President Pomfret's statement that the contract was "not dependent on games won or lost" drew much national attention and editorial comment. The *Charlotte* (North Carolina) *News* said, "It is still reassuring that William and Mary, at least, places the character and personality of the coach a notch higher than his skill at winning all his football games."

The *Alumni Gazette* aptly described the 1950 W&M football season: "The famine came a year earlier than was anticipated. Instead of the [Biblical] seven years of plenty, there were but six." The Big Green had six straight winning seasons under head coach McCray, but no seventh. In fact, for the first time since he began his coaching career in 1930, he had a losing record—4-7. After spring practice, McCray had hesitated when asked about prospects for the fall. There were some signs of another successful campaign. W&M still would run the single-wing offense, but McCray had decided to introduce some variations, like a double wing and buck-lateral of Michigan and a "Y" formation similar to that introduced by Southern Methodist.

But challenges were also apparent. The schedule included Michigan State, Houston, and Boston University, as well as the always tough Southern Conference teams. And, after an absence of a decade, the University of Virginia returned, a scheduling feat that almost took an act of the General Assembly. There was another factor—another war. The Korean Conflict, as it was called, erupted on the Asian peninsula in June of 1950. By the beginning

Michigan State's Carey brothers (86 and 85) zero in on W&M quarterback Ed Magdziak (10). From the 1951 *Colonial Echo.*

Joe Mark (foreground) makes a block on Michigan State defender for Dickie Lewis (15) to scoot through the hole. From the 1951 *Colonial Echo.*

Ed Weber (17) hauls in a Dickie Lewis screen pass and heads toward the end zone in the 14-13 triumph over Duke University in 1951. From the 1952 *Colonial Echo.*

Tommy Koller (10) at the start of an 80-yard touchdown gallop in the second period against Duke. From the 1952 *Colonial Echo.*

of football season, twenty-one of the sixty-seven players who had participated in spring practice had been called into the service.

The pattern was set at the opening game against VMI when the Keydets came from behind in the last minute of the game to defeat the Indians, 25-19, breaking W&M's decade-long state winning streak. In the next three games there was only one win. While the team was beaten handily by Wake Forest, 47-0, and Michigan State, 33-14, it defeated Cincinnati, 20-14. Following a 54-0 Tribe blow-out against Virginia Tech, the Indians suffered successive losses against North Carolina, Boston University, Virginia, and Houston.

Of those games, the Virginia loss was probably the most disappointing. The W&M athletic department, with the help of alumni and some politicians, had worked hard to get the Cavaliers to agree to play the Indians again. The promotional hype for the game was intense. Pep rallies were held, and thousands of W&M faithful made the trek to Charlottesville to rally the Indians, who were 13-point underdogs. In the end, the Cavaliers matched the odds with a 13-0 victory. W&M's defense played a good game and held Virginia on several drives with the assistance of 15 penalties. The Indians also had at least three scoring chances in the second half, but the drives bogged down inside the U.Va. 10-yard line. One drive ended at the 1-yard line.

Marvin Bass

In his college days, they called him "Big Moose," and, when he returned to the Williamsburg campus, the label was "Coach!" To those with whom he associated over the years, he was simply considered one of the finest linemen ever to play the college game and one of the best line coaches ever.

Marvin Bass '45, the captain and a defensive star of W&M's outstanding 1942 football team, began his College career as a member of the "Fabulous Freshman" team of 1939. He came to Williamsburg from Petersburg High School, where he had won All-State honors four times. In fact, he was named All-State eight times, including three times at W&M—1940, 1941, and 1942—and for the 1943 season at the University of Richmond, where he participated in a Navy training program.

In a 1995 interview, Bass praised W&M Coach Carl Voyles for instilling in him many of the attributes he would carry through his own coaching career:

Coach Voyles and his staff prepared us for a lot of things. They made us gentlemen and they made us into a good football team. ...In those days I would envision a stadium of 50,000 people and W&M as prominent as any national football team in the country. It was a school where you could recruit good athletes. It didn't take near the recruiting budget that it took in other places.

Most of his teammates in those years considered Bass in the same athletic category as All-American "Buster" Ramsey, and most of the W&M players he coached felt he and backs coach Eric Tipton were their best coaches.

In 1945, following the war, Bass returned to W&M as line coach for Rube McCray and remained until 1949. He then went to UNC as assistant coach under Carl Snavely. That year the Tar Heels played in the Cotton Bowl. He returned to W&M as an assistant in 1950. After that season's game against UNC, which the Tribe lost, 40-7, the Tar Heel players whom he had coached a year earlier, came across and carried Bass off the field on their shoulders. "It was a great compliment to me," he recalled.

In 1951, just a few weeks before the football season, he was named head coach on the Reservation succeeding McCray. Bass took the job, he said, because "I loved the school and felt like it was a good chance for me to be a head coach. I wasn't thrilled about getting the job under the circumstances, but I knew we had some great talent. The players were unbelievable, and I felt I owned them a lot of loyalty."

A year later, however, Bass was gone. He resigned even though his team had a 7-3 season, winning five of the last six. But Bass did not leave football. He became a highly respected college and professional coach during the next four decades.

His collegiate stops included UNC (a second time), the University of South Carolina (as assistant coach and later as head coach and athletic director), and assistant jobs at Georgia Tech and the University of Richmond.

That journey also took him through the professional ranks numerous times—with the National Football League's Washington Redskins, to Montreal's Beavers of the Canadian Football League as head coach and general manager, twice with the Buffalo Bills of the NFL, as both assistant and head coach with the Birmingham Americans of the World Football League, the Canadian Football League's Calgary Stampeders, and the last eleven years with the Denver Broncos of the NFL under former South Carolina star Dan Reeves.

While at Denver, Bass served initially as a special assistant and offensive line coach and for the last several years as special assistant for quality control.

Bass finally retired to South Carolina in 1993 after nearly sixty years of playing and coaching football. Retirement, however, was not forever. Following the death of his wife, Audrey, in the fall of 1996, Bass yearned again for football and Reeves sensed it. Since he had become head coach of the Atlanta Falcons in 1997, Reeves called upon Bass to return as his special assistant.   (—WK)

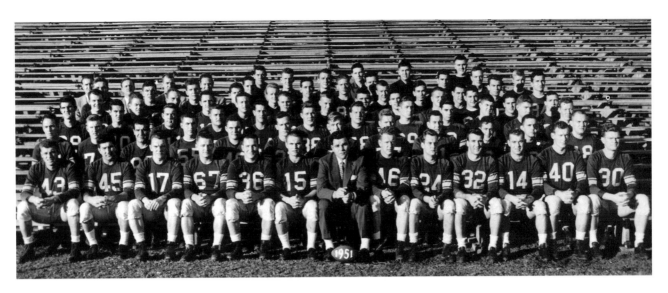

With a mark of 2-7, the worst for a W&M team in fourteen years, the Big Green enjoyed a redemption of sorts in the final two games. Amid a freak snow-ice-and-wind storm in Norfolk's Oyster Bowl, W&M shutout N.C. State, 34-0, with Dickie Lewis and Ed Magdziak scoring twice. The season-ending 40-6 rout of arch-rival Richmond also soothed some aching alumni hearts. Lewis again scored two touchdowns, and Magdziak, Ed Mioduszewski (Meadows), Ragazzo, and Weber contributed one each.

The season was a downer but worse—much worse—loomed ahead. During the spring practice in 1951, while the gridders were going through the paces on the fields surrounding Cary Field's stadium, the football program was being scrutinized by faculty members concerned that improprieties had taken place. In fact, by the third week in August, McCray submitted his resignation to President Pomfret, and line coach Marvin Bass, who had returned as an assistant for the 1950 season after one year at UNC, was named head coach. (See Chapter 4 for details.) Thus, with fall practice just days away and the season only a month off, Bass took control of W&M's fortunes. Only assistant coach Eric Tipton stayed, and Bass faced the immediate task of hiring a staff. Jackie Freeman, who had played with Bass before the war, was hired as backfield coach, and Herb Miller became line coach.

The 1951 team was the last during the "glory years" of W&M's big-time football program. Coach Marvin Bass (center in suit) resigned after only one year because the College's administration could not decide what athletic course to take. Courtesy of the W&M Sports Information Department.

W&M's Tommy Koller (10) runs around end during the Virginia Tech game in 1951. Courtesy of the W&M Sports Information Department.

Charlie Sumner gets moving on an 89-yard kickoff return against the University of Pennsylvania at Franklin Field. W&M defeated the Quakers, 20-12. From the 1952 *Colonial Echo.*

The 1951 squad was a "tested" team that had suffered greatly the previous year. It faced another stiff schedule with newcomers Oklahoma, Pennsylvania, and Duke in addition to a return game with Boston University and Southern Conference powers UNC and Wake Forest.

Strategically, Bass abandoned McCray's single-wing and introduced the split-T formation handled by assistant coach Charley Ellis. The opening game against Boston University was not a real test, with the Tribe earning a 35-24 win, but the next two games were disasters. Oklahoma blew the Indians out, 49-7, and VMI won its second straight over the Indians, 20-7.

These two big defeats came after the team and the campus were affected by the announced resignation of President Pomfret. Negative publicity was rampant and the football players suffered along with everyone else. Team morale was at its lowest ebb since the 1939 arrival of Voyles and McCray at the Reservation.

Then came a turnaround that everyone credits to Bass. A six-game winning streak, one of the biggest comebacks in W&M gridiron history, turned a dismal season into a respectable one.

In Richmond's Tobacco Bowl against Wake Forest, the Indians simply out-played, out-fought, and out-hustled the unbeaten and untied Deacons. An extra-point kick by Lloyd Quinby Hines provided the winning margin in the 7-6 victory.

W&M came from behind three times in the fourth quarter to defeat N.C. State, 35-28. The Wolfpack led 14-0 at halftime, but the Indians came roaring back in the last 20 minutes of the game to score five touchdowns.

Coach Marvin Bass and co-captains George Zupko (left) and Dickie Lewis (right) pose for a 1951 publicity shot. From the 1952 *Colonial Echo.*

Frank Lipski scored twice and Tommy Koller added another, before Ed Mioduszewski tallied on runs of 75 yards and 19 yards.

A 20-14 defeat of Richmond pushed the Indians into a big contest against Ivy League leader Pennsylvania. Dickie Lewis, who led the scoring against Richmond, continued his efforts by scoring in the first quarter; Lipski scored early in the second, while Paul Yewcic added the third and last tally in the 20-12 victory over the Quakers.

W&M's domination of Virginia Tech continued with a 28-7 Homecoming Day. Again, Lewis passed to Tommy Koller resulting in a 7-7 halftime score, but three quick touchdowns by Koller, Lewis, and Mioduszewski in the third quarter buried the Hokies.

Duke University felt W&M's power in the first half, but the second half was all Blue Devils, even though the Indians hung on for a 14-13 squeaker. Lewis tossed a pass to Ed Weber in the first quarter, while Koller took a Lewis pitchout and raced 80 yards for a second-quarter score. Then it was clutch time as Jerry Sazio (Ralph's brother), John Kreamcheck, and Ted Filer played tops in the Indian forward wall, keeping Duke away from a game-winning score.

Going into the final game of the season, the Indians were 7-2. A disastrous, 46-0 loss to Virginia dimmed an otherwise very good season and foreshadowed greater difficulties.

Problems for the Athletic Department and W&M's football program that began in 1949 and culminated with McCray's resignation in August 1950, would not go away. No one knew that 1951 would be Marvin Bass's one and only season as Indian head coach. The sun had set on the glory days.

Power blocking by Indians Sam Lupo (45), Jim Shatynski (62), Ed Weber (17), and Jim Smith (35) opens up the Boston University line for Ed Mioduszewski (25). From the 1952 *Colonial Echo*.

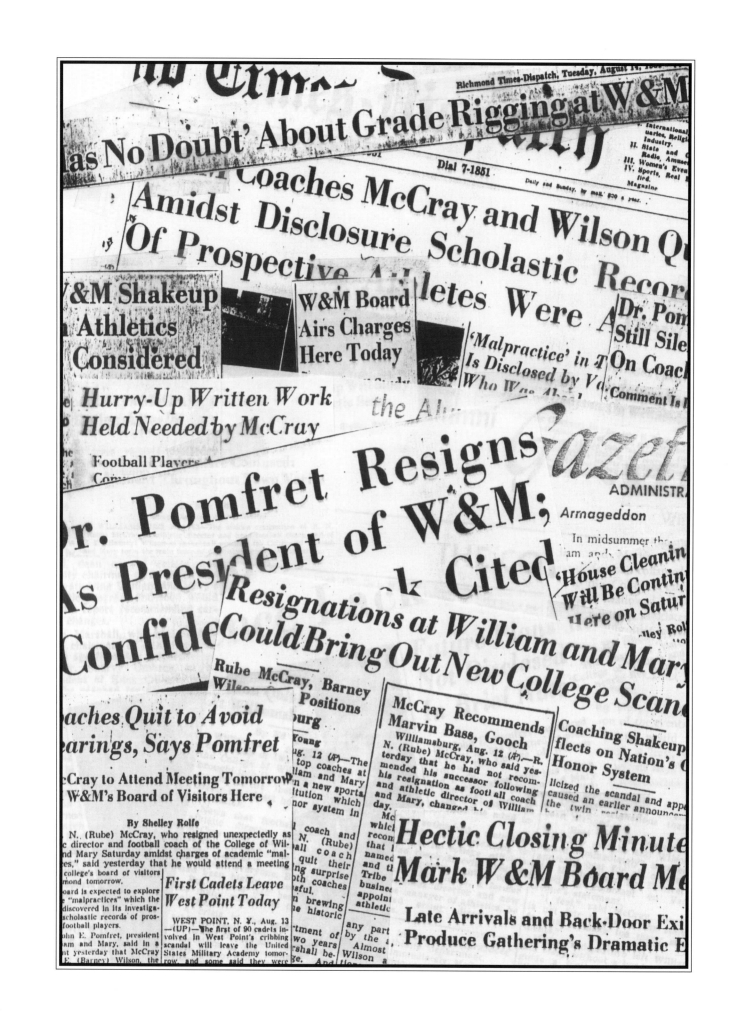

4
The Dark at the End of the Tunnel
The Athletic Controversy
1949 to 1951

Wilford Kale

"**B**ig-time" football ended at William and Mary in the winter of 1951–52 following an athletic controversy, that some have dubbed the "football scandal." The glory days of Carl Voyles and Rube McCray came to an abrupt, ignominious end locked in the grasp of rumors, investigations, and resignations.

Ultimately, the controversy, which became public and consumed activities on the campus for much of August and September 1951, resulted in the resignations of McCray, football coach and athletic director, and Barney Wilson, basketball coach and chairman of the Department of Physical Education for Men. The complexity of the situation, however, had its own ripple effect and far-reaching consequences that resulted in the surprising resignation of W&M President Dr. John E. Pomfret.

Three others not directly involved in the scandal, but caught in its undertow, also resigned their posts—Dr. Nelson Marshall, dean of the College; Charles P. McCurdy, Jr., alumni secretary; and McCray's football coaching successor, Marvin C. Bass.

The saga of the controversy traces a highly complex series of events that began in 1949 with allegations that high school transcripts for certain athletes wanting to attend the College

Coach "Rube" McCray (with papers) is surrounded by his assistants in 1949. Standing (left to right), coaches Tom Powers and Al Thomas had no involvement in the athletic controversy; Barney Wilson and McCray ultimately resigned. Marvin Bass (kneeling at left) succeeded McCray, then resigned after the 1951 season. Eric Tipton (third from left), along with Bass, said he knew nothing of the scandal. Al Vandeweghe (at right), implicated by some, was absolved by the College of any wrongdoing. From the 1949 *Colonial Echo*.

had been altered. It continued into mid-1951 with charges of unethical conduct and academic malpractice raised against McCray and Wilson. Eventually the two coaches admitted to only one element of a broad range of academic charges.

Minutes of several meetings of the College's Board of Visitors held during August and September 1951 outlined many details of the scandal and provide the basis of a 1990 master's thesis: "Kickoffs and Kickbacks: The 1951 Football Scandal at William and Mary" by Joan Gosnell. After skillfully laying out the entire scenario, including the selection of a new William and Mary president, she concluded the dispute boiled down to a fight between the Board and the faculty.

As a result of the controversy, the last forty-five years of William and Mary's first century of football were played out against the backdrop of scandal that forever altered the College's gridiron history and permeated the relationships between football, the College's faculty, and the athletic program for decades. Even today there is residual distrust of football by some academics on campus.

There was never an "official" investigation by the Board of Visitors or the College administration, although Dean of Students J. Wilfred Lambert investigated the handling of transcripts in 1949, and Dean Marshall, in 1951, conducted his own investigation and reported the results to President Pomfret and the Board of Visitors. McCray denied most of the allegations and, in the end, chose to resign without defending himself. As some of his friends later said, whatever his personal involvement, the controversy happened "on his watch," and he took responsibility for it.

Dean J. Wilfred Lambert

Like many scandals, William and Mary's began as a small, isolated incident that expanded and compounded as new sensational rumors and charges surfaced.

The College's postwar athletic success, especially on the gridiron, was attributed in large part to the significant number of returning veterans who were excellent athletes. Eligibility rules were lax or enforced in an uneven manner throughout the intercollegiate ranks.

Although the College's quest for an expanded and enhanced football schedule was strongly supported by the Board of Visitors, it did not, after the war, have the support of President Pomfret. In fact, in the spring of 1946 he proposed a return to the football formula of the early 1930s—playing liberal arts colleges with non-subsidized athletic programs.

This apparent disagreement prompted the Board of Visitors in October 1946 to adopt a new athletic policy that, according to the Board minutes, "would produce athletic teams that could compete successfully with other teams in the State of Virginia belonging to the Southern Conference (i.e., Virginia Tech, University of Richmond, and Virginia Military Institute) and to such extent as it could be reasonably expected that the College teams would win more games than they lost and that such a program be established on a sound financial basis."

In the late 1940s the College had difficulty meeting eligibility requirements for some athletes. While the eligibility rules for the Southern Conference and the National Collegiate Athletic Association (NCAA) had been modified for postwar years, they returned to the pre-1941 rules by the summer of 1948. The NCAA's "Sanity Code" of 1949 was an effort to take some professionalism out of the student athletic programs throughout the nation. Specifically, it restricted the amount of money student athletes could be paid for campus jobs, limited amounts available for individual athletic grants-in-aid, and allowed schools to provide only one "training table" meal per day for the athletes.

President
John E. Pomfret

Dr. Pomfret told the Board of Visitors on June 4, 1949, that W&M needed to sign the Code or "the college would be placed at a great disadvantage in its program of intercollegiate athletics." The Board authorized the endorsement. Pomfret, however, reported to the Board on February 11, 1950, that W&M "is not in compliance with the code in every particular." The major violation was that W&M athletes, like those at many other colleges and universities throughout the nation, were being paid more than regular students for the same campus work.

It was about this time, and within the above context, that the first element of the scandal developed. Lambert, at that time dean of students, registrar, and chairman of the College's admission committee, discovered that the high school transcripts of several William and Mary athletes had been altered. Specifically, one student wanted to take an entry-level Spanish course, but was told he would not get credit for it since he had taken Spanish in high school. The student said he had never taken a Spanish course. Lambert contacted the student's high school and received a transcript that was different from the one on file in the Registrar's Office. Years later, Lambert said in an interview that he brought the altered transcript to the attention of Pomfret, who told him to continue his investigation.

Later, it was determined that four more transcripts from other high schools were also altered. Grades and class standings of the students were changed, and one student's high school suspension was removed from his transcript. All these forged documents, however, carried a similar characteristic. The top loop of the typed "e" was filled. Lambert and his colleagues discovered that a type-writer in the women's athletic office in Blow Gymnasium had the same "e" feature.

When all of the alterations had been uncovered, Dr. Pomfret initiated im-mediate changes in the procedure for handling the transcripts for athletics. Instead of the transcripts going to the athletic department and then being conveyed to the Registrar's Office, all transcripts were to be sent directly from the high school to the registrar, in that case, to Lambert.

The investigation also determined that none of the students involved knew anything about the changes. By early 1950, three of the five students had left campus because of poor grades, one was suspended and one was on academic warning. In addition, Assistant Football Coach Alfred B. Vandeweghe, one of Voyles's "Fabulous Freshmen" of 1939, was implicated in the transcript alter-ations and his contact was not renewed. Almost two years later Dean of the College Dr. Marshall absolved Vandeweghe of any wrongdo-ing.

Dean Nelson Marshall

In 1949, everything appeared to be going well for W&M athletics. In the spring, the men's tennis team captured its second straight national title under Coach Sharvey Umbeck, who was also Dean of the College and chairman of the Fac-ulty Committee on Athletics. But Umbeck left in the fall to become a college president himself, and the deanship—and later the chairmanship of the faculty's athletic committee—fell to Marshall. In October, the Board of Visitors gave McCray a five-year extension as head football coach.

In February 1950, the College's Board of Visitors voted to continue membership in the NCAA, acknowledging that the College's athletic eligibility policy might be out of com-pliance with the NCAA's Sanity Code. Dean Marshall's first academic session report for 1949–50 questioned the position of the faculty's athletic committee; he said it was relegated to making only minor recommen-dations.

Unlike his predecessor, Marshall voiced strong opposition to William and Mary's athletic program and to arrangements made to keep freshman athletes in College. According to his report, the process allowed those students to take upper-level physical education courses that would allow them to get A's or B's and keep them academically in school. He also raised the question, again, about the disposition of financial (work payments) assistance that was higher for athletes than regular students. Neither Pomfret nor the Board of Visitors responded to Marshall's concerns.

At Marshall's urging, the faculty athletic committee, in the spring of 1950, recommended to Pomfret and the faculty that the committee's chairman be authorized to cast votes at the NCAA meetings in absence of the College president. The Board of Visitor's Committee on Athletics did not agree and determined "in the best interests of the College" that the athletic director would cast such votes.

At its June 8, 1950, meeting the Board of Visitors heard a recommendation from its own Athletic Committee that William and Mary's athletic policy be made by the College president, the athletic director, and the Board's athletic committee with the approval by the entire Board. It added that the faculty's committee on athletics should not make athletic policy.

Dr. George Oliver

By September, the Board's athletic committee offered suggestions to overhaul the faculty's athletic committee. Dr. George Oliver, professor of education, was recommended to replace Marshall as committee chairman, rationalizing that committee members should be "men who are interested in athletics and at the same time willing to cooperate fully with the athletic authorities," according to the Board's minutes. It was obvious from this report and subsequent action that the W&M Board of Visitors was not about to surrender its control over the athletic program. A few days later, Marshall resigned as chairman after learning of the Board's action.

During the November 14, 1950, faculty meeting, a committee was appointed to examine faculty concerns that athletic teams' scheduling was affecting students' academic performance. On May 8, 1951, the special faculty committee made its report. The faculty wanted to reduce the number of games in minor sports such as golf, tennis, and cross-country and the number of games during class time and the examination/reading period; to require faculty athletic committee approval for student participation in all-star games; and to request the distribution of all team schedules to the faculty athletic committee before public announcements of those schedules.

It was probably not a coincidence that on April 20, 1951, just two weeks before the faculty's special committee report, Dean Marshall wrote to President Pomfret charging that "the present administration of our intercollegiate athletic program is dishonest, unethical and seriously lacking in responsibility to the academic standards of William and Mary." At that time Dr. Marshall also offered his resignation as dean.

In subsequent discussions with Pomfret, Marshall's resignation was not accepted, and he was told "if possible that specific cases indicating a lack of standards should be presented." Marshall's personal investigation of William and Mary's athletic program began. Athletic Director McCray and Men's Physical Education Department Chairman Wilson were informed of Marshall's investigation and accepted it.

James Rehlaender

Ironically, at the Board of Visitors' next meeting—May 26, 1951—Pomfret recommended that McCray be promoted from associate professor to full professor, but did not tell the Board of Marshall's on-going investigation of McCray and Wilson. Matters on campus began to move swiftly.

According to the time line in Gosnell's thesis, students then joined with the faculty in expressing their concern about athletics. On June 10, James Rehlaender, student body president, and James S. Kelly, president of the 1951 senior class, wrote a joint letter to Pomfret complaining about the current athletic emphasis at the College. They felt the athletic program was expanding too rapidly and that many student leaders wanted William and Mary not to play opponents who were obviously bigger and against competition that was better.

James S. Kelly

The report of Marshall's personal probe, received by Pomfret on June 11, described indications of "dishonesty and a lack of ethical standards" in the physical education department organization. He suggested that his nine examples of ethical misconduct "do not begin to represent the many people who have complained of first-hand experiences." According to Marshall, many people would not talk to him because they feared repercussions of some form. In this kind of atmosphere, Marshall added, "dishonesty can readily flourish if not checked."

Four former secretaries went to College officials in June 1951 with information that McCray had altered the transcripts, according to Board of Visitors minutes, but some other sources said it was Wilson who personally made the changes. Both men denied the charges.

In addition to the 1949 transcript tampering, the allegations included two cases of students earning credit for courses when they were at home instead of in Williamsburg attending classes; two grades given to a student for classes never held; one case of a student whose earned "B" in a course, was reported by the athletic department as an "A"; a student grade upgraded by a professor under pressure; a transcript sent to Lynchburg College omitting the information that the student had been required to withdraw from William and Mary because of an Honor Code violation; and an instance of a student having an illegal car on campus. Marshall also reported that there was a disregard of the College's Honor Code by personnel in the Department of Physical Education.

On June 29, Marshall disclosed four additional cases of dishonesty. Three involved students working in the physical education supply room who received no pay, but rather were given credits for an upper-level physical education course. According to the faculty minutes, the fourth concerned a female student who was "coerced by Wilson" to exaggerate her work records; the excess payment was given to Wilson "to buy books for athletes."

The faculty held a special meeting on July 3 and was brought up-to-date on Marshall's allegations. A special faculty committee was established to investigate the charges of unethical practices made against Wilson and McCray. Dr. Richard H. Morton, professor of history, was named committee chairman.

McCray's attorney, Walter E. Hoffman of Norfolk (who later became a respected federal judge), visited Pomfret that afternoon and recommended that McCray be allowed to resign on February 1, 1952, and that he be freed of his teaching duties, since the Athletic Association and the Department of Physical Education were being separated. Hoffman said McCray would cooperate with College officials regarding the matter of students receiving unearned credits.

Al Vandeweghe

The next day, Pomfret met with Dr. Morton's newly formed faculty committee and discussed two options that Pomfret had outlined in two draft letters. One option was to tell McCray that a special faculty committee had been appointed and that the Rector of the Board of Visitors had been notified of the investigation. McCray would be advised to defend himself or resign. The second option adopted Hoffman's suggestions. Pomfret told the committee he planned to suggest to McCray that he either defend himself against Marshall's allegations or resign under the terms of Hoffman's compromise. However, he assured the committee that he would not offer McCray the second option if they did not approve. The committee members said they would respond to Pomfret as individuals, not as faculty representatives. They had four concerns about accepting the compromise: 1) would McCray cooperate in the course credit investigation? 2) would McCray make no athletic [scheduling] commitments beyond June 1952? 3) would the compromise satisfy the various agencies that accredited the College? and 4) would

Dean Marshall be satisfied? After considerable discussion, everything was arranged, and Marshall, at the urging of several professors, agreed to the compromise.

On July 5, Pomfret informed the faculty committee that McCray had been given both letters and had asked for two days to make a decision. At about the same time, as a result of his investigation, Dean Marshall wrote to Alfred Vandeweghe, clearing him of any accusations of altering high school transcripts in 1949. Vandeweghe said later he had not even known that allegations had been made and that he had been a "scapegoat."

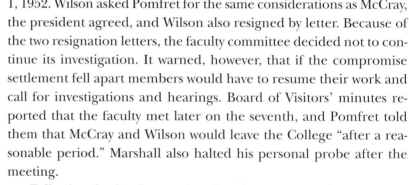

Coach "Rube" McCray

On July 7, McCray tendered his resignation effective, February 1, 1952. Wilson asked Pomfret for the same considerations as McCray, the president agreed, and Wilson also resigned by letter. Because of the two resignation letters, the faculty committee decided not to continue its investigation. It warned, however, that if the compromise settlement fell apart members would have to resume their work and call for investigations and hearings. Board of Visitors' minutes reported that the faculty met later on the seventh, and Pomfret told them that McCray and Wilson would leave the College "after a reasonable period." Marshall also halted his personal probe after the meeting.

Following the faculty meeting, Pomfret announced to news media that the Athletic Department would be separated from the Department of Physical Education and that all coaching and teaching jobs would also be separated.

It looked as though the athletic controversy was settled—until everything went public.

Press speculation began to mount immediately. On July 10, the *Norfolk Ledger Star* broke a story that McCray would resign following the 1951 football season. On July 11, the *Richmond Times-Dispatch* reported that McCray said he would not resign.

Dean Marshall had been asked by Pomfret to clear up the matter of students' unearned academic credit. Marshall wrote McCray on July 30 asking some questions regarding these credits, but McCray's response did not satisfy him. Marshall told McCray he would refer the matter to Pomfret and the special faculty committee. In communications with Pomfret, the special faculty committee concluded that McCray was not cooperating with College officials and that it must reopen the investigation.

In early August, Pete Franklin, a sports writer with the *Newport News Times Herald* newspaper, talked with Vandeweghe about the letter he had received from Dean Marshall absolving him of any wrongdoing in the earlier transcript tampering. Sports Editor Chauncey Durden of the *Richmond Times-Dispatch,* also learned about the letter and called Marshall before writing his own story.

On August 10, McCray and Wilson traveled to Cape May, New Jersey, to meet with a vacationing President Pomfret and personally submitted their resignations, effectively immediately. The next day the two coaches read their resignations to several newspaper reporters.

The *Newport News Times Herald* published an article on August 12 about athletic trouble at William and Mary and included Marshall's July letter to Vandeweghe. The *New York Times* picked up the story. Pomfret issued a press release on August 13, when he returned to Williamsburg, noting that the coaches were "afforded the opportunity of a hearing by a special committee of the Faculty. They declined a hearing, deciding instead to resign."

After receiving Marshall's letter, Vandeweghe tried several times to see Pomfret to discuss the situation and finally barged into the President's Office. While Pomfret saw Vandeweghe at this confrontation, he offered no satisfaction. "I was not trying to hurt the College," the former student and coach explained during a 1997 interview.

Rector Oscar L. Shewmake

Vandeweghe, then turned to the Board of Visitors. Marshall's letter said, in part, "We want to assure you that, in probing into the matter further, we have discovered no basis whatsoever for suspecting your participation. Before writing to you to this effect I have checked with both President Pomfret and Professor McCray and find that, in their opinion, such implications are not justified."

But even the implication that he might have been involved disturbed Vandeweghe. "I wanted to clear my name; I was associated with something that looked bad, and I had done nothing."

Judge Oscar L. Shewmake, Rector of the Board of Visitors (a position now called Rector of the College), who was involved and associated with the College's Athletic Department since his student days, called an unscheduled meeting of the Board for August 15 to discuss, for the first time, all the matters that had taken place regarding athletics during June and July. (Shewmake's College career is discussed in Chapter I.) He wrote each Board member that the matters to be discussed "cannot well be deferred" until the regular October meeting. He stressed that the meeting was "of paramount importance."

Addressing the Board at the beginning of the athletic discussions, Rector Shewmake said, "You have all seen copies of the [news]papers, I have no doubt, and we now find ourselves in an exceedingly regrettable and humiliating situation. I think the College has been done harm that may take years to repair and where the fault is I don't know, but it will be the purpose of this Board to discover that."

President Pomfret presented his report to the Board, outlining the information gathered by Dean Marshall during his personal investigation. All the faculty meetings were summarized and the position of the special faculty committee explained. Pomfret also focused on the compromise arranged with McCray and Wilson and emphasized that during all the proceedings he had tried to protect the integrity and reputation of William and Mary. The compromise would also allow McCray to find another position and "save his family from embarrassment and undue hardship." Pomfret stressed that there was "ample precedent for tempering justice with mercy."

Later in the Board meeting, attorney Hoffman representing McCray and Wilson, who were present but did not speak, said the two coaches "acknowledged their guilt with reference to the giving of credits which had not been actually earned, but denied any participation in the alteration of any records of grades" on admission applications. Vandeweghe said, in a 1997 interview, that he had a football player in a summer school class in 1949. The player attended only one class and went back home to work. McCray and Wilson asked Vandeweghe to give the student credit for the class, but he refused.

Coach Barney Wilson

In a reconvened Board meeting, on August 18, Marshall continued to report on his investigation, stressing, "I must do all I can do to protect the academic honor of the College." Dean Lambert also discussed his findings regarding the transcript alterations that were discovered in 1949.

The Board's Athletic Committee then reported, recommending the appointment of Dr. George Oliver as acting Athletic Director, H. Lester Hooker, Jr., of Hopewell as the new basketball and baseball coach, and Marvin Bass, currently line coach, as the new football coach at an annual salary of $6,500. John V. Bauserman, Board Athletic Committee Chairman, praised Bass as a "William and Mary man."

He is eminently qualified, has the full support and confidence of the student body and the football squad; in fact, in fairness and simply justice to the student body as a whole and the football squad in particular, there can be no other recommendation. His record and personal history are too well known to need repeating.

Bass, in a 1995 interview, said he took the job "because I loved the school and felt like it was a good chance for me to be head coach.

I wasn't thrilled about getting the job under the circumstances, but I knew we had some great talent. The players were unbelievable and I felt I owed them a lot of loyalty. I wanted to see William and Mary do well in athletics, to keep the program going and to stabilize everything.

Pomfret also had recommended Bass to the Board, but had asked that faculty member Dr. Wayne Kernodle be named part-time Athletic Director through June 30, 1952. No prospective basketball coach was offered by the president. Pomfret had also proposed "that the College reiterate its policy of maintaining football competition on the level of the Big Six, and play out-of-state teams of comparable level." The Board rejected that proposal outright and restated the Athletic Policy adopted on October 12, 1946, which Pomfret, apparently, had never known about and which had never been publicly discussed.

John Garland Pollard, Jr.

The Board minutes of that meeting state:

> Resolved that the Board adopts as its athletic policy a program that would produce athletic teams that could compete successfully with other teams in the State of Virginia belonging to the Southern Conference and to such extent as it could be reasonably expected that the College teams would win more games that they lost and that such a program be established on a sound financial basis.

This was the policy that McCray as Athletic Director had been employing for the past five years.

The Board of Visitors' minutes are very incomplete and omit much of the discussions on August 15 and 18. In an oral history, Board member John Garland Pollard, Jr., son of a former Virginia governor, described the meetings as confrontational. "I was amazed further at the hostility shown against Pomfret when they were questioning him as if in a court of law," he said.

In drafting its report, the Board asked Dean Marshall for the February 1950 Resolution from the Faculty Committee on Athletics and any other records regarding his own investigation. On September 8, the Board met again and put its "findings of fact" into the record as unanimously adopted. In its conclusion, the Board said:

> This entire situation is one which could and should have been handled with dispatch by the administrative officers of the College. As a result of its investigation the Board is convinced that the malpractices have been discontinued and that they will not reoccur.

The Board's findings were made public, and many in the William and Mary community, including faculty members and administrators, felt Pomfret was placed in an untenable position. Dean Marshall, in his personal papers, wrote, "I don't know how to express it other than to say the Board made Pomfret the 'goat' in order to clear itself as though it was pure and free from guilt." Dr. Harold Lees Fowler, professor of history and fifteen years later dean of the faculty, said in his oral history that the Board, "was trying to put the rap for this on the president."

Dr. James W. Miller

On September 13, Pomfret resigned as the College's president. In his resignation letter, he wrote: "Since it is apparent that I do not possess the confidence of the full membership of the Board of Visitors, I deem it to be in the best interests of the College for me to resign." The letter, however, did not refer to his future plans.

Pomfret had been in discussions with the Board of Directors of the Henry E. Huntington Library and Art Gallery in San Marino, California, for many months and had apparently been offered the newly created director's job sometime before any of the athletic controversy became public. According to former Virginia Governor Colgate W. Darden, who served briefly during Pomfret's presidency as William and Mary Chancellor, Pomfret wrote the Huntington Board of the situation in Williamsburg and offered to withdraw, but the Board still wanted him as the director. There are no records in the Huntington Library Archives about Pomfret's letter and the Board's response. Before his appointment, Pomfret was well known to the Huntington Board and Library staff through his research work. In 1951 he was completing a history of the province of West New Jersey from 1609 to 1702 for Princeton University Press.

The Executive Committee of William and Mary's Board met on September 18 in the Richmond office of the Rector to accept Pomfret's resignation, to name an acting president, and to receive from the faculty a "Statement" on athletics, which covered not only football, but the entire gamut of intercollegiate sports.

The statement, which became known around campus as the "Manifesto" said, in part, that the faculty was "deeply troubled by the recent disclosed academic irregularities in the physical education and athletic departments of the College."

> For over a decade the College of William and Mary has been laboring under conditions imposed by an increasingly ambitious intercollegiate athletic program. These conditions have been increasingly detrimental to the educational ideas to which the College is dedicated. The insidious influences of the athletic program have eaten at the most vital elements of academic life.

We have seen an exaggerated athletic program steadily sap the academic standards of the College. ... Steadily and inevitably the intercollegiate athletic program has usurped a dominating position in the College. Instead of a healthy and indispensable extracurricular activity, it has become a commercial enterprise demanding winning teams at any cost, even the cost of dishonest academic practice. [The athletic program] has tarnished the bright tradition of the Honor System which William and Mary has cherished for generations. ... One set of principles cannot be applied in one relationship and not in another. There is no double standard of honor.

The Manifesto proclaimed that since 1942 "football players as a group have been only a little more than half as successful as the rest of the study body in completing the requirements for the degree." The College must establish, the statement concluded, a "sound and healthy program of athletics" based upon the foundation promulgated in the Regulations of the Southern Association of Colleges and Secondary Schools, what said "faculty control of all phases of intercollegiate athletics is required."

Charles P. McCurdy

The Board took no action on the faculty's statement, but did appoint Dr. James W. Miller, Chancellor Professor of Philosophy, chairman of the philosophy department, and former dean of the faculty, as "acting president" of William and Mary. Rector Shewmake was elected chairman of a Board committee "to investigate possible candidates" for a permanent College president "and make a report, if possible" at the Board's October 6 meeting.

The entire Board, meeting October 6, formally accepted Pomfret's resignation and approved the Executive Committee's action in naming Miller acting president. A resolution was adopted thanking Miller for serving and "for the commendable manner in which he has discharged his duties." To the surprise of outsiders, the Board later in the meeting heard a report from its presidential search committee and selected Vice Admiral Alvin Duke Chandler, son of former William and Mary President Julian A. C. Chandler, as the new College president. The saga of Chandler's selection is a story best left for another time.

In a related event, a series of articles about the athletic controversy was being planned for publication in the *Alumni Gazette*. Charles P. McCurdy, alumni secretary and *Gazette* editor, published an article in the September edition about the campus turmoil—including the allegations of altered high school transcripts and other charges. It also reported Pomfret's resignation and Miller's appointment. The primary article said the beginning of the football downfall could be traced to 1939 "when the College first undertook its large football operation and gave athletic coaches professorial rank."

McCurdy also published a two-page editorial (the first of three he planned to produce) on the College's football program. He emphasized that the College had an athletic program in place that stressed football rather than academics or a college education. Supporting his point was the fact that from 1943 to 1951 only 32.6 percent of the football players graduated, compared to 55.93 percent of all non-football players.

Coach Marvin Bass

The next issue of the *Gazette,* scheduled for December, was slated to discuss the financial cost of William and Mary football. Everything was ready for publication, but on November 17, 1951, the Society of the Alumni's Board of Directors voted not to continue the series and removed McCurdy's editorial from the publication. Upset and in protest over the action, McCurdy resigned his post on November 23, 1951, effective June 30, 1952.

Other personnel changes resulted from the dissension and upheaval. Before Chandler became president, Marshall resigned as dean, feeling he could no longer serve the College. The last resignation in the athletic controversy came the next year when McCray's football successor, Marvin Bass, departed after only one year at the helm.

Bass, a member of the highly successful 1942 team, had already established a distinguished coaching career. He was a line coach at the College under McCray, 1945–49, and was assistant coach in 1949 at the University of North Carolina under head coach Carl Snavley. He had returned to McCray's staff for the 1950 season and was a logical choice for head football coach.

Despite the athletic turmoil that floated across the campus, the student body, according to *The Flat Hat,* continued to support the football program, the team members, and the new coach. The paper reported that the first pep rally of the year was enthusiastic and that Coach Bass noted great team enthusiasm had helped in the College's first game of the season, a victory over Boston University.

Bass compiled a 7-3 record in 1951, but the controversy never faded for him and the team. "They were a most courageous group of athletes," Bass said of the 1951 squad. "They knew they had obstacles to face; they did it like men and went out and gave every ounce of energy and didn't let adversity stop them from reaching their objective."

When interviewed years after the controversy, both he and longtime College assistant football coach Eric Tipton said they never heard of any wrongdoing within the athletic department. "I don't believe Tip or I would have been told because they knew we simply wouldn't tolerate it. We probably would have quit. I still do not know all of the details of charges or suggestions of problems," Bass said in a 1995 interview. "I didn't know anything was going wrong. It's hard for me to believe Rube did anything wrong. He was a hard worker and good recruiter and a tireless worker and such a likeable person."

President Alvin Duke Chandler

In early February 1952, Bass resigned as head football coach. Several newspaper accounts suggested that he left because the College administration would not give his assistant coaches long-term contracts. That was not altogether true, Bass said in 1995.

> I resigned because of the uncertainty of the [football] program. I remember that Chauncey [Durden, sports editor of the *Richmond Times-Dispatch*] wrote that it was insecurity for me, but it wasn't that. At the time there was no defined program. They were talking about de-emphasis and there was a faculty meeting that I attended when de-emphasis was discussed. But I decided to leave because I didn't know where the program was going and the administration could not give me any answers.

His successor, James E. "Suey" Eason, a high school football coach from Hampton, was given a ten-year contract as William and Mary head coach. "I felt it was a slap in my face," Bass recalled. "I really felt bad about it because I cared so much about the school."

At the May 31, 1952, Board of Visitors meeting, President Chandler presented a summary of salient points of the College's new intercollegiate athletic policy as formulated by the College administration.

> The College firmly believes that intercollegiate athletic competition is a legitimate extracurricular activity and that a well-balanced program of intercollegiate competition will make a definite contribution to a sound William and Mary educational program.

The Administration wanted the College to continue as a member of the Southern Conference, abiding by its rules and regulations.

> The College will continue to schedule athletic contests with Southern Conference members, Virginia colleges, and other institutions which the College considers its natural rivals. This scheduling policy will be carefully followed after the existing commitments have been fulfilled.

Gone was any reference to "win more games that they lost" and gone forever was "big-time" football at William and Mary.

5
A Trying Time
The Aftermath and Repercussions
1951 to 1963

Bob Moskowitz

Jimmie Eason remembers those late-winter, early-spring days in 1952. He was 10 years old, and his daddy had just switched jobs. Jimmie grew up to become a successful accountant and politician who would easily recall those three months when his father, James M. "Suey" Eason, reigned as William and Mary's football coach and athletic director.

In 1952, Coach Eason was 44 and not necessarily a popular choice to take over a badly shaken football program. He had been a standout, multi-sport athlete for the Indians (class of 1924), one who became a highly successful football coach at Virginia high schools in Crewe and Hampton. By the time Eason abruptly turned down the ten-year contract with William and Mary, he had already gone through spring practice to install the seldom-used double-wing formation, an innovation that left many alumni in a state of discontent.

Peace and stability hardly stormed into place in Eason's wake. Many alumni had felt from the outset that diminutive Jackie Freeman, who would be Eason's replacement, was a more logical selection. Freeman, like Eason, was another former Indian football player, but one who stood only 5'6" tall and whose approach to offense was much easier for many alumni to digest. Still, Freeman's tenure would at best become a study of peaks and valleys. When Freeman finally threw in the towel, Milt Drewer—like Freeman a successful young high school coach who had just begun to work at the University of Richmond—was selected.

James M. "Suey" Eason became head coach of W&M for a few months in the spring of 1952, but resigned before his team could head out onto the field (below) to open the fall season. Eason photo courtesy of Jimmie Eason; team photo from the 1953 *Colonial Echo*.

New W&M head coach Jack Freeman (center) gathered a group of assistants to help him in 1952. From left to right: Herb Miller, Eric Tipton (the only holdover from Marvin Bass), Gil Joyner, Boydson Baird, Tom Mikula, and Johnny Clements. From the 1953 *Colonial Echo*.

No matter. The pattern of dissatisfaction, both within and without the William and Mary athletic family, was to remain, at least through Drewer's seven seasons.

The step from the exodus of Marvin Bass back to what appeared to be relative calm on the Reservation was anything but simple. One source of initial irritation to many was that Eason had received a ten-year dual contract, something never before offered a Southern Conference or Virginia college coach. Secondly, there was the double-wing formation, about which few knew much and about which many complained. Skeptics claimed college defenders would too easily control that style of attack. There were plenty of doubters, even though the formation had already carried Eason to a great twenty-three-year high school coaching record that included three state titles at Hampton (one shared) and three second-place finishes en route to, at that time, 212 victories against 74 losses. His Crewe teams won 114 and lost only 8 times in eleven years!

"One of the reasons he took the job is that he was intrigued with the potential of running the double-wing in college," recalled Jimmie Eason, who by 1996 had become the first elected mayor in the city of Hampton. "We ran some innovative stuff off that," the younger Eason said, referring to the days when he starred as tailback for his father at Hampton High School in the late 1950s. "So, Dad was convinced the double-wing would work in college. That intrigued him most. He wanted to prove that it would work, and he knew that William and Mary had some good athletes coming back" from the final Bass team that had won seven of ten games.

Despite open alumni objection to Eason and his double-wing, his decision to leave Williamsburg was even more unexpected than his selection. His appointment had come, he said, after only two weeks of negotiations with College President Alvin Duke Chandler. The Board of Visitors, reported the Newport News *Daily Press* on February 9, 1952, "voted quickly ... in a surprise move ... to name Eason."

After spring practice in which Eason installed the double-wing, it is doubtful if anyone, including his staff, expected the resignation. At the time, Eason shed little light on the matter, although he did issue a lengthy statement, which ran in its entirety in the *Daily Press* of April 10, 1952.

Coach Jack Freeman (right) poses with Hadacol Hines, the team's kicker, for a promotional photograph prior to W&M's game with Navy in October 1952. The coach is holding the game ball from the Navy game in 1942 that the Indians won, 3-0, on a field goal. W&M lost the 1952 Navy contest, 14-0. Courtesy of Richmond Newspapers, Inc.

Another *Daily Press* article that day, one by Larry Fox (later a longtime sports writer for the New York *Daily News*), said Eason "has elected to remain at Hampton High School rather than to assume the duties of head football coach and athletic director at William and Mary College." The story revealed that "at the same time, Chandler announced that Jackie Freeman, a former W&M great (class of 1947) and assistant to Marvin Bass … had been named to fill" the two jobs.

"Bullet" Bill Bowman (center with ball) races up field with the opening kickoff in the 1952 Wake Forest game. His return was for 30 yards. From the 1953 *Colonial Echo*.

However, in 1973 Abe Goldblatt, veteran sports writer for the *Virginian-Pilot*, interviewed the then-retired Eason about the matter. Eason said that at the time of his first interview for the W&M posts, "I didn't know that Bass had quit." He said he didn't think he would get the ten-year contract, but stuck with his request after the College first turned him down.

After his spring practice, Eason recalled,

> I really felt we'd have a good team my first season. Most of the players were seniors, and I was concerned about the future. I thought about the years I had already put in at Hampton, the retirement and other benefits. Most important, however, was the fact that I loved coaching in high school. You didn't have to worry about all this recruiting business.

He said he talked with Chandler for four hours "and I decided the job wasn't for me, and back to Hampton I went." He also told Goldblatt that "maybe I would have stayed at William and Mary as athletic director and baseball coach with no pressure of football." Eason had been a standout college and semipro baseball player.

Eason's resignation statement said that he had accepted the posts because the school "was still receiving much adverse criticism and unfavorable publicity which I … sincerely wanted to see discontinued." He emphasized there "was no misrepresentation" from the school and pointed out that spring practice "was held under tremendous difficulty." As a new coach, Eason enjoyed only a week of preparation for the twenty practice sessions

Garrard Ramsey's Chicago Cardinal professional football card and Knox Ramsey's Los Angeles Dons card from the late 1940s. From the collection of Bob Sheeran.

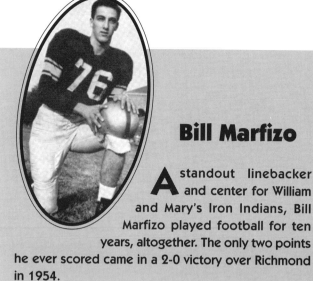

Bill Marfizo

A standout linebacker and center for William and Mary's Iron Indians, Bill Marfizo played football for ten years, altogether. The only two points he ever scored came in a 2-0 victory over Richmond in 1954.

Exploding through a hole made possible by the rush of tackle Jerry Sazio, Marfizo blocked a fourth-quarter punt by Spiders' Tommy Theodose. "Those are two points that I will never forget," he recalled.

Marfizo and the rest of the "Iron Men" mostly played before colleges embraced the practice of using face masks. They came into vogue in 1953 and 1954, he said. He also said that the early ones simply were a bar that ran across the middle of the face, going from one side of the helmet to the other.

Marfizo, who became a dentist and was consequently more conscious of facial protection, recalled once hearing former W&M line great, Tommy Thompson, talk about the masks in the National Football League. Thompson, a Cleveland Brown, was discussing Chicago Bear John Kreamcheck, another Indian lineman. At the time, the NFL had just started using the face masks that had a bar across the face. Thompson recalled, "Lou Groza [a Cleveland kicking star and end] told me that because of that bar that scrunched his face together, Kreamcheck was the ugliest player he ever saw!" (—RM)

Bill Marfizo is carried off the field, in 1954, at Richmond's City Stadium after blocking a Spider punt in the end zone and giving W&M a safety for a short, 2-0 victory. From the 1955 *Colonial Echo*.

allowed by the Southern Conference. Drills were marred by "two snows and hardly a day when the field was not muddy."

Jimmie Eason conceded years later that he and his father didn't talk about the departure. However, Jimmie had learned about some of Suey's feelings that led to the decision.

> There were those tough times before him. Academic problems needed to be cleaned up, and he was under some orders to de-emphasize football. He tried to get administrative assurance and when he didn't get it, he saw no need to stay. He saw it as a no-win situation.

There also were aftereffects of the scandal.

> A lot of players apparently were still in academic trouble. That was a big uncertainty, and it was pretty clear that the administration was cutting back scholarships. Dad had transcripts and knew that a lot who were practicing were marginal when it came to eligibility.

However, in the *Daily Press* article, Coach Eason's stance was pictured differently. "The fact that many members of the varsity squad were on the borderline of flunking out of school had no part in his decision," the newspaper reported.

Only five days earlier, Jackie Freeman had been named backfield coach at the University of Richmond. Eason had rejected keeping Freeman on his staff, even in the face of pressure from alumni, who wanted the transplanted Pennsylvanian to head the offense and run the split-T.

Tommy Koller raced for 12 yards in the first period against Richmond behind some precision blocking. From the 1953 *Colonial Echo.*

One player under Bass, Eason, and Freeman was Jerry Sazio, who went on to coach high school athletes for more than forty years in Norfolk, Virginia. His take on Eason's departure was this:

> He was used to the high school kids. College athletes are different. Some coaches enjoy one level more than others. From what he later told me on the golf course, I think Suey felt restricted at William and Mary. He just liked coaching in high school better.

Three days after Eason's resignation, an Associated Press article, written in Richmond by Ed Young, discussed at length "a five-point statement of athletic policy" by the College of William and Mary. It was, the story said, the "first clear-cut definition of the college's new attitude toward sports since confusion began to set in after a scandal in the Department of Athletics last year."

As Freeman took over, he said his team would operate from the split-T. Interestingly, in retrospect at least, some players didn't seem to have a problem adjusting to the dif-

W&M's "Lonesome Foursome" backfield of Ed Mioduszewski, Bruce Sturgess, Bill Bowman, and Tom Koller pose for a promotional photo prior to the 1952 Thanksgiving game with Richmond. Courtesy of the *Richmond Times-Dispatch.*

ferent formations. Bill Marfizo, who became a Pennsylvania dentist, was a center under Bass and the split-T. He went through Eason's tenure and then became one of the famed "Iron Indians" for Freeman in 1953. He said, "I always liked the split-T from a center's perspective, but I had no trouble at all with the double-wing. We had a lot of good players. I don't think any of them thought about problems in switching."

Tommy Lewis had been an excellent double-wing running back under Eason at Hampton High. He continued to excel under Bass and Freeman at William and Mary. "The formation was a problem for those who had no previous association with it, but I don't think there were any major problems," Lewis said.

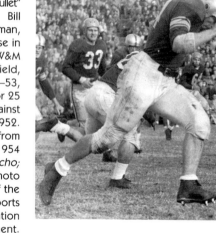

In the offing, however, lurked plenty of "major problems." With the exception of three successive winning years under Marv Levy, the twenty-eight years that followed were mostly ones of frustration for coaches Jackie Freeman, Milt Drewer, Marv Levy, Lou Holtz, and Jim Root. Only Root won as many as seven games—7-4 in 1976—and he also enjoyed a three-year span without a losing season that included a 5-5-1 campaign in 1978.

The climb back to respectability was slow and painful, but certainly the College attracted numerous excellent athletes. There simply weren't enough of them, especially in the Freeman and Drewer years. Combined, the two coaches produced just one winning season (Freeman's). That came in 1953, a football year that would live forever in the minds of William and Mary's athletic family. The campaign was Freeman's second, and a plucky band of only twenty-four players (when healthy) carved out five victories, four losses, and one tie. No William and Mary team would mount a winning season again until the 1965 contingent won six of ten under Levy.

The 1953 team was known as the Iron Indians. Freeman isn't sure, but he credits an article in the *Richmond Times-Dispatch* for being the first to apply the nickname. He said, "I didn't think much about it, really, but it [the name] turned out to be right." Catchy labels weren't new to Freeman, who was only 32 when he took over the dual load of coach and athletic director. As far back as 1942, when he starred for the Indians and they went 9-1-1 to win the Southern Conference championship, newspapers dubbed Freeman a "dynamic mite of 155 pounds." Among other things, the former Notre Dame recruit would be cited for being a "superb punter ... and tricky runner."

"Bullet" Bill Bowman, workhorse in the W&M backfield, 1951–53, rambles for 25 yards against U.Va. in 1952. Top photo from the 1954 *Colonial Echo;* game photo courtesy of the W&M Sports Information Department.

His first team at William and Mary—1952—included a backfield known as the Lonesome Foursome. The group included quarterback Ed Mioduszewski (a second-team Associated Press All-American), halfbacks Tom Koller and Bruce Sturgess, and fullback Bill Bowman. In Freeman's words, "they ran up a helluva lot of yardage" en route to a record of 4 wins and 5 losses.

In Freeman's first game as a head coach, the Indians beat Virginia Military Institute 34-13 in Roanoke. The VMI coach was Tom Nugent, who would gain a reputation as an exciting offensive innovator at several schools. Even considering the

inaugural win, it took the next season and the "Iron Indians" to produce the most memorable Freeman scenario. Little time was needed to figure out that this squad was something special. It upset Wake Forest, 16-14, in the season-opener, and the stage was set. That was followed by a tie with favored Navy, and momentum increased. So, however, did injuries.

But the "Iron Indians" kept competing successfully enough to impress state sports writers and coaches who selected Freeman Coach of the Year in what was called the Big Six. Members were Richmond, University of Virginia, Virginia Military Institute, Virginia Tech, Washington and Lee, and William and Mary.

Years later, Iron players seemed to cling to individual favorite tales of gore. For Jerry Sazio, a junior guard and linebacker from Irvington, New Jersey, "That season was excruciating. We played with injuries you can't believe." He missed two games with torn knee ligaments and, on his return, was shifted to defensive end. "Favoring my leg, I broke my hand in the last game. I fell on my elbow and dislocated my shoulder. All of that was on my left side."

Another who went through the Bass-to-Eason-to-Freeman progression and endured the "Iron Indian" adventures was Bill Marfizo. He appeared to be typical in his approach to his four years of football. Asked if he ever thought of quitting, Marfizo snapped, "Never! It was all like a challenge." He said of the 1953 season, "We had

such great support from fans, newspapers, people like Dusty Rhodes [a volunteer trainer who would help Green and Gold teams for

This "Iron Indian" team photo shows twenty-five players, but only twenty-four were finally on the squad, which compiled a 5-4-1 record, upsetting Wake Forest and tying Navy. From the W&M Sports Information Department.

Eric "The Red" Tipton

Hard-core devotees of big-time football know Eric "The Red" Tipton, as a star and co-captain of the famous "Iron Dukes" football team at Duke University that went undefeated, untied, and unscored upon in 1938 before losing, 7-3, in the 1939 Rose Bowl game against the University of Southern California. But that is another story.

The same Eric Tipton, who graduated from Duke in 1939, joined the William and Mary Athletic Department several months later. For the next eighteen years—a period that encompassed the "Golden Age" of W&M football—Tipton was an assistant football coach responsible for the backfield. From 1953 until 1957 he also was head baseball coach. It was during those years, 1939–57 that "Tip" became a W&M legend. He breathed green, gold, and silver just as he had breathed the royal blue and white of his alma mater.

The young men of W&M who played football under Tipton and the members of his five baseball teams knew him as a man of utmost integrity, unfailing loyalty, and incredible knowledge that made him probably one of the best coaches W&M has ever seen.

Tipton, a talented athlete, signed a professional baseball contract right out of college, but spent his time in Williamsburg when baseball was not in season. His baseball career included 1939 with the Philadelphia Athletics, 1940 and 1941 with Toronto in the International League, playing the most of both years again in the majors. In 1942 he played for the Kansas City Blues of the American Association. From 1942 through 1945 he played for the Cincinnati Reds. In the spring of 1946 he was sold to the St. Paul Saints of the American Association for whom he played until 1952 when he moved to Portland, Oregon, for a season before retiring.

The dual career was not difficult for Tipton, who successfully juggled coaching the offensive and defensive backs with playing outfield. The football season was frequently under way when he arrived in Williamsburg in the fall, but instead of being tired from playing baseball, the football coaches and players said he was enthusiastic for their sport. The enthusiasm gained from W&M in the fall and winter also seemed to rub off on his baseball playing the following spring and summer.

His collegiate career put him in the College Football Hall of Fame (1965), the Duke University Sports Hall of Fame (1976), and the Virginia Sports Hall of Fame (1978). He was a collegiate All-American tailback and defensive back. In 1992, he became a member of the William and Mary Athletic Hall of Fame.

Tipton is probably best known for his punting during a snowstorm in 1938 during Duke's 7-0 defeat of a powerful University of Pittsburgh team. With coaxing, he pulled out a large scrapbook and found a clipping from the game. Statistics revealed twenty punts for an average of 41.3 yards against a return average of only 1.2 yards. He had fifteen of those twenty punts downed inside the Pitt 20-yard line, with two inside the 5-yard line, five between the 5- and 10-yard lines, five between the 10- and 15-yard lines, and three between the 15- and 20-yard lines.

Regarding his tenure at W&M, Tipton explained, "To stay here nearly twenty years, you had to enjoy it. I enjoyed my association with the players, whether it was football or baseball." He was freshman coach primarily in 1939–41 and spent a year as coach and business manager of athletics in 1942 before moving to varsity football in 1943.

"Lots of these guys who came back to coach here were W&M guys in school when I was coach," Tipton said, adding that he very much enjoyed seeing his former players these days at various reunions and other Williamsburg visits.

The first head coach he worked under was Carl Voyles, the man who brought big-time football to W&M. Voyles "was a real disciplinarian," Tipton recalled.

He had everybody really scared of him, including the players and some coaches. He would not let any player get real close to him. Recruiting was his main forte. He also was very thorough. I had known him at Duke, where he was an assistant coach before coming to W&M.

During World War II, "Rube" McCray took over from Voyles and "was a little more easy going and got along with the players very well," Tipton explained.

Many football players from those winning teams of the 1940s, including Knox Ramsey '48 and "Flyin'" Jack Cloud '50, when asked about the coaches who influenced them the most, routinely listed Tipton and W&M's own Marvin Bass.

In the early 1950s W&M football was injured by a scandal. "I never knew anything was going on," Tipton related.

During much of the time, I was away playing baseball, but no one ever talked to me about anything. I never heard a thing. But the truth is that W&M football didn't recover from it until the mid-1960s, about the time [Marv] Levy became head coach.

As assistant football coach, Tipton was part of the great teams of 1947 and 1948 that went to two postseason bowl games, but probably the team that stands out in his mind is the "Iron Indians" of 1953. Although the team was 180 degrees from the "Iron Dukes" of 1938, "those men in 1953 were special. We only had about twenty-two players that season. Those guys often played hurt," he said.

Players then, as in the 1930s and 1940s, played both offensively and defensively. "You had to have a big reason to be taken out of a game that year," he said with a big grin, recalling that W&M's team of about two dozen often faced an opponent with three times that many men suited up for a game.

Today, people easily associate W&M and Duke in the same academic league. Tipton said the relationships also were similar fifty years ago. He said he appreciates Duke and W&M much more today because of their approach to athletics.

I would not want Duke or W&M to turn out to be like an Oklahoma, because of the way many schools now put pressure on athletes.

The crux of the situation now can best be explained by the number of people flunking out of school with 700 scores on the college entrance exam. I can tell you 700 is pretty low and a lot of these name schools are involved. I know you can get a 400 score just for putting your name on the test. I think it's very wrong for these young people. It's really a shame to make college teams so professional these days.

There was not such a professional athletic climate in the 1930s and 1940s, he said, partly because professional teams were not very big and drew less attention, "but that, too, was a different era. At Duke and W&M then you didn't have to be a top-notch student, but you had to know and do your studies."

Tipton (left) and Freeman talk over quarterback problems with three 1953 candidates.
They are (left to right) Al Grieco, Charlie Sumner, and Bob Elzey. Courtesy of the *Richmond Times-Dispatch.*

In 1957, Tipton accepted an offer to be baseball coach and coach of the 150-pound football team at the U.S. Military Academy at West Point. Twenty years later, he retired and returned with his wife, Gertrude, to Williamsburg. They have four children and nine grandchildren.

"To be honest, after thirty-nine years [of coaching], I had had enough," Tipton said. "Of course I miss my association with some of the boys, but I don't miss the coaching angle of it."   (—WK)

four decades]. It all encouraged us. I don't think anyone wanted to quit, but we all wanted to do better."

In the 6-6 tie with Navy, he played six positions. "Freeman would send me in, and I would have no idea what position would be next." After that, sports writers referred to Marfizo as "Mr. Versatility." No wonder. He was a center and linebacker who, against Navy, also played offensive tackle and end, as well as end and halfback on defense. The last four spots "were all new to me."

Late in that game, Navy fullback Joe Gattuso was punting from his 4-yard line. "As we lined up to rush, Jerry Sazio and I talked about blocking the punt by having Jerry open the hole [to allow] me to rush through from my linebacking position." Sazio did his part, and "I rushed through the hole toward Gattuso; the ball was kicked and went through my outreached arms, and the kicking foot smashed into my face, rendering me unconscious." The deadlock, said Marfizo, "was a moral victory. It was a test between David and Goliath."

Playing before facemasks were used obviously could be painful, but that didn't deter people like Marfizo. He would team up with Sazio to produce another blocked kick before the season's end.

The "Iron Indian" defense, led by co-captain Steve Milkovich, John Bednarik, and Bill Marfizo held Navy to six points in the "moral victory" over the Midshipmen. Coach Jack Freeman (left) wipes tears of joy from his eyes as his undermanned squad held nationally ranked Navy to a 6-6 tie. Photos by *Life Magazine*; from the collection of Jack Freeman.

Not all the memories glowed of success, moral victory, or otherwise. The hard-to-forget 57-7 loss at Cincinnati in the third game of the season was one example. Marfizo held a sour view of that contest. "Mostly, they had depth, and we were exhausted." In that era, when face guards were a novelty, drinking liquids during a game also was a novelty. "We had nothing to drink. No liquid, no salt tablets." Then he added: "But we did have lemons."

Freeman, too, nurtured memories of his iron team.

> We could have been six and three easy with only a few more players. We just didn't have any

A special convocation to recognize the "Iron Indian" team was held in old Phi Beta Kappa Hall at the close of the 1953 season. The reception of the team by the students was so overwhelming that Coach Freeman was at a loss for words to express his pride in his team and the College's appreciation. From the 1954 *Colonial Echo*.

bodies. That was the first year players had to go both ways, which was a godsend for us. If we had to platoon, we wouldn't have won a game, not with eighteen or nineteen people. We couldn't have made it.

Despite the relative success, statistics for 1953 were modest at best. In 1952 the 4-5 season saw W&M score 236 points while relinquishing 177. During the next season, even with the improved record, the Indians scored only 122 points and allowed 191. The offense lost more punch the following year, 1954, when W&M went 4-4-2 and scored only 82 points while yielding 137.

Still, a number of individuals sparkled, not the least of whom was Charlie Sumner. One of the all-time Tribe greats, Sumner went on to enjoy a long-time National Football League career as player and assistant coach.

In 1953, as a junior quarterback from Salem, Virginia, Sumner was busy, to say the least. He accounted for 903 yards out of his team's total offense of 2,382. He also scored 30 points, threw two touchdown passes, led the team with 88 yards in punt returns, averaged 35.1 yards a punt, gained 67 yards on four kickoff returns, and intercepted six passes. He attained enough success to be named team co-captain the next year along with "Jarring" Jerry Sazio, as the College's *Football Handbook* called him.

Jerry Sazio, following in the footsteps of his brother Ralph, was a tackle and linebacker, whose prowess on the field for the "Iron Indians" is well documented. From the 1954 *Colonial Echo*.

In 1953 Charlie Sumner, quarterback, did it all. He rushed for 903 of the team's total offense of 2,382 yards; scored 30 points; threw two touchdown passes; led the team with 88 yards in punt returns; averaged 35.1 yards punting; gained 67 yards on four kickoff returns; and intercepted six passes. From the 1954 *Colonial Echo*.

The 1954 William and Mary *Football Handbook* cover was a montage of photographs from the 1953 season of the "Iron Indians." Courtesy of the W&M Sports Information Department.

The 1954 season was a respectable, if not a winning, one. It included more great play from Sumner that emphasized once again his dazzling versatility. Although his running and passing figures shrank, he had four pass interceptions, six pass receptions for 100 yards, a 93-yard punt return for a touchdown in a 27-7 conquest of Pennsylvania, and an average of 36 yards in forty-five punts.

The 4-4-2 record in 1954 also included triumphs by 14-7 over Rutgers and 13-9 over Wake Forest. The ties were with George Washington, 13-13, and Virginia Tech, 7-7.

The fourth success was 2-0 over arch rival Richmond in the season's finale. The lone points were scored on a safety after Marfizo again capitalized on efforts by Sazio to break through the blockers on a crucial punt situation. This time Marfizo physically "saved face" and blocked the punt. That enabled the Indians to extend two streaks. It was their second shutout in a row over

The Keydets of VMI upset the Indians in 1954 in Roanoke, 21-0, signaling trouble on the horizon for W&M's football program. Courtesy of the W&M Sports Information Department.

Richmond and their fifteenth successive triumph over the Spiders, eight of which were shutouts.

Victory in Richmond was all the sweeter then because the Spiders had insisted, starting that year, that all football games with William and Mary be played on Thanksgiving Day in Richmond. Prior to that the sites were switched.

As it turned out, the 2-0 triumph would be a last hurrah. It preceded a long and painful slump for the Indians. The 1955 season ended in a 6-6 tie (with Richmond), one of two in a stretch of twenty-one contests that produced only one victory. In the 1955 season, the record was 1-7-1 and in 1956, 0-9-1, the latter campaign ending Freeman's Williamsburg tenure.

In all, after a 20-13 triumph over visiting Virginia Military Institute on October 29, 1955, the Indians would weather fifteen successive games before enjoying another triumph. That one came over Virginia Tech by a 13-7 score in 1957, when Freeman was no longer the coach. That season had started with two more setbacks, but that's getting ahead of the story.

If the public was surprised at the dearth of victories, Freeman wasn't. In the *Alumni Gazette* of October 1955, he hinted of the troubles that stared him and his players in the face. A preseason story on the football team ended with Freeman's words:

Jack Yohe breaks through the Navy line for 30 yards and a first down at the Midshipmen's 5-yard line. The Indians, however, failed to score in the 1954 Navy 27-0 triumph. From the 1955 *Colonial Echo*.

> What we have has been largely made possible by the Educational Foundation—the organization formed to provide scholarship grants for academically qualified athletes. This is the only way we can hope to maintain teams that will be able to compete on even terms with our natural rivals and neighboring schools. How well our alumni back the Educational Foundation will be the key to our ability to field representative teams in coming years.

Halfback Charlie Sumner gets encouragement from his teammates along the sidelines as he races for a 93-yard punt return and W&M's second touchdown against the University of Pennsylvania. It was a record punt return for Philadelphia's Franklin Field and one of the longest in Tribe history. From the 1955 *Colonial Echo*.

Jack Freeman

The signs were up for all those who cared to see, is the way Jack Freeman recalls things at William and Mary following the 1956 football season. After a 13-13-3 ledger in his first three seasons, W&M endured a demoralizing 1-16-2 record in his final three years.

"I retired then because it just didn't look like the school would do anything to improve the program." Years later, he recalled that improvement did not happen until the Jimmye Laycock era began in the 1980s. Before then, there were "a lot of good tries, but they never could quite make it."

Freeman, a brilliant high school athlete at McKeesport, Pennsylvania, was recruited by Notre Dame, but elected to transfer to William and Mary, in 1941. There, his diminutive frame caught the fancy of Indian football fans from the outset. His popularity never waned, even following his troubled coaching years.

After he left W&M, in the spring of 1957, Freeman remained in touch with sports only through coaching Little League football and baseball. That was when "I was trying to take care of my sons." From 1957 to 1977, he was a warehouse manager and then operating superintendent in Baltimore, Maryland, and Raleigh, North Carolina for A&P.

Following that, he eagerly accepted an invitation in 1978 from Bob Thallman to help coach at VMI in Lexington, Virginia. That lasted until early in 1984 when Thallman and his staff were released.

After a one-year stint as head coach at Lexington High School, Freeman says he has spent "lots of time with my wife and playing golf."   (—RM)

The 1956 *William and Mary Football Yearbook* (today it's called a media guide) rightfully described Coach Freeman as "a man with a mission." Unfortunately, the mission was not accomplished, even though he was blessed once again with some truly brilliant individual players, especially among his ends. Walt Brodie would become a second-team choice on the Associated Press All-American team and was named the Southern Conference Player of the Year. It was the first time the honor was bestowed on someone from William and Mary. Junior Larry Peccatiello gained notice as a future All–Southern Conference end.

Despite the presence of some top-notch talent, Big Green ranks were once again simply too thin to stand firm against the likes of Wake Forest, Navy, Virginia Tech, West Virginia, George Washington, VMI, Army, Rutgers, and Richmond. The record sank to 0-9-1, and only the 18-18 tie with visiting Boston University in the third game of the season averted total failure.

The tie emerged as a microcosm of the entire year. The Indians had charged to an 18-6 lead, only to relinquish two fourth-quarter touchdowns and then fall one agonizing yard short of the Terriers' goal line—and sweet success—as time ran out.

Both teams encountered chances galore to salvage victory, but the Tribe had more of them. Both teams failed on all their attempts at extra points—the Indians blocked two and the New Englanders one. Boston also missed a passing attempt on a conversion, and the Indians had a second-period touchdown nullified by penalty on a pass interception and return.

The final, telling agony for most of the crowd of 5,000 at Cary Field unfolded in the waning seconds. The

Pro Football card of John Kreamcheck when he played for the Chicago Bears in 1953–55. From the collection of Bob Sheeran.

Charlie Sidwell gets a strong block from Grieco to help open a hole in the George Washington line. The Colonials, however, won 16-0 in their first victory over W&M since 1932. From the 1956 *Colonial Echo*.

comeback charge was triggered by junior halfback Charlie Sidwell's 29-yard punt return. Sidwell enjoyed a day of brilliance that had already included a punt runback of 65 yards for William and Mary's second touchdown and a 1-yard run around left end to produce a 6-6 deadlock. For the day, he gained 100 yards in twenty-five carries.

After Sidwell's last punt return, he carried the ball five consecutive times to give the Indians first down on the Boston 5. Then sophomore quarterback Tom Secules sneaked to the 1, but the gun went off, ending play. As it turned out, gone, too, were any hopes of victory in that painful campaign.

William and Mary had scored more than 100 points each season without letup since 1936, when the Indians totalled only 51 points and were shut out in six of nine contests. In Freeman's last three years at the helm, his attacks produced only 82, 81, and 84 points and were shut out twice in each season. No other droughts would be as severe through the remainder of the College's first hundred years of football.

Of significant interest at the end of the 1955–56 school year was a small article in the *Richmond Times-Dispatch*. According to State Budget Director J. W. Bradford, William and

In 1955, W&M snaps the season-starting, five-game losing streak as Tom Secules carries over for one of three Indian touchdowns against VMI. From the 1956 *Colonial Echo*.

Mary spent $31,434 for athletic salaries and special payments in 1955–56. The figure stood in stark contrast to those of some intrastate rivals. Virginia Military Institute's total was $40,609, and Virginia Tech's was $81,379. The stature of the Indians' football program could hardly have been stated more concisely.

Obviously, administrative status quo ruled, even though alumni unrest mounted. The dissatisfaction caused Howard M. Smith, head of the Department of Men's Physical Education, to write a letter to President Chandler strongly supporting both Freeman and basketball coach Boyd Baird. Dated March 2, 1957, the letter pointed out that the two had supported the "generally recognized College Policy as of 1951" and

Walt Brodie

For much of the 1990s, Walt Brodie spent time catching Chesapeake Bay area winds in the sails of his small boat. Four decades earlier, he spent Saturday afternoons catching passes as well as opposing ball carriers.

Brodie, out of Hopewell, Virginia, was one of a string of small, brilliant ends who excelled for William and Mary's football teams during the fifteen years or so that followed World War II.

As a senior in 1956, he became an Associated Press second team All-American end. He also was a first-team pick by the Williamson National Football Rating System. Another Brodie highlight that season was becoming the first from the Reservation ever to be selected as Southern Conference Football Player of the Year. He also collected the most votes on the All-Conference team.

Standing five feet, ten inches tall, Brodie weighed 180 pounds, but as a high school recruit had been told by University of Virginia Coach Art Geuppe that "we like our ends bigger than you are."

While earning All-American honors was "flattering," Brodie would say later that being recognized despite playing for a team that struggled with a 0-9-1 record also was "strange." In fact, a headline in the *Norfolk Ledger-Star* called it the "Surprise of the Year."

He said the selection "was a combination of things." That combination included his "guess" that "I did pretty well." He said to his knowledge "I was selected on the all-opponents' team by all the teams we played that picked one."

He also felt he received "good press" from newspapers in Richmond and Newport News. That included being selected as a "Star of the Week" by the *Richmond Times-Dispatch* for a particularly devastating day on defense against VMI. In the 20-13 W&M victory he sacked the quarterback six times for losses totaling 42 yards, recovered a fumble and made the key block on a long pass play that set up the first Big Green touchdown.

He also pointed out that being 25 and having served two years in the Army, where he played football at Fort Lee, Virginia, "helped." His first two years came in 1951 and 1952. Then "I was suspended for a year" and during that time was drafted in the Army.

Brodie had played during a monstrously successful football era at Hopewell High School and in 1949, as a junior, his team outscored the opposition by 373 to 24. Brodie actually went to West Point, New York, but after three summers of life in the Military Academy, he decided to go elsewhere. That kind of decision was NCAA approved in those days.

I chose William and Mary, because of Les Hooker, who was from Hopewell [and was the W&M basketball coach]. He actually went out looking for money from the alumni to pay my tuition. He got small amounts here and there. Les did it. He recruited me.

A football scholarship didn't include meals then. The team ate at a training table and somebody got hurt against VMI my freshman year and he left school. I was working by waiting on tables and a player told me that a place was open to eat. So I did.

Brodie got into banking, from which he is now retired, and lives sometime in the Richmond area and much of the time in what Virginians call the Northern Neck near the Chesapeake Bay. When he is not sailing, he tries his hand at writing novels.   (—RM)

maintained that "on too many occasions this may have worked against their respective personal interests." He said both coaches readily allowed cramped facilities to be used by other sports and activities. "It is very doubtful whether any two other men with so much personally at stake would have shown other departments as much cooperation." The letter also stated:

> To my knowledge, neither of these gentlemen has ever made promises to their assistant coaches, to their players, or to prospects when recruited, which they personally knew in advance could never be fulfilled. This statement could not be written in defense of many of our previous athletic department operational techniques.

Such practices over the past five years, Smith concluded, "although highly commendable and recommended by the College, have none the less indirectly contributed to their respective lacks of coaching successes here at William and Mary."

As accurate as Smith's defense was, it turned out to have been a case of too little and too late. On March 25, Freeman resigned. He wrote to Chandler requesting "that, at the termination of my present contract [June 30, 1957], my name not be considered for reappointment" as athletic director and head football coach. He expressed displeasure that he had only been offered a one-year extension, which amounted to seven months beyond his current contract. "The connotation of the extension is 'you have one more chance.' If my services of the past five years can not be measured with any greater security than the extension, I feel it is best to terminate," he wrote.

He also offered some striking figures in his defense, pointing out that "in 1951–52 there were 110 students aided by the men's athletic department in comparison with approximately eighty in 1956–57." And he pointed out that there had been 84 men on football aid and six coaches in

Halfback Charlie Sidwell (23) barrels ahead on a muddy field against George Washington in a 16-14 loss to the Colonials. That evening he rushed for 88 yards on seventeen carries or 5.1 yards per gallop. From the 1957 *Colonial Echo.*

Larry Peccatiello, end, awaits a pass as West Virginia defenders converge in the Mountaineers' 1956 20-13 victory at Cary Field. From the 1957 *Colonial Echo.*

Guard Lloyd Hicks (62) nails the West Virginia quarterback for a 12-yard loss in the 1956 battle at Cary Field. Courtesy of the W&M Sports Information Department.

1951–52 compared to 52 and three in 1956–57. Finally, the budget during the period had shrunk by $40,000.

His conclusion was: "In light of the above it is no secret to me or anyone who understands iintercollegiate athletics [what is] the real cause of our decline." As obvious as the administration's shortcomings were, the time was not yet ripe to shake off the specter of the scandal and treat intercollegiate athletics with more respect. That would require more losing seasons.

Decades later, Freeman said the offer of only a one-year extension "wasn't so much a matter of the school having no confidence in me."

I just didn't think it would do anything to help us get back where we needed to be. ... The big reason I left was that they weren't going to provide money for scholarships and staff. Listen, today William and Mary has as many coaches and trainers as we did players.

Milt Drewer (center) came to W&M in 1957 as football coach and athletic director. He arrived on campus in time to conduct spring practice on Cary Field (right). Drewer hired Edmund Derringe (right above) and Bill Chambers as assistant football coaches. Chambers later became a successful Indian head basketball coach, and Derringe, in 1963, became business manager of athletics and remained at the post for about twenty-five years. From the 1957 and 1958 *Colonial Echo*.

Freeman never regretted his decision. "To begin with, you always have a dream, but I think I did the right thing. I'm not sorry, and I would do it again," he said nearly forty years later. He reminded a listener that, at the time, he was married and had four children (eventually five). "Even if I would have put off the decision another year, I still might have left, because school athletics were in such a state of flux."

To Freeman, members of the Educational Foundation "were fighting with each other." It wasn't the best of times, to be sure. Freeman recalled asking his wife, Jane, if he had made the right decision. He laughed and said she told him, "You went to work with A&P and educated all your kids."

During that era of struggle, the Indians almost annually seemed to recruit standout receivers. Larry Peccatiello was one. Only 5'10" tall, the 190-pounder from Newark, New Jersey, went on to be an assistant coach at William and Mary, Navy, Florida State, and Rice before embarking on a National Football League career. That included thirteen years with Washington, as well as stints with Seattle, Houston, Cincinnati, and Detroit.

Peccatiello was recruited by Freeman and played for him three years and one for Drewer. The turmoil that seemed to hover around the program wasn't obvious to the players. "In college, as a player, you always have that air of optimism," Peccatiello said in 1996, when he was defensive coordinator for the Cincinnati Bengals.

Students rush onto Cary Field following W&M's 13-7 upset of Virginia Tech. The Gobblers held a statistical advantage of 268 yards to 232 yards for the Indians, but lost five fumbles and two interceptions to the Tribe. When they got to the locker room, players and Coach Drewer continued the celebration of their victory over Virginia Tech. From the 1958 *Colonial Echo;* locker photo courtesy of the *Richmond Times-Dispatch.*

> I remember that I was sorry Freeman was leaving, and I thought he was bettering himself. It didn't register that a big change had been made. Drewer was very optimistic, so the players just went from there.

Dave Edmunds (with ball) goes over the top of the pile into the end zone during the 1957 Navy game, while end Larry Peccatiello (84) and senior tackle Tom Kanas provide the landing. Peccatiello was co-captain of the 1957 team with Bill Rush (left). From the 1958 *Colonial Echo*.

The difficult schedules of those days, combined with very high entrance requirements that remain today, "made the coaching job very difficult. A break-even season was about as well as you could do."

Peccatiello, who, in 1997, joined the Detroit Lions, thought that from a coach's standpoint, "when you bring a recruit to visit, there's a favorable feeling on [the W&M] campus. I had good success for a stretch." Indeed, Peccatiello's recruiting helped attract sixteen players who were All–Southern Conference selections.

Speaking in the present tense, Peccatiello dealt with the past this way:

> William and Mary being small, academic people there are very much aware of what sports are doing. We're trying to be competitive and recruiting kids who can compete. So, sometimes there are questions about the direction we are going, and you wonder if at larger schools, the same attitude prevailed. The fact that there was a problem before I got there was always in the back of people's minds. So the program was pretty well policed by academic people and rightfully so.

Although dealing with the past, Peccatiello's references could hold today. Certainly, he covered that span of 1957 through 1963 when Drewer, the energetic, dark-haired son of a commercial fisherman from Saxis on Virginia's Eastern Shore, assumed the duties of head football coach and athletic director.

A former Randolph-Macon College fullback and track star, Drewer initially excited area football observers by successfully employing the belly series—a variation of the T-formation. He had been head coach at high schools in Cradock, Hopewell, and Warwick before becoming an assistant coach at the University of Richmond.

In his position at the Indians' helm, the 34-year-old Tribe football boss went about his job energetically. He had not changed much in that respect thirty-some years later. Drewer remained anxious to bang the drums loudly for William and Mary, and to prove it, he served several years on the College's Board of Visitors. He also retained great affection for his days on the Reservation. "I wouldn't have missed those seven years for anything. They were great years, and I'm talking about everything—players, coaches, public. They all did so much for me as a banker," a profession he embraced successfully in Northern Virginia after his Williamsburg stay.

At William and Mary, his verve typified that of a new head coach. "Most coaches with their first chance for a big-time job think they can conquer the world," he said. It was with that attitude, shortly after his appointment, that Drewer visited the campus of Georgia Tech, where legendary coach Bobby Dodd was still running things. "You made a mistake," Dodd snapped. "William and Mary doesn't want football." The remark "hit me between the eyes," Drewer said years later. Nevertheless, his enthusiasm persisted.

His initial season produced four victories against six losses and truly ricocheted from the pits to the peak. The first six outings produced but one victory—a third-game, 13-7 success against Virginia Tech. The seventh game turned into a 14-12 squeaker over the Citadel that preceded one of the school's tastiest upset triumphs.

Unbeaten in eight games, but tied twice, North Carolina State's Wolfpack was trapped in its own den in Raleigh. In a string of enthusiastic words from Raleigh on November 9, 1957, Newport News *Daily Press* sports writer Hank Maloney wrote:

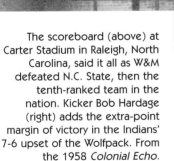

> Underdog William and Mary stopped previously undefeated North Carolina State two inches from the goal line here today in a brilliant second-period defensive stand and then chopped

The scoreboard (above) at Carter Stadium in Raleigh, North Carolina, said it all as W&M defeated N.C. State, then the tenth-ranked team in the nation. Kicker Bob Hardage (right) adds the extra-point margin of victory in the Indians' 7-6 upset of the Wolfpack. From the 1958 *Colonial Echo*.

Milt Drewer

Asked if he had made a mistake going into coaching college football, successful banker Milt Drewer quickly erased any doubts.

"First of all, I was very fortunate in life. Then, no, I didn't make a mistake going into coaching at William and Mary. It prepared me to be a successful banker."

Then, he listed four reasons.

1) I learned how to get along with people, both our employees and customers. 2) Organization. In football, it's a must and it's a major need in banking. 3) You develop leadership talents in football that you can use anywhere. 4) You learn to put forth an image . . . one with confidence. Boy! Do you need that in banking.

Assuming you have some economic background, I found that in banking you don't work as hard as you do in football.

Milt Drewer said having learned to be organized as a college football coach helped him in the financial world after he left William and Mary in 1963. Figures don't dispute him.

Active professionally and in civic affairs ever since, his major accomplishment was rising to the presidency of the First American Bank of Virginia in 1966 and then guiding its increase in assets from $42 million to $3.5 billion.

Eventually, he also held the positions of chairman of the board and chief executive officer before retiring in 1990. By then, the bank had more than 100 offices throughout the state of Virginia. During the same period, he was chairman of the board of the First American Metro Corp. in the metropolitan Washington, D.C., area. The group's net worth was $7 billion.

Along the way, Drewer served on the William and Mary Board of Visitors from 1976 to 1984. He also served as president of the Virginia Bankers' Association, the Virginia State Chamber of Commerce, and the Washington Golf and Country Club; chairman of the state chapter of the American Cancer Society; and a member of the boards of the Virginia Foundation of Independent Colleges, Randolph-Macon College, Chevy Chase Bank, Virginia Power, and Virginia Resources.

He has long been an avid golfer.   (—RM)

down the Wolfpack 7-6 with a stirring 16-play, 67-yard touchdown drive in the final quarter climaxed by quarterback Bob Hardage's game-deciding extra point.

For Coach Earle Edwards, defeat was more difficult to accept than usual since he was "celebrating" his birthday. On the other hand, for William and Mary, it was a particularly satisfying day, especially considering that the Indians triumphed without half their starting backfield. Quarterback Secules was nursing an injured thumb, and the brilliance of Sidwell had apparently flickered out. Earlier that week, after a 14-12 triumph over the Citadel, he had quit the team.

Sidwell, a Portsmouth, Virginia, native and an All–Southern Conference back the year before, had been drafted as a sophomore by the Cleveland Browns of the National Football League. He was eligible to continue playing in college because he had served two years in the armed forces. However, after a lackluster seven games in 1957, he came to Drewer and said he was quitting.

"I asked him not to and warned him that when someone quit, that was it. He wouldn't be allowed to return." Why did he decide to leave? "Let's just say he had lost interest in college football," Drewer said, both at the time of the departure and again decades later. He was, added the former coach, "a remarkable-looking athlete."

The tragedy that would accompany Sidwell's decision didn't become evident until late on November 28, 1957. Hours after he had watched the Indians' 12-7 season-ending loss in Richmond, Sidwell was killed in a one-car crash six miles east of Richmond on U.S. Highway 60. "Police said Sidwell ap-

1958 W&M co-captains Tom Secules (left) and Dan Plummer
pose before the season. From the 1959 *Colonial Echo.*

parently fell asleep at the wheel," the Associated Press
reported. He was 25.

Years later, Drewer would cite the victory over North
Carolina State as a high point of his tenure. "However,
my greatest appreciation goes to an overall feeling …
of being the football coach there [at W&M] and what
went with it."

There were limits, to be sure. One concerned Davis
Y. Paschall, who succeeded Alvin D. Chandler as College president. Drewer said:

> There was pressure from Dr. Paschall. From Dr. Chan-
> dler, never. Dr. Chandler was a realist. He recognized
> the limitations of what you can do. He knew I was loyal. He believed in me. I felt
> pressure from Dr. Paschall, and that's fine. You're supposed to feel pressure and
> know it's necessary to win. Dr. Paschall's attitude was different to me than Dr.
> Chandler's was. We weren't winning, so Dr. Paschall wasn't satisfied, so there wasn't
> any way I was going to be successful under him. He wouldn't give us the where-
> withal he would eventually give others. He had made his decision about Milt
> Drewer.

Drewer pointed out that his scholarship numbers hovered around fifty and that
the figure doubled after his departure. It also is true that the next four coaches following him didn't have winning records, either. "So maybe I wasn't as bad as I thought."

Paschall insisted that he harbored great respect for Drewer. He also felt pressure
himself. In 1996 he recalled things this way:

> I was getting complaints from all over. I met with twelve or thirteen of the alumni
> the year before Mr. Drewer left. They felt that he had done a good job, but that
> the time had come for a change. It was a sweatbox for a college president trying
> to keep an even keel amidst an ocean of athletic turbulence.

A William and Mary president has to know some things. He has to know that if the
football team loses too many games, the alumni will
get after the president. If the team wins too many,
the faculty will get after him. So, he has to balance
the situation, keep an ear open all the time. That's
why the athletic director has to report to the president [something that wasn't true before Freeman's
era].

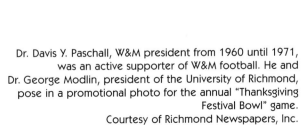

Dr. Davis Y. Paschall, W&M president from 1960 until 1971,
was an active supporter of W&M football. He and
Dr. George Modlin, president of the University of Richmond,
pose in a promotional photo for the annual "Thanksgiving
Festival Bowl" game.
Courtesy of Richmond Newspapers, Inc.

This caricature of an Indian decorated the football pages of the yearbook. From the 1960 *Colonial Echo*.

Paschall also admitted that after a 9-7 loss to Virginia at Cary Field in 1963, "my confidence was somewhat weakened, but not enough to make any change to be interpreted as firing." When Drewer did leave, Paschall felt that "it turned out to be the best thing in the interest of his career that could have happened."

Drewer agreed. "Coaching," he said, "prepared me to be a successful banker." Nevertheless, he endured many low points. One event, in particular, haunted him for years.

The incident was an aftershock of the 1961 season when the record fell to 1-9. That, Drewer recalled, "was a year I was pointing towards." He had recruited successfully, and optimism was high. Instead of smooth going, something he called "the cheating scandal" unfolded. Players didn't cheat, "but, some knew something was going on and didn't report it. It was strictly a matter of not being willing to tell on the others. Twelve players were suspended for a year in violation of the honor code." Five, Drewer said, were starters; four were second-stringers.

One night following that season, "I was backing the car out of our driveway and Suzy [Mrs. Drewer] came out of the house and stopped me. She said, 'I know you

Two Indians, including Dave Edmunds (21) cut down a North Carolina State runner, halting a Wolfpack scoring attempt. W&M defeated N.C. State for the second season in a row. The final score was 13-6. From the 1959 *Colonial Echo*.

have other things on your mind, but this is Christmas Eve. You should get a tree.'" A father of four children, he had completely forgotten the approaching holiday. Instead of heading for the office, he drove some twenty-five or thirty miles to Newport News before he could locate and purchase a tree. "That was really a low time for me," he said.

With or without the confidence of the administration, Drewer would have on-field problems of his own making. He conceded after a year that the belly series wasn't clicking, and he switched to the winged-T. It was while attending a clinic on the T that he met, and hired for $5,000 a year, a young coach as the lone W&M full-time assistant.

The man was short, slender, well-spoken, and appeared to be a teenager, despite his deep voice and habit of smoking a pipe. Lou Holtz was his name, and he would leave Williamsburg after a short stay, only to return as head coach in 1969. From there he would embark on world-famous careers as coach and prestidigitator.

Another of Drewer's on-field problems concerned the brilliant offensive guard and linebacker, Bob Soleau, one of those who had been suspended for a year. Soleau spent part of 1961 in the Army, playing for nearby Fort Eustis, and returned to the Tribe in 1962. The next year, Drewer decided to play the burly fellow from Pittsburgh at fullback.

"It probably wasn't a good thing, but I was looking for a fullback," said Drewer. "I didn't enjoy it," said Soleau, who had played the position a year in high school. It was suggested to Soleau that he might have refused to make the change.

> I wouldn't do that. I always would give something like that a shot. What the heck. I remember that spring; we had a scrimmage, and pro scouts were there. Dan Henning threw a screen pass, and I was behind two linemen with 60 open yards to a touchdown in front of me. I fell right on my rear. I thought then it was a good time to go back to guard."

That didn't happen right away. The pro scouts, however, must have liked what they saw, and Soleau played two years as a linebacker for the Pittsburgh Steelers. He also played a year in Canada and three for Hartford, Connecticut, in the Continental Football League.

Soleau was named to the All–Southern Conference teams in 1962 and 1963. In 1962, he was conference Player of the Year, and the next season he became a second-team Associated Press selection at guard, winning the Jacobs Blocking Trophy for a rare second successive season.

Memories of his career at William and Mary came across as a mixed bag. "Disappointing? Very. I thought we had more talent [than the record showed]. My senior year, we should have gone 8-2 or 7-3." Instead, the ledger was 4-6. "But that's history. I like to think of the good times. I'm very proud to have gone there."

Soleau settled in Connecticut, where he became an insurance executive who remained fun-loving and extremely fond of animals. His "family" included three children and a large collection of pets. He also developed an active interest in equestrian competition, which prompted friends to observe that he "still horses around."

Bob Soleau was an All–Southern Conference player in 1962 and was named the Conference's Player of the Year in 1962 and 1963. From the 1963 *Colonial Echo.*

Lauren Kardatzke makes a jarring tackle of Florida State's Billy Majors as Mike Lashley (78) comes on to help. The Tribe upset the heavily favored Seminoles, 9-0, in one of the South's major upsets in 1959. From the 1960 *Colonial Echo.*

The Athletic Department office mantel contains a number of trophies and awards, but the football from the 37-0 rout of Virginia takes prominent place. From the 1960 *Colonial Echo*.

Because of, or in spite of, the frustrations, in four of his seven years, Drewer's teams won four games. Numerous other times, they came oh-so-close to upsetting a powerful team. As is often the case in troubled football seasons, close defeats became the name of the game. Typical was the 1958 season-opening loss at Navy, which outweighed its visitors by an average of 11 pounds per man.

A game-long downpour didn't help either side in the contest that was the last in Thompson Stadium. The press box had already been dismantled, and reporters were forced to endure fierce winds and gallons of water with no protection whatsoever. Typewriters—those were the pre-computer days—quickly disappeared into their cases. Even then, some reporters still insisted on trying to take notes. They could be seen attempting to splash-write on the backs of less-inspired or more memory-rich compatriots.

Halfback Roger Hale (25) demonstrates why he was the offensive player of the 1960 Furman night game. The Tribe, however, lost a squeaker, 25-23, in the waning minutes. Hale was co-captain of the 1961 squad. From the 1961 *Colonial Echo*.

The Midshipmen were up 8-0 late in the first half when the Tribe stormed to the Navy 4 on second down with twenty-five seconds showing on the clock. With precious seconds clicking away, Referee Henry G. Munder moved the ball three times to what he apparently thought would be drier turf. The clock was not stopped. That left the Indians with one final and futile shot at the goal. The effort by Dave Edmunds fell a yard short as the half ended. It might as well have been a mile. Drewer left the field literally screaming and gesticulating wildly at Munder. Those exertions, too, were in vain.

The 1958 record was 2-6-1. The next year, credentials improved to 4-6, but then came 2-8 and 1-9 years in 1960 and 1961. Drewer went 4-5-1 and 4-6 his final two seasons, but the handwriting was on the wall. He would leave.

Initial clues surfaced before the 1963 football season, when H. Lester Hooker, Jr., a William and Mary alumnus and its former basketball coach, was named athletic director. The move ended an era that had put the football coach in charge of all sports. Like Drewer and Freeman before him, Hooker came to Williamsburg from the University of Richmond, where he had coached basketball for about a dozen years.

His recollections were that the football schedule was arranged so "there would be four home games and four away games as well as two money contests. It didn't take long to figure out that if we sold every seat, we couldn't make money. It was impossible." Hooker also remembers that "the budget for all sports was $243,000. Dr. Paschall told me that if I didn't make the budget, we would drop sports. Also, 67 percent of what we spent went to football."

Despite such stringent—absurd, really—financing, many alumni chose to express dissatisfaction with William and Mary's lack of football successes. Even when success came in single games, enthusiastic approval was absent because winning seasons were totally lacking.

One particularly vexing loss to a favored foe unfolded on October 12, 1963. West Virginia spoiled the Indians' Homecoming before 11,500 Cary Field fans, whose emotions ran the gamut from joyous peaks to woeful valleys. The Indians led by 14-7 at the half but killed themselves with fumbles. They set up two touchdowns for the victors with fumbles and then, seemingly en route to a successful rally, dropped the ball again. This time, the muff came at the West Virginia 30-yard line with a little more than three minutes to play. Final score: WVU 20, W&M 16.

W&M sophomores John Sapinski, Dan Henning, and T. W. Alley prepare for the 1961 season. News bureau photo by John T. Kinnier; courtesy of the *Richmond Times-Dispatch.*

John Sapinsky and T. W. Alley were two of the larger offensive tackles in the league that year. They were huge by William and Mary standards, although in the modern era, Sapinsky's 255 pounds and Alley's 240 would be no more than average. Like many others from the Reservation, both became coaches. Alley's career peaked when he served as head coach at the University of Louisville before an untimely death, and Sapinsky, after surgery prevented a tryout with the Oakland Raiders, settled down at Mark Morris High School in Longview, Washington.

An All–Southern Conference selection in 1962, Sapinsky, like most college players, went through his college days with little awareness of the stress his coaches felt.

Indian players Dan Barton (left) and Roger Hale go over game plans with W&M coaches Milt Drewer and Lou Holtz (right). News bureau photo by John T. Kinnier; courtesy of the *Richmond Times-Dispatch*.

He had been recruited by Penn State, among others, but chose the Williamsburg school "because I liked the concept." He also liked the recruiting effort by former Penn State star Danny DeFalco, who was then a Tribe assistant coach. "I had no knowledge of pressure on the head coach, but I guess there was a sense there was some. I knew he worked hard to build a winning program."

Sapinsky recalled playing with an injured knee as a senior. "I kept playing because we didn't have any depth. I went through the year because that's the way things went." He underwent knee surgery after the season. As times changed, he felt the modern-day Division I-A schedule against Ivy League–type schools had been a good move for the Indians. Dropping teams like Tulane, Vanderbilt, Army, and Navy (strong in Sapinsky's playing days) "is proper."

The loss to West Virginia was the first of five in a row during a 4-6 season. "All those losses do something to you," Drewer told Dick Heller of the *Richmond Times-Dispatch*. Prior to the Davidson contest, Heller wrote that Drewer's future "is best described as uncertain." Still, the Tribe finished with a surge that saw it whip Davidson by 34-5 and favored Richmond by 29-6. Such success, it turned out, did little for Drewer's cause. The two-game total of 64 points scored stood in stark contrast to the eight previous outings in which the Indians' high score had come in a 27-17 defeat of Furman. That was the only other time in which W&M scored more than 16 points.

Bill Corley leads the way as halfback Charlie Weaver scores the winning touchdown against The Citadel, 29-23. The Indians compiled 449 yards in total offense, then a school record. From the 1963 *Colonial Echo*.

The romp over Davidson saw the Wildcats take a 5-0 first-quarter lead before W&M's Dan Henning began to throw the kind of passes that would lead to a National Football League showing with the San Diego Chargers. Henning eventually became a coach, both in the college ranks and in the NFL, where he achieved prominence as head coach of the Atlanta Falcons.

Against Davidson that day, Henning passed for 231 yards while helping halfback Charlie Weaver set a Southern Conference record of ten pass receptions. Henning also tossed touchdown passes to Weaver and George Pearce.

Dick Kern (40) on his way to score in the 29-23 victory over The Citadel in 1962. From the 1963 *Colonial Echo.*

That same afternoon, Syracuse thrashed Richmond, 50-0. Nevertheless, rating services thought the Spiders were about a touchdown better than the Indians. On Thanksgiving Day, William and Mary again fell behind, this time by 6-0 before scoring 29 unanswered points, and once again Henning sparkled. He recorded touchdown passes of 29 yards to Pearce and 55 yards to Bill Corley. Henning also set three season records of 100 pass completions, 1,333 yards gained passing, and 178 career pass completions. The showing prompted Drewer to enthuse: "He's the finest passer I've had here, and he's never been better than he was today."

The triumph also included a touchdown on a 50-yard return of an intercepted pass by Dick Kern. The theft was his conference-leading eighth of the year.

That was November 29. The Newport News *Daily Press* headlines read, "W&M Rips Spiders" on one line over a second line claiming, "Drewer to Quit Job." The article stated,

> For Drewer, the contest quite probably was his last as head coach at William and Mary and possibly his last in the coaching field.

> The Daily Press has learned that the veteran of seven seasons at Williamsburg had apparently made up his mind to forsake the post, no matter what the outcome on Thanksgiving Day.

On November 30, *Daily Press* sports editor Charles Karmosky took W&M alumni to task, saying they "really had no right" to target Drewer, "nor is there the remotest chance that they will step up their financial aid." He also wrote that "there's a great likelihood that W&M will begin switching away from such

Navy and W&M developed an exciting rivalry between 1952 and 1967. A painting of Commodore William Bainbridge salutes Navy destroyer history on the cover of the Navy-W&M program in 1962 at the U.S. Naval Academy. Courtesy of the W&M Sports Information Department.

Coach Drewer is carried off Cary Field by his players after W&M defeated preseason conference favorite Furman, 19-6, to break a ten-game losing streak. From the 1962 *Colonial Echo.*

Quarterback Dan Armour, unable to spot an open receiver, heads up field against Richmond. The Indians lost, 15-3, giving up two touchdowns in the last five minutes of the game. From the 1963 *Colonial Echo.*

major power opponents (as Pittsburgh and Navy) in favor of smaller though still tough schools who will offer fairly sizeable monetary guarantees."

On December 9, the *Times-Dispatch* reacted to what it still felt were rumors that Drewer was through and published a story that was limited to little more than a "no comment" from Drewer and President Paschall. Even then, what was to become a monumental guessing game had already begun, and possible successors to Drewer were being suggested. Early front-runners included Tribe assistant coaches Lou Holtz, Larry Peccatiello, and freshman coach Roger Neilson.

The next day, December 10, the *Times-Dispatch* was again guarded, issuing another "no comment" from Paschall on a story headlined "Drewer to Be Ousted as W&M Grid Coach." The article mentioned that a year earlier Drewer had received "strong editorial support in the W&M student newspaper, 'The Flat Hat.'" As a result, the *Times-Dispatch* story said, Paschall kept Drewer the extra year. Finally, on December 11, the official announcement was made, but it did not state that Drewer was fired.

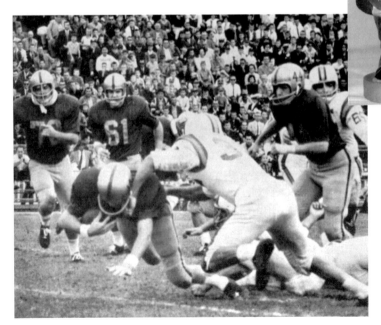

Quarterback Dan Henning (with the ball) in a rare moment when he could not find a pass receiver during the George Washington game. W&M linemen Bob Soleau (61) and T. W. Alley (76) and back Scott Swan (44) are too late to assist. From the 1964 *Colonial Echo.*

"Bouncing head" dolls were popular in the early 1960s. This one is painted in W&M's green and gold. From the collection of Wilford Kale.

Halfback Charlie Weaver picks up good yardage against George Washington although the Tribe lost to the Colonials, 32-14. From the 1964 *Colonial Echo.*

Paschall's statement said, in part, "after careful consideration of the factors involved, Mr. Drewer has concluded that it is best not to renew his contract, which expires in June, 1964." The story by Shelley Rolfe reported that Drewer said he was leaving "on cordial terms" with the College. Ironically, the story also quoted Hooker as saying the school had a total of sixty scholarships, counting freshmen, and that twenty more "will make us competitive." The irony was that the number represented what both Drewer and Freeman had sought all along.

The *Daily Press* that day went out on a limb that proved to be worse than shaky. Drewer, it said, "is expected to be replaced by a member of his staff"—something that would not happen. Peccatiello, Augie Tammarello, and Neilson were listed as candidates. The story said that "the college was, in fact, quite willing to keep Drewer in its family, but it was not willing to offer a contract for more than one year, nor was it willing to extend every effort to prevent the Tribe's football fortunes from diminishing further." The article also pointed out that at Warwick High School, Drewer had coached standout professionals Henry Jordan and Norman Snead, and five others from William and Mary had been NFL draft selections.

The guessing game was growing, and names of possible Drewer successors included Navy's 150-pound coach, Jack Cloud, and University of North Carolina assistants Joe Mark and Vito Ragazzo, all of whom were William and Mary graduates. On November 11, a *Daily Press* headline claimed "It Could Take 30 Days to Pick W&M's Coach." The story said that a "little over a dozen applications" had been received already. The number would increase steadily, but it would not include Milt Drewer's ultimate replacement.

It was hard to tell then, but better times were ahead. A new era, no. Still, the next three coaches combined would produce more encouraging won-lost ledgers. Teams under Freeman and Drewer won only 32 percent of their games. In the next sixteen years, the percentage of wins would climb to 45 percent. So, while he didn't know it then, Drewer's efforts were hardly in vain. Respectability was at last within reach.

Wade Johnson, riding Wampo (Feather), given to the College in 1960 by alumnus Arthur Hansen, leads the team onto Cary Field during the 1963 season. The pony raced around the stadium after every Tribe touchdown. From the 1964 *Colonial Echo.*

W+M, a
college of the
STUDENTS & FACULTY
by the

Indians Stun Middies by 27-16

6
The Almost Years
A Struggle for Respectability
1964 to 1979

Bob Moskowitz

Starting in 1964, the Indians once again sought football respectability. The best they could do was come close through three coaching tenures that lasted sixteen seasons. Only four times were there six or more victories, and only in 1976 were there as many as seven wins. The cumulative record was 75-93-3. Still, if just nine of those losses had been victories, there would have been a break-even ledger.

So, it is not surprising that throughout the span there were more than a few special times. One in particular left William and Mary partisans in a state of euphoria. The date was October 21, 1967. The site was Navy–Marine Corps Memorial Stadium in Annapolis, Maryland. The drama began enveloped in Navy Blue. By sunset the chameleon-like hue had shifted to Indian Green. The slow-to-materialize 27-16 triumph over the United States Naval Academy became accepted by the NCAA as one of the top ten upsets of its lengthy football history. The Indians had trailed by 16-0 before charging to a victory that was all the sweeter because it unfolded before a Navy Homecoming crowd of 19,542.

Sports writer Andrew Beyer described the unexpected dramatics this way in the next day's *Washington Post:*

> It started as a laugher, one of those typical, absurd Navy-William and Mary mismatches. It ended as a nightmare for the Midshipmen, who in the last 5 1/2 horrifying minutes of play allowed three touchdowns and suffered a 27-16 defeat.

Quarterback Dan Darragh dives over for a W&M score against Navy in the historic 1967 game. Photo by Del Vecchio/*Washington Post;* from the 1968 *Colonial Echo.*

W&M's Burt Waite (61) grabs a Navy back, ending another short run. Photo by Del Vecchio/ *Washington Post;* from the 1968 *Colonial Echo.*

End Jim Cavanaugh catches a touchdown pass in the 1967 game against Navy. Photo by Del Vecchio/*Washington Post*. From the 1968 *Colonial Echo*.

William and Mary quarterback Dan Darragh, woefully ineffective during the first half, ran for one touchdown and passed for two others to insure the end of Navy's reign as the top football team in the East.

In the *Richmond Times-Dispatch,* Shelley Rolfe wrote: "The old grads turned out en masse to celebrate another Navy win over its annual patsy, and instead watched William and Mary shake off a quarter century of frustration."

Heroics were supplied by others besides Darragh. Among them were receiver Jim Cavanaugh and wingback Steve Slotnick, who caught Darragh's two scoring passes (the one to Slotnick covering 51 yards). Tailback Jeff Lund, temporarily filling in for game-long defensive standout Ed Herring, fell on a kickoff that put the Indians 20 yards from the victory-clinching final touchdown. It was scored from 2 yards out by wingback Terry Morton, who caught passes and ran for key yardage throughout the pulsating late stages of the drama.

This wondrous happening for the Indians came during Coach Marv Levy's fourth season in Williamsburg. He had surprised many by accepting the job after four years at the helm of the University of California. Years later, after Levy had become head coach of the Buffalo Bills in the National Football League and guided them to four Super Bowl appearances, he continued to cherish openly that dismantling of the Navy football machine. It had been, he said, one of the three most memorable games in his nearly five decades of coaching.

For anyone at William and Mary, that game would be the high point of the Levy era. Period! The conquest "was a resounding thing," said Davis Y. Paschall, then William and Mary's president. It was "resounding" enough for the *New York Times* to include it in a one-column headline on the front page of its Sunday sports section. "Purdue, Alabama and Navy Upset,"

Navy's Fred Bayer (28) moves to break up a pass for W&M's Steve Slotnick. Associated Press wire photo, courtesy of the *Richmond Times-Dispatch*.

Steve Slotnick (43) catches a 51-yard pass from Dan Darragh for the winning touchdown with 3:05 remaining in the Navy game. Courtesy of the W&M Sports Information Department.

the *Times* proclaimed. Smaller type added: "Oregon St., Tennessee and William and Mary Victors."

The impact of the upset lingered with Darragh long afterward. His wife surprised him on their twentieth wedding anniversary with a gift of a full-length video of that epochal contest. She had obtained the old coaching film from the Naval Academy. Athletic Department people "were most gracious," Darragh recalled. He might have said the same thing about Navy's game performance.

To Levy, the *Times-Dispatch* reported, there were two turning points. One came when Navy led 2-0 and W&M linebacker Adin Brown blocked a punt. The other unfolded late in the first half when "we established our ground game," Levy said. That enabled the Tribe to begin moving both on the ground and in the air. While Levy said he didn't try to stir his charges up emotionally during the week before the game, he conceded, "I did talk about David and Goliath once."

William and Mary had not beaten Navy in twenty-five years. Nothing indicated the pattern would change. Navy had lost once in four starts; William and Mary had broken even in six games. Even the Indians' quarterback situation appeared iffy. Mike Madden, a Darragh classmate who

Terry Morton (45) plunges over from the 2-yard line for W&M's final score against Navy with 1:40 remaining in the fourth quarter. Courtesy of the W&M Sports Information Department.

Editorial cartoonist Dick Stinely of *The Virginia Gazette* drew this cartoon following the Indians' upset of Navy. Copyright *The Virginia Gazette.*

William S. "Pappy" Gooch

William S. "Pappy" Gooch carved out a niche as one of the University of Virginia's greatest athletes, but nevertheless, eventually induced many to call him "Mr. William and Mary."

Beyond his athletic prowess, his attributes were many and included story telling and getting along with people.

"He had a knack for attracting people. Everyone liked him. I never met anyone who didn't," recalled Ed Derringe, who came to William and Mary as a line coach in 1957 and started helping Gooch in 1963 before replacing him as business manager in 1964.

Gooch first came to the College in 1928 as director of athletics. It was under his administration that Cary Field was constructed and the groundwork laid for the Indians' forward surge in sports.

He served as athletic director until 1939, when he became business manager of athletics and held that post until his retirement in 1964. Derringe said "that position pulled everything together. You had contact with all the coaches, so Pappy became a central figure, not only at the College, but with people at the schools we competed with, where he also was very well-liked."

During Gooch's tenure with the Indians, he also coached, or helped coach, football, basketball, baseball, track, golf, swimming, boxing, and wrestling.

Son of a circuit court judge, Gooch was born in Roanoke in 1895. He grew up on the family plantation in Louisa County. After graduation from Jefferson School for Boys in Charlottesville, he attended Fishburne Military Academy in Waynesboro and entered the University of Virginia in 1915.

For the Cavaliers he quarterbacked the football team, played basketball and baseball and starred in track. With Gooch at the gridiron helm, Virginia belted such teams as Yale, South Carolina, North Carolina, and Vanderbilt.

After college, he played professional baseball and football and served the Marines in World War I and was a Navy lieutenant commander in World War II.

He was installed in the Virginia Athletic Hall of Fame in 1986.   (—RM)

sparkled as a runner, had been elevated to the starting role before encountering knee troubles. That put Darragh back in command.

Prior to the season, Levy opted to emphasize running as opposed to Darragh's drop-back passing game. Sitting on the bench as a senior following an outstanding junior year had been understandably frustrating. "From my perspective, it didn't make sense. The period was a downer," Darragh said decades later. He also remembered that he and Levy "didn't have the best relationship for a while."

Nevertheless, after Madden was injured against Virginia Military Institute, Darragh's reinstatement as quarterback couldn't have worked out better—for him and for the Indians. The lanky Pennsylvanian recollected the Navy game this way:

> We were always their Homecoming opponent. The noise would be deafening. It was intimidating. I remember before that game, telling my sister, who was a William and Mary sophomore, that we didn't have a prayer.
>
> However, we did have a very good game plan. Looking at the films, the coaches picked up when Navy was going to blitz, and for the first time we put in an audible system, rather than just an audible play or two. It turned out to be the difference in the game. We must have picked up a half-dozen of their blitzes.

One instance was Darragh's long touchdown pass to Slotnick who "had the option to go either way. He gave the defender a head move and went by him, and I just laid the ball there." Darragh told the Newport News *Daily Press* that the play was a sprint-out pass. "I threw it and prayed. I said, 'oh, man; catch it, catch it, catch it.'" From there, he said, "the momentum built. It was sort of like magic."

Jim Cavanaugh was a precocious sophomore nursing a knee injury that day. At first he responded by dropping several passes. However, his late-game catches, a touchdown among them, erased that stigma. Years later, when Cavanaugh had become a proven assistant college coach, he talked about the night before the Navy game. Levy told the team "we would eat a meal. It turned out to be cereal. What a letdown!" Levy apparently was convinced of the nutritional value of cereal. Also, in those

This *Richmond Times-Dispatch* headline says it all. Players pose for the 1967 team photograph with head coach Marv Levy (far left). From the 1968 *Colonial Echo*.

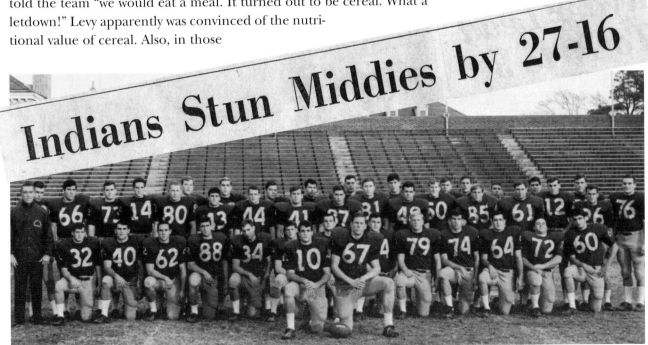

Buttons to show support of W&M were sold at Cary Field in the early 1960s. From the collection of Wilford Kale.

days, meals weren't necessarily a major matter in budget considerations. "So, when we packed our travel bags, everyone would bring food." As it turned out, one bag must have harbored that precious nutrient known as victory.

While the triumph had highlighted the Levy era, an equally major surprise had been the hiring of the coach, himself. After Milt Drewer left William and Mary following the 1963 season, speculation over the selection of his successor ran wild, but it never included Levy. The Chicago-bred Phi Beta Kappa from Coe College had only left the University of California on December 11. Holder of a master's degree in history from Harvard, he seemed to President Paschall to be the answer to a prayer. When Athletic Director Les Hooker approached Paschall about hiring Levy, the spirited school leader was ecstatic. "I'll have peace in my time with the faculty," he told Hooker.

Levy's courtship by William and Mary was certainly fast, if not furious. It came about, as Levy later recalled, because, "I had been fired at California, and I was very disillusioned about coaching. At age 38, I really was going to get out." The Levy psyche didn't rebound until after a call from an old friend—the former and highly successful University of California coach, Lynn "Pappy" Waldorf, who had heard that Levy had been ousted. "He told me that I should be a coach and that he knew the William and Mary

Coach Marv Levy (center) poses with his coaching team in 1965, his second year at W&M. Staff members are (left to right): Larry Peccatiello, Ralph Pucci, August Tammariello, Joe Downing, and Don Roby. Courtesy of the W&M Sports Information Department.

position was available. He told me to give the school a call." For that advice alone, it would seem that Waldorf is entitled to places in the William and Mary Athletic Hall of Fame as well as the National Football League Hall of Fame.

According to Levy, the "negotiating" was almost nonexistent. He called Hooker, who was "noncommittal," but who "called back quickly." Hooker later said that he had pondered calling Levy himself, because he had been unable to contact a man identified by the *Virginia Gazette* in Williamsburg only as "the leading candidate."

Sophomore Chuck Albertson goes through the air for a 5-yard touchdown against VMI. The Indians won, 14-12, giving Coach Levy his first victory and the first defeat of the Keydets since 1958. From the 1965 *Colonial Echo*.

When Hooker reported his findings to Paschall, he told the *Gazette*, "Mrs. [Agnes] Paschall was in the background yelling, 'Hire him! Hire him!'" There was a hastily arranged interview. "They offered, and I accepted. I liked everything about the school," Levy said. The agreement was announced January 3, 1964.

Hiring Levy was Hooker's first trip to the bargaining table on behalf of his alma mater. A former W&M athlete, he had been basketball coach at both the College and the University of Richmond. When he accepted the Tribe position in 1962, he became the first non-coaching athletic director at William and Mary since Dr. George Oliver in 1951. In reflecting on the brevity of the negotiation period, he added one major factor: "We knew that with Levy we wouldn't be de-emphasizing football."

Hooker knew early on that "Marv Levy was a different type coach from what William and Mary had before. He was more intense. Football was everything to him. And he was really into the importance of special teams." Hooker also pointed out that Levy ended the custom of holding "spring practice" in February and switched it to April with its more pleasant weather. On the field, Levy "put his best people on defense," said Hooker, "and he never recruited a high school guard. He would recruit fullbacks and convert them."

Levy also loved signs. He had them everywhere. "A Winner Never Quits, A Quitter Never Wins" was one. It supplied the basic message that he never stopped preaching. He never credited the signs for winning games, but they were ever present.

At VMI, in his first William and Mary game, Levy left six players at home out of a squad of thirty-four. He said

With only thirty-four players on the squad, the 1964 W&M team, Marv Levy's first on the Reservation, compiled a 4-6 record with a tough schedule. Levy was named Southern Conference Coach of the Year. From the 1965 *Colonial Echo*.

Assistant Coach Augie Tammariello (left) is shown with W&M linemen (left to right), guards Jim Dick and Craig Smith and center Tom Feola, before the Richmond game in 1964. Photo by Thomas L. Williams; courtesy of Richmond Newspapers, Inc.

Sophomore quarterback Mike Madden (10) laterals to Chip Young (in left corner) who rambles for an 18-yard gain, while W&M blockers John Shea, Jim Dick, Bill Conaway, Mike Bucci, and Les Beadling lead the way. From the 1966 *Colonial Echo*.

the six had not worked hard enough. His theory, Hooker said, was "if you didn't practice on Thursday, you stayed home on Saturday." It didn't take long to realize that the new coach must be doing something right. The Indians beat the Keydets 14-12, and the Levy era was off and running.

The rest of the season was more of a struggle, and the 4-6 record was no better than Drewer's the year before. Nevertheless, Levy's first W&M squad produced four All-Conference players, the most since 1958. His clubs boasted a total of twenty-three All–Southern Conference players, the best five-season total in school history. That first year also served as a springboard to three successive winning records of 6-4, 5-4-1, and 5-4-1. It was the College's most successful span since the reigns of Carl Voyles and Rube McCray, who combined for ten successive winning years ending in 1949.

Defense may have been first in Levy's mind, but his I-formation offense was hardly neglected. It virtually exploded midway through his second season against Davidson on October 16, 1965. The Indians, winners of only one of four previous games, triumphed 41-7, recording the highest W&M point total in fifty-two games and featuring Darragh's brilliance. He contributed three second-quarter touchdowns and 425 yards in total offense.

Quarterbacks Mike Madden (10) and Dan Darragh (16) pose for a preseason photograph. Courtesy of the W&M Sports Information Department.

Davidson, which had been unscored on in four previous contests, was held to 98 yards in total offense. The Indians held the Wildcats to only 14 first-half yards, all of which came on passing. To put the accomplishment in perspective, consider that erudite Davidson coach Homer Smith said: "Their defense is like Notre Dame's, but they executed much better than Notre Dame."

Running a major college football program involves more than counting victories. Counting fans, too, is a must. So, it followed that, in 1965, Hooker attempted to revitalize a sluggish gate. Among other things, he consulted a nearby minor

Defensive back Bob Gadkowski moves in front of a Virginia Tech receiver to make the interception. From the 1966 *Colonial Echo*.

Indian end Jim Lofrese receives the Most Valuable Player Award at the 1965 Oyster Bowl as W&M upset Southern Mississippi, the number one defensive team in the country, 3-0. The College played in eleven of the Khedive Temple's Shrine games for charity in Norfolk between 1947 and 1993. From the 1966 *Colonial Echo;* sidelines pass from the collection of Wilford Kale.

league baseball executive and attempted to improve Cary Field attendance by giving away tickets to youngsters and providing a pony to the winner of a drawing. Not many years later, animal activists led a move that ended this practice.

The first pony giveaway occurred during the October 23 Homecoming game against George Washington University. If the announced crowd of 11,000 wasn't completely satisfactory, certainly the heroics by the hosts were. Down 14-0, the Indians stormed back to defeat George Washington 28-14, prompting Levy to claim it was the Tribe's "best comeback" in his two years at the College.

The next week the Indians escaped defeat against Southern Mississippi by a 3-0 score. The contest was at Norfolk's Foreman Field in the Oyster Bowl, a game originated by the Shriners to raise money for burned and crippled children. While 24,000 fans helped the Shriners' cause considerably, the chief beneficiary may well have been junior Donnie McGuire. His 31-yard field goal with forty-five seconds remaining in the first half marked the first time he had attempted a field goal in collegiate competition. Ironically, Southern Miss had won its previous two games by 3-0 scores over Virginia Military Institute and Auburn University.

The Indians recorded six triumphs in 1965, five coming in their final six outings. It was the first time since 1953 that the team had won that often in one season. Although several games that year were exciting, victory number five was especially memorable. The 20-6 conquest of The Citadel came about this way, according to the November 7 Newport News *Daily Press* story from Charleston, South Carolina:

> William and Mary's vaunted defense opened the gates to victory and continued heroics by George Pearce here Saturday afternoon. The rampaging Williamsburg Indians scored twice in the first eight minutes and eleven seconds of play and wound up defeating The Citadel, 20-6.

Steve Slotnick (ball circled) is brought down by George Washington's Richard Hester (63) from the bottom and Bob Zier from the top on a punt return in the second quarter. W&M won the Homecoming game, 28-14. Photo by the Richmond Newspapers, Inc.; courtesy of the W&M Sports Information Office.

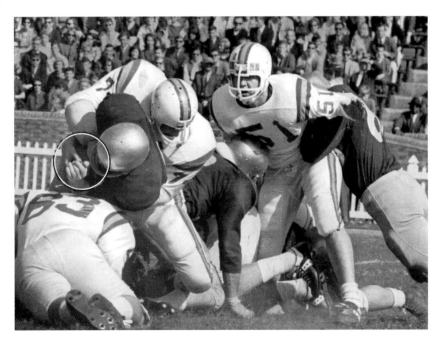

Marv Levy

He most likely would blanche at the comparison, but the Buffalo Bills' Head Coach Marv Levy is easily likened to Ernest Hemingway.

With twenty years of coaching in the National Football League behind him, former William and Mary football boss Levy remains erudite and well-spoken. He can be earthy, even fun-loving. Yet, the former Indians' football coach is organized to the point of severity. To him it is all a matter of discipline.

Hemingway, the master of technique when it came to his profession, also enjoyed life to its fullest and, too, was well-versed in a wide spectrum of subjects.

A Levy legacy at W&M, following his tour of duty there from 1964 through 1968 was a copy of his plan for each player's locker. Helmets went one place, shoulder pads another. And so forth. All of it was for the sake of discipline, something he believed would pay off in many ways.

A Chicago native, Levy served in the Army Air Corps during World War II and following graduation from Coe College as a Phi Beta Kappa, he earned a master's degree in English history from Harvard University in 1951.

At academically rich William and Mary, Levy was heralded for both his academic and coaching exploits. Despite a modest 23-25-2 record, he was named Southern Conference Coach of the Year in each of his first two years in Williamsburg.

Such honors were not new to the former Coe College standout athlete, who came to Williamsburg after four seasons as head coach at the University of California. Earlier, he was Skyline Conference Coach of the Year in 1958 and 1959 at the University of New Mexico. His earliest coaching days produced an exceptional two-season 13-0-1 record at St. Louis County (Missouri) Day School in 1951-52.

In 1996, he was vice president of Buffalo's football operations as well as its head coach. By then, he had been at the helm of NFL clubs for fifteen seasons, eleven in Buffalo. His sparkling credentials there include being twice named NFL Coach of the Year and guiding the Bills into four different Super Bowls.

He solidified a long-time link between the Bills and William and Mary. Harvey Johnson, a standout Tribe lineman from 1940 through 1942, inaugurated the chain when he was hired as a defensive backfield coach in 1960. He had been a kicker with the New York Yankees, making 146 consecutive conversions. Johnson became long-time director of player personnel before and after he coached the Bills in 1968 and 1971. Former W&M great Buster Ramsey also coached there (1978 through 1982) and Levy has been blessed with the playing expertise of W&M's stellar defensive back Mark Kelso and kicking star Steve Christie.

Levy left W&M to begin his pro coaching career as kicking teams' coach of the Philadelphia Eagles under Jerry Williams in 1969. He joined Coach George Allen's staff as special teams coach for the Los Angeles Rams in 1970 and followed Allen to the Washington Redskins as special teams coach in 1971 and 1972, when the 'Skins advanced to Super Bowl VII.

Levy then accepted a post as coach of the Canadian Football League's Montreal Alouettes, who he led to 1974 and 1977 Grey Cup titles. In 1978, Levy became head coach of the NFL's Kansas City Chiefs. He left there after the strike-shortened 1982 season and entered the broadcasting field for nearly two years before joining the Bills.   (—RM)

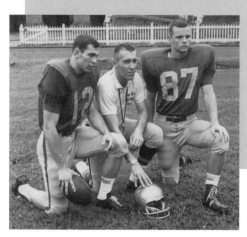

Coach Levy poses with his passing and receiving combination of quarterback Dennis Haglan (left) and end George Pearce. Courtesy of the *Richmond Times-Dispatch.*

Second-team All-American end George Pearce (81) grabs a Dan Darragh pass against VPI. In 1965 Pearce set school and Southern Conference records in pass receptions and yardage. From the 1966 *Colonial Echo.*

Although the Bulldogs were only one-time winners in nine games, they had beaten Richmond 24-0 the week before.

As it was, W&M went on to end its 6-4 season with a 21-0 conquest of Richmond's Spiders, capturing second place in the Southern Conference. Pearce, an All–Southern Conference selection the first two Levy years, caught seven passes that day. The accomplishment, though short of the twelve passes he caught in an earlier 42-14 loss to Navy, prompted teammates to award Pearce the game ball. His catches brought his eight-game total to forty-eight, setting both conference and William and Mary records. For the year, he totalled sixty-one catches for 796 yards and six touchdowns, enabling him also to better both conference and school records for yardage gained.

Pearce, who became a second-team All-American that season and was Southern Conference Player of the Year, also achieved excellence with something Levy dubbed the "poocher" punt. It was a soft kick usually aimed at the sidelines near the goal. The purpose was to give the opposition the poorest ball possession possible. "It was something Levy brought with him from the West Coast, and I was the kicker he inherited from Drewer," Pearce recalled.

The "poocher" was one of several unorthodox approaches embraced by Levy. The quick kick became a specialty of wide receiver Chuck Albertson. Levy conceded he never tried the gimmick during his three decades of coaching in the professional ranks.

The 1966 season opened with a 7-7 deadlock with East Carolina that seemed to typify the period. There was great effort and excellent football, but frustration ruled. The Indians had intercepted four passes, and Chip Young returned a punt 95 yards for a first-quar-

Randy Glesenkamp (88), a solid end, almost has the ball stolen by Bill Edwards of Virginia Tech in the 1965 game in Williamsburg. From the 1966 *Colonial Echo.*

Ned Carr hauls in a Dan Darragh pass against Virginia Tech. The catch was good for six points, but the Gobblers won, 20-18. From the 1967 *Colonial Echo.*

W&M's first network football game was against Boston College in 1966. The game was broadcast by ABC-TV to a large Northeast and mid-Atlantic audience. Quarterback Dan Darragh is shown on a television screen. From the 1967 *Colonial Echo.*

Gordon C. Vliet '54, later executive vice president of the Society of the Alumni, drew the cover of the 1966 W&M *Football Handbook* portraying the ABC television appearance of the Indians. Courtesy of the W&M Sports Information Department.

ter touchdown. The Pirates countered on a third-quarter touchdown return of 75 yards by Bob Ellis that was preceded by two penalties against the Indians. And the tie held up.

By season's end, the Indians were 5-4-1 and tied for the Southern Conference championship. Also, Levy had been selected Southern Conference Coach of the Year for the second straight season. By then, his emphasis on defense had borne fruit, and the Tribe landed four All-Conference selections. Three—end Bob Gadkowski, linebacker Adin Brown, and tackle Joe Neilson—were on defense. Albertson was the fourth pick. The defense had allowed only 144 points, the stingiest yield since 1962 and an accomplishment that would stand up for at least three decades.

The 1967 season's high points weren't limited to beating Navy. After a sluggish start, the Indians sent up warning signals in a 14-12 loss at Vanderbilt and then bested VMI, Ohio University, Navy, and The Citadel in succession before tying West Virginia 16-16. A season-ending 16-7 loss to Richmond marred the impressive late-season binge.

Success against Virginia Military's Keydets in the year's fifth game included a 71-yard touchdown pass on the last play of the third quarter from Darragh to Cavanaugh. The Tribe had charged to a 16-0 first-quarter lead and was still up 23-7 in the second quarter. Levy confided to writers at the Tobacco Bowl in Richmond that "I told the players before the game that if we didn't win, it had been no season." Instead, the Indians ended a three-game losing streak and turned it into a fine season.

The next week at Athens, Ohio, W&M came from behind three times, twice in the second half, the last time at 22-18, to defeat Ohio University by 25-22. At the same time, Navy was beating Syracuse 27-14. The stage was set for that dramatic upset of the Midshipmen the following week.

After Navy came the tie with West Virginia which virtually assured the Mountaineers of another Southern Conference crown. The winners' John Mallory uncorked an 85-yard gain from scrimmage to tie the score

Defensive back Jim Barton transferred to W&M in 1967 after George Washington University discontinued its football program. He became an immediate participant on the defensive team. Photo by Thomas L. Williams; courtesy of the W&M Sports Information Department.

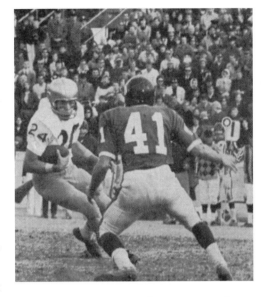

Senior end Chuck Albertson fakes a University of Richmond defender during a 1966 victory that gave the Indians a winning season and a share of the Southern Conference championship. From the 1967 *Colonial Echo*.

at 6-6 in the second quarter. The Tribe went up 16-9 with 3:10 left in the third period, thanks to what the Newport News *Daily Press* called Cavanaugh's "wonderful leaping catch with two defenders on him." West Virginia posted the final score with 4:03 left after recovering a fumble on the William and Mary 24. Mountaineer coach Jim Carlen opted for the tie, and the Mounties kicked the extra point rather than go for a game-winning two points. The November 12 *Daily Press* reported that Carlen conceded that the decision was "my fault. It was a poor call on my part."

In 1968 the shoe showed on the other foot. William and Mary lost a rain-marred 24-21 decision to The Citadel which virtually assured Richmond of winning the Southern Conference crown. In the waning moments of a thriller that saw the lead change hands four times, the Indians shunned a chance to tie on a field goal and went for the touchdown and failed.

In his column, *Daily Press* sports editor Charles Karmosky quoted Levy: "We decided [that going for the field goal] … would be a tarnished type of championship with us not even having a break-even season." If W&M had triumphed against the Mounties and then tied or beaten Richmond the next week, it would have won the title. Instead, the Spiders triumphed 31-6, despite 256 yards gained from passes by junior quarterback Jimmye Laycock. His was a name that would become even more familiar to Tribe football fans in future decades. Halfback Terry Morton's three touchdowns highlighted an afternoon in which he carried a W&M record twenty-nine times for 103 yards. The setback saddled the Tribe with a 3-7 record, the last and worst in the Levy regime.

The W&M team comes on the field for Homecoming Day in 1967 against Richmond. W&M assistant coach August "Augie" Tammariello (at far right of team) concluded his six-year stint with the Tribe that season and moved on to coach in college and the NFL. Charles R. Varner leads the W&M band at far right. From the 1968 *Colonial Echo*.

Lineman David Holland goes after an East Carolina back in the 1968 game. From the 1969 *Colonial Echo.*

"Nothing caused me to leave William and Mary," Levy said nearly thirty years later. "I could have stayed happily the rest of my life. It was a tough school. It would have been a great struggle to develop a dominating team." The major factor causing him to leave, he said, was that "at that time, the pros were becoming more glamorous and interesting." When Levy's longtime friend Jerry Williams became the head coach of the Philadelphia Eagles, the National Football League became even more "interesting."

The attraction was mutual. One reason the NFL was interested in Levy was his long-time love affair with special teams. "I always felt that aspect of football was overlooked. People said it was half the game, but they didn't believe it. I thought we had a good kicking game at William and Mary. We were good at blocking kicks."

In retrospect, Levy felt the "most difficult thing" about coaching at the College "is that you were always fighting the odds. Maybe that made the program better. I don't know. It was difficult to recruit enough players who qualified."

In a 1994 Phi Beta Kappa publication, the *Key Reporter,* Levy was selected to contribute to a space reserved for "articles written by members who have achieved prominence outside academe." One Levy paragraph seemed to project his coaching philosophy best. It read: "Leadership, I concluded, is the ability to get other people to get the very best from themselves. Accomplishing this depends not upon persuading others to follow you but upon succeeding in getting them to join you." Looking back, players like Pearce and Cavanaugh both remained impressed with Levy's organizational skills. "Marv was very professional, very organized," said Cavanaugh.

Levy had been a head coach more than a decade before accepting the W&M job. In contrast, the position was the first at the helm for his successor, Lou Holtz. Taking over in June, well after the completion of spring practice, didn't ease matters for him. Cavanaugh recalled that "things were a little crazy that first year."

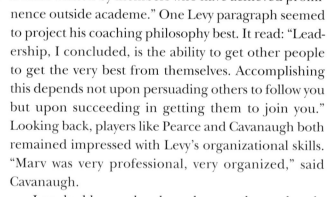

Wes Meeteer rambles for a 26-yard gain as Pittsburgh defenders give chase during a 1968 game. Photo by Don Stetze; courtesy of the W&M Sports Information Department.

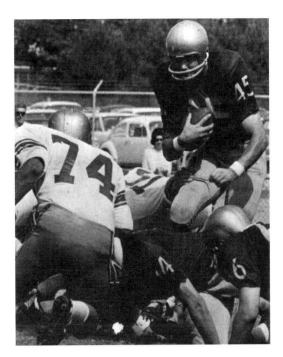

Terry Morton (45) finds the going rough on this run against East Carolina in the 1968 game. From the 1969 *Colonial Echo.*

Les Hooker was still the athletic director when Levy left. Selecting a successor, Hooker recalled, boiled down to a choice between Holtz and former Navy coach Wayne Hardin. "I remember telling Dr. Paschall 'if we hire Lou, he's quick and smart and doesn't look like a coach. Hardin is a pro. There's no telling what will happen to us with him.'" So Holtz got the job and, Hooker recalled, "later, Hardin got the Temple job, and when we played them I really wanted to beat them, but [in 1971] we lost 17-13."

The 1969 Indians, under rookie coach Holtz, split their first six games before losing the final four. That was especially vexing to people like Cavanaugh, because it meant absorbing three successive losses at the hands of Richmond. Worse yet, in those contests, the Spiders out-scored their archrivals 75-30.

In reflecting on his three seasons as the William and Mary head coach, Holtz readily admitted: "It was my first job as a head coach, and I made a lot of mistakes. Dr. Paschall wanted us to build a program" that would survive in the Atlantic Coast Conference. And, in fact, the Indians seemed to approach such status in 1971, Holtz's third year, when they finished 5-6, losing 36-35 to the University of North Carolina and 36-29 to Wake Forest.

Trainer Mont Linkenauger was a 1951 William and Mary graduate who came back to his alma mater during the Levy era. He retired as a trainer in 1973, although he continued on the faculty, as a professor of anatomy and physiology of exercise and kinesiology, until 1988. He compared Holtz with Levy, for whom he coached the punters and kickers: "Lou wasn't as insistent on discipline and work for his assistants. Levy's assistant coaches felt they had to protect the players from him." However, he thought the two coaches' "football philosophies were basically similar."

A Villanova defender just watches as end Jim Cavanaugh makes another super catch in the 33-12 defeat of the Wildcats in 1968. From the 1969 *Colonial Echo.*

Linkenauger accurately recalls the 5-6 record of Holtz's final year as a series of close defeats. The Tribe won its first four games, then lost six of the remaining seven. Of the losses, only one—41-30 at Virginia Tech—

W&M alumnus H. Lester Hooker, Jr., became athletic director in 1963. After Marv Levy became coach, the College arranged to renovate one of the old fraternity lodges as the new football office. Because Levy wanted to stay in Blow Gymnasium until William and Mary Hall was completed, Hooker and business manager Edmund Derringe moved to the lodge. From the collection of H. Lester Hooker, Jr.

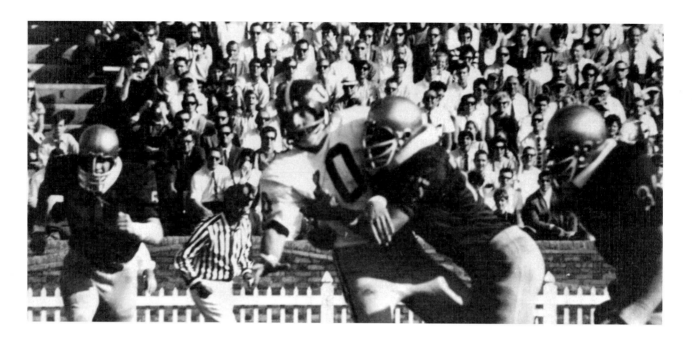

W&M sophomore defensive end Dave Campbell (middle) hits the Villanova quarterback so hard that he loses the football during the 1969 game. Courtesy of the W&M Sports Information Department.

was by more than seven points. A 28-23 conquest by West Virginia especially lingered with Linkenauger. The visiting Mountaineers triumphed in the final seconds, but the Indians' "student section wouldn't leave. They gave the team a standing ovation and wouldn't leave even then."

It was the 1970 season, however, that garnered the most acclaim, because the Indians made it to the Tangerine Bowl. Despite a string of season-opening losses to West Virginia, Miami (Florida), and Cincinnati, the team righted itself and was poised to capture the Southern Conference crown and a bowl berth going into the season's finale with Richmond.

Daily Press sports writer Ray Brown quoted Lou Holtz:

> To be frank, I didn't think that [appearance in a bowl] would be possible after seeing the way we lost to The Citadel [16-7 in Williamsburg]. The way we have played defense, I didn't think we deserved it [the Conference championship].

Success, however, didn't come easily. The team first needed to clear a pair of late-game hurdles. First came a 29-28 conquest of Davidson on a Bill Geiger field goal with fourteen seconds remaining. Then, on November 21, the Indians disappointed most of the 12,000 fans in Richmond's City Stadium by besting the Spiders in a last-ditch 34-33 melodrama. Quarterback Steve Regan, flour-

In 1969, W&M halfback Dennis Cambel (41) and U.Va. defender Rick Gustafson stretch for an Indian pass in an exciting 28-15 Cavalier win. From the 1970 *Colonial Echo.*

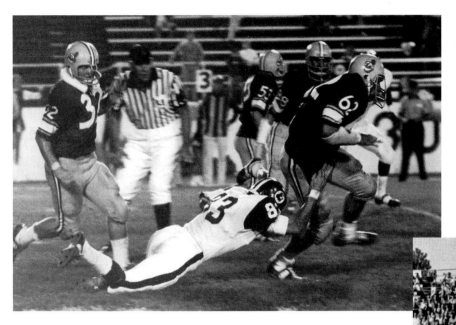

Senior Dave Holland escapes a Temple lineman for a first down in W&M's 7-6 victory over Temple. From the 1970 *Colonial Echo.*

Defensive stalwarts Wally Ake (53) and John Moretz (25) double team the VMI ball carrier in the Indians' 25-17 victory. From the 1970 *Colonial Echo.*

ishing under Holtz's triple-option offense, threw the game-winning touchdown to David Knight with twelve seconds remaining. For a while, Regan's chances of even being around loomed dim. He had been hit on the head early in the game, and Holtz said Regan "asked me to call the plays." Thankfully for the Tribe, Regan's haze lifted quickly. The Indians gained possession prior to the winning score with only fifty-one seconds remaining. Regan passed to Todd Bushnell, and Knight brought the ball to the 12 before the all-telling score. The Indians went for two meaningless extra points and failed.

For the year, the Tribe allowed a school-record 335 points and scored 218 points (including the bowl game), its most since the 236 recorded in 1952. Of course, in 1971, the final Holtz season, the Indians won five, lost six, and scored 278 points, their heftiest total since 1947, when they recorded 320. The major offensive weapon in 1971 was workhorse fullback Phil Mosser, a two-time All–Southern Conference selection, who rushed for 257 yards against Ohio Wesleyan in 1970, a current school record. Mosser was a two-time All–Southern Conference selection, who was the conference Player of the Year in 1970.

Another major source of stellar offensive performances under Holtz was guard Jackson Neall, one of four All–Southern Conference selections that year, and the fifth from William and Mary to receive the Jacobs Blocking Trophy. He remembered that he came to the Williamsburg campus "because I liked it. It was a unique campus, and Coach Levy was

Bobby Ross came from VMI to join Marv Levy's staff in 1967 as an assistant coach and stayed for five seasons before eventually going on to head coaching positions at The Citadel, Maryland, and Georgia Tech, where his team was named number one by UPI in 1990. He then moved into pro football as head coach of the San Diego Chargers and, in 1997, moved to the Detroit Lions. Photo by Andrew Studio, Lexington, Virginia; courtesy of the W&M Sports Information Department.

Lou Holtz

Lou Holtz first caught the College of William and Mary and area residents unaware in 1961. He was just married and professionally boasted only a year as a freshman coach at Iowa University.

When the Peninsula Sports Club, composed of fans from Newport News, Hampton and surrounding localities, asked the Tribe's Head Coach Milt Drewer to speak, he sent Holtz in his place. Members literally laughed when Holtz, peering from behind horn-rimmed glasses, looking undernourished and sounding laid back, told them that at Kent State University he had been a linebacker. The laughter stopped when he began to speak.

In the over three decades since, Holtz has evoked laughter only as a talented magician and entertainer.

His head-coaching career, which began in 1969 with three seasons at the College of William and Mary, has reached storied heights at the University of Notre Dame. Holtz didn't fare badly, either, between jobs in Williamsburg and South Bend, Indiana, where he started in 1986. Holtz was a winning head coach at North Carolina State, 1972–75, and the University of Arkansas, 1977–83. He spent 1984 and 1985 at the University of Minnesota and most of 1976 with the New York Jets of the National Football League.

Before his head coaching days, Holtz served as an assistant at Iowa, W&M, Connecticut, South Carolina, and Ohio State.

His son Skip—one of four Holtz children—was an Irish assistant coach and became head coach at the University of Connecticut in 1993.

Holtz's accomplishments with the Irish were monumental. In addition to a total record of 100-30-2 (a .758 percentage), they included:

- Winning 100 games—more than any other Notre Dame coach except the legendary Knute Rockne.
- Winning a school-best five postseason bowl games.
- Taking Notre Dame teams to an unequalled nine successive January 1 bowl games.

Following the 1996 season, Holtz resigned from Notre Dame and became a football commentator for CBS.   (—RM)

Fullback Billy Gardner (44) carries with blocks by Jackson Neall (66) and Stan Victor (75) against West Virginia in 1971. From the 1972 *Colonial Echo*.

Jim Cavanugh (89) signals touchdown against the Davidson Wildcats. From the 1970 *Colonial Echo.*

very gracious." He felt the 1970 Richmond game was the "high point" of his football career. Going to the bowl as a result of that victory "was such a surprise," considering the season as a whole.

Neall, a 1971 Jacobs Blocking Trophy recipient, remembered that Holtz, who went on to enjoy a successful tenure at several major colleges, especially Notre Dame, "was more in-your-face, very spontaneous. Levy was more an academic. He was cool, calm, and collected most of the time. I remember him as a gentleman."

For Neall, a native of the New Jersey shoreline, football continued to command an important place in his life years later. His daughter's wedding in New Jersey prompted one memory. He invited "a bunch of teammates and they all came." The ex-players included Barry French, Phil Mosser, Todd Bushnell, and Jim Thomas. "It was really exciting. It was the first time we were all together in twenty-five years."

Defensive back Warren Winston received little fanfare during the three Holtz seasons. A Richmonder recruited during the Levy era, he was the first African-American to receive a football scholarship at William and Mary. Years later, when he had become a financial planner, he would say he came to the College "for the academics and because I wanted my family to be able to see me play." The decision, he said, "was a good one. I was never disappointed there."

Holtz left the Green and Gold to accept a job as head coach at North Carolina State. By then an ailing Paschall had been replaced as president by Thomas A. Graves, Jr. In *Davis Y.*

The Indians face off against Ohio Wesleyan in a 1970 game as quarterback Bubba Hooker (10) takes the snap from center Bob Herb, three-year anchor of the offensive line. From the 1971 *Colonial Echo.*

A wall of Davidson defensive linemen stands up W&M halfback John Beck. From the 1970 *Colonial Echo.*

Paschall: A Study in Leadership (1990), Wilford Kale and Harry L. Smith, explained, "Paschall explored, in some detail, membership for William and Mary in the prestigious Atlantic Coast Conference about 1970." According to the authors, after the University of South Carolina left the conference, Paschall said he had "made informal contacts with presidents of four of the remaining seven institutional members and had been 'enthusiastically told' that they would welcome William and Mary as a member."

Paschall said he felt the College's future would be more promising in the Atlantic Coast Conference than in the Southern Conference ... Also William and Mary Hall, which could seat more than 11,000, had just been completed. The first basketball game played in it was with the University of North Carolina. Paschall felt that basketball played there with Atlantic Coast Conference teams would draw capacity crowds ... and [the revenue would] prove a safeguard against future increases in the student athletic fee.

Furthermore, he felt it would enhance the image of the College in many distinctive ways without threatening its sound policy of the student-athlete concept. What happened?

In a 1989 interview Holtz stated:

If it hadn't been for William and Mary, I wouldn't be at Notre Dame today. I believed in Dr. Paschall so strongly. He emphasized to me we didn't want to change academics, but just wanted to play with academic

Center Bob Herb (51) gained national attention in 1970 when he was named to the second-team Associated Press All-American squad and to the first-team All–Southern Conference. Here, at right, Herb paves the way for running-back Phil Mosser (22). Courtesy of the W&M Sports Information Department.

schools like Duke, and that he was going to get W&M into the Atlantic Coast Conference.

Holtz said that a few weeks after Paschall's September 1, 1971, resignation, "President Graves informed me that he wanted the football program to go in a different direction. He was looking more to the Ivy League type." He indicated that if William and Mary had gone into the Atlantic Coast Conference, "I might have stayed there forever." That may have been stretching things, because Holtz's career became somewhat nomadic, starting with his shift from Williamsburg to the ACC's North Carolina State University. He also had stops along the way at Arkansas, the New York Jets, and University of Minnesota, before arriving at Notre Dame for an eleven-year stay that ended after the 1996 football season.

Holtz concedes that he had visited N.C. State just a few months before resigning his position at the College, but states that "it is absolutely untrue" that he had taken another job long before the 1971 season ended for W&M. That rumor prevailed in the media for weeks before the season-ending 21-19 loss at Richmond.

"In my mind, I was going to stay at William and Mary the rest of my life. They wanted to get into the ACC, and that was fine with me." When his name was

Dick Pawlewicz (81) gets a handoff from Bill Deery (13) to begin an end around in the 1972 Vanderbilt game. Barry Beers (74) pulls for a lead block. From the 1973 *Colonial Echo.*

In the Tangerine Bowl, Steve Regan (18) hands off to Phil Mosser, Southern Conference Player of the Year, who gained 100 yards against the University of Toledo, the nation's best defensive team. From the *Alumni Gazette.*

Jim Root

For Jim Root, life after football was quiet and rewarding.

A highly successful life insurance agent, he remained in Williamsburg and eventually became a grandfather of fifteen. He and his wife, Janet, were parents of three and their oldest child, Mistina Athens, had nine children (six boys and three girls). Jim (Skip) Root, Jr., became a Navy pilot and had two boys, while Dale fathered a daughter and three sons and became an art teacher at Winchester, Virginia, High School, where he also excelled in wood carving.

Meanwhile, Root busied himself hunting, fishing, and golfing. He also has always been an active church person and continued to be involved in bettering others.

Such community-oriented activities included serving as president of Williamsburg's Capital Kiwanis Club, being a member of Big Brothers/Big Sisters and Children of Adult Leaders of Young Life, and acting as a reader for Kiwanis Youngsters.

A stroke suffered in 1995 severely limited his physical activities, although his improvement continued slowly but steadily. Mentally, he never lost a step and retained crystal-clear memories of his days—gloried and otherwise—on football fields across the country. (—RM)

mentioned in connection with the job at Raleigh, "I withdrew my name. I never went there until after the William and Mary game at the University of North Carolina" on October 30, 1971. He said that he did talk with NCS athletic director Willis Casey the following Thursday and "told him I would talk when the year was over." After that, "I didn't talk or visit with anyone from N.C. State until after the Richmond game."

Holtz's three-year record at W&M was 13-20, including a bowl game appearance. He did, however, leave a good nucleus of talent in his wake. Successor Jim Root quickly went 5-6 and 6-5, but that hardly heralded the end of the "almost years." Instead, the remainder of Root's eight-year stay—the longest in W&M annals at that point—basically became a study in highs and lows.

While Root's credentials didn't measure up to Levy's, the former Miami of Ohio star, who had been a quarterback with the Chicago Cardinals of the National Football League, had been in the coaching business fourteen years before heading for W&M. His background included four years as head coach at the University of New Hampshire, where he had been NCAA Division Small College Coach of the Year in 1968. He also had worked under Andy Gustafson at Miami (Florida), Andy Pilney (Tulane), Bob Blackman (Dartmouth), and Carmen Cozza (Yale)—all outstanding in their field.

Root came to Williamsburg partly because he had "dreamed of winning" Coach of the Year honors in Division I. "I didn't know what I was getting into," he said laughingly much later on. It wasn't much of a joke.

Root actually came to Williamsburg only after Bobby Ross turned down the job in deference to his family's wishes. Ross, a former VMI

This lamp was created from a W&M football helmet, circa 1975, as a possible item to be sold by the W&M Society of the Alumni. The project did not go forward. From the collection of Wilford Kale.

football star, was an assistant under Levy at both William and Mary and then at Kansas City in the National Football League. In 1972, Ross had only been in Kansas City a short time, and his family didn't want to move again so soon.

About the same time Root was hired, Hooker moved into the recently opened William and Mary Hall and took charge of operations there. In Hooker's place as athletic director came Ben Carnevale. He didn't arrive in Williamsburg until June, and by then Root had handled spring practice.

Carnevale had been a well-known and respected name in athletics since his collegiate days at New York University, beginning in 1934. Included among his credentials were his tenures as basketball coach at North Carolina University and the Naval Academy. After twenty years at Navy, he returned briefly and unhappily to NYU as athletic director. "They kept no promises to me," he said decades later.

Despite the change in scenery, he found himself immersed in new problems at William and Mary. "Here I was a New Yorker who came South alone. I had no assistants. I never had an assistant athletic director."

That situation eased somewhat his second year, when sports information director Barry Fratkin moved up to the position of director of the Athletic Educational Foundation, where his major task was to raise funds. In Fratkin's wake as SID came Bob Sheeran, like Fratkin a W&M alumnus. For the first time, the school had back-to-back full-timers in that position, one that had grown more important during the "almost years."

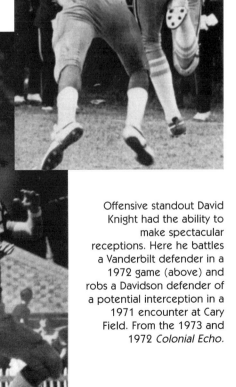

Offensive standout David Knight had the ability to make spectacular receptions. Here he battles a Vanderbilt defender in a 1972 game (above) and robs a Davidson defender of a potential interception in a 1971 encounter at Cary Field. From the 1973 and 1972 *Colonial Echo*.

Greg Freaney (72) tries to stop a Richmond player from getting to quarterback Bill Deery (13) who readies to pass, while Stan Victor (63), Randy Troupe (71), and John Gerdelman (30) set for blocks. Marvin Bass, former W&M player and coach, then an assistant coach at UR stands on the sidelines with arms crossed beside the down marker. From the 1973 *Colonial Echo.*

Carnevale also enjoyed a good relationship with business manager Ed Derringe, who had been an assistant coach under Milt Drewer. Derringe would remain a close friend for decades, said Carnevale. "He was very loyal and dedicated, even though he was one of those who applied for the job that I got."

Carnevale felt that Coach Holtz "had spent money on the program that wasn't in the budget," for items he thought were essential. "We had to face those things. We had to get the Educational Foundation to increase their funding and that was the hardest thing." He said there also was the need to schedule "two or three big-money games a year. Also, the faculty was difficult, too. There was no doubt about some of them being anti-sports. Some athletes weren't allowed to wear their letter jackets to class. It was crazy!"

Other problems swirled around the athletic family that both directly and indirectly involved Root and football throughout his regime. One was consideration of advancing from the newly formed NCAA Division I-AA to Division I. That would have involved expanding the aging Cary Field to hold at least 25,000—nearly 10,000 more than the existing capacity. The project incensed neighboring residents, as well as some faculty and some students. During the same period, there were short-lived demands that the school drop football.

Mark Duffner (77) and Rick Hodgson (64) try to rush a UNC lineman in the close 1973 Tar Heel win, 34-27, at Chapel Hill, North Carolina. From the 1974 *Colonial Echo.*

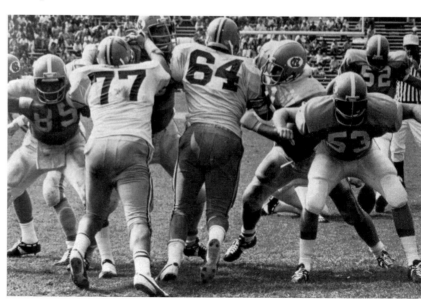

Scheduling also proved to be a bugaboo for Carnevale, even though he helped the Indians make state football history by playing Norfolk State University on September 3, 1977. It was the first time a major state university played a predominantly black school. The Indians hosted the Spartans of the Central Intercollegiate Athletic Association (CIAA) before a capacity throng of 16,500 and triumphed 27-13.

Alumni heatedly objected to playing the predominately black opponent (although the two teams would meet again in 1985) and protested just as vigorously following the game, when it was announced that the Tribe's 1978 Homecoming foe would be James Madison University. At that time, JMU was a non-scholarship, Division III school, not too far-removed from being an all-women's college. As it turned out, the fervor over the stadium, the two games, and the hope that football at the College would be eliminated caused little, if anything, to change.

Despite the hazards and hurdles that cropped up during Root's eight seasons, his tour at the College included plenty of positives. Besides some memorable victories, Root possessed a charisma that attracted hard-working players and assistant coaches.

W&M assistant coach Lou Tepper (far right with W&M hat) gives the defensive team a halftime chalk talk, circa 1974. Tepper went on to become head coach of the University of Illinois in the 1990s. Courtesy of the W&M Sports Information Department.

One such assistant was Bill Casto, a chunky West Virginian who had been a high school coach before joining Root. Later, Casto became athletic director of the Newport News Apprentice School at Newport News Shipbuilding. Apprentice had actually beaten the Indians once, 9-8 in 1938, but by the time Casto took over in 1991, it had become an independent that adhered to NCAA Division III rules.

As a recruiter under Root, Casto felt it was "rewarding" to coach at William and Mary.

> In the face of admission standards, many felt there were restrictions in recruiting. I felt it was a real plus. That's what made it special. That type recruiting was a niche. A coach from the College could point to the high academic standards, and there were enough good players who wanted both good play and good academics. I always felt that if we found the good students, we could compete for them. I used to be astounded at the complaints from the faculty that we wanted to lower admission standards.

W&M's Joe Agee gets off one of his patent punts in The Citadel game in 1974. From the 1975 *Colonial Echo.*

He was at W&M, he recalled, "when the school was struggling to find out where it belonged. It had a very small financial base, really an $18,000 [recruiting] budget. Remember, schools like Pittsburgh, which we played twice, had a million-dollar budget for football." So, what bugged people like Casto for decades was that "the alumni couldn't understand why we didn't win." Changing the Tribe's status from Division I-A to I-AA "was the perfect solution," Casto said.

However, "perfection" seldom develops overnight. Nowhere is this truer than in the William and Mary football story. Particularly vexing to Casto was "the fiasco of some departments at the College trying to drop football and that move to build a new stadium. As a recruiter, it took three or four years to get over it. We kept having to assure high school youngsters, especially in the Northeast, that the school wasn't dropping the sport."

All of those things, Casto said, "were part of that struggle at the school, the struggle of trying to decide where it belonged. Jim Root was caught in the middle of that."

One of the burdens Root shouldered at W&M was dealing with a conception that his offense had that "three-yards-and-a-cloud-of-dust" look. William and Mary's offense was, critics said, patterned after that used by Woody Hayes at Ohio State University. Root had played two years under Hayes at Miami of Ohio, so the connection appeared logical to many. Carnevale said,

Quarterback Bill Deery (14) rolls out looking for a receiver, while Paul Witkovitz, Mark Smith, and Doug Gerek provide protection during the 38-28 loss to Virginia in 1974. From the 1975 *Colonial Echo.*

Quarterback Paul Kruis (12) hands off to Tom Smith (36), whose path is opened up by the Tribe offensive line. From the 1975 *Colonial Echo.*

I encountered a lot of pressure from Root's fifth year on to change coaches. Alumni were disturbed with his Ohio State system. ... It was not an exciting system. I felt the program was going downhill. ... Discipline was down. There were a number of factors, and they included pressure from the Educational Foundation, the Board of Visitors, and the administration.

Nevertheless, Root's credentials were hardly luster-less. His coaching tenure, in which his offense relied heavily on the outside veer, became the longest in school history. The Indians' 7-4 record in 1976 produced the most victories at W&M in a quarter of a century. Despite the ground-oriented offense, quarterbacks Bill Deery (1974) and Tom Rozantz (1976) were All–Southern Conference selections, as was wide receiver David Knight in 1972. Also, tight end Dick Pawlewicz in 1974 and Rozantz in 1978 became W&M's first Blue-Gray All-Star participants since 1952.

Root recalled,

Quarterback Bill Deery (14) talks with fullback John Gerdelman (30) as lineman Kevin Barnes (73) listens during 1974 game. Courtesy of the *Richmond Times-Dispatch.*

I had a fairly complicated system in the sense that we ran the offense from the line of scrimmage. We called a series in the huddle, but the players didn't know where it would go until they got to scrimmage. Linemen had to be smart to adjust quickly. It took a lot of teaching and learning. We always had good quarterbacks and that helped.

He felt that "when I came here, they had good offensive players, but didn't have the [good] defensive players until after 1972." He said that in 1973, recruiters attracted "a great class of freshmen," including Rozantz. On the other hand, "it was one of the

Athletic Director Ben Carnevale (left) joins Rector of the College R. Harvey Chappell, Jr., and W&M President Thomas A. Graves, Jr., to announce the Board of Visitors' decision to continue support of football. From the 1975 *Colonial Echo*.

Students rally in front of the Brafferton to protest against the decision by the W&M Board of Visitors to upgrade athletics, specifically football, but without the win-at-all-cost strategy of one of the proposals. The students' sign reads, "W+M, a college of the students & faculty by the administration for the alumni." From the 1975 *Colonial Echo*.

first years in a long time that we [also] recruited specifically for defense." One such player was Jim Ryan, who became a linebacking standout for the Denver Broncos of the NFL for much of the 1980s.

One reason for Root's difficulty in keeping the Tribe on an even keel, he said, "was the inability of the school to decide what it wanted to do with football." Administratively, the school "was in a quandary." With the threat of the program closing down considered genuine, coaches felt their immediate futures were insecure. Root helped some look for jobs. In particular, he assisted defensive coordinator Lou Tepper (who became head coach at the University of Illinois) in landing a position at Virginia Tech. Hospitalized by a kidney stone, Root recalled, "I phoned Bill Dooley [then the Virginia Tech football coach and athletic director] to recommend Lou, who was as loyal as the day is long."

As Root indicated, he inherited some fine talent, and his first three years sailed along smoothly enough with consecutive records of 5-6, 6-5, and 4-7. That first year, 1972, W&M edged Virginia Tech, 17-16, in the Tobacco Bowl in Richmond behind outstanding play from quarterback Bill Deery. Tech scored the final touchdown and then tried for the game-winning two points on a pass. Defensive back Phil Elmassian "broke it up. He was all enthusiasm. He was all a coach could ever hope for. He was a winner," Root said. (Elmassian would eventually launch a nomadic career as an assistant college coach that took him from one side of the country to the other.)

Ara Parseghian made a surprise visit to W&M football practice in 1976 to see how his former Miami of Ohio quarterback, Coach Jim Root, was doing. The visit occurred just prior to the Ohio University game, while the Indians sported a 4-2 record.

In 1973, William and Mary produced its first winning ledger in six seasons. Highlights included a stunning upset of Virginia Tech and the year-long kicking exploits of Terry Regan, who completed forty-two consecutive attempts at extra points. The season-opening 31-24 W&M triumph ended a Tech winning stretch over the Indians in Blacksburg that had lasted twenty-one years. It also was the first time the Green uniforms had registered two consecutive conquests of the Hokies since 1953. That was near the end of a stretch of fifteen years in which the Hokies went winless against W&M. Included in that period were the seasons of 1943, when the war stopped W&M football, and 1944, when the two teams didn't play each other.

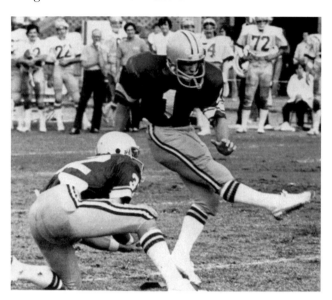

The administration finally took steps at the end of the 1974 campaign that certainly eased the pressures on Root. As Harold Pearson reported in the *Richmond Times-Dispatch* on November 23:

> The Board of Visitors had just concluded two days of meetings with the announcement it had accepted, unanimously, the recommendation of the president.

Dr. Thomas Graves recommended that "there would be no compromising of the academic standards of the nation's second oldest college, but that the athletic program would undergo a re-emphasis." Dr. Graves also said, "I am personally fully committed to this policy and its support."

Kicker Steve Labassi attempts a 47-yard field goal in Cary Field during the 1976 season. He finally kicked two 47-yarders—against Richmond in 1977 and Virginia Tech in 1978—to get into the record books. From the 1977 *Colonial Echo*.

The statements, the *Times-Dispatch* said, were made as the result of a special committee's nine-month study after which most of its recommendations were followed. Committee member Ben Carnevale, the W&M athletic director, said that now "the challenge is there and it's up to us to meet it and do something about it."

The bottom line was that the College would continue to allow grants-in-aid for revenue sports,

A pass intended for UNC's Mike Corbin (83) is intercepted by Kenny Smith (78) during the opening game of the 1975 season. The Tar Heels won 33-7. From the 1976 *Colonial Echo*.

limited by conference regulations. Root's reaction appeared in the *Times-Dispatch:* "You know, you feel tired after a game when you win. After you lose, you feel whipped. I feel tired." Of course, some student and faculty factions were disappointed, although there was satisfaction that no compromises in academic standards would be made.

The day following that announcement, the Indians mauled Richmond, 54-12. "It was one of the best games a team of mine played," Root said afterwards. "And what happened to cause that? I'll tell you—The players suddenly realized they had a school behind them."

Following Root's modestly successful first three years came the 1975 record that plummeted to 2-9. A winless eight-game start included a second-game 20-0 loss at East Carolina, which deserves mention only because of a financial squabble that arose later. The game had been changed to a night contest in order to accommodate ABC, which televised play and paid $250,000 for the privilege. "This was unanticipated revenue," Carnevale said decades later. "We wanted to use the money for raises for the coaches and for all-sports equipment. The administration wanted to use the money to reduce student fees, among several things." Eventually Carnevale had his way, but he said it was not without a struggle.

Another of those eight straight losses was 24-7 to Virginia Tech. But that loss could easily have been

Kevin Barnes (84), at left, prepares to throw a block as quarterback Tommy Rozantz (14) runs the option against UNC in Chapel Hill, North Carolina. From the 1976 *Colonial Echo.*

W&M enjoyed running the quarterback option, which Tommy Rozantz (14) exercised to perfection against Delaware in 1976. Fullback Keith Fimian (44) trails the play. From the 1977 *Colonial Echo.*

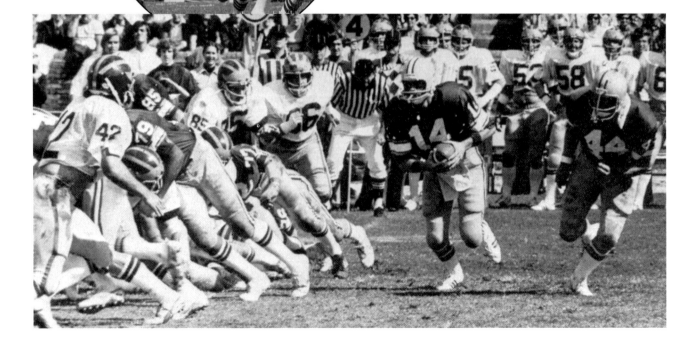

W&M defenders gang up on a Delaware ball carrier. From the 1977 *Colonial Echo.*

Fullback Keith Fimian scores the second of his three touchdowns against Virginia Tech in the Tribe's 27-15 victory in Blacksburg, Virginia. The officials and W&M quarterback Tommy Rozantz signal touchdown. From the 1977 *Colonial Echo.*

labeled a "moral victory," since the Hokies were considered overwhelming favorites. The setting was Norfolk's Foreman Field, home of the Oyster Bowl, and the Norfolk *Virginian-Pilot* predicted a 42-0 Virginia Tech triumph. A crowd of 28,000 saw the game that somehow seemed to trigger a late-year revitalization for what had been a beleaguered Tribe.

The week following the "moral victory," the Tribe defeated Virginia Military Institute, 13-7. That was followed by a 21-17 loss to Colgate before a year-ending 31-21 conquest of Richmond, which saw W&M players celebrate victory by carrying Root off the field. "This bunch has given more than any team I've been associated with," an emotional Root told the media.

The Newport News *Daily Press*—and it wasn't alone—wrote that "the triumph … might save the Tribe coach's job for the second straight year." The story said that a decision was due the following week. Obviously, Root remained, even though Athletic Director Ben Carnevale would say beforehand that "this is one of the toughest decisions I've been involved in."

The late 1975 surge left Root gratified, if nothing else.

The kids came out for those last three games like they were 8-0," he said. "They suddenly had the attitude of an unbeatable team. The coaches couldn't believe it, and the kids' enthusiasm dragged us along.

W&M's kickoff wedge drives forward, opening a hole for Andy Banks (35) in a close game against Rutgers. From the 1978 *Colonial Echo.*

Root insisted that the coaches had known all along that the talent was there.

> We knew we would win. We just didn't know when. An 18-year-old can cause frustration, sure, but you have youthful enthusiasm and excitement that they can transfer to you. Even at zero and eight, they were out there yapping and zipping like they had won the game before. That's when you know you've got a great group.

That "great group" started two opposing trends. The 2-9 record signaled the beginning of steadily growing alumni disenchantment with Root. Conversely, it opened the gates to three consecutive non-losing autumns of 7-4 and 6-5, followed by the 5-5-1 season in 1978.

The Indians' mild, late spurt had carried over into the 1976 season, which opened with a 34-20 upset over VMI and a 14-0 success at the University of Virginia. The surprising of VMI came about mostly because a furious defense caused a flurry of four turnovers in the first thirty-four minutes and then halted a Keydet drive that reached the Indians' 21-yard line with fifty seconds left.

A 20-19 loss to East Carolina followed the victory over Virginia. With 3:22 remaining, the defeat was sealed on a 36-yard field goal by the Pirates' Pete Conaty, at that time the second-leading field goal kicker in the country. On the other side of the ball, a convoluted Tribe kick-

Halfback Jim Kruis (22) takes a break while the Indian defense is on the field. By the end of 1977 he had become W&M's all-time leading rusher with 2,404 yards and currently ranks fifth in that all-time category. From the 1978 *Colonial Echo.*

ing game endured a fumbled punt snap, blocked punt, and missed kick for an extra point.

That defeat, instead of dragging the Indians down, simply set the stage for another Root conquest of Virginia Tech. This one exploded into the books on October 2, 1976, by 27-15 and gave the coach three wins in five contests with the Hokies. For a change, the Tribe's 3-1 record at that juncture made it the only winning team in the state. "It was," shouted Coach Root, "the biggest, best damn win ever for us."

Well, not quite. Nevertheless, Keith Fimian scored three touchdowns while running for 164 yards to help the Tribe control the ball for thirty-eight minutes and charge to a 27-7 lead. Reserves played freely during the final quarter, giving credence to quarterback Tom Rozantz's claim that "we didn't score as much as we could have."

The year included triumphs at Navy, 21-13; at Ohio University, 20-0; and by 23-22 at Cary Field against Appalachian State. What it didn't include was victory over archrival Richmond. The Spiders ended the year by beating the visiting Indians 21-10 and keeping them from becoming the first W&M team since 1947 to win eight games in a season.

The Tribe ledger in 1977 read: six victories against five losses. Still, the season proved to be one fraught with the unexpected. First came the season-opening 27-13 triumph over Norfolk State. On the field, there were few surprises. The Indians' defense sparkled and generally controlled things. End Melvin Martin recorded three sacks, and the visitors from the CIAA were held to only 201 yards in total offense, compared to the victors' impressive haul of 324 yards.

Alvis Lang (29) scoots through a hole provided by the blocking of Rick Wells and John Cerminara (64) in the 1978 VMI game. From the 1979 *Colonial Echo.*

Ed Schiefelbein (86) takes advantage of quickness and a Rob Muscalus (81) block to return a Temple Owl punt in the 22-22–tie game. From the 1979 *Colonial Echo.*

Dusty Rhodes

The story lingers about Dusty Rhodes and a football game at the University of Richmond. An official ran out of patience with the steady verbal attack from Rhodes. He charged Jim Root, then the Indians' coach.

"You get 15 yards for the penalty and 15 more for your coach," said the harassed man in the striped shirt.

"He's not my coach," snapped Root.

"Well, he's on your staff and you'll have to control him," was the retort.

Said Root: "He is on my staff, but I'll never learn to control him!"

John M. "Dusty" Rhodes spent 32 years dedicated to volunteering help of many kinds to William and Mary football players. When he died in 1983 at age 65, he was a recently retired director of the X-ray and EEG laboratory at Eastern State Hospital. That's officially.

Unofficially, he had been described as an assistant trainer at the College. He also was a volunteer member of his local fire department and rescue squad. His hours at games were minimal compared to those he spent attending practices. The combination caused some to accurately describe him as "a classic volunteer."

His involvement with young gladiators ran the gamut from tending injuries to helping solve a seemingly endless span of personal enigmas.

He was no doctor, not even a certified trainer, but he owned the respect of those who were.

He led life to its fullest. Zeal, pride, energy, skill, and an impish sense of humor were all part of the Rhodes legacy. It lives on still.

(—RM)

It was off the field where controversy emerged. William and Mary supporters were against playing the game at all, and others didn't like ending the series. Norfolk State athletic director Bill Archie was one who wanted to keep the relationship alive. When the hosts' athletic director, Ben Carnevale, revealed that Madison, then a Division III school, would replace the Division II Spartans on the Tribe 1978 schedule, Archie said: "I had been looking forward to playing them [W&M] again next year."

Ed Richards wrote in the Newport News *Daily Press:* "It is believed that neither Tribe Head Coach Jim Root nor Madison Coach Challace McMillen were highly in favor of the game."

Late that year, the Tribe defeated East Carolina 21-17 in the Oyster Bowl in Norfolk. Although the game was hard fought and well played, what most remembered was a bizarre development. "I was on the phones in the press box," recalled assistant coach Bill Casto. Quarterback Tom Rozantz, who, the *Daily Press* said, "was simply magnificent," wriggled from tacklers and headed for a long touchdown run. "When Tommy broke loose on the play, I told Root on the phone 'he's gone.' Then I remember shouting 'Oh, my God, what was that?'"

"That" was Jimmy Johnson, who had been the East Carolina head coach from 1946 through 1948. This freezing day he had a sideline pass and a strong hunger for victory. "You could see him in the films as the play broke; he just shot on the field," Casto said. Johnson tackled a surprised Rozantz, who nevertheless kept on going to record a 77-yard touchdown run. Johnson was described in the *Daily Press* as a "giant-sized stranger" … who registered "a good lick that didn't stop Rozantz."

The most poignant part of the incident unfolded later. Casto recalled that Johnson telephoned Root and "apologized and asked to apologize to the team." So, he did before the Indians played in Richmond the next

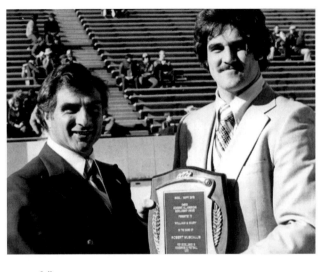

Bob Muscalus receives his All-American plaque from former All-Pro star Nick Buoniconti at the 1978 Sun Bowl. Photo by Cliff Coles, El Paso, Texas; courtesy of the W&M Sports Information Department.

week. Root, said Casto, asked Johnson into the locker room just before the game, and the apology was made. Then Root gave Johnson a W&M cap "and he told him 'we want you on our side.'" Casto's point was simple. "This was a situation that could have been devastating to an older man, and Jim made the guy walk away feeling good."

Daily Press sports editor Charles Karmosky wrote in his column that despite the success, "the Indians must do it all again next Saturday [against Richmond]. Only then can beating East Carolina be fully savored."

As it turned out, lots of Big Green smiles emerged following the season-ender at Richmond. One of the happiest warriors was senior Jim Kruis. He recalled nearly twenty years later that beating Richmond 29-13 before 14,000 was the highlight of his gridiron days. For one thing, Kruis established a Tribe rushing record by gaining 89 yards to give him a career total of 2,404. "They stopped the game to give me the ball," he recalled. He also recanted a bit, adding that "the entire 1977 season was a highlight. Really, the whole atmosphere was great."

Tom Franco (23) turns the corner in a 10-3 win over VMI. From the 1979 *Colonial Echo*.

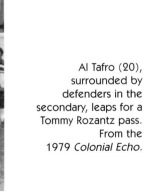

Al Tafro (20), surrounded by defenders in the secondary, leaps for a Tommy Rozantz pass. From the 1979 *Colonial Echo*.

The "Stop the Expansion" sign, on one of the W&M residence halls and the student rally (at right), refer to attempts by supporters of football to get approval to expand Cary Field Stadium in February 1978. A larger stadium, seating at least 25,000 people would be essential for Division I-A football. The Board of Visitors approved the first phase of the expansion, but the project was abandoned when W&M was assigned to Division I-AA football. Hall sign, from the 1980 *Colonial Echo*; rally courtesy of *Richmond Times-Dispatch*.

Kruis remembered the student unrest during his playing days. "I was proud to be a student-athlete. What other students said didn't bother me. I'm proud of having been a player now. I loved it!"

In disposing of the Spiders, the Indians called on substitute senior fullback Craig Cook, who responded by rushing for 138 yards in nineteen carries and a touchdown. Sophomore kicker Steve Libassi gave the hosts a 9-0 lead by kicking field goals of 47, 34, and 38 yards. He also kicked two extra points.

At the end of 1977 and the start of the 1978 season, W&M put together a string of six consecutive wins. Virginia Tech broke the string on September 30, 1978. That's when Tech escaped with a 22-19 victory, much to the delight of 34,000 Lane Stadium patrons and to the long-lasting agony of Root and all William and Mary partisans. Root still insisted in 1996, "I've never had a defeat tear me up so." He called it "the great Lane robbery," a line he readily admitted stealing from the *Richmond Times-Dispatch*.

The stage was set for the painfully bizarre ending when William and Mary took a 19-15 lead. That was strange in itself, because first a 50-yard touchdown pass from Tom Rozantz to Joe Manderfield was negated by a hotly protested call of offensive pass interference. Two plays later, with about 1:30 remaining, the Indians unleashed the same play. This one went in the books as a 59-yard scoring pass from Rozantz to Ed Schiefelbein.

That was only the beginning. Virginia Tech retaliated on the game's last play when officials ruled that end Ron Zollicoffer had scored a touchdown by "catching" a 50-yard pass from David Lamie. The ruling triggered a still-heated debate among those who saw it either in person or on film. Was it a catch, or not?

Tribe defenders Mark Mullady, Steve McNamee, and Terry Havelka seemed to have blanketed the Tech receiver, who maintained, "I caught the ball." The officials agreed. William and Mary players never have. Havelka was quoted in a *Daily Press* story by George Watson as saying that "the ball hit his hands, slid down his chest and hit the ground. It wasn't a touchdown because he never had possession."

Steve Shull (55, far right) rushing to join his teammates to stop a James Madison offensive surge. Madison was first added to the Tribe's schedule in 1978 much to the chagrin of many alumni. From the 1980 *Colonial Echo*.

W&M and James Madison players untangle after an Indian touchdown during a 33-0 shellacking of the Dukes at Cary Field in 1979. From the 1980 *Colonial Echo*.

Halfback Keith Best (18) takes a handoff from Chris Garrity (12), finds an opening, and breaks clear for a touchdown in the 33-0 rout of James Madison. From the 1980 *Colonial Echo.*

Root's distress went beyond the game itself. He "knew we wouldn't get another shot at them," because that was the year the NCAA changed its structure. The Hokies would play at the Division I-A level, and the Tribe would become a Division I-AA member allowed fewer scholarships. (However, the series did continue for several more years.) While many from W&M lauded the change, Root did not. To him it meant the school was "treading water."

> My argument was why shouldn't the top-flight player be able to come to William and Mary for a top-flight education and play a top-flight football schedule? There really is no place for that kind of a student-athlete to go.

As it turned out, that loss to Tech seemed to take the wind out of W&M's sails. The following week, the team played to a 22-22 standoff against Temple and then defeated James Madison 32-7 in a game many howled wasn't worthy of the Indians. However, that win kept them from enduring a losing season. In their final five games, the Indians lost four times, only beating The Citadel by 12-8 to finish at 5-5-1.

The 1979 season, which would be Root's last, saw the record dip to 4-7. Going against Richmond in the next-to-last

Offensive guard Paul Witkovitz (61) celebrates on the sidelines during a 1974 game. Courtesy of the W&M Sports Information Office.

Styles of the game-day football program changed through the years, with the covers often using action photography. Courtesy of the W&M Sports Information Department.

game, the Tribe had only bested Colgate by 28-15; James Madison, 33-0; and Appalachian State, 9-0. Against the Spiders on November 17, 1979, the Indians ended a rut of fifteen scoreless quarters by winning 24-10. That left Root with thirty-nine victories, second most in the history of the College. The year's finale wound up with East Carolina coasting 38-14 before only 9,100 in Cary Field.

Sports editor Charles Karmosky wrote in the next day's Newport News *Daily Press* that Root's career "seems to be hanging in the balance." Carnevale said he hadn't reached a decision. However, Karmosky wrote that "Root's superiors" were concerned about a number of factors, including "the escalating of total scholarships" and the "new stadium situation."

The decision was announced on November 27, 1979. Root and six assistants were fired. Carnevale was quoted in the *Daily Press* saying, "our football program just isn't generating any enthusiasm for the fans. I think it's time for some new leadership and a new attitude."

Root remained in Williamsburg in the insurance business. "At first, I was as depressed as I've ever been. I didn't want anything to do with coaching again." He said in 1996 that he had no regrets. His William and Mary days were, he said, "a real challenge. How many guys get to face down a challenge like we faced, where the administration wavered? First, it said we won't play football, then it said we would. It makes you stop and think."

During that period, when the future of William and Mary football was mired in uncertainty, Root remembered asking alumni: "Two or three years from now what will you do in the fall? You better evaluate what you believe in, or they will do away with football. They're not just fooling around."

Eventually, some influential people listened to him. And thanks to increased financial contributions, slowly the tide did turn. But that didn't happen until the arrival of another—brighter and longer-lasting—era. It hovered just around the corner.

Coach Root talks with quarterbacks on the sidelines at the 1979 Virginia Tech game in Blacksburg. Listening are Alan Drewer (9), starter Chris Garrity (12), and Joe Czerkawski, partially hidden. Photo by Bob Brown; courtesy of the *Richmond Times-Dispatch.*

7
Restoring the Delicate Balance
The Laycock Era
1980 to 1994

Charles M. Holloway

The winds of controversy were still swirling around Cary Field when 31-year-old Jimmye Laycock returned to Williamsburg in the winter of 1979–80 to take charge as the new football coach.

His complex mission: to restore a delicate balance in William and Mary football; to win, of course, but also to measure respectability against victory, to contemplate the difficult distance between aspiration and reality, to weigh pride as well as performance.

Born in Leesburg, Virginia, and a 1970 graduate of the College, Laycock had been a Tribe quarterback under coaches Lou Holtz and Marv Levy in the late 1960s. He began coaching at Newport News (Virginia) High School before moving up to be an assistant coach at The Citadel under Bobby Ross and then offensive coordinator at Clemson.

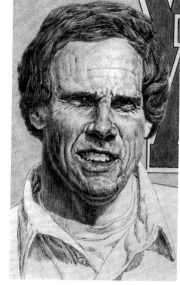

Laycock brought with him some of his assistants from Clemson and The Citadel, and prepared to develop his complex system, rooted in the fundamentals of good football. He owned a powerful will to win and sparkling credentials as player and coach, most recently having directed Clemson's offense during three winning seasons and three consecutive bowl games, most prestigious of which was a 17-15 conquest of Ohio State in the 1978 Gator Bowl.

At William and Mary, he inherited thirty lettermen and six starters on defense, but the offense lacked experience and had an inconsistent record. "There's a lot of work to be done," he remembers thinking. "We only had one quarterback in spring practice—he had to take all the snaps. But," he added, "we hope to have an exciting offense and a hard-nosed defense."

Jimmye Laycock '70 returned to W&M in 1980 as the first alumnus to become head coach since Jack Freeman in 1952. Drawing by Jim Caldwell '82; courtesy of the W&M Sports Information Department.

The new coach arrived in the midst of a rancorous and divisive struggle over the quality and style of football played at the College, a debate that had pitted faculty against administration, students against almost anyone in authority, and alumni against the status quo. "I couldn't pay too much attention to all that," he said. "I came here to coach football."

"I do remember," he recalled later, "that I came into town in the middle of a snowstorm. … The stadium was being renovated, and the locker rooms were all torn up. … It was a little disorganized around here."

As he began preparing his first teams for combat, Laycock was entering a decade still absorbing major sociopolitical changes in the broader society and at the College. Steadily growing numbers of African-American students began to attend previously all-white institutions, and among them were sought-after athletes whose fathers and grandfathers had generally been relegated to black colleges in the South. Title IX of the Education Amendments of 1972 (reinforcing the landmark Civil Rights Act of 1964) prohibited sex discrimination in public educational programs or activities, and sent a widening series of shock waves across almost every campus in the country. The

amendments, followed by a class action suit in 1974, brought major changes in funding for men's and women's programs, including those at William and Mary, and all three of the College's traditional sources for funding intercollegiate athletics were severely challenged.

The Athletic Educational Foundation had to adopt new campaigns to maintain and expand its funding sources; student athletic fees began to rise; and factors like ticket prices and gate receipts had to be reassessed. Yet, by 1976, the College had already begun to award its first grants-in-aid to women athletes.

The federal mandates clearly altered personal and institutional behavior, and helped bring new perspectives to every sport. For a time, there was some resentment and objection to the law. The *Colonial Echo* in 1980 remarked that "Title IX brings money to women's athletics at the students' expenses," and noted that there was "confusion and consternation" over the resulting higher student athletic fees.

Meanwhile, over at Cary Field, Laycock had to play the 1980 season by relying on freshmen and inexperienced players. It would take a transitional year—perhaps two—before he could install his own intricate system of offensive-minded football.

From the outset, his first team was also dogged by injuries to key players, like Andre Hopkins, Bill Swertfager, and Bernie Marrazzo.

Tribe receiver Ed Schiefelbein (86) goes up top to grab one of his six catches in the 27-7 loss to Wake Forest. Photo by John Berry; from the 1981 *Colonial Echo*.

On a hot and humid September evening in Raleigh, using fifty-three of its fifty-five players, William and Mary lost its opener 42-0 to a "very fine North Carolina State team," as Laycock put it. "They executed a nearly perfect football game … and we made too many mistakes."

The Indians developed slowly, losing to VMI by 13-10, and dropping a 7-3 squeaker to a "bigger, stronger, more experienced" Virginia Tech team that scored the winning touchdown with just over half a minute to play.

The Campus Restaurant on Prince George Street catered to College students, frequently athletes, throughout its history. George Dallas (right) operated the eatery for about twenty years until it closed in 1986. Photo by Bob Scott; from the 1981 *Colonial Echo*.

But Navy rolled to an impressive 45-6 victory, and gloom settled in as Homecoming approached with a game against Wake Forest. Despite a supportive home crowd, the young team was clearly outmatched. Although W&M kept it close during the first half (10-7), the team failed to score again and lost 27-7.

Finally, on the season's sixth weekend, Laycock's team scored a comeback win, 17-14, against Dartmouth before a home crowd of 15,000 that included some 2,000 fans from New England. Down 14-3 at the half, the Tribe rallied for two scores after intermission. There were plenty of heroes, led by defensive guard Bo Short, who at 5'10" and 202 pounds had been called "too small" to play, but was named Eastern College Athletic Conference (ECAC) defensive player of the week as well as AP's Lineman of the Week. The ECAC was a loose collection of Eastern colleges and universities, which were not in football conferences.

In the surprise win, Tommy Franco carried thirty-two times for 120 yards, and junior quarterback Chris Garrity completed sixteen of twenty-eight passes for 132 yards, demonstrating a balanced offense.

The next week, William and Mary traveled to New Jersey to play a highly favored Rutgers team, which had narrowly lost to top-ranked Alabama and stood at number seventeen in national polls. Some experts rated the smaller, slower Indians as five-touchdown underdogs, but on a rainy night and with a soggy field, W&M pulled what Laycock called an "unforgettable" upset of the Scarlet Knights, 21-18.

After being down 10-7 at the half, the Indians scored 15 points in the third quarter, with touchdown passes from Garrity to Ed Schiefelbein and then a 2-point conversion. Paul Tyner, a senior defensive end intercepted his second pass, and the Tribe marched 47 yards for a score to lead 21-10. W&M then held on for the win.

"It's been a great feeling to see the football program turn around and see a new positive attitude develop," senior defenseman Steve McNamee said after the game. Others noted that despite a 2-6 record at that point, W&M was beginning to develop the spirit of a winner.

Quarterback Chris Garrity (12) makes sure his team is set before taking the snap from center Bill Swertfager (61) during the Wake Forest game. Photo by John Berry; from the 1981 *Colonial Echo*.

University of Virginia alumnus Jim Copeland served as W&M Athletic Director from 1981 to 1985. Courtesy of the W&M Sports Information Department.

Reality set in, however, at home against Delaware, when the Tribe lost 7-3, partly "because we didn't get the big play," Laycock said. "We played hard, spirited football, and we've lost three games this year by a total of only 11 points. [Garrity] had a rough afternoon. ... He wasn't sharp, and lacked protection." Freshman Laszlo Mike-Mayer kicked "an unbelievable" 41-yard field goal in the driving rain.

The following week a powerful East Carolina team outscored William and Mary 31-23 in a game of "mistakes and big plays," Laycock said. "They had too much speed and strength." The W&M highlight was Garrity's "big league performance," passing for 158 yards and completing fifteen of twenty-three, and Laycock knew he had found an important key to his offense.

On Armistice Day 1980, William and Mary traveled to Cambridge, Massachusetts, to play Harvard in a decrepit Charles River stadium that Sports Information Director Bob Sheeran called a combination of a Greek arena and a Roman circus. On a dark and windy day, the Tribe was doomed by a poor first half and lost 24-13. "Our players weren't mentally ready for the game early on," Laycock said, as his team fell behind 21-0 at the half. "But, we battled back and forced some turnovers. We were erratic on offense, and we never could get the key third down conversions."

The final game of year was a 26-14 loss to Richmond. "Richmond had Redden and too much speed," Laycock said. Barry Redden carried thirty-four times for 191 yards and two touchdowns. W&M started the game as an underdog but closed to 10-7 before faltering. Garrity completed eighteen of forty-four for 192 yards, but the team again made "costly errors, bad snaps, and fumbles."

During 1980, Athletic Director Ben Carnevale announced his retirement, and the College named James Copeland, a 36-year-old native of Charlottesville and U.Va. graduate to replace him. Copeland had played football at Virginia and then with the Cleveland Browns before becoming assistant athletic director at the University of Missouri.

The Cary Field stadium controversy carried over into 1981 and bitterness persisted much of the year. At one point, a student poll showed that 87 percent of the students were against the proposed expansion, whose financial price tag had steadily increased to something over $2 million.

W&M running back Tommy Franco (23) carries into and over the VMI line in the Keydets' 13-10 victory over the Tribe at Cary Field. Photo by John Berry; from the 1981 *Colonial Echo*.

Back Jeff Sanders scores after a 41-yard pass from Chris Garrity against East Carolina in the 1981 game in Greenville. Courtesy of the W&M Sports Information Department.

In the spring of 1981, there were a few rays of sunshine, caused mostly by what Laycock called a "very good spring football practice." He was considerably more sanguine approaching his second season with a good nucleus of veterans, an excellent recruiting year, and a somewhat less demanding schedule with five home games.

Garrity had already set three Tribe passing records in 1980, and one of his talented receivers, Kurt Wrigley, was back as a junior. The line was also bigger and more mature, anchored by Doug Martini at guard. And, the injured Marrazzo became available for service in the backfield.

However, the team got off to a rocky start, losing its first four games. First came a trouncing by Temple in Philadelphia, 42-0; then a closer loss to Miami of Ohio, 33-14; followed by a 47-3 Virginia Tech romp at Blacksburg on September 19. Finally, poor execution cost the Tribe in a 31-14 setback against VMI in Lexington.

Then the team found its stride and won four of its last six games. In an important and satisfying 12-7 win over Dartmouth on October 10 at Hanover, New Hampshire, W&M's confidence returned. Freshman Jeff Powell, an outstanding recruit from Nashville, Tennessee, showed his electrifying speed in a 54-yard touchdown run that helped win the game. He paired with Kurt Wrigley to lead all receivers.

Senior Owen Costello spearheaded a tough defense along with Joe Lucas, and freshman safety Mark Kelso emerged as a potentially great performer in the secondary, leading the team for the year with fifty-six unassisted tackles and six interceptions.

Around 1980, sales of sports related items began to grow. This W&M Indian clock was offered at the Williamsburg Pottery and other area retail outlets. From the collection of Wilford Kale.

Sophomore tailback Bernie Marrazzo (33) drives toward the James Madison goal line in W&M's 31-19 win over the Dukes in 1981. Photo by Rob Smith; from the 1982 *Colonial Echo*.

When the Indians returned home in mid-October to play Marshall College, W&M showed its new-found assurance, trouncing the Herd 38-7, and Marrazzo was in top form, running for 149 yards.

October 24, the team traveled to Annapolis to face a tough Navy team (8-4-0 in 1980) under George Welsh and came away on the short end of a 27-0 score. But by Halloween afternoon, the Tribe was at home and ready for Madison's Dukes and scored a solid 31-19 victory, passing for 241 yards and rushing for another 146.

After a disappointing loss to Harvard (23-14), William and Mary surprised East Carolina on the Pirates' turf 31-21, running up thirty-one first downs and 403 yards passing, while holding ECU to just 19 yards in the air.

Against Richmond at Cary Field, the Tribe won its final game with some ease, pulling ahead in the third quarter en route to a 35-21 win. Garrity passed for more than 300 yards, hitting Powell and Jeff Sanders for key receptions and three touchdowns.

Looking back over the steadily improving Tribe play, the *Colonial Echo* reported that fans at Cary Field were beginning to feel that "football is fun again at the stadium." Cary remained a cozy, friendly place on autumn afternoons with its lush, high-crown field of natural grass, its sheltered brick portico, spongy synthetic oval track, and restful vistas looking onto campus dorms, and later, the new University Center.

There were always the rambunctiously cordial tail-gate parties behind the home stands, the pesky single-engine plane that buzzed the stadium trailing a commercial message, the erratic new scoreboard (that sometimes appeared to be under the control of aliens from space), the primitive restrooms, and the total lack of potable water (though you could buy a cupful for $1.50).

And then there were the bands, the reliable home ensembles, and sometimes bizarre but always entertaining visitors, like the grunge groups from the Ivy League, and, of course, the marching Dukes from James Madison University, at least 200 strong, sometimes garbed in Prussian uniforms with shining helmets.

In December of 1981, after the completion of an encouraging season, the abrasive stadium conflict suddenly ended, not with a bang, but with a bureaucratic whimper as the NCAA voted to move William and Mary and forty-four other college football programs from Division I-A to Division I-AA.

Athletic Director Copeland responded by saying that the change would "have very little effect on the Tribe football program." He told the *Alumni Gazette,* "We plan to continue to play our traditional rivals, including University of Virginia, Virginia Tech, and Navy."

The change, however, did reduce the number of grants-in-aid from eighty-nine to seventy-five over a two-year period. According to the *Alumni Gazette,* Laycock did not expect the change to affect him personally. "I like being here. I'm not caught up in the fact that we are not I-A, and I don't feel I have been pushed back in my career."

When strong-armed Stan Yagiello, a 6', 180-pound sophomore from Livingston, New Jersey, began throwing during the 1982 season, Laycock was sorely tempted to ignore the admonitions of Texas coach Darrell Royal: "When you put the ball in the air three things can happen, and two of them are bad." Laycock was willing to take the chance, and during the season, he put the ball in the air 55 percent of the time, averaging 250 yards per game as compared to 90 on the ground.

Laycock's attitude toward the passing game was clear:

Coach Laycock took time after a spring practice to talk with longtime Newport News Daily Press Sports Editor Charles Karmosky (right). Courtesy of the W&M Sports Information Department.

It's where we should put our emphasis. The system is complicated and it takes time to learn. ... But due to the intellectual nature of our players, we are able to tackle a more intricate offense.

With Yagiello and Dave Murphy at quarterback, and some talented receivers on hand, Laycock was beginning to

Back Jeff Sanders maneuvers through the East Carolina defense at Cary Field. Photo by Mark Beavers; from the 1983 Colonial Echo.

Stan Yagiello

Stan Yagiello came to the College in the fall of 1981 as a slender six-footer from Livingston, New Jersey, bringing with him a strong arm and credentials as an All-State passer. Four years later, he left William and Mary with a box full of records for most passing yards ever by a quarterback, 8,249; total offense, 8,168; and most touchdown passes, fifty-one. He played a key role in turning around the Tribe football program during the early 1980s.

Despite fighting off shoulder injuries that interrupted his career (he missed seven games in 1983), Yagiello improved steadily each year and began setting personal and game records each time he handled the ball.

Against powerful Penn State in 1984, Yag hit twenty-seven of forty passes for 251 yards and two touchdowns. In another "typical" game that the Tribe barely won against Lehigh, 31-29, he tossed for 306 yards and two touchdowns, completing 50 percent of his attempts.

Yagiello, an excellent baseball player, was selected by the Cleveland Indians after high school but turned down the chance, commenting, "The value of an education was much higher than anything Cleveland could offer." He did, however, play a lot of baseball for William and Mary in the spring. Coach Ed Jones said, "Stan is just an all-around outstanding player. He handles the bat well, can bunt. ... At second he made the hard plays look easy."

During his years at the College, Yagiello kept up the standards of the student-athlete despite the demands of two sports. "I've always found that playing a sport makes me budget my time better," he said.

After completing his degree with a major in business administration, he said he hoped that athletics would remain an important part of his life.

If I make it in sports, I'll be able to use my education in the off-season and when my career is over. ...It takes a lot of pressure off you when you have an education to back you up."

After graduation, Yagiello tried his hand at the pros, playing for a time with the Pittsburgh Gladiators (of Arena Football) and then the New York Knights in 1988, but retired to pursue business enterprises in New Jersey. He remains in touch with the College, looks in on occasional games, and actively supports the Athletic Educational Foundation. (—CMH)

Quarterback Stan Yagiello throws one of his perfect spirals. Courtesy of the W&M Sports Information Department.

perfect an offensive philosophy that had roots in his own years as a passer and in his days coaching quarterback Steve Fuller at Clemson. But he still needed to develop and polish a coordinate running game and to strengthen defense.

"We have a promising foundation upon which to build," he said as the year be-gan with thirty-eight lettermen and eighteen starters. He had two speedy tailbacks, Jeff Powell and Marrazzo, but had lost Martini at guard and Bill Wilsey at tackle.

Sophomore Kelso, who had a spectacular 1981 at free safety and was named Rookie of the Year by the Williamsburg Quarterback Club, headed the Tribe's defensive secondary.

Miami of Ohio, playing at home in Oxford, ran back the 1982 open-ing kickoff for a touchdown en route to a 35-17 victory. But the Indians struck back quickly as Yagiello threw for a record 414 yards in his first game, while Jeff Sanders set a school record of twelve receptions. But the William and Mary defense was shaky. "We were our own worst enemy," Laycock said. "We gave up too many big plays."

Senior end Kurt Wrigley in one of his typical moves. In 1982 he surpassed David Knight's mark for season reception yardage with 911 yards. Photo by Mark Beavers; from the 1983 *Colonial Echo.*

Burgesses Day ceremonies September 18, prior to the VMI game, included the ritual payment of quitrents mandated by the College's Royal Charter. Virginia Gover-nor Charles S. Robb, as had his predecessors, received Latin verses as payment for 20,000 acres of land tendered the College by King William and Queen Mary—in this case, two poems translated into Latin by Classical Studies Professor J. Ward Jones. The traditional ceremony affirmed the felicitous blend of academics and athletics that makes the College unique.

In a statistically close game, W&M defeated VMI 24-12 to even its record. Yagiello, Powell, and Wrigley teamed up for 270 passing yards, with Yagiello completing eigh-teen of thirty passes and Powell scoring two touchdowns. Powell, who also ran the hurdles in the NCAA Indoor Championships, possessed blinding speed on the foot-ball field.

The son of a Nashville, Tennessee, pathologist, Powell majored in pre-medical studies and psychology at the College, and became symbolic of the scholar-athlete on campus. "I chose William and Mary because of its outstanding academic programs and the opportunity to compete in both football and track," he said in 1982.

It was a different story the next week, against a big, strong Virginia Tech team in Blacksburg. One headline read "Ouch! Tech 47, William and Mary 3." Coach Laycock said, "We played our poorest game of the season."

W&M defenders Steve Zeuli (99), Joe Lucas (90), and Guy Crittendon (14) cut off the escape route of an East Carolina quarterback in the Tribe's close 31-27 loss to the Pirates. Photo by Mark Beavers; from the 1983 *Colonial Echo*.

The subsequent loss to Rutgers, 27-17, was, according to Laycock "hard to explain."

> There were times when we played good football, times when a crucial mistake erased all the good. ... The front line was inconsistent, but we had good play from [guard] Mario Shaffer and Lee Glenn at center.

Yagiello threw three interceptions, but the team gained 295 yards through the air, with Wrigley leading all receivers with four catches for 68 yards. Murphy alternated at quarterback and tossed for 136 yards while directing two touchdown drives. Marrazzo rushed ten times for 60 yards.

The next week against Dartmouth at home, Murphy and Dave Scanlon led the way to a 24-16 win over a scrappy Dartmouth. Laycock lauded a defense anchored by linebacker Lonnie Moore's fourteen tackles and one interception for 34 yards and a touchdown.

Playing at Annapolis in a 35-mile an hour wind, the Tribe "ran into a buzz saw in the form of the U.S. Naval Academy football team," Laycock said. The Midshipmen piled up 39 points to 3: "They executed flawlessly and played aggressively," Laycock added.

Late in October the Indians played a strong game at James Madison, but lost 24-18 before a Harrisonburg Homecoming crowd of more than 14,000. "Our players were emotionally ready," Laycock commented in the Athletic Educational Foundation newsletter. "They had bounced back from Navy ... and we evened it up when Jeff

Powell ran for 68 yards without one shoe to tie it at 7-7." But fumbles and interceptions took the Tribe out of contention. "I couldn't ask much more from our defense," Laycock said. "They played their hearts out."

After that, Delaware, the nation's second ranked I-AA team, raced to a 62-21 win at Newark. The Blue Hens were "virtually unstoppable," rolling up 646 yards in total offense, but the Indians tried to respond through the air, throwing fifty-eight times for 365 yards. It was not enough.

William and Mary lost a close game to Brown, 23-21, spoiling the Tribe's Homecoming. Laycock said: "I cannot fault the players. … It was heartbreaking to see them come up short. … We were in control of the game most of the day." Yagiello played all the way, making only a couple of "sophomore mistakes." Scanlon, the 158-pound tailback, was player of the week, rushing twelve times for 75 yards and one touchdown.

East Carolina University came to Cary Field the following week, bringing some 1,500 loyal fans, who saw their team take a 7-0 lead on Tribe fumbles. Yagiello led the Tribe to a 14-14 tie at halftime, only to watch ECU swarm back with a quick touchdown in quarter three and add a field goal to lead 24-14. Yagiello responded by hitting Marrazzo in the end zone, but the extra point failed and the visitors were still ahead by four points. Then Wrigley's reception of a toss by Marrazzo moved the Tribe ahead 27-24. Outweighing William and Mary 40 pounds per man, ECU's bulk finally prevailed in the waning moments, and they scored once more to win 31-27.

During the spring of 1983, football practice and a number of other normal College activities were disrupted by events that focused world attention on Williamsburg and the College. In late May, the Summit of Industrialized Nations convened in town and William and Mary Hall became media headquarters. Advance work for the international gathering of seven heads of state actually

At halftime during a winter 1984 basketball game, Coach Laycock presents offensive guard Mario Shaffer with his Kodak All-American Football Team award for play during the 1983 season. Shaffer also was named to the Associated Press First Team I-AA team. Photo by Tim Steeg; from the 1984 *Colonial Echo*.

Chris Hugh and Mike Sutton slap high fives at the end of the Richmond game, which the Tribe won, 25-14. The 1983 victory gave W&M its first winning season since 1977. Photo by Tim Steeg; from the 1984 *Colonial Echo*.

Junior fullback Bobby Wright (30) scraps for every yard against JMU. Photo by Tim Steeg; from the 1984 *Colonial Echo*.

began during the winter. Many members of the athletic department were temporarily moved while extensive renovations were made to "the Hall" in anticipation of the arrival of some 3,000 reporters and broadcasters from a variety of nations.

Having won only 10 of his first 33 games, Laycock regarded 1983 as a pivotal season for him and for his experienced offensive unit, led by Yagiello now a junior. Ten of eleven starters on offense returned, and the team began to take on aspects of a veteran squad. Laycock noted that while the Indians had averaged 345 yards of offense per game during 1982, they had also suffered costly turnovers.

"Our emphasis this year will be on not turning the ball over and not forcing throws," he said. "Stan is as good as there is talentwise—experience will enable him to get better and better." It proved an exciting year, in which the Tribe repeatedly came from behind to post a 6-5 record, its first winning year since 1967. The season also opened the door to the Laycock era of triumphs. Through 1996 there would be only two more losing seasons—1987 (5-6) and 1991 (5-6).

The year began at home with a 28-14 win over VMI. Using a strong and balanced offense, the Tribe showed a quick offensive line that blended with superb passing by Yagiello, who threw for 200 yards and three touchdowns against the Keydets.

Two tough losses followed—one to Delaware, 30-13, and another to North Carolina, 51-20. But against the Tar Heels, who owned one of the nation's top defenses, the Indians nonetheless rolled up 352 yards.

The "Cardiac Kids" revived themselves in a thriller to beat Yale, 26-14, in New Haven. After trailing 14-7 in the third quarter, the team pulled ahead when Scanlon ran for 81 yards and Murphy, filling in for an injured Yagiello, tossed for 179 yards passing. Defensive stars included linebackers Brian Black and Jim McHeffey, tackles Bob Crane and Mike Murphy, and, of course, Kelso at free safety.

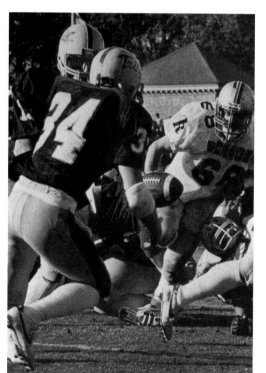

Quarterback Dave Murphy hands off to Dave Scanlon (34), who scored ten touchdowns during the 1983 season. Photo by Tim Steeg; from the 1984 *Colonial Echo*.

After this tight game, the Tribe moved on to play Dartmouth in Hanover, New Hampshire, on October 8. They were not disappointed, though it turned out to be another scary encounter, with William and Mary behind most of the game, before pulling it out 21-17.

Scanlon turned out to be the hero, carrying twenty-two times for 85 critical yards, most of them in the final quarter when he scored three touchdowns. A smallish tailback at 5'9" and 171 pounds, Scanlon scored the last time on a pass from Murphy with only 49 seconds left. Murphy, in his first role as starter, completed sixteen of thirty-three for 135 yards, and guided the team to its sixth straight win over Dartmouth.

Before a crowd of 12,000 on Burgesses Day, William and Mary nosed out James Madison 24-21. Limited to only 69 yards on the ground, the Tribe found alternate ways to win its third straight, using a tough defense to create five sacks.

Next, Rutgers came to Williamsburg and rudely interrupted a gala Homecoming Weekend by beating the Indians, 35-28. Trailing, 35-21, at halftime, the Tribe took the kickoff and marched from its 10-yard line to the Rutgers 10, where Bobby Wright seemingly plunged over the goal. But the officials disagreed, and the Tribe never made up the deficit.

On Sunday, October 30, the headlines read "Hokies Maul W & M 59-21," and that pretty much summarized the feeling. "We didn't tackle, we got blocked, and we gave up long pass plays," Laycock said. On the other hand, the partisan crowd of more than 28,000 at Lane Stadium in Blacksburg was elated, as was the team. Quarterback Mark Cox said, "We thought we could score every time we had the ball." And they did, rolling up 617 yards in offense.

At Huntington, West Virginia, W&M blasted Marshall, 48-24, in an exciting game. It was the team's fifth win in nine starts, and quarterback Murphy was on fire. He

For the first time in decades, sports protests in 1984 were not directed at the football program. Cuts were proposed for six other men's and women's sports, and this sign reflects students' support of those programs. Photo by Tim Steeg; from the 1984 *Colonial Echo*.

Mark Kelso

In his very first year as a defensive back, Mark Kelso quickly made his mark, being selected as rookie and defensive player of the year, leading in unassisted tackles, and being named All-State safety. He also rose quickly in the academic world, and was twice named an Academic All-American. During his years at the College, he maintained a 3.5 GPA in business management.

At about 6' and 180 pounds, Kelso was neither the biggest nor fastest defender, but his innate quickness and intelligence made him one of the Tribe's all-time best players and a draft choice for the pros. At William and Mary, he remains high on the list of top tacklers and made a record number of twenty pass interceptions during his career.

Kelso won a coveted NCAA postgraduate scholarship and received honorable mention on the 1984 All-America team. He recalls, "I never really had any aspirations of playing pro football. I went to William and Mary for the balance of academics and athletics."

After being picked by the Philadelphia Eagles in the tenth round of the draft and later dropped, he went to the Buffalo Bills, and, by 1988, was their defensive captain. That same year he was named All-Pro by *Sports Illustrated* magazine. His Bills coach, Marv Levy, once said Kelso's looks were deceiving: "You look him in the face and you think he's a choirboy. He's tough."

Now retired from the Bills and self-employed, Kelso remains active, as he has been for years, in community work with children, and Buffalo's Roswell Park Cancer Institute. He also works with Athletes in Action and Athletes Against Drunk Driving.   (—CMH)

turned in a memorable performance, completing twenty-eight of thirty-eight passes for just over 400 yards, hitting wide receiver Mike Sutton eleven times including two touchdowns.

The following week, W&M traveled to Greenville, North Carolina, and wished it had not. Apparently irked by a press clip that quoted Mario Shaffer as saying "There's nobody on the rest of our schedule that we can't beat," East Carolina showed little mercy in crushing the Tribe 40-6. "We did it to get respect," one ECU player said later. The Pirates ran up 20 first downs and 325 yards in the first half to lead, 27-0.

In their last game of the year the Indians beat Richmond 24-15 in a continuation of the closely contested series. Laycock's team won with superb defense and sharp passing by Dave Murphy, who completed twenty-three of thirty-nine and finished his record-setting season with 2,093 yards in the air. On a sun-dappled afternoon before 10,000 fans at Cary, Scanlon ran for 140 yards to reinforce a balanced offense that totaled 207 yards on the ground and 223 in the air. "We dominated the game," Laycock said. As players poured champagne over Laycock in the locker room, he said, "This was by far the biggest game the kids have played since I've been here. ... This team learned how to win this year."

At the conclusion of the season, it was announced that two years hence William and Mary would join the new Colonial Football League (Division I-AA). New opponents would include Bucknell, Colgate, Holy Cross, Lafayette, and Lehigh, but state rivals like Richmond and James Madison would remain on the schedule. Ultimately, in 1985 the W&M Board of Visitors decided the College would not become a member of the Colonial Football League because of scholarship

Joe Monaco (96) chases Princeton quarterback Doug Butler during W&M's 33-28 victory in 1985. Courtesy of the W&M Sports Information Department.

and recruiting restraints. It would be another eight years before the Tribe would join a football conference.

The 1984 season turned out to be one of highs and lows for Laycock and his team, but ultimately produced another winning season (6-5). The Indians started strongly, winning three of their first four games, and were ranked as high as number eight in the I-AA national polls.

The *Alumni Gazette* noted at the start of the year that Laycock had "developed one of the most explosive passing offenses in college football. ... During 1983 the Tribe threw the ball an average of almost 40 times per game, completing over 63 percent."

Offense alone had not been the secret of Laycock's success during the first rebuilding years. He assembled a long-lasting nucleus of assistants; his recruiting program began to take hold; and his gift for the game—his intuition and shrewdness—became evident.

Strong defense, led by Kelso, and varied offense won the VMI game early in the new season. The Keydets were held to only 17 yards of second-half offense as W&M won 24-13.

Playing Delaware at home, the Tribe faced the eighth-ranked I-AA team, and came away with a narrow 23-21 victory. It did not begin well, with Delaware intercepting a Yagiello pass on the first play and driving for a touchdown, but W&M struck back, scoring the next 17 points to lead, 17-14, at the half. With eight minutes left, Delaware marched 90 yards to eat up the clock, score, and lead with about one minute remaining. Yagiello directed a 70-yard march, featuring a blend of sideline passes and rushes to end with fourth and one on the Delaware 18 and seven seconds to go. Then he scrambled and hit an open Sanders for the winning touchdown, and the first win over Delaware since 1923.

Home tickets for VMI, Lehigh, and Temple at Cary Field during the 1984 season. From the collection of Wilford Kale.

Merritt "Dirk" Gibson, tailback, shows his form in a 1984 game. Courtesy of the W&M Sports Information Department.

Lonnie Moore (56) comes to aid Joe Lucas (90) with a sack against Dartmouth in a 1982 victory.

Ron Gillam (21) is embraced by Mark Kelso (23) and greeted by Stan Yagiello (7) on the sideline after a successful play. From the 1985 *Colonial Echo*.

On a two-game winning streak, William and Mary traveled north to face perennial powerhouse Penn State before more than 80,000 fans. Despite the lopsided 56-18 score, Yagiello had his best day of the season, completing twenty-seven of forty passes for 251 yards and two touchdowns.

Still on the road against James Madison, William and Mary slipped to a 10-6 halftime deficit, coming back to win 20-10. "It was a case where we overcame some things, and that's what a good team will do," Laycock said.

Although line stalwarts Lee Glenn and Graeme Miller had a great game against Temple, and Yagiello completed twenty-four of forty-three passes for 282 yards, the Tribe fell to a solid Temple team at home, 28-14. William and Mary rebounded the next week to pull off the upset of its season on Burgesses Day, scoring a 24-3 conquest of fifth-ranked Boston University.

But then came two weeks on the downslope of the rollercoaster year with road losses to Virginia Tech, 38-14, and Wake Forest, 34-21. Tech's defense, led by All-American Bruce Smith, dominated play. Against Wake Forest, on a hot and humid day, the Tribe went in physically banged up from the Tech game.

On November 3, the team returned to Cary Field, facing Lehigh and backed by a Homecoming crowd estimated at 17,000. TV star Linda Lavin '59 served as grand marshal of a parade through town before the game and received

A football manager tapes up Graeme Miller's ankle during a 1984 game. Photo by Dan Webster; from the 1985 *Colonial Echo*.

the Alumni Medallion during the festive weekend. This was the last Homecoming for outgoing College President Thomas A. Graves and his wife, Zoë.

Senior Yagiello broke several school passing records, leading a 24-10 march to victory over Lehigh. He completed twenty-five of thirty-seven passes for 280 yards and one touchdown. Tight End Glenn Bodnar caught seven passes for a career high of 111 yards.

The team's late-season 48-39 win at Colgate was a thriller in which W&M trailed, 14-0, until Yagiello hit Bodnar for 26 yards and a touchdown to make it 14-7 at the half. In the third quarter, Bobby Wright stunned the Red Raiders with a 98-yard kickoff return, but Colgate struck back before the Indians ran up three straight touchdowns. Kelso's 84-yard punt return with three minutes left ended the scoring.

In the last game of the year, Richmond's Spiders outlasted the visiting Tribe, 33-31. After the game, the winners' coach, Dal Shealy, said, "I thought it would come down to the last play or the final minute." He was right. In a fast-moving game, the two teams amassed a cumulative total of 883 yards. William and Mary made one desperation drive in the last quarter and scored, but couldn't control an onside kick, and the game was over.

In 1985, W&M witnessed a changing of the guard. In the president's office, Tulane University Law Dean Paul R. Verkuil '61 replaced Dr. Thomas A. Graves as president; in William and Mary Hall, alumnus John Randolph '64 replaced Jim Copeland as athletic director.

It was also a watershed year for Laycock. After five seasons as head coach, his sophisticated system had matured, he had a seasoned staff, and his recruiting

Male cheerleaders selected "formal" attire for the 1984 Homecoming game against Lehigh. Photo by Liz Radday; from the 1985 *Colonial Echo*.

By the 1980s game-day football programs featured action photographs on the cover, like this one for the VMI game, September 8, 1984. Courtesy of the W&M Sports Information Department.

Michael Clemons

Anyone who saw Michael Clemons play football at William and Mary, or anywhere else for that matter, would understand exactly why the exciting runner came to be known as "Pinball." Even though he held all sorts of records at Dunedin High School in Clearwater, Florida, and was named student-athlete of the year, some (including William and Mary coaches) felt that at 5'5" and barely 165 pounds he might be too small to do much in college.

So much for conventional wisdom. An economics major at the College, Clemons helped Jimmye Laycock build the Tribe teams of the mid-1980s into a powerful force. Inevitably known as Mr. All-Purpose for his versatility at running and receiving, Clemons made the ECAC All-Star team in 1985, and set a raft of individual and team records each year he played.

During 1985, he ran for 714 yards on 179 carries, and also set a school record by catching seventy passes and scoring twelve touchdowns. Coach Laycock observed during this period that "Michael is a threat every time he touches the ball."

Clemons capped his college career by being named to the Kodak All-America first team in 1986. That award certificate hangs proudly in Laycock's office along with others for Mario Shaffer, Reggie White, and Steve Christie.

The durability, shiftiness, and speed that helped Clemons become one of the Tribe's all-time rushers, also stood him in good stead when he moved into the pro ranks.

Following graduation, Clemons went to the Kansas City Chiefs in 1987 and, despite a good rookie year, was released. He then moved to Tampa Bay, where he returned punts for a year before finding his niche in the Canadian league.

By 1990, Clemons had been named most outstanding player in the Canadian Football League, where he led the Toronto Argonauts to the Grey Cup championship game. In their fast, wide-open game, which puts a premium on motion and speed, Clemons excelled once again, and, in 1990, set a single-season pro-football record for all-purpose yardage (rushing, receiving, and kick returns).

Clemons has become one of the most popular players in the league. He is sought out by fans wherever he goes in Canada speaking on behalf of the CFL and its programs.   (—CMH)

Michael Clemons (2) makes a spectacular jump over the line for a touchdown against Delaware in the 1985 game. Photo by Lawrence I'Anson; from the 1986 *Colonial Echo.*

techniques had begun to pay off. "The fact that we emphasize our academic framework is why our players come here in the first place," he said.

Laycock had already recruited some Academic All-Americans who were also outstanding athletes. Football players did not live in separate luxury dorms, but in fraternity houses and other student resident halls; they did not eat at special training tables; and they took the same courses that everyone else did. NCAA rules limited their practice time to twenty hours a week.

William and Mary football players maintained a graduation rate of 84 percent, at least as high as the student body as a whole, putting the College in a class with Stanford, Duke, and other highly selective institutions. National publications, such as *U.S. News & World Report,* rated the College as the number one public university, especially in its dedication to teaching. Tranquility had settled over the once-contentious relationships between faculty and athletics.

The *Colonial Echo* characterized 1985 as "the best in 20 years." If nothing else, it was the first time in twenty years that there had been three straight winning seasons. Late in September, Hurricane Gloria laid siege to the campus for forty-eight hours—students

Michael Clemons breaks away from a Delaware lineman only to run into two more Mud Hens. From the 1986 *Colonial Echo.*

hunkered down in dorms, windows were taped, the pizza market thrived, and a quasiholiday atmosphere developed. Torrential rains came, with strong winds, but little damage resulted, and the storm passed. Late one afternoon during the storm, campus police were surprised to find the football team out practicing. "It was part of our preparation," assistant coach Matt Kelchner said. "We need to be ready to play under any conditions."

As the schedule unfolded, the year was tougher than the final 7-4 record suggested; the Green and Gold seemed to live and die in the final minutes of close games. Five were decided in the last three minutes. The loss in early September to Wake Forest, for instance, saw the Deacons score in the last 58 seconds and break a tie to win, 30-23. William and Mary led 14-10 at the half on passes from Yagiello to Harry Mehre and on Michael Clemons runs. Yagiello passed for nearly 300 yards, but the Deacons dominated the rushing game and held on to win.

Next, W&M won a close one against Norfolk State, again using Yagiello passes to Gilliam and a spectacular 94-yard kickoff return by Clemons to pull it out 28-23 after

John Netals reaches for a perfect pass from Stan Yagiello (7) in rear. From the 1986 *Colonial Echo.*

holding a 21-0 lead in the third quarter. The following week, the Tribe eked out a 17-16 win over a tough Delaware team at Cary Field. The Blue Hens dominated the game in total offense and had twenty-seven first downs to W&M's seventeen, but Clemons scored on a short run to put the Tribe ahead, 17-10. Then, with about a minute to play, Delaware scored, but the Indians stifled a 2-point conversion attempt to win. That elevated W&M to seventh in the national I-AA poll.

In a statistically close contest, W&M rode Yagiello's arm for 412 yards to beat James Madison, 31-14, as Clemons scored twice on short runs, and Brian Morris made a 20-yard field goal.

William and Mary then began a grueling series of six road games. "I wouldn't wish that schedule on my worst enemy," Coach Laycock said. The Tribe proceeded to beat Harvard, 21-14, in Cambridge on October 5, passing for 306 yards and running for another 129.

Coaches review plays on the sideline at Cary Field. From the 1986 *Colonial Echo.*

The Indians lost a one-sided decision to Division I-A Virginia Tech at Blacksburg 40-10. Tech led 17-7 at the half and never looked back, holding W&M to 22 yards on the ground.

The following week in Philadelphia, Temple ground out a 45-16 win after leading 38-9 at the half. Yagiello passed for two touchdowns and more than 300 yards, but the running game produced only 43 yards against Temple's 389.

In game eight, the Tribe went to Lexington and lost a heart-breaker to VMI, literally in the last seconds of the game. After being tied 14-all at the half and leading 38-31 in the fourth quarter, W&M saw the

Keydets score twice and then convert a 2-point play to win 39-38. Mixing passes and runs, VMI marched the length of the field with about a minute left and successfully gambled for the two extra points.

Against Lehigh, visiting W&M lost in almost every statistical category—total yards, first downs, even passing yardage—but somehow won, 31-29, in the last quarter. Yagiello passed to Ron Gilliam and Clemons for scores, and hit more than half of his passes.

At Princeton, on November 9, the Tribe built a 27-14 lead at the half, only to see it melt toward the end, but still pulled out a 33-28 win.

In the November 16 Homecoming game against Richmond, before some 18,000 fans, William and Mary won 28-17 as Stan Yagiello completed his career with three touchdown passes. He also compiled a single-season record of 2,962 yards in 1988 and went into the books as one of W&M's great all-time passers.

In beating the Spiders, Clemons ran for 105 yards and caught eight passes for three touchdowns. The 5'6", 160-pound junior set a single-season record with seventy pass receptions.

Students try to tear down a goal post at Cary Field following W&M's 28-17 victory over Richmond. The team finished 7-4 in 1985, then Laycock's best, and good for 16th in the Division 1-AA national rankings. From the 1986 *Colonial Echo*.

Following the victory, William and Mary fans swarmed onto the field and pulled down the goal posts. As one observer put it, "the south goal post looked like a pretzel." "Winning seven games, beating Richmond in Homecoming, and doing it all for seniors were big factors for us," Laycock said.

Several seniors set their sights on professional careers. Yagiello, a three-year starter who had rewritten most of the College's passing records, tried out with the Washington Redskins. Bodnar

Quarterback Ken Lambiotte, here with Laycock, transferred from the University of Virginia and led W&M to its first Division I-AA playoff game in 1986. Photo by M. B. Gleason; courtesy of the W&M Sports Information Department.

John Cannon

When John Cannon first came to William and Mary from Holmdel, New Jersey, he hadn't given much thought to the possibility of playing football in the pro ranks once he graduated. "I took a couple of years in pre-med but then switched to business," he once said. "I never really thought about a football career."

Even after he had demonstrated his strength and special skills in college and then with the Tampa Bay Buccaneers, he still kept his perspective by working to earn his stock-broker's license. From 1982 to 1987, he started seventy-five games with Tampa, and eventually then retired in Florida, where he works as a broker, and involves himself in a number of charitable organizations, including Toys for Tots and the Special Olympics.

Success and commitment came early to Cannon; he graduated second in his high school class, and also saved a child's life when he was a lifeguard at the Jersey Shore.

Though he was sidelined with injuries from time to time, he made his mark on the Tribe teams of the early 1980s, ending 1981 with a total of 50 tackles, and piling up a career total of 218 while at the collegeCollege. Once characterized by a teammate as "a huge man blessed with amazing speed and agility," Cannon, who was 6'4" and 240 pounds, could run the 40-yard dash in 4.7 seconds.

As a senior, Cannon, an All-American candidate, led the team in sacks and was named defensive player of the year by the Quarterback Club. (—CMH)

Ticket stubs from three 1986 home games, two of which the Tribe won, defeating Princeton and Harvard. From the collection of Wilford Kale.

also sought a pro career. Kelso signed as a free agent with the Buffalo Bills and became an all-time great.

As the 1986 season began against Colgate, the big question was, "Who can replace Stan?" The answer came quickly. Laycock had a strong-armed but untested senior, Ken Lambiotte, a 6'4", 190-pound transfer from the University of Virginia. On opening day against Colgate, Lambiotte electrified the crowd by passing for 303 yards and three touchdowns in an easy 42-21 win. Laycock said afterward, "I felt comfortable with Kenny right from the start."

As the season progressed, Clemons demonstrated why he had been characterized as "one of the finest all-purpose backs in the country." A big, seasoned offensive line was anchored by 6'6", 263-pound Archie Harris, called "one of the biggest and strongest men ever to play at William and Mary." Harris was enrolled in law school at Marshall-Wythe, but eligible as a fifth-year senior. Mehre returned, along with Dave Szydlik to lead a strong receiving corps, and freshman kicker Steve Christie from Ontario, Canada, was starting to get rave reviews.

The first three wins were precursors of a potent offensive season that produced 9 wins and 3 losses. Following Colgate, VMI fell, 37-22, and then Bucknell, 30-13, as the Tribe went 3-0, scoring 109 points in the process.

Against VMI, W&M trailed early but roared back with three straight touchdowns. Christie kicked well, including a 28-yard field goal toward the end of the game. At Bucknell, the Indians overcame another sluggish start and put together an explosive second half to win 30-13 over the Bisons.

The Harvard game at home was a 24-0 shut-out for the Indians, a defensive victory, but one-sided in almost every department; Christie added another of his long field goals. Writing for the syndicated Cox News Service about the game, Bob Dart characterized it as "football the way it was meant to be ... played on a sunny Saturday afternoon on God's own grass ... involving the two oldest institutions of higher learning in America."

In the fifth week of the season, William and Mary triumphed, 44-34, at Lehigh and demonstrated its scoring power with three aerial touchdowns, including one flea-flicker that Michael Clemons tossed to Harry Mehre for a score.

Playing Delaware at Newark in mid-October, William and Mary was led again by Lambiotte, who threw two touchdowns in the opening quarter and a total of 288 yards in the air. Michael Clemons ran for another 108, and the defense held All-American Rich Gannon in check. Following this game, the Tribe was ranked third in the nation in the I-AA poll.

Linebacker Dave Pocta (54) was an important factor in W&M's defensive unit. He zeros in on a VMI ball carrier in the 1986 game and later was named to the All-Eastern College Athletic Conference team. Courtesy of the W&M Sports Information Department.

But on October 25, the James Madison Dukes outslogged the Indians, 42-33, in the rain in Harrisonburg. It was close at the half—Madison led 28-24—but the Dukes outgained W&M and most of the Madison scores came on runs. Christie kicked a 43-yard field goal despite the elements.

On November 1 in Charlottesville, William and Mary scored a remarkable 41-37 win over Division I-A Virginia under lowering skies, in a misty rain. Many called it the game of the decade. A Homecoming crowd of 35,000 was stunned when the Tribe matched U.Va. score for score, and the half ended 17-17. Lambiotte beat his former school with 307 yards in the air and five touchdowns, two by himself on short run-

Four University of Virginia defenders go after a Tribe ball carrier in the November 1, 1986, game in Charlottesville. W&M upset the Cavaliers behind the quarterbacking efforts of former U.Va. player Ken Lambiotte, who threw five touchdown passes and passed for 307 yards. Photo by C. James Gleason; courtesy of the W&M Sports Information Department.

Archie Harris

Not much more than ten years ago, Archie Harris was in his first year of law school at Marshall-Wythe, but also striking fear into the hearts of opponents on the football field as a 6'7" 270-pound offensive tackle. He was, and remains, an imposing and remarkable figure both athletically and professionally. After completing his law degree in 1989, he moved to Washington, D.C., where he is an attorney with the firm of Keller and Heckman.

The 1983 media guide characterized Harris as "a big, powerful second-year lineman who has all the tools to be a standout college player." It was eminently accurate. After coming to William and Mary from Richmond, Virginia, with credentials as an All-State star, he had moved easily and quickly into his tackle slot and, by 1986, was playing as a fifth-year senior in law school. In 1985 he won second team ECAC honors and became an on-field leader, carving holes in the opposing line for the likes of Michael Clemons.

Harris began setting precedents early in life and worked as a 13-year-old page in the Virginia General Assembly. His parents and his godfather, former governor L. Douglas Wilder, encouraged him to follow a career in law after he had earned a National Achievement Scholarship in high school and later compiled a near-3.0 GPA as a government major at William and Mary.

While Harris still follows football and sometimes returns to Williamsburg to take in a game, he never seriously considered the pro game and moved directly onto his career path. (—CMH)

ning plays. Christie hit two field goals, one for 40 yards, and Mehre caught a touchdown pass early in the game. Subsequently, Lambiotte was named *Sports Illustrated*'s offensive player of the week.

Laycock's coaching psychology was clearly evident during critical short-yardage conditions at the Virginia goal line, when he twice confidently went for the touchdown instead of the field goal. Both times it worked.

Early in November, the Princeton Tigers came to Cary Field and left with a 32-14 loss. By the third quarter, William and Mary had built a 32-7 lead, and cruised to the win, running up 430 yards total offense. Dave Pocta led a strong defensive effort. After the game, Princeton Coach Ron Rogerson said, "We couldn't stop Michael Clemons, but neither could anyone else."

The tables were turned, however, when a strong Holy Cross team, ranked second in the I-AA poll, visited the stadium. Despite the Homecoming crowd and a rainy afternoon, the Crusaders used a strong rushing game and accurate passing to build a 17-7 lead by the third quarter, and added two touchdowns in the fourth for a relatively easy 31-7 victory.

The final game's 21-14 defeat of Richmond completed a 9-win regular season and assured W&M of a playoff spot. After falling behind 14-7 in the third quarter, the Tribe gathered momentum with strong passing by Lambiotte and consistent running by Clemons, who scored twice.

Just after Thanksgiving and before a surprisingly small home crowd of 5,700, William and Mary entered the I-AA playoffs at home against their old nemesis, Delaware. Unfortunately, it was no contest this time around. As one writer described the game, "Gannon sliced and diced the Tribe." Future pro quarterback Gannon dominated play, and Delaware won easily 51-17 in a dramatic reversal of the season's first meeting in October. The Blue Hens were superior in every department, surging to a 20-9 score at the half, and holding the Tribe to only 8 more points. Christie contributed three field goals.

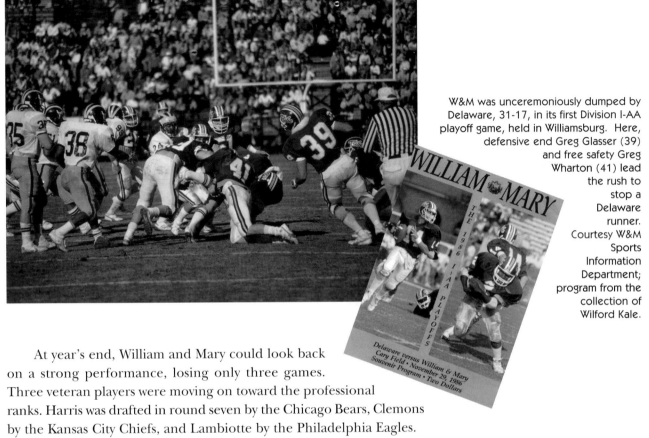

W&M was unceremoniously dumped by Delaware, 31-17, in its first Division I-AA playoff game, held in Williamsburg. Here, defensive end Greg Glasser (39) and free safety Greg Wharton (41) lead the rush to stop a Delaware runner. Courtesy W&M Sports Information Department; program from the collection of Wilford Kale.

At year's end, William and Mary could look back on a strong performance, losing only three games. Three veteran players were moving on toward the professional ranks. Harris was drafted in round seven by the Chicago Bears, Clemons by the Kansas City Chiefs, and Lambiotte by the Philadelphia Eagles.

Different challenges faced the 1987 Indians with the loss of several stars. A host of returnees provided the nucleus. One of the real surprises was rapidly developing junior quarterback John Brosnahan, who joined Dave Wiley as co-captain. Brosnahan came to the team as a walk-on, but before 1987 ended, he was recognized as tenth best passer in the nation in I-AA efficiency, passing for seventeen touchdowns and more than 2,000 yards.

Things did not begin well for the Tribe, which traveled to Johnson City to play East Tennessee State in W&M's first indoor game at ETSU's cozy, 12,000 seat mini-dome. The Tribe could not contain Tennessee's veer offense, which rolled up 348 yards on the ground and 204 more in the air to win, 49-25. It was a learning experience for William and

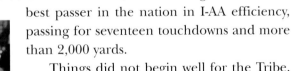

John Brosnahan took over the quarterback job in 1987 and in two years passed for 2,970 yards. Here he brings the crowd to its feet scoring two of the teams for touchdowns against Bucknell in 1987. Photo by John l'Anson; from the 1988 *Colonial Echo*.

Mary as Christie contributed one of the bright spots, hitting a school record 53-yard field goal. Looking back at ETSU, Laycock said, "They didn't make any mistakes. ... They always seemed able to make the big play."

Still on the road, the Tribe played Navy at Annapolis on September 12 and came

away with a convincing 27-12 win. Before a crowd of some 20,000, the inspired Indians shocked the Naval Academy and took a 27-0 lead just before the half. "We corrected our mistakes against ETSU," said linebacker Kerry Gray. Navy Coach Elliot Uzelac summed it up: "We played really bad."

By the time it reached Colgate for the third game, W&M was ranked third in the I-AA poll, but this did not impress the Red Raiders, who surged ahead 17-7 at the half and held on to win 19-7. Brosnahan was rushed all afternoon, and the Tribe running

Erick Elliott (8) crashes through the Bucknell line en route to a 118-yard rushing day. Photo by John I'Anson; from the 1988 *Colonial Echo.*

game sputtered, averaging only 1 yard per carry.

William and Mary returned to Cary Field on October 3 to play Lehigh on a windy, rainy day, salvaging a 28-27 win with a last-minute surge. Despite the weather, Brosnahan hit Mehre for three long touchdown passes.

For game five, the Indians traveled to New Haven and lost a frantic 40-34 decision to Yale. The Bulldogs played well, and took advantage of a porous W&M defense, blocking two Christie punts.

The following week against Delaware at home, W&M saw its early 14-6 lead vanish and fell behind at the half, 21-14. Unable to score after intermission, the Tribe lost 38-14, although Brosnahan threw for 165 yards and two touchdowns.

Home to the James Madison Dukes before another big crowd on October 24, W&M outscored the highly rated visitors in total offense, but not points, and saw victory slip away, 28-22. Brosnahan completed nineteen of thirty

Assistant Coach Don McCaulley, defensive coordinator, talks with linebackers Todd Scruggs (85) and Todd Lee (55) during the 1987 Yale game. McCaulley served for ten years on Laycock's staff retiring in 1990. Photo by Kathleen Durkin; from the 1988 *Colonial Echo.*

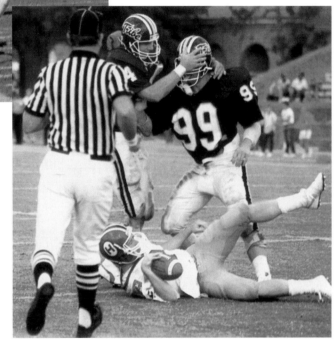

Receiver Harry Mehre scampers down the sideline in the 1986 Harvard game. Courtesy of the W&M Sports Information Department.

passes for 229 yards, including one dramatic strike to Mehre in the end zone. But he also had two interceptions.

Its record sagging at 2-5, William and Mary moved down to Tidewater on October 31 to play VMI in Norfolk's Oyster Bowl and came away with a 17-6 triumph. The defense allowed only 168 total yards, and a strong running game, led by tailback Eddie Davis, made the big difference.

In the next game at home, Bucknell could not mount much offense, scoring only two field goals, as Tribe running backs Erick Elliot, Eddie Davis, and Tyrone Shelton ran roughshod in William and Mary's 31-6 win at Cary Field.

Next, the Tribe visited Holy Cross, again first in the Division I-AA rankings, and went home convinced after a 40-7 drubbing that insured a losing record for the season. W&M played a strong first half and trailed only 14-7, but the Crusaders roared back with 26 straight points to win handily.

At year's end, William and Mary once again faced Richmond. The Spiders came to Cary Field and went home empty, scoring only once in the fourth quarter. The 20-7 victory left the Tribe record at 5-6.

Brad Uhl (99) paced the team with 138 tackles in 1987. Courtesy of the W&M Sports Information Department.

The 1988 season began with a short commute to Charlottesville and ended with a historic 7,000-mile road trip to Tokyo, Japan, where William and Mary competed in the postseason Epson Ivy Bowl, held January 8, 1989, against a team of Japanese all-stars.

Playing a strong Virginia team in its first game, the Tribe actually led 17-10 at the half, but gave up two quick touchdowns in the third quarter and never recovered, losing 31-23.

At VMI on September 10, before a crowd of just over 9,000, the Indians found their stride, piling up 232 yards on the ground and winning easily, 30-7. New leaders began to emerge, among them fullback Shelton, who had come to campus as a walk-on and developed into an offensive weapon. Davis and newcomer Robert Green also showed their running skills, and Craig Argo moved in for his first start at quarterback.

Next came a 14-6 conquest of invading Lehigh. During this game, Mehre set a school record with eleven pass receptions for 158 yards, including two touchdowns on passes from Argo, who hit twenty-one of thirty-three passes for 207 yards.

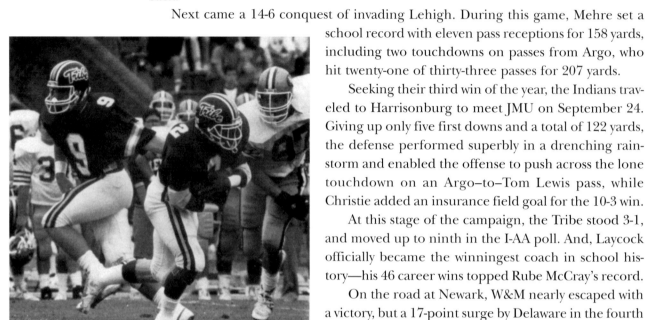

Seeking their third win of the year, the Indians traveled to Harrisonburg to meet JMU on September 24. Giving up only five first downs and a total of 122 yards, the defense performed superbly in a drenching rainstorm and enabled the offense to push across the lone touchdown on an Argo–to–Tom Lewis pass, while Christie added an insurance field goal for the 10-3 win.

At this stage of the campaign, the Tribe stood 3-1, and moved up to ninth in the I-AA poll. And, Laycock officially became the winningest coach in school history—his 46 career wins topped Rube McCray's record.

On the road at Newark, W&M nearly escaped with a victory, but a 17-point surge by Delaware in the fourth quarter downed the Tribe, 38-35. W&M started in a deep hole, but charged back to go ahead, 35-31, on a fourth-down play at the Delaware 10. Laycock eschewed a chip-shot field goal and opted for a successful pass play from Argo to Mehre in the end zone. However, Delaware marched back 58 yards in three plays to win.

A week later, at home, William and Mary revised the script. Christie's late 42-yard field goal gave the team a 33-31 victory over New Hampshire, which missed a long field goal attempt in the waning minutes.

Villanova visited Williamsburg for the season's seventh game, which ended in a 14-14 draw, the first tie for a Laycock team. Christie sought to break the deadlock with a field goal in the final seconds, but the

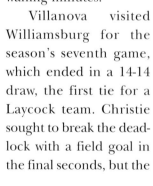

Back Robert Green (2) takes a handoff from quarterback Craig Argo (9), 1988 era. Courtesy of the W&M Sports Information Department.

Fullback Larry Black (35) powers behind right guard Scott Perkins (69), right tackle John Menke (70), and tight end Matt Shiffler (89). From the 1988 *Colonial Echo*.

Members of the W&M football team pay a minute of silent tribute to the late Emperor Hirohito before the start of the Epson Ivy Bowl game at Yokohama Stadium, south of Tokyo. The Emperor, who died the day before the game, at age 87, had visited Williamsburg and the College in 1979. Associated Press LaserPhoto.

Wildcats blocked it. Regardless, this became a memorable day for the peerless Canadian kicker who completed two other field goals to tie the College's single-season record. On the ground, freshman Robert Green put in a full day, rushing for 106 yards and receiving Brosnahan passes for another 77, including one touchdown.

October 29, between the hedges in Athens, Georgia, some 80,000 University of Georgia fans watched W&M take on a major I-A opponent and hold them even for a full quarter. But then form settled in, and the Bulldogs made it 42-17 at the half on the way to a 59-24 final score. Argo, playing in his hometown, passed for 308 yards and two touchdowns, and Green piled up 76 yards rushing and 87 receiving.

At Homecoming the following week, the Tribe beat Division II Wofford, 30-14. Alert defensive play shut out the Terriers in the second half as Green scored three W&M touchdowns.

Defense again prevailed in the win over Colgate. All the Raiders could produce was a field goal from 32 yards out as the Indians won, 28-3. William and Mary penetrated the Colgate line for eight sacks, leaving the visitors with a total of minus-39 yards in offense.

Losing the Richmond game 24-19 on November 19 removed a bit of luster from a 6-4-1 season, but the Spiders pulled off three big plays toward the end, all resulting in touchdowns and victory. Christie kicked two field goals, and Brosnahan threw for 173 yards, but Richmond's strong ground game made the difference.

William and Mary played its first postseason game overseas on January 9, 1989, flying fourteen hours to Japan to participate in the Epson Ivy Bowl against the Japanese all-stars. Football had been played in Japan for some fifty years, and 200 Japanese university teams competed during a season that generally paralleled ours.

Arranged by alumnus Mark McCormack's International Management Group, the exhibition contest was developed to initiate a sports-culture exchange between the two nations and to promote American football in Japan. It had been two full generations since the great Japanese-American quarterback Art Matsu first stepped on the

Coach Laycock displays the first Epson Ivy Bowl trophy in Yokohama, Japan, after the Tribe defeated a Japanese college All-Star team, 73-3. Courtesy of the W&M Sports Information Department.

Fullback Tyrone Shelton was a fire-plug type player, who averaged 4.6 yards per carry in 1987 and 1988. Courtesy of the W&M Sports Information Department.

field in a William and Mary uniform and left his own indelible impression on football at the College.

The Tribe's goodwill visit coincided with the death of Emperor Hirohito, but despite the national concern and general solemnity, the game was played as scheduled. The 73-3 romp by W&M, was one-sided but amiable as the larger, more experienced Americans scored pretty much at will, and Green won MVP honors, gaining 166 yards and making two touchdowns.

Eight months later the Tribe beat Colgate 17-13 at home, starting one of its best seasons ever, losing only two and tying one before a postseason defeat in the NCAA playoffs. Argo played the whole game at quarterback, hitting fourteen of twenty-five for 178 yards. The two-pronged running attack by Green and Alan Williams added 185 yards on the ground.

The following week in Lexington, junior quarterback Chris Hakel substituted for injured Argo and sparked the Tribe to a 24-17 win. Off to a slow start on a soggy, rainy day, the team fell behind 9-3 at the half, but revived, with Hakel's strong passing and running, to score 21 points in a row.

On September 23 at Palmer Stadium, a 14-point, fourth-quarter Princeton surge gave the Tigers a 31-31 tie with William and Mary after the Tribe had led 20-3 at the half. Hakel passed well, especially during the first half, but Princeton ground out 506 yards in total offense for the victory.

Moving on to Scott Stadium at the University of Virginia, William and Mary kept it close for a little while with two Christie field goals in the second quarter, but dropped a 24-12 decision to the Cavaliers.

Game number five saw William and Mary rebound with a come-from-behind 27-24 win over Delaware at Cary Field. Christie kicked two field goals, one a record-tying 53-yarder in the fourth quarter, which proved to be the winning margin in a hard-fought game that pitted Delaware's ground game against Tribe passing under Argo, who had recovered quickly from knee surgery.

Against Boston University in the Oyster Bowl, it was the Argo, Shelton, and Williams show as the Tribe piled up 527 yards in offense and beat a stubborn BU team, 13-10. Argo completed twenty-two of thirty-five passes, Shelton ran for 154 yards, and Williams caught nine passes for 110 yards. Christie's two field goals again provided the victory margin.

Next, at Villanova, William and Mary dropped its second game of the year, 20-17, after playing a strong first half and leading 10-3. Villanova racked up eleven first downs to three in the second half and shut down the usually potent Tribe offense.

Still on the road, William and Mary took on Lehigh in Bethlehem, Pennsylvania, and unleashed its most productive game of the season, winning 55-39. During a four-

Quarterback Chris
Hakel takes the snap
from center Greg
Kalinyak with Reggie
White at left tackle in a
1989 game. Courtesy of
the W&M Sports
Information
Department.

possession onslaught, the Tribe scored four touchdowns in the second quarter and held a 38-17 halftime lead.

Playing East Tennessee State at Cary Field on Homecoming Day, William and Mary was able to extract a measure of revenge for the drubbing it took from the Buccaneers in 1987. This time, the Tribe delighted more than 14,000 fans by pulling out a hard-fought 34-28 triumph in the fourth quarter.

In the next to last game of the regular season, W&M played James Madison on Veterans Day and came away with yet another close victory, 24-21, scoring 11 points in the last quarter. After trailing 21-10 at the half, the Tribe tightened its defense, holding the Dukes to only 75 yards, while the offense generated 200 yards and three touchdowns. Three Christie field goals played a critical role.

With a playoff berth at stake, the Indians played host to Richmond and worked their way to a convincing 22-10 victory. William and Mary controlled the game early, stacking up 15-0 advantage as Christie hit three field goals and Argo ran 18 yards to score his second rushing touchdown of the year.

The good news was that William and Mary made the playoffs; the bad was that the opponent was Furman, the defending national I-AA champions. The Tribe fell behind badly at the start, but cut a 17-0 deficit to 17-10, when Shelton scored on a short run and Christie kicked a 34-yarder to end his career with 279 points, an all-time record. During the second half, the statistics and scoring all went to the Paladins, who rolled up twenty-three first downs on 324 yards rushing and another 78 passing to win going away, 24-10. Nevertheless, the Tribe's season record of 8-3-1 was one of the best in history, and set the scene for an even better performance in 1990.

Linebacker Jeff Neilsen was a walk-on who was an Academic All-American in 1990 and 1991. Courtesy of the W&M Sports Information Department.

Steve Christie

What are the odds that a world-class badminton and soccer player would come to William and Mary from Canada to major in fine arts and end up setting all the College's records for kicking the football?

Alumnus Bill Watson '79, once an All-American soccer player, thought they might be pretty good, at least in the case of Steve Christie. He recommended the young Oakville, Ontario, player to Jimmye Laycock, and the coach took it from there.

Christie already had a fine reputation as a soccer player, and as a pretty good place kicker in American-style football. After a visit to Williamsburg and a tryout, he decided on the College, and became an instant success on the field.

In 1987, Christie was named rookie of the year, and ECAC placekicker of the year. By the time he graduated in 1990, Christie set William and Mary records for career points, 279; field goals, fifty-seven; points after touchdown, 108; and longest field goal, 53 yards—which he hit three times. To show his versatility, he also ranked as the fourth best punter in the nation in 1988.

While at William and Mary, Christie continued his interest in art and art history, and upon graduation married Alison Tabb '90. He began his professional football career with the Tampa Bay Buccaneers in 1990 and 1991, but, in 1992, moved to the Buffalo Bills, coached by Marv Levy, Tribe coach, 1966–68. Christie still plays for the Bills and continues to build a record-setting career.

During 1994, he kicked his 100th field goal, and is already on the books as the most accurate field goal kicker in NFL history, with a percentage of 80.65. In his second championship game, 1994, Christie kicked a 54-yarder to set a Super Bowl record.

Christie, who now lives with his family in Williamsburg, collects impressionist paintings, and with his wife, is involved in the horse racing and breeding business during the offseason. He also works in several community endeavors in Canada, New York, and Virginia.   (—CMH)

The 1990 record-breaking season started badly in the heat and humidity of a late summer evening in Charleston, South Carolina, where the Indians lost a 34-31 decision to The Citadel. An end zone interception of Hakel's final pass in the fourth quarter stopped a desperate 73-yard march and closed out play.

But the next week at home, a strong defense combined with Hakel's passing to push the Tribe past Villanova, 37-14. The junior quarterback completed sixteen of twenty-seven for 222 yards, while Green and Shelton combined to run nearly 200 yards.

On a rainy Parents Weekend, the Tribe defense treated visiting Connecticut rudely and shut them out for three full quarters before the Huskies trimmed the final count to 24-7. Shelton ran 98 yards, and Hakel passed for 235 yards and three touchdowns.

In game four, the Indians traveled to Charlottesville and gave notice of their developing momentum. In a wide-open game against a highly rated Cavaliers, W&M led 27-21 at the half. Unfortunately, Virginia responded with a stunning, 29-point third quarter that effectively ended the game. Despite Hakel's 326 yards passing, Virginia amassed nearly 700 yards and won 63-35.

Steve Christie holds the W&M career scoring mark of 279 points, 1985–89. Courtesy of the W&M Sports Information Department.

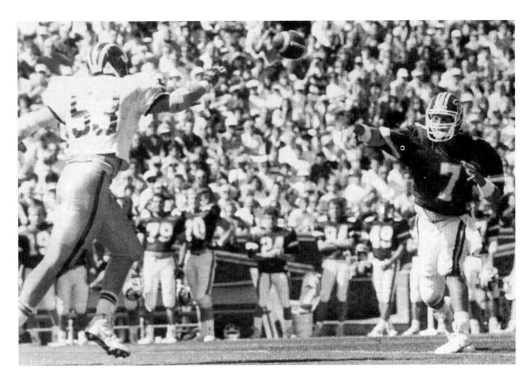

Quarterback Chris Hakel (7) sends one of his "bullets" past a Delaware defender in 1989. Courtesy of the W&M Sports Information Department.

On October 6, the Tribe visited Newark to spoil Delaware's Homecoming celebration, before a crowd of more than 21,000. Behind 12-7 after three quarters, William and Mary mounted a seventeen-play drive that resulted in Hakel scoring on a short plunge and a two-point conversion for a fragile 15-12 lead. Shelton scored an insurance touchdown, and the extra point completed the Indians' 15-point quarter.

The next week, in the 44th annual Oyster Bowl, William and Mary scored almost at will, crushing VMI, 59-47, as Green picked up MVP honors, carrying fifteen times for 163 yards and scoring three times. The game's combined point total was the highest in a W&M football game.

The Tribe then went on another scoring spree, this time against Bucknell at Cary Field, winning 45-17 after building a 10-0 first-quarter lead. Green ran for more than 100 yards and three touchdowns.

Scoring was again the name of the game the following week as Hakel connected for three touchdowns and rushed for another, leading W&M over visiting Lehigh, 38-17.

On a fine November Saturday under blue skies, William and Mary celebrated the 1990 Homecoming by rallying from a 28-24 fourth-quarter deficit and running its season record to 7-2 with a 38-28 win over Furman. The dynamic duo of Green and Shelton combined for 306 yards on the ground, and Hakel hit sixteen of thirty passes for 282 yards.

As a junior, Mackenzie "Mac" Partlow was recognized as the best lineman in 1989 and received the George Hughes Award. Courtesy of the W&M Sports Information Department.

Beyond the solid victory, there was further reason to celebrate during the reunion weekend, because Walter and Betty Zable, classes of 1937 and 1940 respectively, announced their major commitment of $10 million to the College's Campaign for the Fourth Century. They joined College officials in dedication ceremonies on the ancient field, designating it as Walter J. Zable Stadium at Cary Field.

At this point in the football season, William and Mary had risen to ninth in the national I-AA poll and was looking toward the strong possibility of a playoff berth again. The team traveled to Harrisonburg for another encounter with the James Madison Dukes and came away 31-21 winners. The closely contested game saw Green run for 155 yards to spark a steamroller offense that totaled 508 yards.

The Tribe won its final regular season game at Richmond Stadium, 31-10, piling up 21 second-quarter points after shutting out the Spiders in the first half. This victory marked the 100th meeting between the historic rivals in the nation's fourth longest collegiate football series. (In the early years of football, the two teams had sometimes scheduled multiple games in a season.) W&M nosed ahead with 48 wins to 47 losses and five ties.

At Zable Stadium November 24, William and Mary began the NCAA Division I-AA playoffs for the second time in a row and whipped the University of Massachusetts, 38-0. Striking through the air and on the ground, the Indians went ahead 17-0 at the half and never looked back. Alan Williams scored four times on running plays, and Green added a 50-yard touchdown run. Hakel passed for his third 300-yard game in the season, and a powerful Tribe defense held the Minutemen scoreless.

This series captures Coach Laycock on the sidelines in 1989 with his reaction and those of his team as the Tribe scores another touchdown. Photos by Bob Keroack; courtesy of the W&M Sports Information Department.

Tony Tomich urges the alumni crowd in the west stands to cheer louder for the Tribe's defense during the 1990 Furman game. Photo by Vincent Vizachero; from the 1991 *Colonial Echo*.

The second playoff game was another story. Against Central Florida, the Tribe faltered in the last quarter of a high-scoring game to lose, 52-38, in Orlando's huge Citrus Bowl. W&M led 28-24 at halftime and then watched the Knights pile up a three-to-one touchdown margin in the game-breaking fourth quarter. Hakel hit fourteen of thirty passes for 273 yards, and rushing by Williams and Green produced another 201, but the effort was far short of UCF's 578 yards.

Thus ended a gratifying and record-breaking season of 10 wins and 3 losses. Shelton ended the year with 1,082 yards, and Green had 1,408, putting them at the top of the College's career rushing charts. Hakel added his own passing records, and defensive stalwarts—Reggie White, Greg Kalinyak, Brad Ewell, Allen Garlic, and Mark Wilson—played with distinction.

But the final drama of the 1990 season was yet to be played out. Just before Christmas, Coach Laycock announced that he had accepted an offer to become head football coach at Boston College, a Division I-A school. It proved to be, at least for a while, the last of several offers he seriously considered, including one from Duke University. Laycock made his announcement Wednesday, December 19, saying it was a difficult decision to make after eleven successful years at William and Mary—longer than any preceding coach—and that his family ties, friendships, staff, and players in Williamsburg all complicated the decision. Reportedly, Boston would pay him an estimated $140,000 a year, approximately double his salary at William and Mary. "I think it's a tremendous opportunity," Laycock said. "It's a school with academic prestige, plus the football tradition."

J.D. Gibbs (11), a 5'11" corner back, started every game his junior year and continued to be an important element in W&M's defensive secondary his senior year in 1990. Courtesy of the W&M Sports Information Department.

However, a surprising second act of the drama was staged the following day. Laycock, after a sleepless night, called a news conference to say that he had changed his mind and would remain at William and Mary. "It was not any one thing," he said. "Not any one person. … It was just not right for me." Family considerations obviously had a strong influence on him, as did innate loyalty to his alma mater.

A 1990 team captain, offensive guard Reggie White (56) opens a hole for tailback Alan Williams. White was named to four first-team All-American squads that year. Courtesy of the W&M Sports Information Department.

After a record-breaking tenure—68 wins and three trips to the playoffs—Laycock opted to remain at home. And after the holidays, he began plotting the 1991 gridiron campaign.

Interestingly, the first game of what would be the last losing season through 1996 took place on a September evening in Boston, but involved Boston University, not Boston College. The

Senior tailback Alan Williams raises his hand in jubilation as he scores a touchdown in the Tribe's 1990 Division I-AA playoff game against the University of Massachusetts. Courtesy of the W&M Sports Information Department.

Tribe came away with a 48-22 win, with Hakel and Green sparking the offense. Green carried for 140 yards and scored four touchdowns. Strong defensive play was led by senior safety Rich Allaway and linebacker Jeff Nielsen, a two-time Academic All-American with a 3.6 grade point average.

Delaware visited Zable Stadium on a sticky September 14 and captured a narrow 28-21 victory. The Blue Hens held the Tribe to just 75 yards on the ground and demonstrated a strong running attack.

The Indians rebounded against Navy in Annapolis. Big plays made the difference in a 26-21 triumph, which was the Tribe's first in ten starts against the Midshipmen since the dramatic upset in 1967. Williams scored on a 67-yard pass from Hakel, and Green ran 79 yards for the second touchdown. Chris Dawson kicked field goals for 30 and 37 yards to insure the verdict.

Special team members Scott Wingfield (35) and Tom Dexter (36) force a University of Virginia kickoff returner out of bounds in the 1990 game in Charlottesville. From the 1991 *Colonial Echo*.

In game four, James Madison came to Williamsburg and stole a 29-28 victory. Madison's 16-point fourth quarter overcame the Tribe's lead. On the first play of the game, Green raced for 45 yards and scored shortly after that, but JMU persisted.

With a 2-2 record, William and Mary traveled to Chapel Hill to meet a powerful University of North Carolina, whose depth led to a 59-36 romp. One W&M bright spot was a 65-yard pass play for a touchdown that featured two sophomores, quarterback Shawn Knight and receiver Michael Tomlin.

On October 12, the Tribe evened its record again in a 40-26 win over VMI in Lexington. Junior Scott Wingfield was the top rusher with 133 of W&M's 258 yards. William and Mary scored on each of its first four possessions, leaving little doubt of the outcome.

In the Homecoming game against The Citadel, William and Mary did not disappoint the alumni. After trailing 14-7 at the half, the Tribe mounted a strong offense and won 24-17. Returning after injuries, Green carried eleven times for 69 yards, and Alan Williams added another 90 to lead a crunching ground attack.

In the course of the weekend, President Paul Verkuil announced that he would leave the College after Charter Day 1992, to become president of the American Automobile Association, setting in motion the search for a new leader for the impending celebration of the College's tercentenary.

W&M celebrates a late score in the Tribe's 38-28 victory over Furman at newly dedicated Walter J. Zable Stadium. Courtesy of the W&M Sports Information Department.

Alex Utecht celebrates the Tribe's first round Division I-AA playoff shutout of the University of Massachusetts, 38-0. Courtesy of the W&M Sports Information Department.

Walt Zable

Walter J. Zable could be regarded as the epitome of a William and Mary student-athlete. He came to W&M in 1933—amid the Great Depression—with athletic ability that gave him the opportunity to attend college. Like his classmates, he had little money but lots of drive and determination. He also had the mind for academics, majoring in physics, minored in math, and took many chemistry courses.

After an early career with General Dynamics, Sperry Gyroscope Co., and ITT Federal Telecommunications Laboratories, Zable established Cubic Corp. of San Diego, a multimillion-dollar, diversified electronics company in 1951. His company has become an international leader in electronics development and computerized locomotion.

Its ticket system for the Washington Metro system was revolutionary. Similar machines have been installed in the London Underground and in Singapore, Hong Kong, and San Francisco.

Zable and his wife, Betty '40, returned for Homecoming festivities November 3, 1990, and brought with them a pledge of $10 million to their alma mater. The bulk of the money was to provide scholarships for W&M students, including a broad spectrum of athletics.

Zable, the student-athlete, had come full circle to William and Mary. The stadium at Cary Field was named in his honor during that Homecoming visit. In the mid-1930s, there were few student-athletes at W&M. Zable recalls:

A lot of our football players majored in physical education. The last semester they had to take human anatomy. It was tough, and a lot of them never got their degree. I remember a quarterback who came from New York or New Jersey. I would go to this kid's dormitory room in Monroe [Hall], and he would be lying on his bed reading comic books. He lasted one semester here.

Today, W&M boasts many student-athletes. Many scholarship athletes graduate, and in the process make good grades and major in many fields, ranging from Zable's physics and mathematics to philosophy, business administration, and government.

"It's a different ball game here. This is one of the schools where you have to get grades," Zable said. Grades were important to Zable a half century ago. He did not know where his career would ultimately take him, but he knew from the outset that a college education was essential.

I made good grades in physics and math, but not in English literature and some other subjects. I didn't even have a textbook. I didn't have enough money to buy textbooks.

He also recalled that one year he did not have $5 to pay for his photograph in the school yearbook. If he could not buy textbooks, he borrowed books "or read somebody's book. Hell, you would have to, but I didn't spend a lot of time in those courses. I did spend a lot of time in physics and math. I had to make A's and B's."

Zable said he majored in physics because at W&M that was the closest he could get to electronics. He was born in California and raised in Boston, where electronics was taught in grammar school.

I got interested in electronics ,and I had a tremendous education in Boston. The three Rs were drilled into you and there was no hanky-panky.

Zable had originally planned to attend Harvard, but came to W&M because two older football players from his Boston high school had come to Williamsburg. "I was going to leave after my freshman year," he said, "but it was so nice down there that I came back."

And Walter and Betty Zable's love affair with William and Mary began during those days on campus. William and Mary is such a special school, according to the Zables. "It provided me an education ... and without an education, God knows what would have happened to my career," he said.

In his collegiate days, Zable won broad recognition for his athletic ability. He was an honorable mention All-American end and won all–South Atlantic honors on the football team and was Southern Conference low-hurdles track champion. In 1937, the year he graduated, Zable was named Best Athlete in Virginia.

He went on to play football for the Richmond Arrows and the New York Giants and, in 1938, founded the Danville (Virginia) Green Wave semipro team when while he was teaching school there.

His sports honors also have included the 1962 *Sports Illustrated* Silver Anniversary All-American Team and the Distinguished American Award from the National Football Foundation and Hall of Fame's San Diego Chapter. The Foundation also recognized him in 1980 with its Gold Medal Award for athletic and humanitarian excellence. In 1981 he was inducted into the College Football Hall of Fame at King's Island, Ohio.

The NCAA in 1987 acknowledged Zable's contributions to athletics by giving him the Theodore Roosevelt Award, its most prestigious honor, in recognition of his outstanding professional accomplishments. Yet, he admitted that his favorite sport was not football but baseball. "Baseball you could go out at 8 a.m. and play until you couldn't see the ball," he said. "I played infield—shortstop and third base—and at W&M I pitched." He had a "very good" curve ball, "and a fast ball, too."

Nevertheless, W&M named the football stadium at Cary Field, the Water J. Zable Stadium. "It's the premier honor," Zable said of his life full of awards and recognition. It's big "because of having gone to school here."

He played in the football game against the University of Virginia when the stadium was dedicated in 1935. Never in his wildest dreams did he think that, fifty-five years later, that stadium would be named in his honor.

You wish you had the crystal ball to understand what goes on in life," he said. "In the 1930s, I was worried about getting an education and finding out where my next buck was coming from to live. ... William and Mary provided that education, and we had a wonderful time here. (—WK)

Walt Zable, the epitome of the student-athlete when he was at W&M in the 1930s, sits with W&M students just minutes before the dedication ceremony, November 3, 1990, when the stadium at Cary Field was named in his honor. Zable played in the first game in the new stadium in 1934. Photo by C. James Gleason; courtesy of the W&M Sports Information Department.

Peter Reid, offensive tackle, was named Sports Network Honorable Mention All-American in 1991. Courtesy of W&M Sports Information Department.

Against twelfth-ranked Villanova, the Indians were weakened by key injuries to the defense. W&M still put up a good fight, tying the game at 21 in the third quarter, before yielding two late touchdowns, and losing 35-21.

Back on the road in Bethlehem, Pennsylvania, the Tribe escaped from Lehigh, 41-37, as Green rushed for 147 yards and three touchdowns, and Hakel passed for 324 yards and two more touchdowns.

In the season's penultimate game against Samford (Alabama) in mid-November, W&M dropped a 35-13 decision in Zable Stadium, although Hakel added another 273 yards and two touchdown passes to his career totals.

Although W&M went to Richmond on November 23 with three straight losses, the Tribe rediscovered its offense to smash the Spiders, 49-7. Hakel passed for 303 yards; Green and Williams combined for another 223 on the ground.

The 1991 season ended with the team rated seventh nationally in total offense per game, tenth in passing, and seventeenth in scoring. Its four-year run of 30 wins, 16 losses, and 2 ties was the best in William and Mary history.

On June 1, 1992, Timothy J. Sullivan took office as the College's 25th president, just eight months before the beginning of the 300th anniversary celebrations. Sullivan, a law professor and dean of the Marshall-Wythe School of Law since 1985, reaffirmed William and Mary's "enduring commitment" to the highest academic standards.

Three months later, on September 12, the new football season began with VMI at Zable Stadium. The Tribe got off to a slow but winning start, 21-16, holding off the Keydets in the final two minutes and stopping a two-point conversion effort in the process. Actually, the newly emerging defensive strength of the team was only beginning to jell, and versatile junior quarterback Knight com-

Wide receiver Corey Ludwig tries to get away from this U. Mass defender in a 1990 Division I-AA playoff game. In his three years, Ludwig made 88 receptions for 1,399 yards. His biggest year was in 1992 when he had 55 receptions for 893 yards and two TDs. Courtesy of the W&M Sports Information Department.

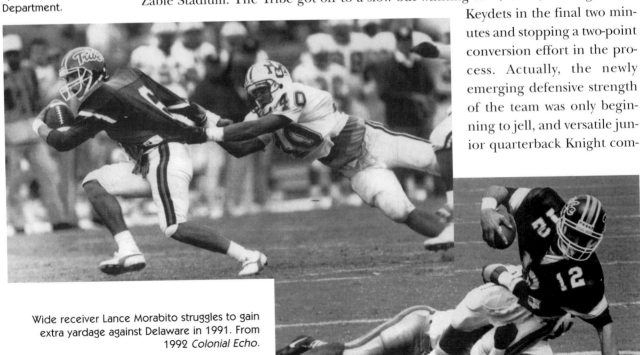

Wide receiver Lance Morabito struggles to gain extra yardage against Delaware in 1991. From 1992 *Colonial Echo*.

pleted eleven passes for 134 yards, while Derek Fitzgerald and James Blocker-Bodley led the rushing attack.

The second game at home against Boston University featured running by Blocker-Bodley, Troy Keen, and Wingfield, who piled up 235 yards in the 31-21 win. William and Mary took a 17-7 lead at the half and scored twice more in the third quarter to seal the victory.

Later in September, the Tribe traveled to Harvard Stadium in Cambridge, Massachusetts, and registered its third win, 36-16. Knight led a balanced passing and running attack, dashing 34 yards to score in the first period and completing thirteen of twenty-two passes for 192 yards.

Linebacker Jason Miller in 1992. Courtesy of the W&M Sports Information Department.

Game four was back at Zable Stadium, where William and Mary unleashed a potent offense to trounce Brown 51-6, and pile up 618 yards in total offense. Knight completed fourteen of eighteen passes for just over 300 yards and threw touchdowns to Corey Ludwig, Tomlin, and Erik Olson.

On October 10, the Tribe went north to Franklin Field to play its second Ivy League opponent in a row, the Penn Quakers. Pennsylvania did not go peacefully, but extra points by W&M's Dawson made the difference, 21-19.

During most of October, William and Mary was ranked tenth nationally in the I-AA polls, and the Tribe validated this assessment by soundly beating Towson State at Zable Stadium, 43-15, though the halftime lead was only 21-12.

Halfway through the season, the Indians made another humbling visit to Scott Stadium in Charlottesville. U.Va. romped, 33-7, after William and Mary had tied the score at 7-7 with a 56-yard pass from Knight to Tomlin. From there, it was all downhill with the Tribe only making 190 yards in total offense.

Moving to Harrisonburg for a Halloween game against James Madison, William and Mary lost to the Dukes, 21-14, but it would be the Tribe's last loss of the year. The Indians took a 14-3 lead at halftime on runs by Fitzgerald and Keen, and Knight passed for just over 200 yards to keep it close. But the Green and Gold ran out of gas in the second half, and JMU scored 15 unanswered points in the fourth quarter to win.

Placekicker Chris Dawson was the primary kicker in 1991, 1992, and 1993, compiling 22 field goals in his career. Photo by Colby Loucks; from the 1993 *Colonial Echo*.

Robert Green

For several years, the Robert Green show was often a feature during televised Chicago Bears football games as the former William and Mary back became one of the team's top runners in a tough division of the NFL. At 5'8" and just about 200 pounds, Green was told regularly that he was probably too short to play football in the big leagues.

Early in his sports career, he began demonstrating why the experts were wrong, and left Friendly High School (in suburban Maryland, near the District of Columbia) as the school's all-time leading rusher with 1,700 yards.

Robert Green excelled in his high school studies as well as in several sports, became a member of the National Honor Society, and worked as a recreation instructor during the summer.

He majored in kinesiology at William and Mary and quickly established himself as a freshman star on the football field. He started racking up 100-yard games with regularity and finished his rookie year with a flair, running for more than 900 all-purpose yards and being named Most Valuable Player of the Epson Ivy Bowl in Japan.

Green started his senior year in 1991 as a prospective All-American candidate and was the Tribe's all-time leading rusher by then, with 2,668 yards. By the time he graduated, he had pushed that record total to 3,543. He also broke the school's single-season rushing mark and scored nineteen touchdowns on the ground.

Green joined the Washington Redskins as a free agent and played on special teams before going to Chicago in 1992, where he became a mainstay in the Bears' backfield during the 1996 season. Caught in the Bears' salary cap problems, he moved on to the Minnesota Vikings for the 1997 season. Green now lives in suburban Maryland with his wife and family.   (—CMH)

Robert Green moves out on a long gainer in 1988. In the rear are quarterback John Brosnahan (15) and fullback Tyrone Shelton (45). Courtesy of the W&M Sports Information Department.

On the road against Colgate, November 7, W&M played four strong quarters and won easily, 44-26, although the statistics were close. Knight passed for three touchdowns and ran for one with just over a minute to play.

In the final home game the following week, William and Mary trailed 7-6 at the half and came back to cement the 26-13 victory in the fourth quarter on two field goals by Dawson and a touchdown plunge by Keen with 10 seconds left.

The week before Thanksgiving, the Indians traveled up I-64 for their traditional combat against Richmond and returned home with a 34-19 win, the ninth of the year. Dawson hit two field goals in the third quarter, helping reinforce a slender 14-13 halftime lead, and his team coasted from there.

At season's end, Dawson was named to the second All-State team, and Fitzgerald was selected Rookie of the Year by the ECAC, having set a freshman rushing record with 835 yards on 175 carries

William and Mary ended the year ranked thirteenth nationally in the final Division I-AA poll and also became the fifth College team to win at least nine games.

Instead of waiting for a possible NCAA bid to the playoffs, William and Mary had, before the beginning of the season, accepted an invitation to participate again in the Epson Ivy Bowl. It traveled to the Far East on January 9, 1993, to play Nihon University, and won, 35-19.

Chris Dawson was four-for-five in field goal attempts outside of 40 yards in 1992, including a career-best 51-yarder against Brown. Courtesy of the W&M Sports Information Department.

The Japanese educational and cultural experiences were probably more valuable than the game itself. As Laycock jokingly put it, one of his challenges in preparing for the game was "overcoming jet lag and the night life of Roppongi" [an entertainment district where the visitors were treated royally].

Against the all-Nihon Phoenix team, William and Mary amassed 28 points in the second quarter and coasted to victory. Knight, and his Japanese counterpart Yamada, each passed for 199 yards. Knight ran for two touchdowns and threw for two more.

Eight months later, on September 4, 1993, William and Mary commemorated the 100th anniversary of its first football season by entering the Yankee Conference. The initial game against conference member New Hampshire was a 27-14 win and heralded another successful year. With fourteen starters and thirty-six letter winners returning, the squad appeared strong. Knight led the way at quarterback, ably supported by Fitzgerald at tailback and Craig Staub anchoring a tough line.

Craig Staub gave no mercy to a Richmond Spider runner in 1992, leading defensive linemen with a career-high seventy-one total tackles. Courtesy of the W&M Sports Information Department.

The second week, hard-running Delaware outscored the invading Tribe, 42-35, even though William and Mary put 28 points on the board in the final quarter.

Game three found the Indians playing in the Louisiana Superdome against Tulane, a 10-0 victor. Senior Todd Durkin passed well, hitting fifteen of twenty-two for 142 yards, but the rushing game was shut down, accumulating a total of only 55 yards.

Back in Zable Stadium on September 25, William and Mary found its stride against Harvard, piling up a 45-17 victory with a balanced passing and running attack featuring Fitzgerald on the ground and Knight in the air.

On October 2, at Foreman Field in Norfolk, William and Mary held VMI to just six points while romping, 49-6 in W&M's last Oyster Bowl appearance. Total offense was as lopsided as the score—651 yards for the Tribe and only 151 for the Keydets.

After a week off, the Tribe traveled to Boston on October 16 and drubbed Northeastern, 53-6 at Parson Field. Knight led the way with twelve of eighteen passes for 131 yards.

Dozens of special events dominated the gala tercentenary Homecoming weekend, including the unveiling of a reproduction statue of Lord Botetourt in the Wren Yard, the dramatic announcement by President Timothy Sullivan that The Campaign for the Fourth Century had surpassed its $150 million goal, and "the mother of all birthday parties" at Busch Gardens.

Following the festive anniversary events on October 23, William and Mary knuckled down to business in Zable Stadium, building a 28-10 lead over Villanova at the half, and nearly doubling it for a devastating 51-17 win to post a 3-1 record in the Yankee Conference. With 17,616 at Cary Field, the Tribe rambled for 564 yards in offense, 433 of them on the ground.

James Blocker-Bodley, a running back, made his biggest team impact as a kickoff return specialist. Here he heads up field against Boston University in 1992. He holds the W&M career record for most kickoff return yards with 1,600 and ranks seventh with a yearly average of 23.9 yards per return in 1992. Courtesy of W&M Sports Information Department.

The next week against James Madison, W&M escaped with a workmanlike 31-26 victory, putting together a 14-point third quarter to wrap it up. Fitzgerald again ran well, with two touchdowns and 139 yards. Knight hit twelve of nineteen for 194 yards, and Dawson made a timely 42-yard field goal in the second quarter.

For the first half of November, William and Mary was on the road in New England, first playing Maine at Orono, and then Massachusetts in Amherst. The Tribe scored a total of 92 points against the two northern rivals, topping Maine, 47-23, and then U.Mass., 45-28.

The Maine game featured an early and spectacular 85-yard touchdown pass from Knight to Tomlin, followed by Fitzgerald's 42-yard scoring dash for 14 first-quarter points and a 35-17 half-time lead. Moving to Amherst, William and Mary again found the terrain to its liking, mounting 542 yards of total offense against the Minutemen, and scoring six touchdowns to win easily.

The series against Richmond continued at Zable Stadium, and the Indians beat the Spiders 31-17 to qualify for the I-AA playoffs. They took a 21-3 lead at the half, but then allowed Richmond to score twice in the third quarter and threaten briefly. Keen plunged in for an insurance touchdown in the third quarter, and Dawson added a little icing with a 24-yard field goal toward the end of the game.

Rain or shine, Tribe defensive players showed little mercy in the rain at Villanova in 1993. Courtesy of the W&M Sports Information Department.

The last weekend in November, William and Mary flew to Lake Charles, Louisiana, to face McNeese State in the Division I-AA playoffs. The locale itself, deep in bayou country, should have been intimidating. Knight, injured early, was ably replaced by Todd Durkin. Fitzgerald and Keen ran well, and the game remained close all the way. The Tribe led 21-20 at the half, but McNeese pushed ahead to lead 31-28 going into the fourth quarter. Knight returned to direct a last-ditch drive, moving his team from its 31-yard line to the McNeese 24 with a minute to play. But the effort fell short on the 20 as a pass to Ludwig failed.

During the season, Knight set a NCAA record for passing efficiency with a 69.4 percent completion rate. He also passed for 2,235 career yards and twenty-two touchdowns and was twice named ECAC Player of the Week. Tackle Craig Staub was recognized as an Academic All-American, an AP second-team All-American, and first-team Walter Camp All-American.

The W&M Athletic Department issued this pin in 1993 to mark the 100th anniversary of the beginning of the College's football program in 1893. Courtesy of the W&M Sports Information Department.

William and Mary began its 100th football season with a solid core of veterans—twelve starters and thirty-four lettermen and a national I-AA ranking of nineteenth. With Knight and Keen in the backfield, Darren Sharper at free safety, and a tough line that included Josh Beyer, All-State guard, and Greg Applewhite at linebacker, the Big Green looked strong.

The team justified pre-season praise by knocking off its first four opponents and taking a 4-0 record into Scott Stadium October 1 against Virginia.

On a beautiful Labor Day weekend in Kingston, Rhode Island, the Indians got off to a slow first half, but gained momentum to lead 23-10 in the third quarter and easily won 38-17. Knight hit nine of nineteen passes for 167 yards, but the ground game produced most of the scoring.

In game two, the Tribe posted a 31-7 victory over Delaware at Cary Field. W&M dominated with 373 yards of total offense, and Terry Hammons pulled off a 95-yard scoring punt return early in the last quarter.

Traveling to Greenville, South Carolina, the Indians next took on their old nemesis, Furman, but this time escaped with a 28-26 victory thanks to Brian Shallcross's kicking. Furman, on the other hand, failed twice on 2-point conversion attempts and lost despite two fourth-quarter scores.

William and Mary entertained VMI on September 24, but allowed the visitors only a fourth-quarter touchdown in a 45-7 mismatch. Again, a devastating ground game and Knight's passing did the job.

On a brilliant early fall day in Charlottesville, the Tribe trailed U.Va., 6-0, when Knight twisted his ankle and left what would be a 37-3 loss. Replacement Matt Byrne completed twelve of twenty passes for 135 yards, but W&M rushers could not penetrate the big, fast Cavalier line.

Quarterback Shawn Knight took charge of the W&M offense in 1992 and led the Tribe for three years. Either rolling out (above) or dropping straight back, Knight excelled as a passer. He set an NCAA record for passing efficiency in 1993 at 204.6 with 125 completions in 177 attempts for twenty-two touchdowns and 2,055 yards with only four interceptions. His career passing efficiency mark of 170.77 is also an NCAA record. Courtesy of the W&M Sports Information Department.

The following week, October 8, Byrne made his first start against Northeastern at Zable Stadium, and led the Tribe to two first-quarter touchdowns and a 17-12 win.

Plagued by injuries at mid-season, William and Mary lost to Massachusetts, 23-14, on October 15. Keen ran for another 122 yards on twenty-nine carries, but the Minutemen piled up 13 last-quarter points.

In a slump and still playing hurt, the Tribe went to Harrisonburg the following week and was whipped by James Madison, 33-7. W&M's only touchdown came early in the second quarter on a long pass from Knight to Tomlin. After having been ranked as high as eighth in the I-AA poll earlier in the year, William and Mary dropped to twenty-third, and Madison rose to tenth.

Some confidence was restored late in October on a trip to suburban Philadelphia, where William and Mary trounced Villanova, 53-28. Knight was back in top form, completing twenty-one of twenty-six attempts for 260 yards and four touchdowns.

As part of the November 5 Homecoming show, a quartet of skydivers, led by alumnus Sandy Taylor Wambach '81 parachuted into Zable Stadium carrying the game ball and updating the 1931 caper in which a biplane had dropped the football to start the game with Roanoke College. The University of Maine Black Bears did not do much better than long ago Roanoke, and were blanked by the Tribe, 17-0.

Cheerleaders continue to play an important role in football festivities at the College. Here the 1994 squad poses on Cary Field. From the 1995 *Colonial Echo.*

Hoping to close out another strong season and make the playoffs, the Tribe went to Richmond Stadium the week before Thanksgiving and squeezed out a 21-20 conquest of the Spiders, thanks to three extra points by Shallcross and Knight's 198 yards passing and two touchdowns.

The victory and an 8-3 season, however, did not send the Tribe into postseason play. W&M's earlier loss to James Madison kept the team from making the Division I-AA playoff field.

Halfback Troy Keen goes through a big hole in the Delaware line and heads for a big gain against the 1994 Blue Hens. From the 1995 *Colonial Echo*.

The culmination of the College's 100th season of football was Laycock's fifteenth year as head of a remarkably stable and successful program. The success of various team members and several individual squads rivaled the records of the glory years of "big time" football at William and Mary in the 1940s.

Defensive tackle Craig Staub (96), shown here against Villanova, made three first-team All-American squads in 1993 and made the All-Yankee Conference team the first time W&M players were eligible, also in 1993. He was also named Yankee Conference Defensive Player of the Year in 1993. Courtesy of the W&M Sports Information Department.

Laycock was the most successful coach compiling a record of 98-70-2 with the 1990 team becoming the first to win 10 games. His long-range, meticulously organized recruiting program combined with a dedicated, disciplined style to produce results year after year. He was able to achieve that delicate balance—gridiron success amid the pressures of an academically respected College.

During his tenure, spanning the administrations of three different W&M presidents, the basic number of scholarships available for football players decreased from eighty-nine in 1980 to seventy in 1990, and currently sixty-three. So the challenge goes on.

William and Mary's eleven or twelve football games each fall take up forty or fifty hours in all. NCAA regulations limit players to just twenty hours a week of practice.

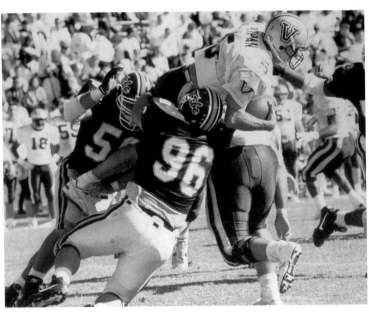

But it is all the other hours and days and weeks of intense preparation, analysis, and critique that combine to explain Laycock's phenomenal success: the secret is in the details.

There is an unquestionable impact of high-tech on the game now, with videotape, slow-motion replays, and fancy ball-throwing machines that look like inverted floor-polishers. There are sophisticated playbooks with dozens, or even hundreds, of formations and routes that must be perfected. And there are sports medicine experts, strength trainers, and an academic support counselor to sustain the program. But on game day, the wins still go to the men who execute the fundamentals best, blocking and tackling just a little better than the other guy.

When they are not on the road throughout the year scouring Virginia and the mid-Atlantic states for prospects, Laycock and his eight assistant coaches regularly put in seventy- and eighty-hour weeks planning, studying films, and conducting a variety of meetings among themselves and with the players. The boss is closely in-volved in every aspect of the game, and in reaching out to the community. He is always ready to talk to local fans at the Quarterback Club and to the media, and, for many years, reached a regional audience through his weekly cable TV show.

When the first whistle blows on Saturday after-noon, it still comes down to Laycock who must take the blame or credit for each game, and he is always there, prowling the sidelines, deeply involved but even-tempered, soliciting earphone advice from coaches high up on the rim of the stadium.

Inevitably, there are echoes of Laycock's former coaches in his style and his technique. "I learned a lot about the fundamentals of football as a player for Marv Levy," he said. And, "Playing for Lou Holtz, I learned the importance of motivation. He had a knack for mak-ing the game fun."

Today, Laycock is regarded with respect and ad-miration by those in many football sectors. Head Coach Frank Beamer of Virginia Tech, for example, says "Jimmye really understands and has a feel for the game of football." And Dwight Clark, former San Francisco 49er star, calls Laycock "a great strategist, communi-cator and teacher."

Coach Laycock gets the "water treatment" following W&M's 34-19 victory over Richmond in 1992. Courtesy of the W&M Sports Information Department.

William and Mary's long-range goals for football—and all athletics—have remained constant: to provide a quality education for its stu-dent-athletes; to field winning teams; to build fianancial stablity; and to produce outstanding graduates. Debated, reshaped, and refined during a turbulent century of games, the modern manifestation of *mens sana in corpore sano* seems to have brought a satisfying sense of equilibrium to academic and athletic endeavors on the ancient campus.

For every John Cannon, Steve Christie, Michael Clemons, or Robert Green, who has graduated from Coach Laycock's football field to achieve distinction in profes-sional football, William and Mary can boast of dozens pursuing successful careers in business, science, medicine, and teaching.

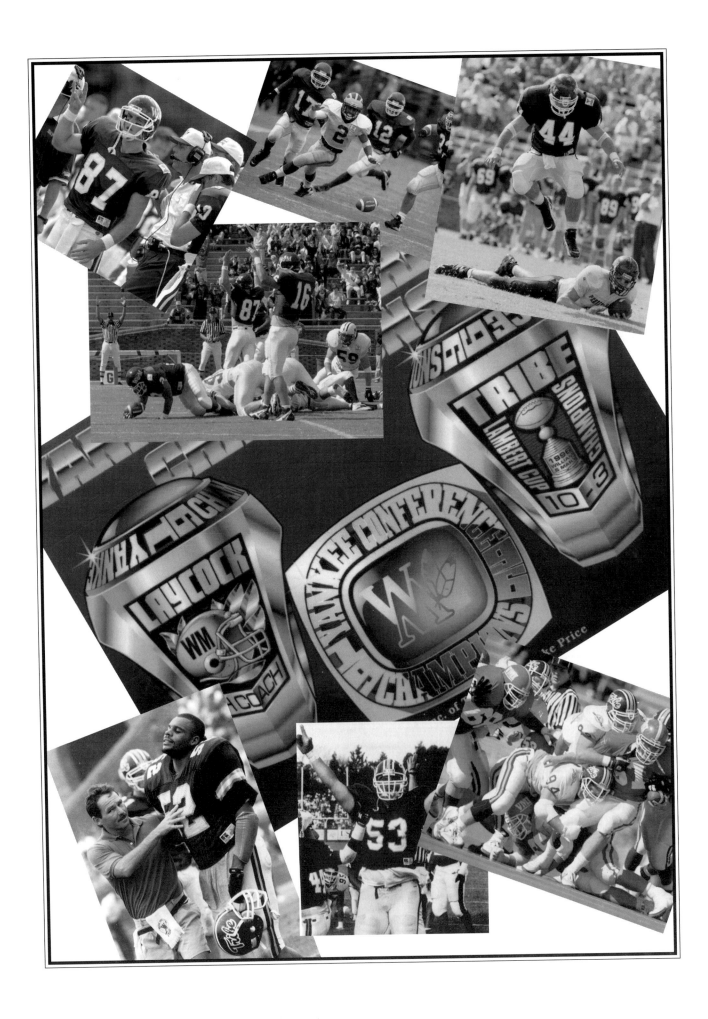

Epilogue
Let the Good Times Roll—
The 101st and 102nd Seasons
1995 to 1996

Wilford Kale

The 102nd season of W&M football equaled its most wins. The 1996 team compared favorably with the 1990 squad, as both compiled records of 10-3, the most season victories in the school's history, and gained the quarterfinals (one of the top eight teams) in the NCAA Division I-AA playoffs.

The squad ended the regular season 9-2 and was ranked fifth in Division I-AA—the highest year-end finish of any W&M football team. Seniors on the 1996 team won 34 games during their four years, the most ever won by a W&M class in any four-year period in the 102 seasons of W&M football.

For only the second time in history, W&M won the Lambert Cup, symbolic of the number one Division I-AA team in the East. The Lambert/Meadowlands Awards Poll, which awards the cup, considers teams from Maine to Virginia.

In a year supposed to be one of "rebuilding," the Tribe's success pointed to Coach Laycock's reputation as one of the finest developers of young talent in the nation. Twelve of the team members received All–Yankee Conference honors, led by two consensus All-Americans—guard Josh Beyer and strong safety Darren Sharper. They were first-team selections on the Associated Press and Walter Camp All-American Division I-AA squads.

Sharper, the Yankee Conference's Defensive Player of the Year, had ten interceptions during the season, tying Jack Bruce's 1947 season record. Sharper's career interception total of twenty-four set a new school record. He also graduated as the NCAA Division I-AA's career leader in interception return yards with 486.

Beyer, a 6'5", 295-pound senior, led an offensive line that helped junior tailback Alvin Porch rush for 1,210 yards in his first year as a starter. Redshirt freshman receiver Dave Conklin was named the Conference's Rookie of the Year, setting W&M freshman records for receptions, 44; receiving yards, 843; and touchdowns, nine. Although inexplicably missing from the All-Conference team, wideout Josh Whipple

Coach Laycock is surrounded by awards won by his 1996 team (10-3), which made the NCAA Division I-AA quarterfinals. The Yankee Conference Championship "Bean Pot" is at right, with the Lambert Cup, symbolic of the best Division I-AA team in the East (large bowl, front). Photo by Bob Keroack. Courtesy of the W&M Sports Information Department.

Dr. George Oliver, Jr.

George J. Oliver, Jr.'s car license plate reads: "W&M Doc." And that's pretty much a fact now. A general surgeon in Williamsburg from 1958 until his retirement in 1987, Dr. Oliver has been the doctor on call for William and Mary athletics for years. Since about 1982 it's been official; he's the team physician.

He began serving as primary care doctor for football team members only a few months after arriving in town and has continued in that capacity, except for about nine years in the 1970s. His work with the basketball team has been continuous since 1958 and the days of Coach Bill Chambers.

As his tenure lengthened, his involvement with different teams increased. Now, as primary care physician, he gets calls from nearly all men's and women's athletic teams.

I am there if they need me. I work now with the head trainer, but the orthopedics get involved in most of the injuries. I've been around so long that I can arrange for the kids to see most of the doctors in town they need to see. I do a lot of the liaison stuff.

Do not expect to see the Doc on the football field unless he's called.

I don't go out unless I'm called. It's better that way. Usually, the trainer is out there trying to determine how we can get an injured player off the field. Once they're off the field, we can get to work if needed.

On a daily basis, Dr. Oliver gets by the training room at least once or twice a day, checks athletes who have reported an illness and is, of course, on call.

A graduate of the University of Richmond (1946) and the Medical College of Virginia (1947), Dr. Oliver has been involved with W&M for many years, because his father was a W&M faculty member, serving as chairman of the College's Department of Education. George J. Oliver, Sr., later moved to Richmond to head Richmond Professional Institute (then a branch of W&M).

The Doc became involved professionally with W&M probably because the College's head football coach in 1958 was Milton Drewer, also from the Eastern Shore. "I got to know him pretty quickly, and we became buddies, and he asked me to help, and I've been here ever since."

Doc Oliver has mixed emotions on days when his alma mater, Richmond, plays W&M. "But after the close association I've had with William and Mary athletics over the years, it's very difficult for me to root against them in any game they play," Dr. Oliver said. "So, I'll root for W&M."

After working with W&M athletics nearly forty years, he believes "they are the finest young people in the world. The W&M students are exceptional. We have a different caliber of students here and there are some schools that have people I wouldn't want anything to do with."

Academics are important to W&M athletics, the Doc explained.

These days there are very few who would major in physical education any more. They major in significant academic pursuits. Kids come here for a quality education, and that's what college should be about, and that's what grants-in-aid should be about.   (—WK)

Orthopedic consultant Dr. Ed Wilhelm works with an injured Tribe player on the sidelines. Other orthopedic surgeons on the W&M staff include Drs. Jeff Moore and Dan Carr, and local chiropractor Bob Pinto. They serve as consultants to the College's sports medicine staff. Courtesy of the W&M Sports Information Department.

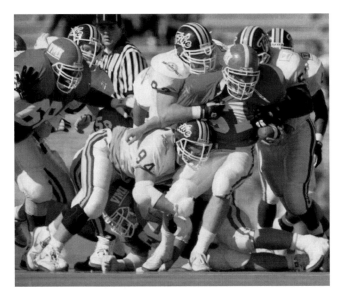

W&M linebacker Jason Miller (center) wraps up a VMI ball carrier in the 1995 game. Miller was the 1995 Yankee Conference Defensive Player of the Year. Photo by Alexa Welch; courtesy of the *Richmond Times-Dispatch*.

had sixty-five receptions for 1,096 yards and twelve touchdowns, a strong year by anyone's standards.

The 1996 success was built to a large degree on 1995—the 101st football year. Although the 1995 season resulted in a 7-4 record, a fine record for most squads, it was a downer for W&M because there was no postseason opportunity. An early season 24-17 loss to James Madison gave the Dukes a game up and ultimately one of the conference's two postseason playoff slots. A 23-20 loss to Delaware on November 4 sealed the postseason door.

The 7-4 record also was remarkable because W&M began the season with losses to U.Va. and James Madison. A tribute to the Tribe's consistent gridiron prowess was the fact that never during the season did the team fall out of The Sports Network's Top-25 Division I-AA standings.

Josh Beyer was a 1996 Division I-AA All-American tackle. Courtesy of the W&M Sports Information Department.

The 1995 team was led by fifth-year quarterback Matt Byrne, who ultimately amassed 1,700 yards through the air, despite the rocky start without any touchdown passes in the first two games. The next two were shutout victories over Northeastern, 32-0, and New Hampshire, 39-0, as the defense grew more confident. Defensive anchors included two seniors—middle linebacker Jason Miller, the Yankee Conference's Defensive Player of the Year, and All-Conference defensive end Jim Simpkins—and juniors outside linebacker Stefon Moody and defensive back Sharper.

At that point, tailback stars Derek Fitzgerald and Troy Keen began to take charge on offense. Keen had two touchdowns and Fitzgerald one against Northeastern; they reversed the numbers at New Hampshire. Working behind Beyer's blocking, Fitzgerald finished the season as W&M's all-time rusher with 3,744 yards, while Keen ended his college career third in

Outside linebacker Stefon Moody was a tri-captain of the 1996 team and finished his career with 217 tackles and 160 assists. Courtesy of the W&M Sports Information Department.

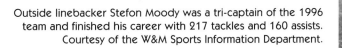

John Randolph, athletic director, 1985–95, worked closely with Laycock to insure that the football program and the rest of W&M's intercollegiate sports worked together. Courtesy of the W&M Sports Information Department.

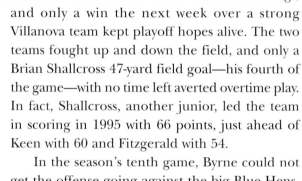

rushing with 2,949 yards and second on the all-time touchdown list with forty-two.

Three mid-season victories against VMI, a good Rhode Island team, and Pennsylvania, ran the win streak to five games and sent the twelfth-ranked squad against unranked but feisty Massachusetts. At Amherst, in a driving rain that made traction virtually impossible, nothing seemed to go right for the Tribe, while the Minutemen took advantage of a lack of offense and some defensive letdowns. U. Mass. triumphed, 20-9.

The loss dropped the Tribe from twelfth to twentieth in the national rankings, and only a win the next week over a strong Villanova team kept playoff hopes alive. The two teams fought up and down the field, and only a Brian Shallcross 47-yard field goal—his fourth of the game—with no time left averted overtime play. In fact, Shallcross, another junior, led the team in scoring in 1995 with 66 points, just ahead of Keen with 60 and Fitzgerald with 54.

In the season's tenth game, Byrne could not get the offense going against the big Blue Hens, who began the fourth quarter with a 23-6 advantage. Two scores were just too late to overcome the advantage, and Delaware won, 23-20.

The season-ending traditional game with Richmond was a 27-7 Tribe victory, the seventh in a row against the Spiders, pushing the series record to 53-47-5.

Running back Derek Fitzgerald finds the way cleared by W&M fullback Jay Hamric in the 1995 game against James Madision. Fitzgerald rushed for 3,744 career yards, making him the number one ground gainer in the College's history. Photo By Alexa Welch; courtesy of the *Richmond Times-Dispatch*.

The 1995 seniors celebrated their 33-12 four-year record as the best in Tribe history—until the following year. They, too, enjoyed four straight winning seasons, and the team ended its four years with fifty successive weeks of top-twenty-five finishes in the national I-AA poll. A league-high thirteen athletes were named to All–Yankee Conference honors. Laycock became the thirteenth Division I-AA coach to win 100 games.

After the 1995 season, W&M and Tribe football lost one of its biggest supporters when Athletic Director John Randolph died after a lengthy battle with lung cancer. Randolph, a 1964 graduate of W&M, had served as head track and field coach from 1968 un-

Tailback Troy Keen moves around a Delaware defender in the 1995 game. In his career, Keen rushed for 2,949 yards, making him the third best rusher in W&M history. Photo by Clement Britt; courtesy of the *Richmond Times-Dispatch*.

When he was not in the game trying to make the big play, wide receiver Josh Whipple (87) was on the sideline helping Coach Laycock (with headset) relay offensive signals to the quarterback during the 1995 James Madison game. Photo by Alexa Welch; courtesy of the *Richmond Times-Dispatch*.

til 1976. After successful track coaching stints at the U.S. Military Academy, 1976–79, and the University of Florida, 1979–85, he returned to his alma mater in 1985 and guided athletics at the College for a decade.

During Randolph's tenure, raising funds to endow numerous sports programs was a major objective. For football in 1990, the Fourth and Goal Drive secured commitments from more than 250 former football players, with the ultimate objective of endowing the entire scholarship program. A gateway at Zable Stadium at Cary Field was dedicated in Randolph's memory during halftime ceremonies of the W&M-Delaware football game, November 2, 1996.

On April 2, 1996, after a national search, Edward C. "Terry" Driscoll, vice president of Eagle International Group, an event management and services company, was named athletic director. He assumed the W&M post July 1, 1996. Associate Athletic Director Barbara Blosser, a W&M athletic department staff member since 1986, twice served as acting athletic director, first from October 1992 to June 1993 and then from August 1995 until Driscoll's appointment.

Driscoll, a 1969 graduate of Boston College, played five years in the National Basketball Association and four years in Italy. He became an athletic sales promotion agent in 1980 and quickly moved up the corporate ladder, becoming president of KSG, Inc., a national sales agency in the sporting goods industry. He later moved from product marketing and sales to sports marketing and management, before coming to W&M.

Defensive end Jim Simpkins (front), co-captain of the 1995 team, was a top pass rusher with twelve career sacks, ninety-two tackles, and sixty-nine assists. Courtesy of the W&M Sports Information Department.

Terry Driscoll, sports promotion and sports management specialist, was named athletic director of W&M in 1996. Courtesy of the W&M Sports Information Department.

W&M defenders Mike Beverly (17), Darren Sharper (12), and Mike Bertoni (33) chase Delaware's Norman Coleman as he tries to recover a fumble in the November 3, 1996, game. Photo by Alexa Welch Edlund; courtesy of the *Richmond Times-Dispatch.*.

Quarterback Mike Cook (4) launchs a pass during a 1996 home game at Zable Stadium. Cook's performance for the season—3,166 yards passing—ranked him second for passing behind Chris Hakel's 3,414 in 1990. Photo by Don Long; courtesy of the *Richmond Times-Dispatch.*

Meanwhile, Laycock's "system" continued to flourish. The 1996 season, purportedly a "rebuilding" year, attested once again to Laycock's coaching ability and his football system. The system "is one that fits the type of players we have—smart, hard working, over achievers."

It is very adaptable and is based upon the personnel. The system is consistent in how we do things," Laycock explained, "but changing in the way we go about doing basic things.

We have a multiple-formation offense, designed to take advantage of personnel in any one given year or any one given week. That is how we've been able to do it. There is a balance in run and pass but the system is adaptable because of the personnel.

Two other elements of Laycock's system have attracted attention: the recruitment and use of "walk-ons" and Laycock's fourth-down game.

W&M has focused on walk-ons since about 1986, Laycock said, "and we've had them. It's been an important factor for our team. We work at walk-ons real hard. We talk to them. We recruit them and we publicize them."

Three top players in 1996—Sean McDermott, junior strong safety; Billy Commons, junior wide receiver; and Whipple, senior wide receiver—were walk-ons. Dean Olson wrote in the *William & Mary News,* that the three were all high school quarterbacks, excellent in academics, who came to the College "with no promise of financial aid to play football."

Not accomplished enough in high school to receive a grant for the gridiron, they were what's called in the parlance of the sport "walk-ons."

But they came also with an assurance from the coaching staff: work hard, win your position on the team on merit and you'll be rewarded. Goal attained, promises kept."

All three gained full athletic grants before graduation.

Another walk-on, Alan Williams '92, compiled more than 2,500 yards at tailback for the Tribe and is now the running backs' coach. He told Olson that the Laycock system and philosophy went beyond football.

What we're all about is developing young men. A walk-on is treated exactly as a full scholarship athlete, from training rules to expectations of how they practice. Coach Laycock talks a lot about teamwork, commitment, character and being accountable for your actions. This applies not only to football; it carries over into their later lives in the job market and building a family.

As for the fourth-down game, Laycock's assistant coaches just smile when asked about it. The team goes for fourth down on many occasions, often when it appears not to be the advisable call. And is successful more often than not.

One W&M coach who requested anonymity said, "those calls help build confidence. The players sense if the coach thinks we can make it on fourth down, then we'll

An unknown until the 1996 season, junior tailback Alvin Porch posted 1,210 yards rushing that season. He squeezes for every yard (above) in the game against VMI and scrambles over for a touchdown in the game against New Hampshire. Top photo by Mark Gormus, bottom photo by Don Long; courtesy of the *Richmond Times-Dispatch*.

Steve Cole

He is not the most visible person on Cary Field, except in an injury or emergency situation when Steve Cole, W&M's director of sports medicine, runs onto the field to aid a fallen gridder.

The injured athlete, whether football player or not, knows when Cole or a member of his staff is around, they are in highly trained and competent hands.

In 1996 Cole celebrated his fifteenth year at the helm of the elaborate sports medicine program that operates out of facilities at Zable Stadium and Adair Gynamsium. Besides supervising full-time staff members and graduate assistants, he oversees thirty undergraduate students who gain valuable on-the-job experience in the athletic training program.

A certified athletic trainer and strength and conditioning specialist, Cole came to W&M in 1983 from Troy State University. He received his bachelor's degree in physical education and athletic training from West Virginia University in 1976 and a master's degree in sports medicine in 1978 from the University of Virginia.

Center Brian Sorrell, praised Cole for his "hard work and the enthusiasm" he brings to the job. "He is willing to help in any way possible. Every team member gets individual attention and he works long hours and is always accessible."

A true fitness buff, Cole is an exemplary model for all the athletes. He is an avid competitor who has participated in a variety of triathlons since 1980, spending many hours of his free time in training. (—WK)

make it." Many scoring drives in 1996 were continued by successful fourth-down plays. "One fourth-down success builds for another and another."

Laycock has always been known for his offensive coaching skills, but, early in his career, defense lagged somewhat. "We started about the 1991 season making progress in defense," Laycock explained.

> It had to do with consistency of defensive coaching and a defensive scheme—one that would fit our personnel. We also started getting speed in our defensive personnel. You can hide people on offense, but not defense.

With a defensive system also in place, Laycock could shift coaches and be confident the team would not suffer. The 1995 team and its defensive attributes "was just part of the evolution," Laycock said.

> I was not surprised at our ability in 1995. We've gotten better every year defensively. We had more of that in 1996. The biggest thing was the front seven. We've had good secondary and the depth to use people. We started the season with two defensive tackles out and we still won and I didn't expect it.

Steve Cole and John Mitrovic attend to Tribe tailback Alvin Porch on the field during the 1996 season. Courtesy of the W&M Sports Information Department.

Senior fullback Jay Hamric proved to be one of the team's best blockers. Here he exhorts his teammates after a good play. Photo by Alexa Welch Edlund; courtesy of the *Richmond Times-Dispatch*.

In 1996, the biggest factor was "consistency in the way we played," Laycock explained early in January 1997, as he looked back over a 10-3 season. "Every week we came to play and every week we played pretty darn well. That was the overriding factor about this team."

Ready to begin his eighteenth season at W&M, Laycock said there is no comparison now with his first years at the College in the early 1980s.

There are so many more things in place now that allow you to coach. It's a much better situation. I now have assistant coaches who have established themselves and I feel comfortable in delegating things. They have a track record of working under me.

Most preseason prognosticators viewed W&M's 1996 team with a degree of skepticism. *Richmond Times-Dispatch* reporter John O'Connor predicted a 6-5 season, noting:

The Tribe needs its veteran blockers to ease ball movement while it breaks in a new quarterback and a pair of new running backs. W&M had the Yankee's third-best defense last year and should maintain that position or improve. If sophomore Mike Cook, who's expected to start at QB, can throw effectively and Alvin Porch or Tony Harris can emerge as a solid runner, the Tribe could be the Yankee's surprise team.

And surprise they did. Cook became the passer, and Porch the runner.

The first game against Central Florida in Citrus Bowl Stadium in Orlando showed more about the squad than many people had envisioned. W&M lost to the Golden Knights, 39-33. The offense made the showing many people had hoped for, but the defense had not jelled.

But solid wins over Rhode Island, 23-16; Virginia Military, 40-21; Bucknell, 47-0; and New Hampshire, 31-7, set the stage for a season-ending run for the playoffs. A roadblock appeared in the sixth game, when nemesis James Madison upset the Tribe 26-21 in Harrisonburg. It was the Dukes' third straight victory over W&M and put the pressure directly on the young squad to defeat equally strong Villanova, Delaware, and Massachusetts teams to have any chance at postseason play.

Villanova, ranked ninth in Division I-AA, fell to the Tribe 30-21 as Cook hit nineteen of twenty-seven passes for 279 yards and Porch rushed for 121 yards, the fifth time in seven games that he had gone over the 100-yard mark. It was, however, the defense that

Tribe pride became an athletic promotional slogan in the mid-1990s. From the collection of Wilford Kale.

Darren Sharper

Darren Sharper, called by many one of the outstanding defensive talents in the nation, became a two-time All-American at free safety in 1996 when he set or tied three W&M records.

He broke Mark Kelso's career mark of twenty interceptions by capturing twenty-four enemy aerials and equaled Jack Bruce's long-time record, set in 1947, for ten interceptions in a season. Sharper also compiled 1,027 in punt return yards for his career, besting the 797-yard mark of Palmer Scarritt.

Sharper lived up to the *1996 W&M Football Media Guide*'s preview that he was "big enough to have a strong presence in the run defense but he also possesses outstanding speed and quickness for [pass] coverage."

His 1996 talents and record-breaking achievements did not go unnoticed. He was named on five Division I-AA first team All-American squads. In 1995 he was named on two first team All-America teams and was an honorable mention pick on one All-American team in 1994.

He was a first-team Yankee Conference All-Conference Team member three times, and the 6'3", 205-pound Sharper was named the 1996 Yankee Conference Defensive Player of the Year.

Recognition, however, continued in the 1997 National Football League Draft when he was selected in the second round (60th selection overall) by the Green Bay Packers, defending Super Bowl champs. Packers Head Coach Mike Holmgren explained:

We drafted him as a safety, but we think he could play the corner. He's got good size, good range and he's a very bright young man. We have good defensive backs now, but a couple of those guys are a little bit older, so if we can bring a young man in and add him to that mix in the secondary and have him play with those guys, I think he can be a real fine player for us.

Green Bay defensive coordinator Fritz Shurmur echoed Holmgren's feelings:

Darren exhibits great skills to make interceptions and to make plays. He's a good tackler and a bright guy. He should contribute.

The Richmond, Virginia, native received his B.A. from W&M in sociology and runs a "mentorship program" in Williamsburg that helps keep kids on the right path academically and socially. (—WK)

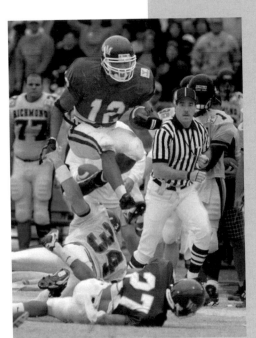

Darren Sharper runs the ball back after an interception during the Tribe's 27-7 win in 1995 over the Richmond Spiders. Photo by Alexa Welch; courtesy of the *Richmond Times-Dispatch.*

Defensive end Luke Cullinane (foreground) was a three-year starter, 1994–96 with nineteen career sacks, sixty-six tackles, and sixty-nine assists. Courtesy of the W&M Sports Information Department.

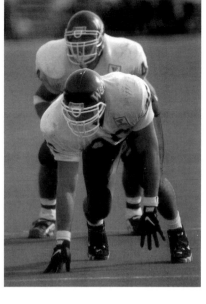

also rose to the occasion sacking the Wildcat quarterback ten times, taking the air out of the conference's most prolific aerial offense, according to *Richmond Times-Dispatch* reporter Vic Dorr, Jr. The Tribe defense held Villanova to a minus-39 yards rushing.

The victory was sweeter because the Tribe trailed 7-0 after Villanova's second offensive play and 14-0 after two offensive series. W&M fought back, however, and scored 17 points in the second quarter and 13 points in the third quarter for the win. Tailback Porch left the game in the third quarter with a separated shoulder; his backup, Tony Harris, also left with a shoulder injury. Freshman Corey Nesmith responded with 53 yards on seventeen carries late in the game.

Mike Bertoni wore number 59 during his junior year, 1995, and turned in a season-high six-tackle performance with a sack against Villanova. Courtesy of the W&M Sports Information Department.

Northeastern, the Homecoming opponent, proved stubborn before succumbing, 21-14, on a fourth-quarter touchdown by Porch with 52 seconds left in the game. Again, W&M fell behind 14-0 in the second quarter as Cook was intercepted four times and did not find his rhythm until the second quarter, according to *Richmond Times-Dispatch* reporter Adam Foldenauer.

> W&M's defense turned in its usual dominating performance. Coming off last week when it registered [nine] sacks. ... The Tribe sacked Huskies QB Jim Murphy five times for 36 yards. End Mike Bertoni led W&M with 12 tackles (three for losses), two sacks, a forced fumble and a fumble recovery.

For the game, Cook completed twenty of thirty-nine passes for 244 yards, hitting receiver David Conklin for a 25-yard touchdown mid-way in the third quarter.

Times-Dispatch reporter O'Connor stressed the impact of W&M's improved defense as the team made preparations for Delaware.

Linebacker Mike Bertoni (33) goes after the New Hampshire quarterback with the help of Brian Giamo (58) in the October 5, 1996, game. Bertoni finished the season with seven sacks for a minus-36 yards. Photo by Don Long; courtesy of the *Richmond Times-Dispatch*.

Never before in Jimmye Laycock's 17 years as W&M's coach has there been a stretch during which the Tribe's defensive front made such a jarring impact. The Tribe went 7-4 last season thanks in part to a defense that finished third in the league. It had 26 sacks. Through eight games this year, W&M has 39 sacks, for 202 yards worth of losses.

The difference? Experience. Across the line, Gang Green features a pair of seniors—end Mike Bertoni and tackle Brian Giamo—and two juniors tackle Pete Coyne and end Luke Cullinane (11 sacks).

Mike Holtzclaw of the Newport News *Daily Press* also wrote about the W&M line. Giamo called the group's effort "relaxed intensity," relaxed out of confidence. The self-proclaimed "Four Horsemen," limited the opposition to an average of 66.5 yards through eight games. "That's what it's all about—it's the whole unit, not the individual," Bertoni said. "We've got four guys working together, and every one can make the big plays. If I don't get the sacks, I know Luke will and if it's not him, then Giamo and Coyne will do the job."

Tribe linebacker Mike McGowan hurdles Pennsylvania receiver Miles Macik during the Tribe's 48-34 win in 1995. Photo by Joe Mahone; courtesy of the Richmond Times-Dispatch.

In the first overtime game in W&M history, the Tribe edged Delaware, 10-7, on Shallcross's redemptive 42-yard field goal. Earlier in the game he had missed attempts from 20 yards (wide right) and 25 yards (wide left).

Again, W&M's defense held Delaware 20 points below its game average. The Blue Hens had only 76 yards rushing, while the Tribe had 190. Porch collected 183 in his biggest running game of his career, which pushed him over 1,000 yards for the season.

Cook hit Whipple for an 11-yard touchdown pass in the first quarter, but Shallcross's misses and an interception of Cook on the Delaware 7, blunted three other scoring opportunities. Delaware scored early in the fourth quarter to tie the game, ultimately forcing overtime.

Times-Dispatch sports writer Dorr summed up W&M's 30-6 victory over Massachusetts:

The game, the Yankee Conference championship and an invitation to the Division I-AA playoffs were very much up for grabs. So

Jude Waddy, linebacker, was a three-time All-Yankee Conference selection. He recorded 195 tackles and 115 assists, while starting thirty of thirty-four games. Courtesy of the W&M Sports Information Department.

15th ranked W&M did the only sensible thing. It permitted its talented wide receivers to do the grabbing.

A procession of remarkable catches by Josh Whipple and David Conklin touched off a second-half explosion. ... Between them Whipple and Conklin provided eight second-half receptions for 161 yards. By doing so, they helped the Tribe transform a 6-6 halftime tie into something resembling a romp.

Tribe quarterback Cook continued to excel, hitting fifteen of twenty-six passes for 226 yards and a touchdown, while rushers combined for 138 yards. The Minutemen, who had upset W&M in 1994 and 1995, accounted for only 77 yards rushing and were hit with three interceptions, all by defensive back Sharper. In addition to breaking Mark Kelso's career interception mark (20), Sharper set a new school career record by returning five punts for 47 yards, raising his career total to 1,027.

The win set up the season finale with Richmond. A victory assured a conference championship and playoff. Two fourth-quar-

W&M wide receiver Josh Whipple (87) uses some fancy footwork to elude Richmond's Keith Middleton to score the Tribe's first touchdown in its 28-13 win on November 16, 1996, against the Richmond Spiders. Photo by Clement Britt; courtesy of the *Richmond Times-Dispatch.*

ter touchdowns sealed W&M's 28-13 triumph over the Spiders. Wide receiver Whipple caught two first-half touchdown passes of 67 and 3 yards from Cook to give the Tribe a lead that was never lost. "If it was a rebuilding year, it was a pretty darn good one," Whipple told the *Times-Dispatch*. Cook also had a good day passing, connecting on thirteen of twenty-five for 234 yards. Two lost fumbles and an interception, however, gave Richmond opportunities to stay close.

Following the game, Laycock told O'Connor that he decided to condense and simplify his offensive scheme after the 1995 season. Instead of the two-back, ball-sharing setup he used with Fitzgerald and Keen, Laycock opted to go with a one-back plan that featured Porch. Fullback Jay Hamric was used as a blocker and pass receiver, not a runner.

Pass protection that forced Byrne to read on the run in 1995, O'Connor wrote, was simplified and sophomore quarterback Cook became the conference's leading quarterback. "We changed a good bit of our terminology too," Laycock said.

It was stuff we all knew as coaches, but you add things through the years and sometimes it becomes more difficult to convey it to the players.

No matter what you do each year, you've got to re-evaluate it. You've got to be careful or you can get into bad habits and get in ruts and do things just because you've done them before.

Terry Hammons, wide receiver, was co-captain of the 1995 squad and became the fifth W&M receiver to break the 2,000-yard mark, gaining 2,134 yards with 756 yards in 1995 his career best. Courtesy of the W&M Sports Information Department.

"Fix it, even if it ain't broke?" O'Connor wrote. Laycock did just that.

The W&M juggernaut continued on November 30, 1996, on Cary Field as the Tribe blasted Jackson State, 45-6, in the first round of the Division I-AA playoffs. The team piled up 480 yards of total offense and could have had many more if Laycock had not brought in the reserves.

Sharper, whose ten interceptions had blitzed opponents' offenses all season, this time returned a punt 80 yards for a touchdown that quickly pushed Jackson State into a 14-0 second-quarter deficit. It just got worse.

W&M, the eighth seed in the playoffs, was in the final field of eight when it traveled to Cedar Falls, Iowa, to play third-seeded Northern Iowa, a similar team with a good defense and an explosive offense. It was the second time W&M had advanced to the second round. In 1990, the Tribe lost to Central Florida. Playing in UNI-Dome on artificial turf, W&M looked like a sure loser, down 17-0 after the first 15 minutes of play and trailing, 27-0, at halftime. The team just came out flat, Tribe linebacker Mike McGowan told O'Connor. The W&M offensive line also endured five sacks, and the running game was kept in check.

The second half was another story. Cook got some much needed pass protection and hit on four third-quarter touchdown passes: 11 and 13 yards to Whipple and 50 and 36 yards to Conklin. Down only 35-28 going into the fourth quarter, W&M tied the score with 5:40 remaining on another Cook-to-Whipple, this time for 8 yards.

The 1,000 or so W&M faithful who made the trek to Iowa could not believe what they were seeing. The Tribe held Northern Iowa on the next set of downs, but punt return artist Sharper could not handle the ball, losing the fumble with 4:28 remaining and giving Northern Iowa the ball at the W&M 30. On fourth down, Northern Iowa connected on a 32-yard field goal, for a 38-35 lead. W&M's final drive, and its season, ended on downs at mid-field.

Daily Press sports writer Holtzclaw reported that the team felt its second half rally made the loss easier to take. "I'm very, very pleased with the attitude of this team," Laycock told Holtzclaw.

On the road in a tough place to play and down 27-0, it would have been easy to fold up the tent and say, "Let's just get out of here." Instead, we could have won it. Out on the field [before the team made it to the locker

Bumper sticker denotes W&M athletic slogan. From the collection of Wilford Kale.

room] I told the guys that the big thing is that we can't let this loss take away from what we accomplished this year.

"In the end," Holtzclaw wrote, "the Tribe made the coaches look smart. The defense went after opponents like a tidal wave. The offense became a powerhouse, with sophomore quarterback Mike Cook and junior tailback Alvin Porch, both first-year starters, having seasons that put them among the best-ever at William and Mary."

The second-half rally enabled linebacker Mike McGowan and his teammates to walk off the field for the last time, Holtzclaw wrote, holding their heads high. "It hurts now," McGowan said of the loss at Northern Iowa. "But in 20 years we'll all get together with our [Yankee championship] rings on our fingers, have a beer and talk about how this year was the best time of our lives. It really was."

The 1996 season had just ended when rumors began to circulate that Laycock was again being sought by another school to be head coach. This time it was Southern Methodist University in Dallas and the athletic director doing the interviews was none other than former W&M Athletic Director Jim Copeland, a longtime friend of Laycock's.

On December 19, 1996, the *Richmond Times-Dispatch* and the Newport News *Daily Press* reported that Laycock had interviewed at SMU and was believed to be tops on Copeland's list. The *Daily Press* quoted W&M Athletic Director Driscoll as saying: "My best guess is that it's his [Laycock's] job to turn down. He'd have to be the one to say that for sure, but that's the impression I got."

The next day Laycock announced that he would not accept the SMU job offer and would remain at W&M. This was the latest of several Division I-A football jobs Laycock has turned down. "There are a lot of circumstances you have to consider. Obviously, there is another level at Division I and if a position on that level comes up, you certainly have to think about it, but right now I am happy to be here and am happy where I am."

Laycock still likes his alma mater. "I'm comfortable here and, of course, it's fine here." He looked at the Southern Methodist University head football job "because it is important to me and the staff that you explore things, not for the sake of doing it, but because it strengthens you and your belief in what you have already. It's part of the growing process."

Thus, Laycock entered 1997 making preparations for his eighteenth year at the helm of W&M football, where, since 1986, his teams have compiled an 86-40 record

Place-kicker Brian Shallcross scored 200 points with field goals and extra points in 1994, 1995, and 1996, collecting 84 points in 1996 on thirteen field goals and 45 points after touchdown. Courtesy of the W&M Sports Information Department.

and a winning percentage of .686 percent. According to W&M Assistant Sports Information Director for football Pete Clawson, W&M and Laycock had the Yankee Conference's most successful program (by percentage) during that decade.

Since becoming a member of the Yankee Conference in 1993, W&M compiled a 25-7 record, which tied Delaware's victory mark as the best in the conference during that time. But, as of July 1, 1997, the Yankee Conference was no more. Beginning in the fall of 1997, the twelve "Yankee" football programs play as the Atlantic 10 football conference. Sports writer John O'Connor called the changeover "a marriage of necessity" in the *Times-Dispatch* on November 14, 1996.

> The upcoming NCAA restructuring will allow voting privileges only to those conferences that have a full complement of sports. The 50-year old Yankee, which includes the University of Richmond, William and Mary and James Madison, plays only football. The A10 plays 21 sports, but football is currently not among them. Without the merge, schools from both leagues would have a weak voice in NCAA matters.

At the time of the change, the Atlantic 10 was known as a basketball conference that included Virginia Tech in all sports except football. The Atlantic 10 football conference operates a separate entity under the Atlantic 10 umbrella, with its own constitution, bylaws, and budget.

Prior to the Yankee move, W&M, Richmond, James Madison, and VMI (which is in the Southern Conference), discussed the formation of a football wing under the Colonial Athletic Association, along with Delaware, Villanova, The Citadel and Furman. Those talks, however, were suspended when NCAA restructuring became imminent, O'Connor explained.

The Yankee Conference champion traditionally received the old "Bean Pot" trophy. Since the Tribe became the last conference champion in 1996, the trophy has sat in the W&M football office, a fitting tribute to the College's emergence as a perennial winner.

W&M football players received this ring as winners of the 1996 Yankee Conference Championship. It was the fiftieth and last season for the conference, which merged into the Atlantic 10 Conference on July 1, 1997. Photo by Jostens Inc. of Tidewater; courtesy of the W&M Sports Information Department.

Part II

The Games
The Statistics
The Honors

Oh, we will fight, fight, fight for the Indians—
When the Indian team appears.
And we will pull like Hell for the Indians
When they hear our mighty cheers.
We will circle the ends for the Indians,
And we'll romp right down the field.
Touchdown! Touchdown! Indians.
And Richmond's line will surely yield.

—William and Mary Fight Song
Colonial Echo, 1924

W&M Sports Information Director

Around 1937, the responsibility for publicizing sports—primarily football and ultimately basketball—fell to the Athletic Publicity Director and was considered part of the duties of the College's Director of Public Relations. With the increased popularity and success of W&M football after World War II, the posiition expanded to full time in 1946. Then, from 1953 until 1964, it reverted to a primarily part-time job, handled by W&M students. In 1964, a full-time position was again created, and the first assistant was hired in 1973. Eventually, as responsibilities increased to include all sports, the position was renamed Sports Information Director (SID).

Pete
Clawson
and Jean Elliott

Richard Velz+		
& Spike Moore*	1937–40	
Spike Moore	1941 & 1942	
Laurence Leonard+	1946–47	
John Cox+	1947–49	
Tom Joynes* & Sam Banks*	1949	
Jim Jackson	1949–51	
Sam Banks	1951–53	
Rene A. Henry*		1953
Pete Franklin		1954–55
Peter M. Kalison*		1955–57
Frank Simmons*		1957–60
Bill Bryant*		1960–61
Barry Fratkin*		1961–73
(Wilford Kale* & Frank Simmons, acting, football season, 1966)		
Bob Sheeran, Assistant Director		1973
Bob Sheeran		1974–85
Kevin O'Rourke, Assistant Director		1977
Matt Seu, Assistant Director		1984–85
Bill Sullivan		1985–88
Bernie Cafarelli, Assistant Director		1985–87
Marty Benson, Associate Director		1987–88
Jean Elliott		1988 to present
Marty Benson, Associate Director		1988–90
Brian Haave, Assistant Director		1990–92
Jeff Nygaard, Assistant SID/Football		1992–95
Pete Clawson, Assistant SID/Football		1995 to present

Frank Simmons

Bob Sheeran

Barry Fratkin

+ Also served as Director of Public Relations for the College
* Were full-time students when they held the post. Frank Simmons was a student in the post from 1957 until 1959 and then became full-time SID, 1959–60. Barry Fratkin was a student in the post from 1961 until 1964 and then became full-time SID, 1964–73.   (—WK)

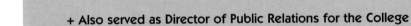

Appendix 1

Football Schedule

Date	Opponent Location and Event	Score W&M-Opp
1893 (2-1)		
Nov. 11	Norfolk Norfolk	4-16
Nov. 18	Old Dominion Club Williamsburg (campus)	14-4
Nov. 30	Capitol City Athletic Club Richmond (Thanksgiving Day)	8-4
1894 (0-1)		
Nov. 12	Hampden-Sydney Hampden-Sydney	0-28
1895 (No Games)		
1896 (0-2)		
Oct. 31	Randolph-Macon Williamsburg (campus)	0-10
Nov. 16	Randolph-Macon Ashland	0-4
1897 (0-1)		
Nov. 6	Columbian (George Washington) Washington, D.C.	0-26
1898 (1-1)		
Nov. 7	Randolph-Macon Williamsburg (campus)	5-0
Nov. 19	Richmond Richmond (Broad Street Park)	0-15
1899 (2-3)		
Oct. 21	Richmond Richmond	0-14
Oct. 30	Hampden-Sydney Williamsburg (campus)	0-6
Nov. 11	Portsmouth Athletic Club Williamsburg (campus)	5-10
Nov. 18	Hampton Athletic Club Williamsburg (campus)	41-0
Dec. 2	Baltimore City Club Newport News (Soldiers Home)	6-5

Date	Opponent Location and Event	Score W&M-Opp
1900 (1-2)		
Nov. 2	Newport News Athletic Club Williamsburg (campus)	5-0
Nov. 3	Hampden-Sydney Williamsburg (campus)	0-17
Nov. 24	Randolph-Macon Ashland	0-11
1901 (2-1-1)		
Oct. 22	Old Point Comfort College Williamsburg (campus)	11-6
Oct. 29	Randolph-Macon Williamsburg (campus)	0-0
Nov. 9	Richmond Williamsburg (campus)	11-27
Nov. 16	Fredericksburg College Williamsburg (campus)	6-0
1902 (1-1-1)		
Oct. 18	Old Point Comfort College Williamsburg (campus)	6-0
Oct. 25	Hampden-Sydney Hampden-Sydney	0-42
Nov. 6	St. Vincent's Academy Newport News	0-0
1903 (1-3)		
Oct. 17	Norfolk High School Williamsburg (campus)	15-0
Oct. 26	Old Point Comfort College Williamsburg (campus)	0-23
Oct. 31	Randolph-Macon Richmond (Broad Street Park)	0-39
Nov. 14	Richmond Richmond	0-24
1904 (3-3)		
Oct. 1	Norfolk High School Williamsburg (campus)	18-0
Oct. 15	Portsmouth Athletic Club Williamsburg (campus)	36-0
Oct. 22	Virginia Tech Blacksburg	0-30
Oct. 24	Roanoke Roanoke	5-6

Date	Opponent / Location and Event	Score W&M-Opp
Nov. 4	Richmond Williamsburg (campus)	15-6
Nov. 19	Randolph-Macon Williamsburg (campus)	0-6

1905 (2-4-1)

Date	Opponent / Location and Event	Score W&M-Opp
Sept. 30	Hampton Athletic Association Williamsburg (campus)	6-0
Oct. 11	Richmond Richmond	0-0
Oct. 21	Richmond Richmond	4-0
Oct. 28	VMI Lexington	0-23
Nov. 4	Maryland Agricultural College (University of Maryland) Williamsburg (campus)	0-17
Nov. 12	Richmond Richmond (Broad Street Park)	5-23
Nov. 19	Randolph-Macon Richmond (Broad Street Park	0-27

1906 (2-6)

Date	Opponent / Location and Event	Score W&M-Opp
Oct. 6	Virginia Tech Roanoke	0-12
Oct. 8	Virginia Tech Blacksburg	0-28
Oct. 13	Norfolk High School Williamsburg (campus)	10-0
Oct. 18	North Carolina A&M (State) Raleigh, N.C. (State. Fair Grounds)	0-40
Oct. 27	Brambleton Business College Williamsburg (campus)	10-0
Nov. 3	Richmond Williamsburg (campus)	0-24
Nov. 17	Randolph-Macon Williamsburg (campus)	4-6
Nov. 29	Richmond Newport News (Thanksgiving Day)	0-6

1907 (6-3)

Date	Opponent / Location and Event	Score W&M-Opp
Oct. 5	VMI Lexington	0-58
Oct. 12	Randolph-Macon Norfolk (Lafayette Field)	4-0
Oct. 19	North Carolina Chapel Hill, N.C.	0-14
Oct. 26	Old Point Comfort College Williams burg (campus)	16-6
Nov. 2	Medical College of Virginia Petersburg (Riverside C.C.Field)	19-0
Nov. 9	Fort Monroe Williamsburg (campus)	15-0
Nov. 16	Randolph-Macon Ashland	12-4

Date	Opponent / Location and Event	Score W&M-Opp
Nov. 23	Hampden-Sydney Hampden-Sydney	4-0
Nov. 28	Richmond Newport News (Thanksgiving Day)	0-48

1908 (4-6-1)

Date	Opponent / Location and Event	Score W&M-Opp
Sept. 26	Virginia Charlottesville	0-11
Oct. 3	VMI Lexington	0-21
Oct. 12	North Carolina State Raleigh, N.C.	0-24
Oct. 17	Randolph-Macon Petersburg	0-6
Oct. 24	Brambleton Business College Williamsburg (campus)	0-0
Oct. 31	Hampden-Sydney Petersburg	0-10
Nov. 7	Fort Monroe Williamsburg (campus)	5-0
Nov. 14	Randolph-Macon Richmond (Broad Street Park)	0-15
Nov. 21	Richmond Richmond (Broad Street Park)	21-18
Nov. 26	Hampden-Sydney Newport News (Casino Field)	17-0
Dec. 4	St. Vincent's Academy Newport News	6-5

1909 (6-4)

Date	Opponent / Location and Event	Score W&M-Opp
Sept. 25	Virginia Charlottesville	0-30
Oct. 2	Norfolk Blues Williamsburg (campus)	3-0
Oct. 9	VMI Lexington	0-6
Oct. 11	Norfolk High School Williamsburg	11-0
Oct. 16	Medical College of Virginia Williamsburg (campus)	6-0
Oct. 23	Episcopal High School Williamsburg (campus)	9-0
Oct. 30	Randolph-Macon Richmond (Broad Street Park)	3-15
Nov. 6	Hampden-Sydney Hampden-Sydney	3-22
Nov. 20	Richmond Richmond (Broad Street Park)	15-0
Nov. 25	Hampden-Sydney Newport News (Thanksgiving)	15-8

1910 (1-7-1)

Date	Opponent / Location and Event	Score W&M-Opp
Sept. 24	Virginia Charlottesville	0-10
Oct. 1	University College of Medicine Williamsburg (campus)	3-5

Date	Opponent Location and Event	Score W&M-Opp
Oct. 8	Norfolk High School Williamsburg (campus)	5-5
Oct. 15	VMI Lexington	0-33
Oct. 22	Norfolk Blues Norfolk	0-41
Oct. 29	Hampden-Sydney Williamsburg (campus)	6-17
Nov. 5	Randolph-Macon Williamsburg (campus)	2-11
Nov. 12	St. Vincent's Academy Williamsburg (campus)	6-18
Nov. 19	Richmond Richmond	18-6

1911 (1-5-2)

Date	Opponent Location and Event	Score W&M-Opp
Sept. 30	Virginia Charlottesville	0-81
Oct. 7	Georgetown Washington, D.C.	0-66
Oct. 14	University College of Medicine Williamsburg (campus)	0-0
Oct. 21	Fredericksburg College Williamsburg (campus)	0-0
Oct. 28	Medical College of Virginia Williamsburg (campus)	0-6
Nov. 4	Randolph-Macon Newport News	11-14
Nov. 11	Richmond Williamsburg (campus)	3-0
Nov. 18	Hampden-Sydney Hampden-Sydney	0-19

1912 (0-7)

Date	Opponent Location and Event	Score W&M-Opp
Sept. 29	Virginia Charlottesville	0-60
Oct. 5	Norfolk Blues Norfolk (Lafayette Field)	0-13
Oct. 12	University College of Medicine Williamsburg (Old Cary Field)	0-20
Oct. 26	Medical College of Virginia Williamsburg (Old Cary Field)	0-66
Nov. 2	Randolph-Macon Williamsburg (Old Cary Field)	0-20
Nov. 9	Richmond Richmond	0-20
Nov. 16	Hampden-Sydney Petersburg	0-27

1913 (0-5-1)

Date	Opponent Location and Event	Score W&M-Opp
Oct. 4	VMI Lexington	3-33
Oct. 11	Richmond Blues Williamsburg (Old Cary Field)	0-0
Nov. 1	Randolph-Macon Ashland	3-37

Date	Opponent Location and Event	Score W&M-Opp
Nov. 8	Richmond Newport News	13-20
Nov. 15	Hampden-Sydney Farmville	0-32
Nov. 22	Richmond Williamsburg (Old Cary Field)	13-20

1914 (1-7)

Date	Opponent Location and Event	Score W&M-Opp
Oct. 3	Richmond Blues Williamsburg (Ol d Cary Field)	9-13
Oct. 10	VMI Lexington	0-38
Oct. 17	Randolph-Macon Williamsburg (Old Cary Field)	10-7
Oct. 24	Richmond Williamsburg (Old Cary Field)	3-7
Oct. 31	Hampden-Sydney Newport News (Horwitz Field)	0-19
Nov. 7	Randolph-Macon Ashland	0-63
Nov. 14	Hampden-Sydney Williamsburg (Old Cary Field)	0-41
Nov. 21	Richmond Richmond	0-32

1915 (0-9-1)

Date	Opponent Location and Event	Score W&M-Opp
Sept. 29	Union Theological Seminary Williamsburg (Old Cary Field)	0-7
Oct. 2	VMI Lexington	6-19
Oct. 9	Richmond Blues Williamsburg (Old Cary Field)	0-0
Oct. 16	Hampden-Sydney Hampden-Sydney	0-28
Oct. 23	Richmond Williamsburg (Old Cary Field)	0-28
Oct. 30	Randolph-Macon Ashland	7-34
Nov. 6	Hampden-Sydney Newport News	0-38
Nov. 13	Randolph-Macon Williamsburg (Old Cary Field)	7-15
Nov. 20	Richmond Richmond	0-45
Nov. 25	Delaware Newark, Del. (Thanksgiving Day)	0-93

1916 (2-5-2)

Date	Opponent Location and Event	Score W&M-Opp
Sept. 30	Union Theological Seminary Williamsburg (Old Cary Field)	7-0
Oct. 7	VMI Lexington	0-66
Oct. 14	Portsmouth Naval Training Portsmouth	13-13
Oct. 21	Randolph-Macon Williamsburg (Old Cary Field)	0-17

Date	Opponent Location and Event	Score W&M-Opp
Oct. 28	Richmond Richmond	0-48
Nov. 4	Hampden-Sydney Williamsburg (Old Cary Field)	0-31
Nov. 11	Randolph-Macon Ashland	14-7
Nov. 18	Richmond Williamsburg (Old Cary Field)	0-0
Nov. 30	Hampden-Sydney Norfolk (Thanksgiving Day)	0-9

1917 (3-5)

Date	Opponent Location and Event	Score W&M-Opp
Oct. 7	VMI Lexington	0-53
Oct. 13	Richmond Richmond (Boulevard Field)	0-28
Oct. 20	Randolph-Macon Williamsburg (Old Cary Field)	13-0
Oct. 27	Hampden-Sydney Farmville	0-21
Nov. 3	Emory & Henry Emory	7-0
Nov. 10	Randolph-Macon Ashland	21-6
Nov. 17	Richmond Williamsburg (Old Cary Field)	0-19
Nov. 24	Hampden-Sydney Newport News	0-32

1918 (0-2)

Date	Opponent Location and Event	Score W&M-Opp
Nov. 16	Lynchburg College Lynchburg	0-13
Nov. 30	Richmond Williamsburg (Old Cary Field)	0-7

1919 (2-6-1)

Date	Opponent Location and Event	Score W&M-Opp
Oct. 4	Lynchburg College Lynchburg	0-0
Oct. 10	VMI Richmond (Boulevard Park)	3-21
Oct. 18	Richmond Williamsburg (Old Cary Field)	7-0
Oct. 27	Randolph-Macon Williamsburg (Old Cary Field)	3-0
Nov. 1	Hampden-Sydney Norfolk	3-7
Nov. 8	Richmond Richmond (Boulevard Park)	0-17
Nov. 15	Randolph-Macon Richmond	6-7
Nov. 22	Hampden-Sydney Williamsburg (Old Cary Field)	6-7
Nov. 27	Richmond Richmond (Thanksgiving Day)	0-21

1920 (4-5)

Date	Opponent Location and Event	Score W&M-Opp
Sept. 25	Virginia Charlottesville	0-27
Oct. 2	Virginia Tech Blacksburg	0-21
Oct. 9	Gallaudet College Richmond (Boulevard Park)	14-7
Oct. 16	Lynchburg College Williamsburg (Old Cary Field)	36-0
Oct. 23	Union Theological Seminary Williamsburg (Old Cary Field)	34-0
Oct. 30	Richmond Norfolk	0-13
Nov. 6	North Carolina A&E (State) Raleigh, N.C.	0-81
Nov. 20	Randolph-Macon Richmond (Boulevard Park)	34-0
Nov. 25	Hampden-Sydney Newport News (Thanksgiving Day)	7-14

1921 (4-3-1)

Date	Opponent Location and Event	Score W&M-Opp
Oct. 1	Virginia Tech Blacksburg	0-14
Oct. 8	Trinity (Duke) Durham, N.C.	12-0
Oct. 15	George Washington Norfolk	7-7
Oct. 22	Wake Forest Norfolk	21-14
Oct. 29	Randolph-Macon Williamsburg (Old Cary Field)	35-0
Nov. 5	Catholic University Newport News	13-27
Nov. 12	Union Theological Seminary Williamsburg (Old Cary Field)	76-0
Nov. 24	Richmond Richmond (Thanksgiving Day)	7-17

1922 (6-3)

Date	Opponent Location and Event	Score W&M-Opp
Sept. 30	Penn State State College, Pa.	7-27
Oct. 7	Virginia Tech Blacksburg	6-20
Oct. 14	Randolph-Macon Williamsburg (Old Cary Field)	33-7
Oct. 21	Trinity (Duke) Norfolk	13-7
Oct. 28	Hampden-Sydney Richmond	32-6
Nov. 4	Wake Forest Norfolk	18-0
Nov. 11	Roanoke Williamsburg (Old Cary Field)	14-0
Nov. 18	Gallaudet College Newport News	45-0
Nov. 30	Richmond Richmond (Thanksgiving Day)	3-13

Date	Opponent Location and Event	Score W&M-Opp

1923 (6-3)

Date	Opponent Location and Event	Score
Sept. 29	Navy Annapolis, Md.	10-39
Oct. 6	Syracuse Syracuse, N.Y.	3-63
Oct. 13	Guilford Williamsburg (Old Cary Field)	74-0
Oct. 20	Trinity (Duke) Rocky Mount, N.C.	21-0
Oct. 27	Randolph-Macon Williamsburg (Old Cary Field)	27-0
Nov. 3	Hampden-Sydney Norfolk	20-0
Nov. 10	Delaware Williamsburg (Old Cary Field)	14-0
Nov. 17	Roanoke Roanoke	7-9
Nov. 29	Richmond Richmond (Thanksgiving Day)	27-6

1924 (5-2-1)

Date	Opponent Location and Event	Score
Oct. 4	Navy Annapolis, Md.	7-14
Oct. 11	Syracuse Syracuse, N.Y.	7-24
Oct. 18	Randolph-Macon Williamsburg (Old Cary Field)	27-7
Oct. 25	Trinity (Duke) Norfolk	21-3
Nov. 1	King Richmond (Mayo Island Park)	27-0
Nov. 8	Albright Williamsburg (Old Cary Field)	27-0
Nov. 15	Roanoke Newport News	7-7
Nov. 27	Richmond Richmond (Thanksgiving Day)	20-6

1925 (6-4)

Date	Opponent Location and Event	Score
Sept. 26	Lenoir-Rhyne Williamsburg (Old Cary Field)	44-0
Oct. 3	Navy Annapolis, Md. (Farragut Field)	0-25
Oct. 10	Syracuse Syracuse, N.Y.	0-33
Oct. 17	Randolph-Macon Richmond (Mayo Island Park)	54-0
Oct. 24	Duke Norfolk	35-0
Oct. 31	Harvard Cambridge, Mass.	7-14
Nov. 7	Albright Williamsburg (Old Cary Field)	27-0

Date	Opponent Location and Event	Score
Nov. 11	Haskell Richmond (Mayo Island Park)	13-14
Nov. 20	Roanoke Roanoke	23-0
Nov. 26	Richmond Richmond (Thanksgiving Day)	14-0

1926 (7-3)

Date	Opponent Location and Event	Score
Sept. 25	Randolph-Macon Williamsburg (Old Cary Field)	35-0
Oct. 2	Loyola Williamsburg (Old Cary Field)	19-0
Oct. 9	Syracuse Syracuse, N.Y.	0-35
Oct. 16	Harvard Cambridge, Mass.	7-27
Oct. 23	George Washington Williamsburg (1st Homecoming)	14-0
Oct. 30	Lynchburg Newport News (High School Field)	48-0
Nov. 6	Columbia New York City, N.Y.	10-13
Nov. 13	Wake Forest Norfolk	13-6
Nov. 25	Richmond Richmond (Thanksgiving Day)	14-0
Dec. 4	Chattanooga Chattanooga (First Post Season Game— Southern Title)	9-6

1927 (4-5-1)

Date	Opponent Location and Event	Score
Sept. 24	Catholic University Williamsburg (First Night Game)	0-12
Oct. 1	Syracuse Syracuse, N.Y.	0-18
Oct. 8	Lenoir-Rhyne Williamsburg (Old Cary Field) (N)	19-0
Oct. 15	Quantico Marines Newport News	14-20
Oct. 22	Concord State Williamsburg (2nd Homecoming)	13-7
Oct. 29	Princeton Princeton, N.J.	7-35
Nov. 5	Chattanooga Norfolk	7-12
Nov. 11	Roanoke Roanoke	18-7
Nov. 19	Hampden-Sydney Norfolk	33-7
Nov. 23	Richmond Richmond	0-0

Date	Opponent Location and Event	Score W&M-Opp

1928 (6-3-2)

Date	Opponent / Location and Event	Score
Sept. 22	Lynchburg Williamsburg (Old Cary Field) (N)	41-0
Sept. 29	Marshall Williamsburg (Old Cary Field) (N)	0-0
Oct. 6	Syracuse Syracuse, N.Y.	0-32
Oct. 13	Wake Forest Williamsburg (Old Cary Field) (N)	0-0
Oct. 20	Catholic University Williamsburg (Old Cary Field) (N)	12-13
Oct. 27	Emory & Henry Williamsburg (Old Cary Field) (N)	0-3
Nov. 3	George Washington Washington, D.C. (Central Stadium)	24-0
Nov. 12	Roanoke Richmond (Mayo Island Park)	32-6
Nov. 17	Bridgewater Williamsburg (Old Cary Field)	68-0
Nov. 24	Hampden-Sydney Newport News	34-0
Nov. 29	Richmond Richmond (Thanksgiving Day)	7-0

1929 (8-2)

Date	Opponent / Location and Event	Score
Sept. 28	St. John's Williamsburg (Old Cary Field) (N)	19-0
Oct. 5	Navy Annapolis, Md.	0-15
Oct. 12	Emory & Henry Emory	7-6
Oct. 19	Virginia Tech Richmond	14-25
Oct. 26	Bridgewater Williamsburg (Old Cary Field) (N)	59-0
Nov. 2	George Washington Williamsburg (Homecoming) (N)	51-6
Nov. 9	Roanoke Roanoke	19-6
Nov. 16	Catholic University Williamsburg (Old Cary Field) (N)	36-13
Nov. 28	Richmond Richmond (Thanksgiving Day)	25-0
Dec. 7	Hampden-Sydney Hampden-Sydney	20-6

1930 (7-2-1)

Date	Opponent / Location and Event	Score
Sept. 27	Guilford Williamsburg (Old Cary Field) (N)	24-0
Oct. 4	Navy Annapolis, Md.	6-19
Oct. 11	Wofford Williamsburg (Old Cary Field) (N)	19-0
Oct. 18	Virginia Tech Richmond (Mayo Island Park)	6-7
Oct. 25	Bridgewater Williamsburg (Old Cary Field) (N)	81-0

Date	Opponent / Location and Event	Score
Nov. 1	Harvard Cambridge, Mass.	13-13
Nov. 8	Roanoke Williamsburg (Homecoming) (N)	39-0
Nov. 15	Emory & Henry Williamsburg (Old Cary Field) (N)	27-0
Nov. 26	Richmond Richmond (Thanksgiving Day)	19-0
Dec. 6	Hampden-Sydney Richmond (Richmond Stadium)	13-0

1931 (5-2-2)

Date	Opponent / Location and Event	Score
Sept. 26	Guilford Williamsburg (Old Cary Field)	32-0
Oct. 3	Navy Annapolis, Md.	6-13
Oct. 10	Randolph-Macon Williamsburg (Old Cary Field)	9-2
Oct. 17	Virginia Tech Richmond	6-6
Oct. 23	Bridgewater Williamsburg (Old Cary Field)	95-0
Oct. 31	Washington & Lee Norfolk	0-0
Nov. 7	Roanoke Roanoke	13-6
Nov. 14	Emory & Henry Emory	24-0
Nov. 26	Richmond Richmond (Thanksgiving Day)	2-6

1932 (8-4)

Date	Opponent / Location and Event	Score
Sept. 17	Roanoke Williamsburg (Old Cary Field) (N)	6-0
Sept. 24	Randolph-Macon Williamsburg (Old Cary Field) (N)	27-13
Oct. 1	Navy Annapolis, Md.	6-0
Oct. 8	Guilford Williamsburg (Old Cary Field) (N)	47-0
Oct. 15	Virginia Tech Richmond	0-7
Oct. 22	Washington & Lee Norfolk (Band Field)	7-0
Oct. 29	Army West Point, N.Y.	0-33
Nov. 2	Bridgewater Williamsburg (N)	77-0
Nov. 5	VMI Norfolk (Foreman Field)	20-7
Nov. 11	George Washington Washington, D.C.	6-12
Nov. 19	Emory & Henry Williamsburg (Homecoming)	18-6
Nov. 24	Richmond Richmond (Thanksgiving Day)	7-18

Date	Opponent Location and Event	Score W&M-Opp

1933 (6-5)

Date	Opponent Location and Event	Score W&M-Opp
Sept. 16	Roanoke Williamsburg (Old Cary Field) (N)	7-6
Sept. 23	Randolph-Macon Williamsburg (Old Cary Field)	12-0
Sept. 30	Navy Annapolis, Md.	0-12
Oct. 7	Washington & Lee Lexington	0-7
Oct. 14	Virginia Tech Richmond	7-13
Oct. 21	Guilford Williamsburg (Old Cary Field)	37-7
Oct. 28	Georgetown Washington, D.C.	12-6
Nov. 4	VMI Norfolk	14-0
Nov. 11	Emory & Henry Emory	6-25
Nov. 18	Davidson Williamsburg (Homecoming)	7-12
Nov. 30	Richmond Richmond (Thanksgiving Day)	6-0

1934 (2-6)

Date	Opponent Location and Event	Score W&M-Opp
Sept. 29	Navy Annapolis, Md.	7-20
Oct. 6	Emory & Henry Williamsburg (Old Cary Field)	20-8
Oct. 13	Virginia Tech Richmond	0-6
Oct. 20	Georgetown Washington, D.C.	0-3
Oct. 27	Roanoke Williamsburg (Old Cary Field)	15-6
Nov. 3	VMI Norfolk	6-13
Nov. 17	Washington & Lee Williamsburg (Homecoming)	0-7
Nov. 29	Richmond Richmond (Thanksgiving Day)	0-6

1935 (3-4-3)

Date	Opponent Location and Event	Score W&M-Opp
Sept. 21	Virginia Wmsbg (New Cary Field Opened)	0-0
Sept. 28	Navy Annapolis, Md.	0-30
Oct. 5	Army West Point, N.Y.	0-14
Oct. 12	Virginia Tech Richmond	0-0
Oct. 19	Guilford Williamsburg	44-0
Oct. 26	Roanoke Williamsburg	14-7

Date	Opponent Location and Event	Score W&M-Opp
Nov. 2	VMI Williamsburg (Homecoming)	0-19
Nov. 9	Dartmouth Hanover, N.H.	0-34
Nov. 15	Emory & Henry Williamsburg	22-0
Nov. 27	Richmond Richmond (Thanksgiving Day)	6-6

1936 (1-8)

Date	Opponent Location and Event	Score W&M-Opp
Sept. 26	Navy Annapolis, Md.	6-18
Oct. 3	Virginia Norfolk	0-7
Oct. 10	Virginia Tech Richmond (City Stadium)	0-14
Oct. 17	Guilford Williamsburg	38-0
Oct. 24	Roanoke Williamsburg	0-13
Oct. 31	Hampden-Sydney Williamsburg	0-19
Nov. 7	VMI Williamsburg (Homecoming)	0-21
Nov. 14	Washington & Lee Norfolk	7-13
Nov. 26	Richmond Richmond (Thanksgiving Day)	0-7

1937 (4-5)

Date	Opponent Location and Event	Score W&M-Opp
Sept. 25	Navy Annapolis, Md.	0-45
Oct. 2	VMI Norfolk (Foreman Field)	9-20
Oct. 9	Virginia Tech Richmond (City Stadium)	12-0
Oct. 16	Guilford Williamsburg	37-0
Oct. 23	American University Williamsburg	38-0
Oct. 30	Virginia Charlottesville	0-6
Nov. 6	Hampden-Sydney Williamsburg	21-12
Nov. 13	Washington & Lee Williamsburg (Homecoming)	12-14
Nov. 25	Richmond Richmond (Thanksgiving Day)	0-6

1938 (2-7)

Date	Opponent Location and Event	Score W&M-Opp
Sept. 24	Navy Annapolis, Md.	0-26
Oct. 1	Apprentice School (Newport News) Williamsburg	8-9

Date	Opponent Location and Event	Score W&M-Opp
Oct. 8	Virginia Tech Blacksburg	0-27
Oct. 15	Guilford Williamsburg	45-0
Oct. 22	VMI Williamsburg (Homecoming)	0-14
Oct. 29	Virginia Charlottesville	0-34
Nov. 5	Hampden-Sydney Williamsburg	18-7
Nov. 12	Washington & Lee Lexington	0-27
Nov. 24	Richmond Richmond (Thanksgiving Day)	7-10

1939 (6-2-1)

Date	Opponent Location and Event	Score W&M-Opp
Sept. 23	Guilford Williamsburg	31-6
Sept. 30	Navy Annapolis, Md.	6-31
Oct. 7	Apprentice School (Newport News) Newport News	39-6
Oct. 14	Virginia Tech Richmond (City Stadium)	6-6
Oct. 21	Hampden-Sydney Williamsburg	26-0
Oct. 28	Virginia Norfolk (Foreman Field)	6-26
Nov. 11	Randolph-Macon Williamsburg	19-6
Nov. 18	Washington & Lee Williamsburg (Homecoming)	18-14
Nov. 30	Richmond Richmond (Thanksgiving Day)	7-0

1940 (6-2-1)

Date	Opponent Location and Event	Score W&M-Opp
Sept. 21	N.C. State Norfolk (Foreman Field)	0-16
Sept. 28	Navy Annapolis, Md.	7-19
Oct. 5	Apprentice School (Newport News) Williamsburg	42-0
Oct. 12	Virginia Tech Richmond (City Stadium)	20-13
Oct. 19	Hampden-Sydney Williamsburg	41-0
Oct. 26	Virginia Williamsburg (Homecoming)	13-6
Nov. 2	VMI Lexington	0-0
Nov. 9	Randolph-Macon Williamsburg	46-6
Nov. 28	Richmond Richmond (Thanksgiving Day)	16-0

1941 (8-2)

Date	Opponent Location and Event	Score W&M-Opp
Sept. 20	Apprentice School (Newport News) Williamsburg	53-0
Sept. 27	Navy Annapolis, Md.	0-34
Oct. 4	Randolph-Macon Williamsburg	57-7
Oct. 11	Virginia Tech Richmond (City Stadium)	16-7
Oct. 18	Hampden-Sydney Hampden-Sydney	28-0
Oct. 24	George Washington Norfolk (Foreman Field) (N)	48-0
Nov. 1	Dartmouth Hanover, N.H.	3-0
Nov. 8	VMI Williamsburg (Homecoming)	21-0
Nov. 20	Richmond Richmond (City Stadium)	33-3
Nov. 29	N.C. State Williamsburg (Cary Field)	0-13

1942 (9-1-1)

Date	Opponent Location and Event	Score W&M-Opp
Sept. 18	Hampden-Sydney Norfolk (Foreman Field) (N)	27-0
Sept. 26	Navy Annapolis, Md.	3-0
Oct. 3	Virginia Tech Blacksburg	21-7
Oct. 10	Harvard Cambridge, Mass.	7-7
Oct. 24	George Washington Williamsburg (Homecoming)	61-0
Oct. 31	Dartmouth Williamsburg (Cary Field)	35-14
Nov. 7	Randolph-Macon Williamsburg (Cary Field)	40-0
Nov. 14	VMI Norfolk (Foreman Field)	27-6
Nov. 21	N.C. Pre-Flight Williamsburg (Cary Field)	0-14
Nov. 26	Richmond Richmond (City Stadium) (Thanksgiving)	10-0
Dec. 5	Oklahoma Norman, Okla.	14-7

1943

(No Varsity Games—World War II)

1944 (5-2-1)

Date	Opponent Location and Event	Score W&M-Opp
Sept. 30	Fort Monroe Williamsburg	46-0
Oct. 6	Hampden-Sydney Richmond (City Stadium) (N)	38-0

Date	Opponent Location and Event	Score W&M-Opp
Oct. 14	Pennsylvania Philadelphia (Franklin Field)	0-46
Oct. 21	Richmond Air Base Williamsburg	39-0
Oct. 28	N.C. State Norfolk (Foreman Field)	2-19
Nov. 11	North Carolina Chapel Hill, N.C.	0-0
Nov. 18	VMI Portsmouth (City Stadium)	26-0
Nov. 30	Richmond Richmond (Thanksgiving Day)	40-0

1945 (6-3)

Date	Opponent Location and Event	Score W&M-Opp
Sept. 29	Catawba Williamsburg	19-6
Oct. 6	Tennessee Knoxville, Tenn.	13-48
Oct. 13	Virginia Tech Richmond (City Stadium)	38-0
Oct. 20	VMI Richmond (City Stadium)	13-9
Oct. 26	N.C. State Norfolk (Foreman Field) (N)	6-20
Nov. 3	Maryland College Park, Md.	33-14
Nov. 10	North Carolina Norfolk (Foreman Field)	0-6
Nov. 17	Merchant Marine Williamsburg (Homecoming)	25-7
Nov. 29	Richmond Richmond (Thanksgiving Day)	33-0

1946 (8-2)

Date	Opponent Location and Event	Score W&M-Opp
Sept. 21	Ft. McClelland Williamsburg	61-0
Sept. 27	Miami (Fla.) Miami, Fla. (Orange Bowl) (N)	3-13
Oct. 5	The Citadel Charleston, S.C.	51-12
Oct. 12	Virginia Tech Williamsburg	49-0
Oct. 19	Washington & Lee Roanoke	34-18
Oct. 26	VMI Williamsburg (Homecoming)	41-0
Nov. 2	Maryland Williamsburg	41-7
Nov. 9	North Carolina Richmond (City Stadium)	7-21
Nov. 16	George Washington Washington, D.C. (Griffith Stadium)	20-0
Nov. 28	Richmond Richmond (Thanksgiving Day)	40-0

1947 (9-2)

Date	Opponent Location and Event	Score W&M-Opp
Sept. 27	Davidson Norfolk	21-0
Oct. 4	The Citadel Williamsburg (Cary Field)	56-7
Oct. 11	Virginia Tech Richmond	21-7
Oct. 18	North Carolina Williamsburg (Cary Field)	7-13
Oct. 25	Boston University Boston, Mass. (Fenway Park)	47-13
Nov. 1	Wake Forest Williamsburg (Cary Field)	21-0
Nov. 8	VMI Williamsburg (Homecoming)	28-20
Nov. 15	Washington & Lee Roanoke	45-6
Nov. 22	Bowling Green Williamsburg	20-0
Nov. 27	Richmond Richmond (Thanksgiving Day)	35-0
Jan.1 '48	Arkansas Birmingham, Ala. (Dixie Bowl)	19-21

1948 (7-2-2)

Date	Opponent Location and Event	Score W&M-Opp
Sept. 25	Davidson Charlotte, N.C. (Memorial Stadium)(N)	14-6
Oct. 2	Wake Forest Williamsburg	12-21
Oct. 9	VMI Norfolk (Oyster Bowl)	31-0
Oct. 16	Virginia Tech Blacksburg	30-0
Oct. 23	St. Bonaventure Olean, N.Y.	6-7
Oct. 30	Richmond Williamsburg (Homecoming)	14-6
Nov. 6	North Carolina Chapel Hill, N.C.	7-7
Nov. 13	Boston College Boston, Mass (Braves Fields)	14-14
Nov. 20	North Carolina State Williamsburg	26-6
Nov. 27	Arkansas Little Rock, Ark.	9-0
Jan. 1 '49	Oklahoma A&M (State) Memphis, Tenn. (Delta Bowl)	20-0

1949 (6-4)

Date	Opponent Location and Event	Score W&M-Opp
Sept. 17	Houston Houston, Tex. (N)	14-13
Sept. 24	Pittsburgh Pittsburgh, Pa.	7-13
Oct. 1	Virginia Tech Williamsburg	39-13

Date	Opponent Location and Event	Score W&M-Opp
Oct. 8	VMI Williamsburg (Homecoming)	54-6
Oct. 15	Michigan State East Lansing, Mich.	13-42
Oct. 22	Wake Forest Wake Forest, N.C.	28-55
Oct. 29	Richmond Richmond	34-0
Nov. 5	North Carolina Williamsburg	14-20
Nov. 19	Arkansas Little Rock, Ark.	20-0
Nov. 26	North Carolina State Williamsburg	33-7

1950 (4-7)

Date	Opponent Location and Event	Score W&M-Opp
Sept. 23	VMI Roanoke (N)	19-25
Sept. 30	Cincinnati Williamsburg	20-14
Oct. 7	Wake Forest Williamsburg (Homecoming)	0-47
Oct. 14	Michigan State East Lansing, Mich.	14-33
Oct. 21	Virginia Tech Blacksburg	54-0
Oct. 28	North Carolina Chapel Hill, N.C.	7-40
Nov. 4	Boston University Boston, Mass.	14-16
Nov. 11	Virginia Charlottesville	0-13
Nov. 18	Houston Houston, Tex.	18-36
Nov. 25	North Carolina State Norfolk (Oyster Bowl)	34-0
Dec. 2	Richmond Williamsburg	40-6

1951 (7-3)

Date	Opponent Location and Event	Score W&M-Opp
Sept. 22	Boston University Williamsburg	34-25
Sept. 29	Oklahoma Norman, Okla.	7-49
Oct. 6	VMI Williamsburg	7-20
Oct. 13	Wake Forest Richmond (Tobacco Bowl)	7-6
Oct. 20	North Carolina State Raleigh, N.C.	35-28
Oct. 27	Richmond Richmond	20-14
Nov. 3	Pennsylvania Philadelphia, Pa. (Franklin Field)	20-12
Nov. 10	Virginia Tech Williamsburg (Homecoming)	28-7

Date	Opponent Location and Event	Score W&M-Opp
Nov. 17	Duke Williamsburg	14-13
Nov. 24	Virginia Charlottesville	0-46

1952 (4-5)

Date	Opponent Location and Event	Score W&M-Opp
Sept. 20	VMI Roanoke (N)	34-13
Sept. 27	Wake Forest Williamsburg	21-28
Oct. 4	Penn State State College, Pa.	23-35
Oct. 11	Navy Annapolis, Md.	0-14
Oct. 18	Boston University Boston, Mass.	28-33
Oct. 25	Richmond Williamsburg (Homecoming)	42-13
Nov. 8	Virginia Tech Blacksburg	34-15
Nov. 22	North Carolina State Williamsburg	41-6
Nov. 29	Virginia Williamsburg	13-20

1953 (5-4-1)

Date	Opponent Location and Event	Score W&M-Opp
Sept. 19	Wake Forest Richmond	16-14
Sept. 26	Navy Annapolis, Md.	6-6
Oct. 3	Cincinnati Cincinnati, Ohio (N)	7-57
Oct. 17	Virginia Tech Williamsburg	13-7
Oct. 24	George Washington Williamsburg (Homecoming)	12-7
Oct. 31	North Carolina State Raleigh, N.C.	7-6
Nov. 7	VMI Roanoke	19-20
Nov. 14	Richmond Richmond	21-0
Nov. 21	Washington & Lee Williamsburg	7-33
Nov. 28	Boston University Williamsburg	14-41

1954 (4-2-2)

Date	Opponent Location and Event	Score W&M-Opp
Sept. 25	Navy Annapolis, Md.	0-27
Oct. 2	Pennsylvania Philadelphia, Pa.	27-7
Oct. 9	North Carolina State Norfolk	0-26

Date	Opponent Location and Event	Score W&M-Opp
Oct. 16	Rutgers New Brunswick, N.J.	14-7
Oct. 22	George Washington Washington, D.C. (N)	13-13
Oct. 30	Virginia Tech Blacksburg	7-7
Nov. 6	VMI Roanoke	0-21
Nov. 13	West Virginia Williamsburg (Homecoming)	6-20
Nov. 20	Wake Forest Williamsburg	13-9
Nov. 25	Richmond Richmond (Thanksgiving Classic)	2-0

1955 (1-7-1)

Date	Opponent Location and Event	Score W&M-Opp
Sept. 24	Navy Annapolis, Md.	0-7
Oct. 1	Virginia Tech Williamsburg	7-14
Oct. 8	Duke Durham, N.C.	7-47
Oct. 15	West Virginia Morgantown, W. Va.	13-39
Oct. 22	George Washington Williamsburg	0-16
Oct. 29	VMI Williamsburg (Homecoming)	20-13
Nov. 5	Wake Forest Wake Forest, N.C.	7-13
Nov. 19	North Carolina State Raleigh, N.C. (N)	21-28
Nov. 24	Richmond Richmond (Thanksgiving Classic)	6-6

1956 (0-9-1)

Date	Opponent Location and Event	Score W&M-Opp
Sept. 22	Wake Forest Williamsburg	0-39
Sept. 29	Navy Annapolis, Md.	14-39
Oct. 6	Boston University Williamsburg	18-18
Oct. 13	Virginia Tech Blacksburg	7-34
Oct. 20	West Virginia Williamsburg (Homecoming)	13-20
Oct. 26	George Washington Washington, D.C. (N)	14-16
Nov. 3	VMI Lynchburg	6-20
Nov. 10	Army West Point, N.Y.	6-34
Nov. 17	Rutgers New Brunswick, N.J.	6-20
Nov. 22	Richmond Richmond (Thanksgiving Classic)	0-6

1957 (4-6)

Date	Opponent Location and Event	Score W&M-Opp
Sept. 21	George Washington Williamsburg	0-7
Sept. 28	Navy Annapolis, Md.	6-33
Oct. 5	Virginia Tech Williamsburg	13-7
Oct. 12	Penn State University Park, Pa.	13-21
Oct. 19	VMI Williamsburg	13-14
Oct. 26	West Virginia Morgantown, W. Va.	0-19
Nov. 2	The Citadel Charleston, S.C.	14-12
Nov. 9	North Carolina State Raleigh, N.C.	7-6
Nov. 16	Rutgers Williamsburg (Homecoming)	38-7
Nov. 28	Richmond Richmond (Thanksgiving Classic)	7-12

1958 (2-6-1)

Date	Opponent Location and Event	Score W&M-Opp
Sept. 27	Navy Annapolis, Md.	0-14
Oct. 4	Virginia Tech Blacksburg	15-27
Oct. 11	VMI Bluefield, W. Va.	6-6
Oct. 18	North Carolina State Williamsburg	13-6
Oct. 24	George Washington Washington, D.C. (N)	0-7
Nov. 1	Boston University Boston, Mass.	7-33
Nov. 8	Davidson Williamsburg (Homecoming)	7-16
Nov. 15	West Virginia Williamsburg	6-55
Nov. 27	Richmond Richmond (Thanksgiving Classic)	18-15

1959 (4-6)

Date	Opponent Location and Event	Score W&M-Opp
Sept. 19	Virginia Charlottesville	37-0
Sept. 26	Navy Annapolis, Md.	2-29
Oct. 3	Virginia Tech Roanoke	14-20
Oct. 10	Furman Williamsburg (Homecoming)	7-8
Oct. 17	VMI Norfolk	7-26
Oct. 24	George Washington Williamsburg	14-7

Date	Opponent Location and Event	Score W&M-Opp
Oct 31	The Citadel Williamsburg	13-38
Nov. 7	Davidson Davidson, N.C.	25-7
Nov. 14	Florida State Tallahassee, Fla.	9-0
Nov. 26	Richmond Richmond (Thanksgiving Classic)	12-20

1960 (2-8)

Date	Opponent Location and Event	Score W&M-Opp
Sept. 17	VMI Williamsburg	21-33
Sept. 24	Virginia Norfolk (N)	41-21
Oct. 1	George Washington Williamsburg	19-9
Oct. 8	Furman Greenville, S.C. (N)	23-25
Oct. 15	Virginia Tech Williamsburg (Homecoming)	0-27
Oct. 22	Florida State Tallahassee, Fla. (N)	0-22
Oct. 29	Tulane New Orleans, La. (N)	8-40
Nov. 5	The Citadel Charleston, S.C. (N)	0-14
Nov. 12	Vanderbilt Nashville, Tenn.	8-22
Nov. 24	Richmond Richmond (Thanksgiving Classic)	0-19

1961 (1-9)

Date	Opponent Location and Event	Score W&M-Opp
Sept. 16	Virginia Tech Roanoke (N)	6-20
Sept. 23	Virginia Charlottesville	6-21
Sept. 30	Navy Annapolis, Md.	6-44
Oct. 7	Furman Williamsburg	19-6
Oct. 14	The Citadel Williamsburg (Homecoming)	8-10
Oct. 20	George Washington Washington, D.C. (N)	12-49
Oct. 28	VMI Williamsburg	7-14
Nov. 4	Davidson Williamsburg	30-31
Nov. 11	Army West Point, N.Y.	13-48
Nov. 23	Richmond Richmond (Thanksgiving Classic)	18-36

1962 (4-5-1)

Date	Opponent Location and Event	Score W&M-Opp
Sept. 15	Virginia Tech Williamsburg	3-0
Sept. 22	Virginia Williamsburg	7-19
Sept. 29	Navy Annapolis, Md.	16-20
Oct. 6	The Citadel Charleston, S.C.	29-23
Oct. 13	Davidson Davidson, N.C.	7-7
Oct. 20	Furman Williamsburg (Homecoming)	21-7
Oct. 27	VMI Lexington	0-6
Nov. 3	West Virginia Morgantown, W. Va.	13-28
Nov. 10	George Washington Williamsburg	10-6
Nov. 22	Richmond Richmond (Thanksgiving Classic)	3-15

1963 (4-6)

Date	Opponent Location and Event	Score W&M-Opp
Sept. 21	The Citadel Charleston, S.C. (N)	7-0
Sept. 28	Navy Annapolis, Md.	0-28
Oct. 5	Furman Greenville, S.C. (N)	27-17
Oct. 12	West Virginia Williamsburg (Homecoming)	16-20
Oct. 19	Virginia Tech Blacksburg	13-28
Oct. 25	George Washington Williamsburg	14-32
Nov. 2	VMI Williamsburg	6-26
Nov. 9	Virginia Charlottesville	7-9
Nov. 16	Davidson Williamsburg	34-5
Nov. 28	Richmond Richmond (Thanksgiving Classic)	29-6

1964 (4-6)

Date	Opponent Location and Event	Score W&M-Opp
Sept. 19	VMI Lexington	14-12
Sept. 26	Navy Annapolis, Md.	6-35
Oct. 3	Pittsburgh Pittsburgh, Pa.	7-34
Oct. 10	Furman Williamsburg	21-14
Oct. 17	The Citadel Williamsburg (Homecoming)	10-0

Date	Opponent Location and Event	Score W&M-Opp
Oct. 23	George Washington Washington, D.C. (N)	0-21
Oct. 31	Virginia Tech Williamsburg	20-27
Nov. 7	Virginia Williamsburg	13-14
Nov. 14	West Virginia Morgantown, W. Va.	14-24
Nov. 26	Richmond Richmond (Thanksgiving Classic)	33-13

1965 (6-4)

Date	Opponent Location and Event	Score W&M-Opp
Sept. 18	VMI Williamsburg	32-21
Sept. 25	West Virginia Williamsburg	14-34
Oct. 2	Virginia Tech Blacksburg	7-9
Oct. 9	Navy Annapolis, Md.	14-42
Oct. 16	Davidson Davidson, N.C.	41-7
Oct. 23	George Washington Williamsburg (Homecoming)	28-14
Oct. 30	Southern Mississippi Norfolk (Oyster Bowl)	3-0
Nov. 6	The Citadel Charleston, S.C.	20-6
Nov. 13	Boston College Boston, Mass.	17-30
Nov. 20	Richmond Williamsburg	21-0

1966 (5-4-1)

Date	Opponent Location and Event	Score W&M-Opp
Sept. 17	East Carolina Williamsburg	7-7
Sept. 24	West Virginia Morgantown, W. Va.	13-24
Oct. 1	George Washington Washington, D.C. (N)	10-3
Oct. 8	Villanova Williamsburg	34-14
Oct. 15	The Citadel Williamsburg (Homecoming)	24-6
Oct. 22	Navy Annapolis, Md.	0-21
Oct. 29	VMI Lexington	22-15
Nov. 5	Boston College Chestnut Hill, Mass. (Reg. ABC-TV)	13-15
Nov. 12	Virginia Tech Williamsburg	18-20
Nov. 19	Richmond Richmond	35-19

1967 (5-4-1)

Date	Opponent Location and Event	Score W&M-Opp
Sept. 9	Quantico Williamsburg	38-7
Sept. 16	East Carolina Williamsburg	7-27
Sept. 23	Virginia Tech Blacksburg	7-31
Sept. 30	Vanderbilt Nashville, Tenn.	12-14
Oct. 7	VMI Richmond (Tobacco Bowl)	33-28
Oct. 14	Ohio University Athens, Ohio	25-22
Oct. 21	Navy Annapolis, Md.	27-16
Nov. 4	The Citadel Charleston, S.C.	24-0
Nov. 11	West Virginia Williamsburg	16-16
Nov. 18	Richmond Williamsburg (Homecoming)	7-16

1968 (3-7)

Date	Opponent Location and Event	Score W&M-Opp
Sept. 21	East Carolina Greenville, N.C.	14-0
Sept. 28	Virginia Tech Williamsburg	0-12
Oct. 5	Pittsburgh Pittsburgh, Pa.	3-14
Oct. 12	Ohio University Williamsburg (Homecoming)	0-41
Oct. 19	West Virginia Richmond (Tobacco Bowl)	0-20
Oct. 26	VMI Lexington	20-10
Nov. 2	Villanova Williamsburg	33-12
Nov. 9	Syracuse Syracuse, N.Y.	0-31
Nov. 16	The Citadel Williamsburg	21-24
Nov. 23	Richmond Richmond	6-31

1969 (3-7)

Date	Opponent Location and Event	Score W&M-Opp
Sept. 20	Cincinnati Cincinnati, Ohio (N)	18-26
Sept. 27	Temple Philadelphia, Pa. (N)	7-6
Oct. 4	Virginia Williamsburg	15-28
Oct. 11	The Citadel Charleston, S.C. (N)	21-14
Oct. 18	Davidson Williamsburg (Homecoming)	15-17

Date	Opponent Location and Event	Score W&M-Opp
Oct. 25	VMI Williamsburg (Burgesses Day)	25-17
Nov. 1	Virginia Tech Roanoke (Harvest Bowl)	7-48
Nov. 8	West Virginia Williamsburg	0-31
Nov. 15	Villanova Villanova, Pa.	21-35
Nov. 22	Richmond Williamsburg	17-28

1970 (5-7)

Date	Opponent Location and Event	Score W&M-Opp
Sept. 12	West Virginia Morgantown, W. Va.	7-43
Sept. 18	Miami Miami, Fla. (N)	14-36
Sept. 26	Cincinnati Williamsburg	10-17
Oct. 3	Ohio Wesleyan Williamsburg	33-29
Oct. 10	The Citadel Williamsburg (Homecoming)	7-16
Oct. 17	VMI Lexington	24-10
Oct. 24	Virginia Charlottesville	6-33
Oct. 31	Virginia Tech Williamsburg	14-35
Nov. 7	Connecticut Williamsburg	28-15
Nov. 14	Davidson Davidson, N.C.	29-28
Nov. 21	Richmond Richmond	34-33
Dec. 28	Toledo Orlando, Fla. (Tangerine Bowl)	12-40

1971 (5-6)

Date	Opponent Location and Event	Score W&M-Opp
Sept. 11	The Citadel Charleston, S.C. (N)	35-28
Sept. 18	East Carolina Greenville, N.C.	28-10
Sept. 25	Davidson Williamsburg	40-14
Oct. 2	Tulane New Orleans, La. (N)	14-3
Oct. 9	West Virginia Williamsburg	23-28
Oct. 16	Virginia Tech Blacksburg	30-41
Oct. 23	VMI Williamsburg (Homecoming)	12-7
Oct. 30	North Carolina Chapel Hill, N.C.	35-36
Nov. 6	Wake Forest Winston-Salem, N.C.	29-36

Date	Opponent Location and Event	Score W&M-Opp
Nov. 13	Temple Philadelphia, Pa.	13-17
Nov. 20	Richmond Williamsburg	19-21

1972 (5-6)

Date	Opponent Location and Event	Score W&M-Opp
Sept. 9	Furman Williamsburg	31-7
Sept. 16	Navy Annapolis, Md.	9-13
Sept. 23	Villanova Villanova, Pa.	17-20
Sept. 30	The Citadel Williamsburg	31-12
Oct. 7	West Virginia Morgantown, W. Va.	34-49
Oct. 14	Vanderbilt Williamsburg (Homecoming)	17-21
Oct. 21	VMI Lexington	31-3
Oct. 28	Virginia Tech Richmond (Tobacco Bowl)	17-16
Nov. 4	Davidson Davidson, N.C.	56-9
Nov. 11	East Carolina Williamsburg	15-21
Nov. 18	Richmond Richmond	3-20

1973 (6-5)

Date	Opponent Location and Event	Score W&M-Opp
Sept. 8	Virginia Tech Blacksburg	31-24
Sept. 15	North Carolina Chapel Hill, N.C.	27-34
Sept. 22	Wake Forest Winston-Salem, N.C. (N)	15-14
Sept. 29	The Citadel Charleston, S.C. (N)	24-12
Oct. 6	Villanova Williamsburg	33-21
Oct. 13	Vanderbilt Nashville, Tenn. (N)	7-20
Oct. 20	Davidson Williamsburg (Homecoming)	51-35
Oct. 27	VMI Williamsburg	45-14
Nov. 3	East Carolina Greenville, N.C. (N)	3-34
Nov. 10	Colgate Williamsburg	42-49
Nov. 17	Richmond Williamsburg	0-31

Date	Opponent Location and Event	Score W&M-Opp

1974 (4-7)

Date	Opponent Location and Event	Score W&M-Opp
Sept. 7	Mississippi State Starkville, Miss.	7-49
Sept. 14	Wake Forest Winston-Salem, N.C.	17-6
Sept. 21	Virginia Charlottesville	28-38
Sept. 28	Furman Greenville, S.C. (N)	0-10
Oct. 5	The Citadel Williamsburg	16-12
Oct. 12	Boston College Chestnut Hill, Mass	16-31
Oct. 19	Rutgers Williamsburg (Homecoming)	28-15
Oct. 26	VMI Lexington	20-31
Nov. 9	Virginia Tech Williamsburg	15-34
Nov. 16	East Carolina Williamsburg	10-31
Nov. 23	Richmond Richmond	54-12

1975 (2-9)

Date	Opponent Location and Event	Score W&M-Opp
Sept. 6	North Carolina Chapel Hill, N.C.	7-33
Sept. 20	East Carolina Greenville, N.C. (N)	0-20
Sept. 27	Pittsburgh Pittsburgh, Pa.	0-47
Oct. 4	The Citadel Charleston, S.C. (N)	6-21
Oct. 11	Ohio University Williamsburg (Homecoming)	8-22
Oct. 18	Rutgers New Brunswick, N.J.	0-24
Oct. 25	Furman Williamsburg	6-21
Nov. 1	Virginia Tech Norfolk (Oyster Bowl)	7-24
Nov. 8	VMI Lexington	13-7
Nov. 15	Colgate Williamsburg	17-21
Nov. 22	Richmond Williamsburg	31-21

1976 (7-4)

Date	Opponent Location and Event	Score W&M-Opp
Sept. 11	VMI Williamsburg	34-20
Sept. 18	Virginia Charlottesville	14-0
Sept. 25	East Carolina Williamsburg	19-20
Oct. 2	Virginia Tech Blacksburg	27-15
Oct. 9	Delaware Williamsburg (Homecoming)	13-15
Oct. 16	Navy Annapolis, Md.	21-13
Oct. 23	Ohio University Athens, Ohio	20-0
Oct. 30	Furman Greenville, S.C.	7-23
Nov. 6	Appalachian State Williamsburg	23-22
Nov. 13	The Citadel Williamsburg	22-0
Nov. 20	Richmond Richmond	10-21

1977 (6-5)

Date	Opponent Location and Event	Score W&M-Opp
Sept. 3	Norfolk State Williamsburg	27-13
Sept. 10	VMI Lexington	13-23
Sept. 17	Pittsburgh Pittsburgh, Pa.	6-28
Sept. 24	Louisville Louisville, Ky. (N)	21-7
Oct. 1	Villanova Williamsburg	28-8
Oct. 8	Virginia Tech Richmond (Tobacco Bowl)	8-17
Oct. 22	Navy Annapolis, Md.	17-42
Oct. 29	Rutgers Williamsburg (Homecoming)	21-22
Nov. 5	The Citadel Charleston, S.C.	14-13
Nov. 12	East Carolina Norfolk (Oyster Bowl)	21-17
Nov. 19	Richmond Williamsburg	29-13

1978 (5-5-1)

Date	Opponent Location and Event	Score W&M-Opp
Sept. 9	VMI Williamsburg	10-3
Sept. 16	Connecticut Storrs, Conn.	27-3
Sept. 23	Villanova Villanova, Pa.	21-17
Sept. 30	Virginia Tech Blacksburg	19-22
Oct. 7	Temple Williamsburg	22-22
Oct. 14	James Madison Williamsburg (Homecoming)	32-7
Oct. 21	Navy Annapolis, Md.	0-9

Date	Opponent Location and Event	Score W&M-Opp
Oct. 28	Louisville Louisville, Ky.	21-33
Nov. 4	The Citadel Williamsburg	12-8
Nov. 11	East Carolina Greenville, N.C.	3-20
Nov. 18	Richmond Richmond	3-17

1979 (4-7)

Date	Opponent Location and Event	Score W&M-Opp
Sept. 8	VMI Lexington	3-7
Sept. 15	Colgate Williamsburg	28-15
Sept. 22	Virginia Tech Blacksburg	14-35
Sept. 29	Georgia Tech Atlanta, Ga.	7-33
Oct. 6	James Madison Williamsburg	33-0
Oct. 13	Navy Norfolk (Oyster Bowl)	7-24
Oct. 20	Rutgers Williamsburg (Homecoming)	0-24
Oct. 27	Delaware Newark, Del.	0-40
Nov. 10	Appalachian State Boone, N.C.	9-0
Nov. 17	Richmond Williamsburg	24-10
Nov. 23	East Carolina Williamsburg	14-38

1980 (2-9)

Date	Opponent Location and Event	Score W&M-Opp
Sept. 6	North Carolina State Raleigh, N.C. (N)	0-42
Sept. 13	VMI Williamsburg	10-13
Sept. 20	Virginia Tech Blacksburg	3-7
Sept. 27	Navy Annapolis, Md.	6-45
Oct. 4	Wake Forest Williamsburg (Homecoming)	7-27
Oct. 11	Dartmouth Williamsburg	17-14
Oct. 18	Rutgers New Brunswick, N.J.	21-18
Oct. 25	Delaware Williamsburg	3-7
Nov. 1	East Carolina Greenville, N.C. (N)	23-31
Nov. 8	Harvard Cambridge, Mass.	13-24
Nov. 15	Richmond Richmond	14-26

1981 (5-6)

Date	Opponent Location and Event	Score W&M-Opp
Sept. 5	Temple Philadelphia, Pa. (N)	0-42
Sept. 12	Miami (Ohio) Williamsburg	14-33
Sept. 19	Virginia Tech Blacksburg	3-47
Sept. 26	VMI Lexington	14-31
Oct. 10	Dartmouth Hanover, N.H.	12-7
Oct. 17	Marshall Williamsburg	38-7
Oct. 24	Navy Annapolis, Md.	0-27
Oct. 31	James Madison Williamsburg	31-19
Nov. 7	Harvard Williamsburg (Homecoming)	14-23
Nov. 14	East Carolina Greenville, N.C.	31-21
Nov. 21	Richmond Williamsburg	35-21

1982 (3-8)

Date	Opponent Location and Event	Score W&M-Opp
Sept. 11	Miami (Ohio) Miami, Ohio	17-35
Sept. 18	VMI Williamsburg	24-12
Sept. 25	Virginia Tech Blacksburg	3-47
Oct. 2	Rutgers New Brunswick, N.J.	17-27
Oct. 9	Dartmouth Williamsburg	24-16
Oct. 16	Navy Annapolis, Md.	3-39
Oct. 23	James Madison Harrisonburg	18-24
Oct. 30	Delaware Newark, Del.	21-62
Nov. 6	Brown Williamsburg (Homecoming)	22-23
Nov. 13	East Carolina Williamsburg	27-31
Nov. 20	Richmond Richmond	28-17

1983 (6-5)

Date	Opponent Location and Event	Score W&M-Opp
Sept. 10	VMI Lexington	28-14
Sept. 17	Delaware Williamsburg	13-30
Sept. 24	North Carolina Chapel Hill, N.C.	20-51

Date	Opponent Location and Event	Score W&M-Opp
Oct. 1	Yale Norfolk (Oyster Bowl)	26-14
Oct. 8	Dartmouth Hanover, N.H.	21-17
Oct. 15	James Madison Williamsburg	24-21
Oct. 22	Rutgers Williamsburg (Homecoming)	28-35
Oct. 29	Virginia Tech Blacksburg	21-59
Nov. 5	Marshall Huntington, W. Va.	48-24
Nov. 12	East Carolina Greenville, N.C.	6-40
Nov. 19	Richmond Williamsburg	24-15

1984 (6-5)

Date	Opponent Location and Event	Score W&M-Opp
Sept. 8	VMI Williamsburg	24-13
Sept. 15	Delaware Newark, Del.	23-21
Sept. 22	Penn State College Station, Pa.	18-56
Sept. 29	James Madison Harrisonburg	20-10
Oct. 6	Temple Williamsburg	14-28
Oct. 13	Boston University Williamsburg	24-3
Oct. 20	Virginia Tech Blacksburg	14-38
Oct. 27	Wake Forest Winston-Salem, N.C.	21-34
Nov. 3	Lehigh Williamsburg (Homecoming)	24-10
Nov. 10	Colgate Hamilton, N.Y.	48-39
Nov. 17	Richmond Richmond	31-33

1985 (7-4)

Date	Opponent Location and Event	Score W&M-Opp
Sept. 7	Wake Forest Winston-Salem, N.C. (N)	23-30
Sept. 14	Norfolk State Williamsburg	28-15
Sept. 21	Delaware Williamsburg	17-16
Sept. 28	James Madison Williamsburg	31-14
Oct. 5	Harvard Cambridge, Mass.	21-14
Oct. 12	Virginia Tech Blacksburg	10-40
Oct. 19	Temple Philadelphia, Pa. (N)	16-45

Date	Opponent Location and Event	Score W&M-Opp
Oct. 26	VMI Lexington	38-39
Nov. 2	Lehigh Philadelphia, Pa.	31-29
Nov. 9	Princeton Princeton, N.J.	33-28
Nov. 16	Richmond Williamsburg (Homecoming)	28-17

1986 (9-3)

Date	Opponent Location and Event	Score W&M-Opp
Sept. 6	Colgate Williamsburg	42-21
Sept. 13	VMI Williamsburg	37-22
Sept. 20	Bucknell Bucknell, Pa.	30-13
Oct. 4	Harvard Williamsburg	24-0
Oct. 11	Lehigh Philadelphia, Pa.	44-34
Oct. 18	Delaware Newark, Del.	24-18
Oct. 25	James Madison Harrisonburg	33-42
Nov. 1	Virginia Charlottesville	41-37
Nov. 8	Princeton Williamsburg	32-14
Nov. 15	Holy Cross Williamsburg (Homecoming)	7-31
Nov. 22	Richmond Richmond	21-14
Nov. 29	Delaware Williamsburg (Div. I-AA Playoffs)	17-51

1987 (5-6)

Date	Opponent Location and Event	Score W&M-Opp
Sept. 5	East Tennessee State Johnson City, Tenn. (N)	25-49
Sept. 12	Navy Annapolis, Md.	27-17
Sept. 19	Colgate Hamilton, N.Y.	7-19
Oct. 3	Lehigh Williamsburg	28-27
Oct. 10	Yale Hartford, Conn.	34-40
Oct. 17	Delaware Williamsburg	14-38
Oct. 24	James Madison Williamsburg (Homecoming)	22-28
Oct. 31	VMI Norfolk (Oyster Bowl)	17-6
Nov. 7	Bucknell Williamsburg	31-6
Nov. 14	Holy Cross Worcester, Mass.	7-40

Date	Opponent Location and Event	Score W&M-Opp
Nov. 21	Richmond Williamsburg	20-7

1988 (6-4-1)

Date	Opponent Location and Event	Score W&M-Opp
Sept. 3	Virginia Charlottesville (N)	23-31
Sept. 10	VMI Williamsburg	30-7
Sept. 17	Lehigh Williamsburg	14-6
Sept. 24	James Madison Harrisonburg	10-3
Oct. 8	Delaware Newark, Del.	35-38
Oct. 15	New Hampshire Williamsburg	33-31
Oct. 22	Villanova Williamsburg	14-14
Oct. 29	Georgia Athens, Ga.	24-59
Nov. 5	Wofford Williamsburg (Homecoming)	30-14
Nov. 12	Colgate Williamsburg	28-3
Nov. 19	Richmond Richmond	19-24
Jan. 9, 1989	Japan All-Stars Tokyo, Japan (Epson Ivy Bowl)	73-3

1989 (8-3-1)

Date	Opponent Location and Event	Score W&M-Opp
Sept. 9	Colgate Williamsburg	17-13
Sept. 16	VMI Lexington	24-17
Sept. 23	Princeton Princeton, N.J.	31-31
Sept. 30	Virginia Charlottesville (N)	12-24
Oct. 7	Delaware Williamsburg	27-24
Oct. 14	Boston University Norfolk (Oyster Bowl)	13-10
Oct. 21	Villanova Villanova, Pa.	17-20
Oct. 28	Lehigh Philadelphia, Pa.	55-39
Nov. 4	East Tennessee State Williamsburg (Homecoming)	34-28
Nov. 11	James Madison Williamsburg	24-21
Nov. 18	Richmond Williamsburg	22-10
Nov. 25	Furman Greenville, S.C. (Div. I-AA Playoffs)	10-24

1990 (10-3)

Date	Opponent Location and Event	Score W&M-Opp
Sept. 8	The Citadel Charleston, S.C. (N)	31-34
Sept. 15	Villanova Williamsburg	37-14
Sept. 22	Connecticut Williamsburg	24-7
Sept. 29	Virginia Charlottesville	35-63
Oct. 6	Delaware Newark, Del.	22-12
Oct. 13	VMI Norfolk (Oyster Bowl)	59-47
Oct. 20	Bucknell Williamsburg	45-17
Oct. 27	Lehigh Williamsburg	38-17
Nov. 3	Furman Williamsburg (Homecoming)	38-28
Nov. 10	James Madison Harrisonburg	31-21
Nov. 17	Richmond Richmond	31-10
Nov. 24	Massachusetts Williamsburg (Div. I-AA Playoffs)	38-0
Dec. 2	Central Florida Orlando, Fla. (Div. I-AA Playoffs)	38-52

1991 (5-6)

Date	Opponent Location and Event	Score W&M-Opp
Sept. 7	Boston University Boston, Mass. (N)	48-22
Sept. 14	Delaware Williamsburg	21-28
Sept. 21	Navy Annapolis, Md.	26-21
Sept. 28	James Madison Williamsburg	28-29
Oct. 5	North Carolina Chapel Hill, N.C.	36-59
Oct. 12	VMI Lexington	40-26
Oct. 19	The Citadel Williamsburg (Homecoming)	24-17
Oct. 26	Villanova Villanova, Pa.	21-35
Nov. 2	Lehigh Philadelphia, Pa.	37-41
Nov. 16	Samford Williamsburg	13-35
Nov. 23	Richmond Williamsburg	49-7

Date	Opponent Location and Event	Score W&M-Opp

1992 (9-2)

Date	Opponent Location and Event	Score
Sept. 12	VMI Williamsburg	21-16
Sept. 19	Boston University Williamsburg	31-21
Sept. 26	Harvard Cambridge, Mass.	36-16
Oct. 3	Brown Williamsburg	51-6
Oct. 10	Pennsylvania Philadelphia, Pa.	21-19
Oct. 17	Towson State Williamsburg (Homecoming)	43-15
Oct. 24	Virginia Charlottesville	7-33
Oct. 31	James Madison Harrisonburg	14-21
Nov. 7	Colgate Hamilton, N.Y.	44-26
Nov. 14	Lehigh Williamsburg	26-13
Nov. 21	Richmond Richmond	34-19
Jan. 9, 1993	Nihon University Tokyo, Japan (Epson Ivy Bowl)	35-19

1993 (9-3)

Date	Opponent Location and Event	Score
Sept. 4	New Hampshire Williamsburg	27-14
Sept. 11	Delaware Newark, Del.	35-42
Sept. 18	Tulane New Orleans, La. (N)	0-10
Sept. 25	Harvard Williamsburg (100th Anniversary of First Football Game)	45-17
Oct. 2	VMI Norfolk (Oyster Bowl)	49-6
Oct. 16	Northeastern Brookline, Mass.	53-6
Oct. 23	Villanova Williamsburg (Homecoming)	51-17
Oct. 30	James Madison Williamsburg	31-26
Nov. 6	Maine Orono, Me.	47-23
Nov. 13	Massachusetts Amherst, Mass	45-28
Nov. 20	Richmond Williamsburg	31-17
Nov. 27	McNeese State Lake Charles, La. (Div. I-AA Playoffs)	28-34

1994 (8-3)

Date	Opponent Location and Event	Score
Sept. 4	Rhode Island Kingston, R.I.	38-17
Sept. 11	Delaware Williamsburg	31-7
Sept. 17	Furman Greenville, S.C. (N)	28-26
Sept. 24	VMI Williamsburg	45-7
Oct. 1	Virginia Charlottesville	3-37
Oct. 8	Northeastern Williamsburg	17-12
Oct. 15	Massachusetts Williamsburg	14-23
Oct. 22	James Madison Harrisonburg	7-33
Oct. 29	Villanova Villanova, Pa.	53-28
Nov. 5	Maine Williamsburg (Homecoming)	17-0
Nov. 19	Richmond Richmond	21-20

1995 (7-4)

Date	Opponent Location and Event	Score
Sept. 2	Virginia Charlottesville (N)	16-40
Sept. 9	James Madison Williamsburg	17-24
Sept. 16	Northeastern Brookline, Mass.	32-0
Sept. 23	New Hampshire Durham, N.H.	39-0
Sept. 30	VMI Lexington	27-7
Oct. 7	Rhode Island Williamsburg	23-14
Oct. 14	Pennsylvania Williamsburg	48-34
Oct. 21	Massachusetts Amherst, Mass.	9-20
Oct. 28	Villanova Williamsburg (Homecoming)	18-15
Nov. 4	Delaware Newark, Del.	20-23
Nov. 11	Richmond Williamsburg	27-7

Date	Opponent Location and Event	Score
1996 (10-3)		
Aug. 29	Central Florida Orlando, Fla.	33-39
Sept. 7	Rhode Island Kingston, R.I.	23-16
Sept. 14	VMI Williamsburg	40-21
Sept. 21	Bucknell Lewisburg, Pa.	47-0
Oct. 5	New Hampshire Williamsburg	31-7
Oct. 12	James Madison Harrisonburg	21-26

Date	Opponent Location and Event	Score
Oct. 19	Villanova Villanova, Pa.	30-21
Oct. 26	Northeastern Williamsburg (Homecoming)	21-14
Nov. 2	Delaware Williamsburg	(Overtime) 10-7
Nov. 9	Massachusetts Williamsburg	30-6
Nov. 16	Richmond Richmond	28-13
Nov. 30	Jackson State Williamsburg (Div. I-AA Playoffs)	45-6
Dec. 7	Northern Iowa Cedar Falls, Iowa (Div. I-AA Playoffs)	35-38

Scheduled Games, 1997–2000

Date	Opponent	Location and Event
1997		
Aug. 30	Hampton University	Williamsburg
Sept. 6	Georgia Southern	Statesboro, Ga.
Sept. 13	VMI	Lexington
Sept. 20	New Hampshire	Durham, N.H.
Sept. 27	Boston University	Williamsburg
Oct. 4	Northeastern	Brookline, Mass.
Oct. 11	James Madison	Williamsburg
Oct. 18	Connecticut	Storrs, Conn.
Oct. 25	Villanova	Williamsburg
Nov. 1	Delaware	Newark, Del.
Nov. 15	Richmond	Williamsburg
1998 (Tentative)		
Sept. 5	Open	
Sept. 12	VMI	Williamsburg
Sept. 19	Northeastern	Williamsburg
Sept. 26	Villanova	Villanova, Pa.
Oct. 3	Open	
Oct. 10	Delaware	Williamsburg
Oct. 17	James Madison	Harrisonburg
Oct. 24	New Hampshire	Williamsburg
Oct. 31	Hampton University	Hampton
Nov. 7	Open	
Nov. 14	Connecticut	Williamsburg
Nov. 21	Richmond	Richmond

Date	Opponent	Location and Event
1999 (Tentative)		
Sept. 4	Open	
Sept. 11	VMI	Lexington
Sept. 18	Furman	Williamsburg
Sept. 25	Delaware	Newark, Del.
Oct. 2	Open	
Oct. 9	Maine	Williamsburg
Oct. 16	James Madison	Williamsburg
Oct. 23	Rhode Island	Kingston, R. I.
Oct. 30	Villanova	Williamsburg
Nov. 6	Northeastern	Brookline, Mass.
Nov. 13	Massachusetts	Amherst, Mass.
Nov. 21	Richmond	Williamsburg
2000 (Tentative)		
Sept. 2	Open	
Sept. 9	VMI	Williamsburg
Sept. 16	Furman	Greenville, S.C.
Sept. 23	Open	
Sept. 30	Villanova	Villanova, Pa.
Oct. 7	Maine	Orono, Me.
Oct. 14	Delaware	Williamsburg
Oct. 21	Rhode Island	Williamsburg
Oct. 28	James Madison	Harrisonburg
Nov. 4	Northeastern	Williamsburg
Nov. 11	Massachusetts	Williamsburg
Nov. 18	Richmond	Richmond

Appendix 2

Record against All Opponents

Teams	W	L	T	W&M Points	Opp Points
Albright	2	0	0	54	0
American	1	0	0	38	0
Appalachian State	2	0	0	32	22
Arkansas	2	1	0	48	21
Army	0	4	0	19	129
Baltimore City College	1	0	0	6	5
Boston College	0	3	1	60	90
Boston University	6	4	1	278	235
Bowling Green	1	0	0	20	0
Brambleton AC	1	0	1	10	0
Bridgewater	5	0	0	380	0
Brown	1	1	0	73	29
Bucknell	4	0	0	153	36
Capitol City AC	1	0	0	6	4
Catawba	1	0	0	19	6
Catholic University	1	3	0	61	65
Central Florida	0	2	0	71	91
Chattanooga	1	1	0	16	18
Cincinnati	1	3	0	55	114
The Citadel	18	7	0	520	339
Colgate	6	3	0	273	206
Columbia	0	1	0	10	13
Concord State	1	0	0	13	7
Connecticut	3	0	0	79	25
Dartmouth	6	1	0	112	102
Davidson	9	4	1	377	194
Delaware	8	12	0	360	572
Duke (Trinity)	6	1	0	123	70
East Carolina	4	11	1	228	348
East Tennessee	1	1	0	59	77
Emory & Henry	7	2	0	131	48
Episcopal High	1	0	0	9	0
Florida State	1	1	0	9	22
Fort McClellan	1	0	0	61	0
Fort Monroe	3	0	0	66	0
Fredericksburg	1	0	1	6	0
Furman	7	6	0	238	216
Galludet	2	0	0	59	7
Georgetown	1	2	0	12	75
George Washington	12	9	2	377	258
Georgia	0	1	0	24	59
Georgia Tech	0	1	0	7	33
Guilford	10	0	0	409	13

Teams	W	L	T	W&M Points	Opp Points
Hampden-Sydney	16	22	0	421	546
Hampton AC	1	0	0	5	0
Hampton HS	1	0	0	41	0
Harvard	4	4	2	187	155
Haskell	0	1	0	13	14
Holy Cross	0	2	0	14	71
Houston	1	1	0	32	49
James Madison	10	8	0	427	369
Jackson State	1	0	0	45	6
*Japan All-Stars	1	0	0	73	3
King	1	0	0	27	0
Lehigh	8	1	0	297	216
Lenoir-Rhyne	2	0	0	63	0
Louisville	1	1	0	42	40
Loyola (Baltimore)	1	0	0	19	0
Lynchburg	3	1	1	125	13
Maine	2	0	0	64	23
Marshall	2	0	1	86	31
Maryland	2	0	0	74	21
Maryland Ag. College	0	1	0	0	17
Massachusetts	3	2	0	136	77
McNeese State	0	1	0	28	34
Merchant Marine Acad.	1	0	0	25	7
Miami (Florida)	0	2	0	17	49
Miami (Ohio)	0	2	0	31	68

William and Mary vs. the University of Richmond

Quite simply, it's the fourth longest series in college football history. Only Lehigh-Lafayette, Yale-Princeton, and Yale-Harvard are longer. Through 1996—W&M's 102nd season—the teams had played 106 games.

The series began in 1898 and has been played continuously except for 1900, 1902, and 1943, when the College did not field a varsity team because of World War II. Twice—in 1905 and 1919—the teams met three times in one season, and double games were scheduled in 1906 and 1913–17. Annual games have been held since 1920.

Lawrence Leonard, longtime sports editor of *The Richmond News-Leader* (1947–68) and for one year (1946–47) W&M's sports publicity director, says, when W&M and Richmond play, "you can throw away the season record, toss out the script and be prepared for surprises and plenty of upsets."

The game often becomes a psychological contest, and the breaks of the ball game often help determine the victor. I'm sure the rivalry ranks up there with Duke–University of North Carolina, Tennessee-Alabama, Georgia–Georgia Tech, Army-Navy and many others. I've seen Richmond come in with some fine players and good teams and W&M the same way and lose games they were favored to win by many points.

Early in the series many of the games were played on Thanksgiving Day. Other rivalries also met on "Turkey Day," including the old "Military Classic of the South," between Virginia Military Institute and Virginia Tech and the universities of Virginia and North Carolina in the 1910s–30s.

A record of the 1925 game in the *Colonial Echo* already called W&M and Richmond "ancient rivals." It was the first time in many years (eight games) that Richmond had failed to score. The game was tied 0-0 until the fourth quarter. Center Lee Todd recovered a punt and ran 30 yards for a touchdown. Quarterback Art Matsu kicked the extra point and four minutes later W&M scored again with halfback W. H. "Dicky" Charles scoring and Matsu kicked again.

Robert Green (2) and teammates— Tom Dexter (38) and Jeff Neilsen (47) hold the I-64 trophy that goes to the winner of the W&M/Richmond game. Courtesy of the W&M Sports Information Department.

Like many other games in the long series, the 1925 victory gave the winner a championship—the undisputed state intercollegiate crown. The season-ending game through the years also has crowned conference champions and given boosts to postseason bowl and playoff hopes.

From 1921 through 1947 the W&M-Richmond game was played on Thanksgiving Day in Richmond, but between 1948 and 1953 it was switched away from the day and was played on a home-and-home basis. It returned to Thanksgiving Day in Richmond in 1954. Newspaper accounts indicate that a special commemorative ceremony was usually held at the game, including a re-enactment of the first Thanksgiving, staged as part of the halftime ceremonies in 1963 and 1964.

Leonard recalled how Dr. Davis Y. Paschall, then W&M president, moved to end the "Turkey Day" classic in 1964. "The change came about because both institutions have an extended Thanksgiving holiday and to move the game date would be fairer to the students of both schools," Dr. Paschall said. "Secondly, we're old-fashioned enough to feel that Thanksgiving should be reserved for family reunions and church services. For years we've come up here to play and have been unable to attend services. We've also lost a lot of time we'd like to spend with our families."   (—WK)

Teams	W	L	T	W&M Points	Opp Points
Michigan State	0	2	0	27	75
Mississippi State	0	1	0	7	49
Navy (Annapolis)	6	35	1	277	985
New Hampshire	4	0	0	130	52
Newport News	1	0	0	5	0
Newport News App.	3	1	0	142	15
*Nihon University	1	0	0	35	19
Norfolk Blues	1	2	0	3	54
Norfolk Collegians	1	0	0	3	0
Norfolk H.S.	4	0	1	59	5
Norfolk State	2	0	0	55	28
Norfolk YMCA	0	1	0	0	16
N.C. A&M	0	1	0	0	44
N.C. State	8	8	0	225	249
North Carolina	0	11	2	167	334
N.C. Pre-Flt	0	1	0	0	14
Northeastern	4	0	0	123	32
Northern Iowa	0	1	0	35	38
Ohio University	2	2	0	53	85
Ohio Wesleyan	1	0	0	33	29
Oklahoma	1	1	0	21	56
Oklahoma A&M	1	0	0	20	0
Old Dominion Club	1	0	0	14	4
Old Pt. Comfort	3	1	0	33	34
Penn State	0	4	0	61	139
Pennsylvania	4	1	0	116	118
Pittsburgh	0	5	0	23	136
Portsmouth AC	1	1	0	36	6
Portsmouth Training Base	0	0	1	13	13
Princeton	2	1	1	103	108
Quantico Marines	1	1	0	52	27
Randolph-Macon	22	19	1	580	431
Rhode Island	3	0	0	84	47
Richmond	54	47	5	1533	1386
Richmond AB	1	0	0	39	0

Teams	W	L	T	W&M Points	Opp Points
Richmond Blues	0	1	2	9	13
Roanoke	11	3	1	219	79
Rutgers	4	6	0	173	199
Southern Miss.	1	0	0	3	0
St. Bonaventure	0	1	0	6	7
St. John's	1	0	0	19	0
St. Vincent's Academy	1	1	1	12	23
Samford	0	1	0	13	35
Syracuse	0	7	0	10	236
Temple	1	4	1	72	160
Tennessee	0	1	0	13	48
Toledo	0	1	0	12	40
Towson St.	1	0	0	43	15
Tulane	1	2	0	22	53
Union Theo. Seminary	3	1	0	117	7
University Col. of Med.	0	2	1	3	25
Vanderbilt	0	4	0	44	77
Villanova	10	4	1	428	291
VMI	39	33	2	1345	1317
Virginia	5	26	1	343	825
Virginia Tech	18	39	4	800	1142
Virginia Medical	2	2	0	25	72
Wofford	2	0	0	49	14
Wake Forest	9	10	1	289	399
Washington & Lee	4	6	1	130	139
West Virginia	0	15	1	188	470
Yale	1	1	0	60	54
Totals	**445**	**452**	**41**	**15,715**	**15,717**

Attendance Records

Home Games

1949 vs. University of North Carolina, 19,000+ (est.)
1985 vs. Richmond, 18,000+ (est.)

Away Games

1984 vs. Penn State University, 80,000+ (est.)
1988 vs. University of Georgia, 80,000+ (est.)

The Southern Conference

For 31 years—1936 through 1977—William and Mary was a member of the Southern Conference, which at one time or another included most of the major football playing colleges and universities in the South.

Beginning in 1921 as the nation's fifth intercollegiate athletic conference, the Southern included such teams as Alabama, Auburn, Clemson, Georgia, Georgia Tech, Kentucky, Maryland, Mississippi State, North Carolina, North Carolina State, Tennessee, Virginia, Virginia Tech, and Washington & Lee.

A year later, Florida State, Louisiana State, Mississippi, South Carolina, Vanderbilt and Tulane joined. VMI and Duke became members in 1924, making the Southern a gigantic twenty-two-member athletic conference.

William and Mary initially sought entrance into the Southern as early as 1929 after the football fortunes in Williamsburg turned around with eight out of nine winning seasons between 1921 and 1929. The *Alumni Gazette* reported in its Feb. 29, 1936 edition that "after seven years of watchful waiting and fitful hopes, and with the constancy of Jacob's wooing of Rachel, William and Mary was finally admitted to the Southern Conference at its recent session in Richmond.

"The admission, which might have come much earlier but for a split-up of the conference several years ago when [twelve Deep South schools] seceded and left their former colleges to form the Southeastern Conference," the *Gazette* said.

In 1932 a dozen schools—Alabama, Auburn, Florida, Georgia, Georgia Tech, Kentucky, Louisiana State, Mississippi, Mississippi State, Tennessee, Tulane and the University of the South—left to form the Southeastern Conference.

In 1936 William and Mary led a seven-school entrance class that also included The Citadel, Davidson, Furman, George Washington, Richmond, and Wake Forest.

The College's entrance into the Southern was not auspicious. The school lost all four conference games and ended the season with a 1-8 overall record, last of the league's fifteen teams. W&M fortunes didn't improve much until Carl Voyles became head coach in 1939. His four-year record of 29-7-3, and winning percentage of .782 ranks third among the all-time conference coaches with a minimum of three seasons.

The Southern remained big-time, good-time football for the next seventeen years until 1953, when Duke, Wake Forest, North Carolina, North Carolina State, Clemson, South Carolina, and Maryland withdrew to join Virginia (which had left the Southern in 1935) to form the Atlantic Coast Conference.

W&M withdrew in 1977, after the conference started admitting schools that the administration felt were not in the same academic league as the College. Independent status, at the time, offered W&M teams a better opportunity for the right competitive mix, according to members of the Board of Visitors.

W&M remained independent until 1993, when it joined the Yankee Conference. The Yankee, with its dozen schools spanned the East Coast from Williamsburg to Orono, Maine, and included two traditional W&M rivals—Richmond and James Madison.

During W&M's thirty-one years in the Southern, the College's teams and athletes were successful and set an unusual number of records and precedents. In games against Southern Conference opponents, W&M won 113, while losing 95 and tying 11, for a .541 winning percentage. In all games played while in the conference, W&M won 184, lost 203, and tied 15, for a .476 winning percentage. The Indians won three Southern Conference football championships—1942, 1947, and 1970—and tied for the 1966 title with East Carolina.

The most unusual championship season came in 1970, under coach Lou Holtz, when the Indians won their last two games by a total of two points to take the title and a trip to the Tangerine Bowl, now the Florida Citrus Bowl.

W&M participated in two other postseason bowl games while in the Southern. In the 1947 Dixie Bowl game, the Indians lost to Arkansas, 21-19, while winning the 1948 Delta Bowl, 20-0, against Oklahoma A&M (now Oklahoma State).

League records prior to 1948 have been lost, but since then, W&M coaches have won Coach of the Year titles three times: Marv Levy in 1964 and 1965 and Jim Root in 1976.

Player of the Year also went to four W&M players: end Walt Brodie in 1956; guard Bob Soleau in 1961; end George Pearce in 1965; and running back Phil Mosser in 1970. W&M players who won the coveted Jacobs Blocking Trophy were: Lou Creekmur in 1950, Bob Soleau in 1962 and 1964, Bob Herb in 1970, and Jackson Neal in 1970. (—WK)

Conference Titles

1996	Yankee Conference Champion
1970	Southern Conference Champion
1966	Southern Conference Co-champion with East Carolina
1947	Southern Conference Champion
1942	Southern Conference Champion
1930	Virginia Athletic Conference Champion
1929	Virginia Athletic Conference Champion
1926	Virginia Intercollegiate Athletic Association Class-B Champion
1925	Virginia Intercollegiate Athletic Association Class-B Champion
1924	Virginia-North Carolina Athletic Association Virginia Intercollegiate Athletic Association Class-B Champion State-Champion
1907	Eastern Division, Virginia College Athletic Association Co-champion

Yankee Conference

The Yankee Conference, an athletic organization for all sports, was established on December 3, 1946, the effective date of a preamble and code drafted on August 24, 1946. The first league championships were conducted in 1947.

The original membership was Rhode Island State College (now the University of Rhode Island), the University of Connecticut, the University of Maine, Massachusetts State College (now the University of Massachusetts), the University of New Hampshire, and the University of Vermont.

With the creation of Division I-AA in 1978, the conference disbanded for all sports except football. Vermont, which had eliminated its football program in 1974, dropped out of the organization. The league remained a six-team group, however, since Boston University had joined in 1973.

Originally established as a conference for the New England land grant colleges, the league in 1996 consisted of twelve schools along the East Coast, ranging from Maine to Virginia and including five of the original six schools.

The University of Delaware and the University of Richmond joined the conference in 1984 and became eligible for the championship in 1986. Villanova University, added in 1985, became eligible in 1988. In 1993, James Madison University, Northeastern University, and William and Mary became eligible for the conference crown.

The league was an original conference to receive an automatic bid to the NCAA Division I-AA national play-offs. When the Yankee Conference was a Division II league, New Hampshire represented the conference in the NCAA play-offs twice and Massachusetts once.

The Yankee Conference celebrated its 50th year in 1996—its last season. Because, beginning in 1997, the NCAA decided to recognize for inclusion in the football play-offs only those conferences with full-time sports programs, the Yankee Conference folded, effective July 1, 1997. All members immediately became the football members of the Atlantic 10 Conference.

From 1993 through 1996, the Yankee Conference operated in two divisions, the New England Division—Boston U., Connecticut, Maine, Massachusetts, New Hampshire, and Rhode Island—and the Mid-Atlantic Division—Delaware, James Madison, Northeastern, Richmond, Villanova, and William and Mary.

In the Conference's fifty-year history, the champions or co-champions were Massachusetts with seventeen titles; Connecticut, fifteen; New Hampshire, eleven; Maine, nine; Rhode Island, seven; Boston U., six; Delaware, five; Villanova, two; and Richmond and W&M, one each.

Although only a member for four years, W&M finished with the best all-time percentage in the conference, .781, based on a record of 25-7-0.

The annual Yankee Conference winner was awarded the Bean Pot, a trophy donated by the University of New Hampshire's 1947 Glass Bowl team. (The Glass Bowl was the conference's first formal football championship.) The trophy currently sits in the football office in William and Mary Hall, because the Tribe won the 1996 Yankee Conference championship. (—WK)

Appendix 3

All-Time Head Coaches & Captains with Season Records

Year	Coach Captain/Co-Captains	Record Postseason
1893	None H.G. Humphreys	2-1-0
1894	None R.K. Slaughter	0-1-0
1895	None Ralph Leigh	None
1896	R. Armstrong W.P. Cole	0-2-0
1897	W.J. King P.B. Jones	0-1-0
1898	W.J. King J.E. Elliott	1-1-0
1899	W.H. Burke F.S. McCandlish	2-3-0
1900	W.J. King C.J. Corbitt	1-2-0
1901	None O.L. Shewmake	2-1-1
1902	None O.L. Shewmake	1-1-1
1903	H.J. Duvall S.C. Blackiston	1-3-0
1904	J.M. Blanchard H. Blankenship	3-3-0
1905	J.M. Blanchard C.E. Johnson	2-4-1
1906	H.W. Withers G.G. Hankins	3-7-0
1907	James H. Barry G.A. Dovell	6-3-0
1908	G.E. O'Hearn C.A. Taylor, Jr.	4-6-1
1909	G.E. O'Hearn J.G. Driver	6-4-0
1910	J.M. Blanchard W.B. Lee	1-7-1
1911	W.J. Young W.B. Lee	1-5-2
1912	W.J. Young R.C. Tilley	0-7-0
1913	D.W. Draper Jack Wright	0-5-1
1914	D.W. Draper S.L. Bertschley	1-7-0
1915	D.W. Draper C.R. Heflin	0-9-1
1916	S.H. Hubbard J.F. Wilson	2-5-2
1917	H.J. Young W.K. Close	3-5-0

Year	Coach Captain/Co-Captains	Record Postseason
1918	V.M. Geddy Unknown	0-2-0
1919	J.G. Driver R.W. Copeland	2-6-1
1920	J.G. Driver W.K. Close	4-5-0
1921	W.E. Fincher J.F. Wilson	4-3-1
1922	Bill Ingram F. Chandler	6-3-0
1923	J.W. Tasker John Todd	6-3-0
1924	J.W. Tasker John Todd	5-2-1
1925	J.W. Tasker F. Elliott	6-4-0
1926	J.W. Tasker Art Matsu	7-3-0 (First postseason game)
1927	J.W. Tasker Meb Davis	4-5-1
1928	Branch Bocock W. Carmichael	6-3-2
1929	Branch Bocock Ted Bauserman	8-2-0
1930	Branch Bocock Jim Murphy	7-2-1
1931	John Kellison Otis Douglas	5-2-2
1932	John Kellison Hap Halligan	8-4-0
1933	John Kellison Gerald Quirk	6-5-0
1934	John Kellison Joe Bridgers	2-6-0
1935	Tommy Dowler M. Bryant	3-4-3
1936	Branch Bocock Joe Marino	1-8-0
1937	Branch Bocock John Coiner, H. McGowan	4-5-0
1938	Branch Bocock Herb Krueger	2-7-0
1939	Carl M. Voyles John Dillard, Lloyd Phillips	6-2-1
1940	Carl M. Voyles Charles Gondak	6-2-1
1941	Carl M. Voyles Bill Goodlow	8-2-0
1942	Carl M. Voyles Marvin Bass	9-1-1

Year	Coach / Captain/Co-Captains	Record / Postseason
1943		No Varsity Team
1944	Rube McCray / John Clowes	5-2-1
1945	Rube McCray / Eugene Holloway	6-3-0
1946	Rube McCray / Denver Mills	8-2-0
1947	Rube McCray / Bob Steckroth, Ralph Sazio	9-2-0 (Dixie Bowl)
1948	Rube McCray / Harry Caughron, Lou Hoitsma	7-2-2 (Delta Bowl)
1949	Rube McCray / George Hughes, Jack Cloud	6-4-0
1950	Rube McCray / Vito Ragazzo, Joe Mark	4-7-0
1951	Marvin Bass / Dickie Lewis, George Zupko	7-3-0
1952	Jack Freeman / Ed Miodusewski, John Flannigan	4-5-0
1953	Jack Freeman / Tommy Martin, Steve Milkovich	5-4-1
1954	Jack Freeman / Charlie Sumner, Jerry Sazio	4-4-2
1955	Jack Freeman / Al Grieco, Bill Marfizo	1-7-1
1956	Jack Freeman / Jack Yohe	0-9-1
1957	Milt Drewer / Bill Rush, Larry Peccatiello	4-6-0
1958	Milt Drewer / Dan Plummer, Tom Secules	2-6-1
1959	Milt Drewer / Gray Lynn, Lauren Kardatzke	4-6-0
1960	Milt Drewer / Jim Porach, Wayne Woolwine	2-8-0
1961	Milt Drewer / Roger Hale, Eric Erdossy	1-9-0
1962	Milt Drewer / Stan Penkunas, Dennis O'Toole	4-5-1
1963	Milt Drewer / Bob Soleau	4-6-0
1964	Marv Levy / Scott Swan	4-6-0
1965	Marv Levy / Tom Feola, Jim Dick	6-4-0
1966	Marv Levy / Chuck Albertson, Bill Conaway	5-4-1
1967	Marv Levy / Adin Brown, Mike Madden	5-4-1
1968	Marv Levy / Jim Barton, Burt Waite	3-7-0
1969	Lou Holtz / Dave Holland, Jim Cavanaugh	3-7-0
1970	Lou Holtz / Joe Pilch, Bob Herb	5-7-0 (Tangerine Bowl)
1971	Lou Holtz / Phil Mosser, Wally Ake	5-6-0
1972	Jim Root / Paul Scolaro, Todd Bushnell	5-6-0
1973	Jim Root / Joe Montgomery, Randy Rovesti	6-5-0
1974	Jim Root / Mike Stewart, Dick Pawlewicz	4-7-0
1975	Jim Root / Craig McCurdy, Paul Kruis	2-9-0
1976	Jim Root / Jack Kroeger, Jeff Hosmer	7-4-0
1977	Jim Root / Joe Agee, Keith Fimian	6-5-0
1978	Jim Root / Melvin Martin, Jim Ryan, Tom Rozantz	5-5-1
1979	Jim Root / Steve Shull, Bill Scott	4-7-0
1980	Jimmye Laycock / Steve McNamee, Dennis Fitzpatrick	2-9-0
1981	Jimmye Laycock / Owen Costello, Chris Garrity	5-6-0
1982	Jimmye Laycock / Wayne MacMasters, Kurt Wrigley	3-8-0
1983	Jimmye Laycock / Steve Zeuli, Bernie Marrazzo	6-5-0
1984	Jimmye Laycock / Mark Kelso, Bobby Wright, Bobby Crane, Lee Glenn	6-5-0
1985	Jimmye Laycock / Bob Solderitch, Todd Leeson, Graeme Miller	7-4-0
1986	Jimmye Laycock / Dave Pocta, Dave Szydlik, Michael Clemons	9-3-0 (NCAA Playoffs)
1987	Jimmye Laycock / Joe Monaco, Dave Szydlik, Dave Wiley	5-6-0
1988	Jimmye Laycock / John Brosnahan, Dave Wiley	6-4-1 (Epson Ivy Bowl Win)
1989	Jimmye Laycock / Craig Argo, Greg Kimball	8-3-1 (NCAA Playoffs)
1990	Jimmye Laycock / Alan Garlic, Brad Uhl, Mac Partlow, Reggie White, Tyrone Shelton	10-3 (NCAA Playoffs)
1991	Jimmye Laycock / Tom Dexter, Robert Green, Chris Hakel, Jeff Nielsen	5-6-0
1992	Jimmye Laycock / Joe Person, Palmer Scarritt, Alex Utecht	9-2-0 (Epson Ivy Bowl Win)
1993	Jimmye Laycock / Todd Durkin, Eric Lambert, Craig Staub, Tom Walters	9-3-0 (NCAA Playoffs)
1994	Jimmye Laycock / Greg Applewhite, Mike Tomlin	8-3-0
1995	Jimmye Laycock / Terry Hammons, Jim Simpkins	7-4-0
1996	Jimmye Laycock / Josh Beyer, Stefon Moody, Mike McGowan	10-3-0 (NCAA Playoffs)
1997	Jimmye Laycock / Peter Coyne, Sean McDermott, Dan Rossettini, Jude Waddy	

Appendix 4

Assistant Football Coaches since 1915

Name	Dates	Head Coaches
"Doc" Marrow	1915	Draper
W. B . Lee	1916	Hubbard
G. A. Dovell	1916	Hubbard
Bobby Gooch	1920	Driver
J. S. Counselman	1920–21	Driver & Fincher
Vernon M. Geddy Sr.	1922–24	Ingram & Tasker
Bob Wallace	1922–25	Ingram & Tasker
Arthur Nilsson	1924–25	Tasker
Paul M. Keister	1925	Tasker
John B. Todd	1925–27	Tasker
Art Matsu	1927	Tasker
Walter "Beef" Hoffman	1928	Bocock
Cy Young	1928–30	Bocock
"Honest" John Kellison	1929–30 & 1935–38	Bocock & Dowler
Fetzer	1930–32	Bocock & Kellison
"Meb" Davis	1930–32	Bocock & Kellison
Bill Scott	1931–36	Kellison & Bocock
Otis W. Douglas Jr	1932–38	Kellison & Bocock
Tommy Dowler	1933–34	Kellison
Joseph Chandler	1933	Kellison
Joseph R. Flickinger	1937–38	Bocock
Eric Tipton	1939–56	Voyles, McCray, Bass & Freeman
Dwight Stuessy	1939–44	Voyles & McCray
Reuben N. "Rube" McCray	1939–43	Voyles
Albert "Pop" Werner	1939–42	Voyles
Glenn Knox	1943–44	McCray
Marvin Bass	1944–48 & 1950	McCray
Dick Gallagher	1945–46	McCray
S.B. "Frosty" Holt	1945	McCray
Kenneth Rawlinson	1946	McCray
Thomas Power	1946–49	McCray
Alfred Thomas	1947–48	McCray
Alfred Vandeweghe	1947–49	McCray
Barney Wilson	1947–50	McCray
Henry "Red" Caughron	1949	McCray
Tom Mikula	1949&1950 & 1952	McCray & Freeman
Lou Hoitsma	1949&1950	McCray
Buddy Lex	1950	McCray
Irwin "Red" Newell	1950	McCray
Jackie Freeman	1951	Bass
Ralph Floyd	1951	Bass
Charlie Ellis	1951	Bass
Lester H. Hooker Jr.	1951	Bass
Herb "Neepie" Miller	1951–55	Bass & Freeman
Johnny Clements	1952	Freeman
Gil Joyner	1952–55	Freeman
Boydson Baird	1952–58	Freeman & Drewer
Frank "Sonny" Cowling	1953	Freeman
Dick Lewis	1954–55	Freeman
Jim Smith	1954–55	Freeman
Jack Cloud	1954	Freeman
Joe Mark	1953, 1956–59	Freeman & Drewer
Robert Hunt	1957	Drewer
Bill Chambers	1957–59	Drewer
Ed Derringe	1957–63	Drewer
David Nusz	1958–60	Drewer
Larry Peccatiello	1958, 1961–68	Drewer & Levy
Joe Agee	1958–63, 1965	Drewer & Levy
Buddy Chandler	1959	Drewer
Dante Defalco	1960–61	Drewer
Jack Prater	1960	Drewer
Lou Holtz	1961–63	Drewer
Eric Erdossy	1962	Drewer
Roger Nielson	1962–63	Drewer
August Tammariello	1962–67	Drewer & Levy
John Harvey	1964	Levy
Jim Roe	1964	Levy
Bob Banner	1964	Levy
Charlie Weaver	1964	Levy
Joe Downing	1964–66	Levy
Don Roby	1964–68	Levy
Dick Besnier	1965	Levy
Craig Smith	1965	Levy
Ralph Pucci	1965–71	Levy & Holtz
Bobby Ross	1967–70	Levy & Holtz
Mont Linkenauger	1967–68	Levy
Joe Teefey	1967–69	Levy & Holtz
Larry Beightol	1968–71	Levy & Holtz
Dick Harmison	1969	Holtz
John Konstantinos	1969–71	Holtz
Chuck Clausen	1969–70	Holtz
Bo Rein	1970	Holtz
Brian Burke	1971	Holtz
George Foussekis	1971	Holtz
Bob Morrison	1971	Holtz

Team Records

Most Points Scored

Game: 95 vs.
          Bridgewater, 1931
Season: 467 in 1990

Most Points Allowed

Game: 93 vs.
          Delaware, 1915
Season: 333 in 1982

Most Total Yards Gained

Game: 681 vs.
          Richmond, 1991
Season: 6,438 in 1990

Most Plays

Game: 100 vs. Virginia
          Tech, 1971
Season: 1,004 in 1990

Rushing Yards

Game: 453 vs. Ohio
          Wesleyan, 1970
Season: 3,024 in 1990

Pass Attempts

Game: 55 vs. Virginia
          Tech, 1982
Season: 458 in 1985

Consecutive

Victories:	9, 1985–86
Losses:	9, 1956–57
Shutouts:	5, 1923; 1930–31; 1941
Shutouts in one season:	7, 1928
Winning seasons:	6, 1921–26
	6, 1928–33
	6, 1944–49
Southern Conference wins:	7, 1970–71
Yankee Conference wins:	9, 1993–94
Games scored:	132, 1981–93
State games without a loss:	31, 1939–50
Games without a victory:	12, 1955–57
Quarters without a touchdown:	42, 1911–13
Losing seasons:	11, 1910–20
	11, 1954–64

Pass Completions

Game: 35 vs. Rutgers,
          1983
Season: 270 in 1986

Passing Yards

Game: 414 vs. Miami,
          1982
Season: 3,414 in 1990

First Downs

Game: 36 vs. VMI,
          1991; vs. VMI,
          1993
Season: 324 in 1990

Most Interceptions

Game:
          6 vs. Wake Forest,
          1947
Season:
          25 in 1972

Most Yards Penalized

Game: 197 vs. Furman,
          1962

Name	Dates	Head Coaches
Ralph Kirchenheiter	1972–78	Root
Jim Goodfellow	1972–73	Root
Dick McLean	1972–73	Root
Paul Schudel	1972–73	Root
Bob Sherman	1972–79	Root
Lou Tepper	1973–77	Root
Phil Elmassian	1974	Root
Bill Casto	1974–79	Root
Dave Zimmerman	1974–76	Root
John Akers	1976–78	Root
Ivan Fears	1977–79	Root
Steve Schnall	1978–79	Root
Wally Ake	1979	Root
Phil Janaro	1979–90	Root & Laycock
Ralph Friedgen	1980	Laycock
Mike Mahoney	1980	Laycock
Charles Rizzo	1980	Laycock
Kelvin Rogers	1980–82	Laycock
Dan Smith	1980–83	Laycock
Don McCaulley	1981–90	Laycock
Bill Stewart	1981–83	Laycock
Cliff Schwenke	1982	Laycock
Tom Brattan	1983–91	Laycock
Gene Epley	1983–85	Laycock
Mike Faragalli	1983–84	Laycock
Kenny Martin	1983	Laycock
Sean Kelly	1984	Laycock
Mike Kolakowski	1984–88	Laycock
Zbig Kepa	1984 to present	Laycock
Matt Kelchner	1984 to present	Laycock
Derwin Cox	1985–87	Laycock
Russ Huesman	1985 to present	Laycock
Joe Bottiglieri	1990–95	Laycock
Mike London	1991–94	Laycock
Chris Thatcher	1992–94	Laycock
Warren Belin	1995–96	Laycock
Jeffery Fela	1995	Laycock
Bob Solderitch	1996 to present	Laycock
Alan Williams	1996 to present	Laycock
Brian Vaganek	1997 to present	Laycock

Appendix 5

All-Time Football Roster, 1893–1996

A

Abbitt, John	1905
Abbotts, Bill	1941, 1942
Accurso, Aaron	1991
Adams, David	1994, 1995
Adams, Dick	1940
Adams, Timothy	1986, 1987
Addington, Ray	1914
Addison, Edward	1913, 1914
Agee, Joe	1975, 1976, 1977
Aguilar, Scott	1986
Ahles, Ken	1973, 1974
Ake, Wally	1969, 1970, 1971
Albert, Peter	1980, 1981
Albertson, Chuck	1964, 1965, 1966
Alessi, Mike	1979, 1980
Ali, Hameen, Jr.	1996
Alkire, H.	1925
Allaway, Richard	1988, 1989, 1990, 1991, 1992
Allen, David	1987, 1988, 1989
Allen, Dewey	1978
Allen, J.	1945
Allen, Kingsley	1952
Alley, T.W.	1961, 1962, 1963
Allison, Henry	1908
Allison, Marvin	1943
Allums, Jeff	1985
Alvis, Jeffery	1996
Ambrosino, Brian	1994
Ames, Richard	1935
Amico, Fred	1982
Amon, Ollie	1943
Amos, Ed	1975, 1976, 1977
Anderson, Alfred S.	1897
Anderson, Clifton	1925
Anderson, Jeremy	1993, 1994
Anderson, Ralph	1932
Anderson, Ray	1968
Andrews, Billy	1989
Andrews, Corky	1980
Andrews, William	1919
Applegate, Todd	1990, 1991
Applewhite, Chris	1990, 1991, 1992, 1993, 1994
Applewhite, Greg	1990, 1991, 1992, 1993, 1994
Archer, Carl	1956, 1957, 1958
Argo, Craig	1986, 1987, 1988, 1989

Armour, Dan	1961, 1962, 1963
Arnold, Allen	1908
Ashmore, Kip	1969
Ashton, Kendrick	1994, 1995, 1996
Atherton, Mark	1983
Ayers, Thomas	1929, 1930, 1931

B

Baber, Jim	1949, 1951
Back, Scott	1973, 1974, 1975
Bahner, Eric	1974, 1975, 1976
Baierl, Bob	1989, 1990
Baker, Julius	1944
Baker, Michael	1996
Baker, Tommy	1987, 1988, 1989
Baklarz, Keith	1975, 1976, 1977, 1978
Baldacci, Paul	1926, 1928, 1929, 1930
Balderson, Leroy	1944
Balkan, Harold	1930
Banks, Andy	1975, 1977, 1978
Banner, Bill	1961, 1962, 1963
Barber, Stanley	1905, 1907, 1908
Barber, Wayne	1958, 1959, 1960
Barble, Yates	1904
Barclay, Thomas	1929, 1930
Bardsley, T.	1943
Barger, Ray	1966, 1967, 1968
Barley, Dave	1961
Barnard, Daniel	1909
Barnes, Eric	1976, 1977, 1978, 1979
Barnes, Kevin	1973, 1974, 1975
Barnett, Cedric	1990, 1991, 1992, 1993
Barnhardt, Troy	1988, 1989, 1990
Baron, J.S.	1898
Baron, O.	1898
Baroulette, Ashley	1995, 1996
Barr, William	1910
Barret, Bob	1942
Barrett, Joe	1973, 1974
Barthol, Bart	1970
Bartnicki, Steve	1979
Bartolich, Allan	1984
Barton, Dan	1959, 1960, 1961
Barton, Jim	1967, 1968
Baskett, Carol	1951, 1952
Bass, Marvin	1940, 1941, 1942
Bates, Chip	1974, 1975, 1976
Bates, Harold	1948, 1949, 1950, 1951

Bates, Rodger	1963, 1964, 1965
Bauserman, John	1926, 1927, 1928, 1929
Bauserman, Robert	1927, 1929, 1930
Baxter, Robert	1966
Beach, Dick	1964
Beach, George	1934, 1935
Beadling, Les	1965, 1966, 1967
Beatty, Ralph	1967, 1968
Bechtold, Loye	1958, 1959, 1960
Beck, John	1969, 1970, 1971
Becker, Jack	1964
Bednarik, John	1951, 1952, 1953
Beers, Barry	1971, 1972, 1973
Behrman, Jim	1960, 1961, 1962
Beitner, Geoff	1967, 1968, 1969
Belmear, Michael	1987, 1988, 1989, 1990
Benedetto, Elmo	1934, 1935
Benjamin, Jr., Ernest	1995, 1996
Benner, Bill	1978, 1979, 1980
Bennett, A.C.	1921
Bennett, Terry	1975
Bentley, John	1919
Benton, William S.	1929
Benzing, Marty	1990, 1991, 1992
Bergin, Edward	1931, 1932, 1933
Berry, Bill	1963
Berry, Cary	1939, 1940
Berry, John	1993, 1994
Bertoni, Mike	1992, 1993, 1994, 1995, 1996
Bertschey, Stanton	1913, 1914
Best, Keith	1978, 1979, 1980
Bettge, Brett	1975
Beverly, Mike	1995, 1996
Beyer, Josh	1992, 1993, 1994, 1995, 1996
Biehl, Bruce	1968, 1969, 1970
Bilbo, Jon	1968, 1969, 1970
Billcheck, Justin	1993, 1994
Biondi, Lou	1975
Bisczat, Ray	1981, 1982, 1983
Bishop, Jeff	1981, 1982, 1983
Black, Brian	1981, 1982, 1983
Black, Larry	1985, 1986, 1987
Blackburn, Mike	1976, 1977, 1978, 1979
Blackiston, Slater	1901, 1902, 1904
Bladergroen, Mark	1972, 1973, 1974

Blagg, Andy 1942
Blake, Everett 1934, 1935, 1936
Blake, Howard 1900
Blaker, Arthur 1934, 1935
Blanc, Henry 1945, 1946, 1947, 1948
Blanchard, T.M. 1904
Blaninship, H. 1904
Blanks, Lawrence 1946
Blitzer, Max 1912
Blocker-Bodley, James 1989, 1990, 1991, 1992, 1993
Bloxsom, Welton 1926, 1927, 1928
Bly, T. E. 1898, 1900, 1901
Bodnar, Glenn 1982, 1983, 1984
Bogan, Larry 1968
Boggs, Chris 1993
Bonfardin, Bob 1955, 1956
Booker, G. S. 1894
Booker, Keith 1989, 1990, 1991, 1992
Booker, Phil 1959, 1960, 1961
Boone, Lawrence 1943
Booth, Bob 1973, 1974, 1975
Booth, G.W. 1915
Bosiack, Greg 1969
Bottalico, Joe 1941
Bourne, Jeff 1994, 1995
Bowen, B.T. 1901, 1902
Bowers, Don 1974, 1975
Bowler, Jr., Mike 1995, 1996
Bowman, Bill 1951, 1952, 1953
Boyd, Gregg 1989
Boyer, Shawn 1990, 1991, 1992, 1993
Boyle, Tim 1985
Brady, Pat 1973
Brady, Tim 1993, 1994, 1995, 1996
Brantly, John 1954, 1955, 1956
Braun, Mark 1975, 1976, 1977
Braxton, Mike 1985
Brenner, Steve 1981, 1982, 1983
Brickell, Marshall 1934
Bridgers, Joe 1932, 1933, 1934
Bridges, Herbert 1919
Bright, Tom 1967, 1968, 1969
Brinkley, E.S. 1901
Brinkley, Wade Hampton 1893
Britt, Michael 1990, 1991, 1993, 1994
Brittingham, Lafayette 1916
Brockwell, Raymond 1910
Broderick, P.F. 1929, 1930
Brodie, Glenn 1964
Brodie, Walt 1952, 1955, 1956
Brodka, John 1939, 1940
Brookins, Mike 1972
Brooks 1951
Brooks, Julian 1919
Brosnahan, John 1985, 1986, 1987, 1988
Brostrom, Steve 1989
Brown, Adin 1965, 1966, 1967

Brown, Arthur 1963, 1964
Brown, Charles 1909
Brown, Charles 1993
Brown, Daryl 1996
Brown, Dennis 1966
Brown, Jack 1893
Brown, Jed 1987
Brown, Jeffrey 1993
Brown, John 1946
Brown, Ken 1974, 1975
Brown, Mike 1977, 1978, 1979
Brown, Oliver 1956
Brown, Regis 1942, 1946
Brown, Russ 1971, 1972, 1973
Brown, Ted 1963
Brown, Thomas 1897
Brown, William 1996
Bruce, Jack 1944, 1946, 1947, 1948
Bruce, Jackie 1990
Bruno, Al 1934, 1935, 1936
Bruno, Howard 1967, 1968, 1969
Brunson, Ernest 1984, 1985, 1986
Brusko, Ed 1956, 1957, 1958
Bryan, Arthur 1910
Bryan, Robert 1968
Bryant, Melville 1933, 1934, 1935
Bucci, Mike 1963, 1964, 1965
Buccino, Tony 1963, 1964, 1965
Buchanan, Gordon 1965, 1966, 1967
Bucher, Dave 1941, 1942, 1945
Bujakowski, Mike 1972, 1973, 1974
Bunch, G. 1935, 1937
Bunch, Melvin 1939, 1940
Bunch, Otis 1935, 1936
Bunting, Clinton 1987
Burchfield, Harold 1939
Burford, E.S. 1916
Burgess, Mike 1975, 1976, 1977, 1979
Burgwyn 1943
Burke, Tom 1949, 1950
Burklow, Tom 1973
Burnick, Dan 1976, 1977, 1978, 1979
Burns, Brendan 1939
Burton, Marvin 1900
Bushnell, Todd 1970, 1971, 1972
Butler, Tom 1975, 1976
Byrd, Charles 1972
Byrne, Bill 1938
Byrne, Matt 1991, 1992, 1993, 1994, 1995

C

Cafferty, Bruce 1977, 1978, 1979
Cain, C.H. 1922, 1923, 1924, 1925
Calabrese, Dan 1951, 1952
Caldwell, Carey 1990
Caldwell, William 1945
Callas, George 1975, 1976

Calos, Gus 1946, 1947
Calvert, George 1983, 1984
Cambal, Dennis 1969, 1970, 1971
Campbell, Chris 1985
Campbell, Dave 1968, 1969, 1970
Campbell, Dwayne 1982
Campbell, John G. 1893, 1994
Campbell, Ross 1943
Campbell, Tom 1944
Canada, Drew 1982
Cannon, John 1979, 1980, 1981
Capitano, Sam 1951
Capps, Bruce 1951
Carawan, Rolfe 1975, 1976, 1977
Carbonaro, Victor 1939
Cardaci, Joe 1950, 1951
Cardamone, Joe 1954
Carey, Mickey 1973, 1974, 1975
Carmichael, William 1926, 1927
Carr, Charles 1987
Carr, James 1914
Carr, Ned 1964, 1965, 1966
Carr, Peter 1900
Carroll, Dan 1976
Carroll, Mike 1968, 1969, 1970
Carter, Billy 1955, 1956
Carter, Henry 1906, 1907
Carter, Herb 1977
Caruso, Henry 1943
Cary, Cornell 1978, 1979, 1980
Case, Louis 1973, 1974, 1975
Casey, Jesse 1994, 1995, 1996
Cashman, Brad 1967
Cauffiel, Joseph 1951
Caughron, Harry 1946, 1947, 1948
Cavallaro, Sam 1981
Cavanaugh, Jim 1967, 1968, 1969
Cerminara, John 1976, 1977, 1978, 1979
Chabot, Steve 1972
Chalkley, J. 1921
Chalko, William 1931, 1932, 1933
Challender, Timothy 1990, 1991, 1992
Chandler, Ferdinand 1919, 1922
Chandler, Henry 1944
Chapman, H.L. 1904
Chapman, Matt 1988
Chappell, Bo 1943
Chappell, Harvey 1943, 1944
Chappell, Ronnie 1971, 1973
Charles, Winston H. 1922, 1923, 1924, 1925
Chattin, Jeff 1991, 1992, 1993, 1994, 1995
Cheatham, Alvin 1966, 1967, 1968
Cheek, Carl Wayne 1958, 1959, 1960
Cheek, Dave 1979
Chestnut, Al 1938, 1939, 1940

Chiarmonti, Chuck	1944
Chiesa, Ray	1954, 1955, 1956
Childress, Deak	1969
Childs, Chris	1982, 1983, 1984, 1985
Childs, John	1992, 1993, 1994
Chipok, Steve	1942, 1946, 1947
Chisholm, Walter	1919
Chrisman, Dave	1956, 1957, 1958
Christian, Pete	1934
Christie, Steve	1986, 1987, 1988, 1989
Christinson, Osborne	1930
Christner, Mike	1964
Chunta, Mike	1956, 1957, 1958
Churchill, Bill	1967
Cisik, David	1986, 1987, 1988, 1989
Clark, Dale	1946
Clark, Dave	1945, 1946
Clark, Kevin	1985, 1986
Clark, Scott	1971
Clarke, Bill	1966
Clauer, John	1946
Clements, Russell	1950
Clemons, Michael	1983, 1984, 1985, 1986
Close, W.H.	1916, 1919, 1920
Cloud, Jack	1946, 1947, 1948, 1949
Cloud, Kenneth	1975, 1976, 1977, 1978
Clough, Max	1972, 1973, 1974
Clowes, John	1944
Coblentz, Dave	1971
Cofer, C.V.	1922
Cofer, John	1908
Cohen, Whitfield	1907, 1908
Coiner, John Scott	1935, 1937
Colclough, Phil	1954, 1955, 1956
Cole, W.P.	1896
Coleman, Robert	1946
Columbo, Dick	1957
Comiskey, Charlie	1981, 1982, 1983
Commons, Billy	1993, 1994, 1995, 1996
Como, Richard	1966, 1967, 1968
Compher, Mark	1987, 1988, 1989, 1990
Compton, Scott	1984
Compton, Wayne	1978
Conaway, Bill	1964, 1965, 1966
Condon, John	1985, 1986
Conklin, David	1995, 1996
Connelly, Charles	1973
Connery, Cliff	1977, 1978, 1979
Connors, Jim	1981, 1982, 1983
Connors, Joe	1950, 1952
Constantino, Anthony	1928, 1929, 1930, 1931
Conway, Dick	1966
Cook, Craig	1975, 1976, 1977

Cook, James Allan	1926, 1927
Cook, Mike	1994, 1995, 1996
Cook, Scott	1985, 1986, 1987, 1988
Cooke, Giles	1919
Cooke, Howard	1989
Copeland, Charley	1951, 1952, 1953
Copeland, Richard	1914, 1915, 1916
Copeland, Richard	1919
Copenhaver, M.H.	1898, 1900
Corbett, Lou	1954, 1955
Corbett, Louis	1951
Corbitt, Wylie	1900
Corley, Bill	1961, 1962, 1963
Costello, Owen	1977, 1978, 1979, 1980, 1981
Counselman, John	1897
Cowling, Sonny	1950, 1951, 1952
Cox, Calvin	1959, 1960, 1961
Cox, Linwood	1951, 1952, 1953, 1954
Cox, Tom	1987
Coyne, Peter	1993, 1994, 1995, 1996
Craft, Steve	1965
Craig, Floyd	1952
Craig, Jeff	1962, 1963, 1964
Crane, Robert	1982, 1983, 1984
Creekman, Jim	1939, 1940
Creekmur, Lou	1944, 1947, 1948, 1949
Crim, J.W.H.	1901
Cripe, David	1970, 1971
Crisco, Richard	1979
Crittenden, Guy	1981, 1982, 1983
Crocco, Gary	1985
Crockett, Clint	1942
Cross, Glenn	1973
Crossman, Renny	1987
Crow, Al	1957, 1958
Crow, Marvin	1951
Cullinane, Luke	1994, 1995, 1996
Cullum, Paul	1974
Cumbo, David	1985, 1986, 1987
Cunningham, Scotty	1940, 1941
Cunningham, Tom	1946
Curtis	1899
Cuseo, Frank	1937, 1938
Czerkawski, Joe	1976, 1977, 1978, 1979

D

D'agostino, James	1995, 1996
Dade, R.B.	1901, 1902
Dade, Robert	1905, 1906
Dalton, Steve	1973, 1974, 1975
Daniel, Jim	1968, 1969
Daniels, Chris	1987, 1988

Darden, Frank	1927, 1928, 1929
Darden, Jackson	1932, 1933
Darragh, Dan	1965, 1966, 1967
Davidson, John	1937, 1938
Davies, Bill	1934, 1936
Davies, Ernest	1919
Davies, J. Jenkyn	1893, 1994
Davis George M.	1944, 1945
Davis, Colin R.	1946, 1947, 1948, 1949
Davis, Bill	1969, 1970, 1971
Davis, Chris	1991
Davis, Ed	1985, 1986, 1987, 1988
Davis, George H.	1944, 1945, 1946, 1947
Davis, Gerald	1989, 1990, 1991, 1992, 1993
Davis, H.J.	1901
Davis, M.C.	1924, 1925, 1926
Davis, Paul	1902
Davis, Shawn	1987, 1988, 1989, 1990
Davis, Walt	1975, 1976, 1977, 1978
Dawson, Andrew	1989, 1990
Dawson, Chris	1990, 1991, 1992, 1993
Dawson, Frank	1990, 1991, 1992, 1993, 1994
Dean, Jack	1966, 1967, 1968
Deanes, Terrance	1992, 1993
Debranski, Mike	1962, 1963
Deel, O.	1911, 1912
Deery, Bill	1972, 1973, 1974
Defazio, Brian	1993
Deforest, W.	1944
Degennarro, Greg	1985, 1986
Degrado, John	1934
Degutis, Albert	1934, 1936
Dekaney, Mark	1982
Della Torre, Tommy	1937, 1938
Deluca, Donald	1938
Demary, Tony	1965, 1966, 1967
Denault, Bill	1945
Denner	1945
Dennis, Steve	1940
Dennis, Todd	1982, 1983, 1984
Dewey, Craig	1971, 1972
Dexter, Thomas	1987, 1988, 1989, 1990, 1991
Deyoung, Eric	1995
Dick, Jim	1963, 1964, 1965
Dietz, E.	1921
Diggs, Richard	1929
Dildine, Robert	1990
Dillard, John	1937, 1938, 1939
Dinardo, Jim	1978, 1979, 1980
Dinsmore, Paul	1957, 1958, 1959
Dinunzio, Chad	1995, 1996
Disharoon, James	1945

Voice of William and Mary Football

Jay Colley (left) and Bob Sheeran broadcast the weekly games of William and Mary on a statewide radio network. Colley has been handling the play-by-play since 1983, and Sheeran, who served for twelve years as Sports Information Director, has been providing color commentary since 1985. Courtesy of the W&M Sports Information Department.

In 1946, WRVA-AM in Richmond provided the first regular-season broadcasts of W&M football games. The Delta Bowl Football Game on January 1, 1949, was broadcast over WXGI-AM in Richmond. WLEE-AM in Richmond took over the broadcasts for the 1950 and 1951 seasons. From 1952 through 1959 no single station carried all the games each year. Stations in Hampton Roads, including WVEC-AM in Hampton; WTAR-AM in Norfolk; WGH-AM in Newport News; and WACH-AM in Portsmouth, carried W&M games only when arrangements could be made with the opponents' broadcasting networks. . In 1960, WBCI-AM in Williamsburg (the station became WMBG-AM in 1972) resumed broadcasts of the yearly schedule and continued annually through 1993, with the exception of 1964 when WDDY-AM in Gloucester broadcast the games. The W&M Football Network was established in 1967 and has operated since. WXGM-AM & FM in Gloucester became the flagship of the network in 1994.

Play-by-Play, Station	Years
Hugh Carlyle (WRVA)	1946–49
with John Tansey, color, 1947 & 1948	
with Dave Findlay, color, 1949	
Joe Mason (WLEE)	1950 & 1951
No regular broadcasts	1952–59
Fred Rawlinson (WBCI)	1960–61
with Ken Bradby, color, 1960 & 1961	
Ray Schreiner (WBCI)	1962
Fred Rawlinson (WBCI)	1963
with Ken Bradby, color, 1963	
Dave Van Horn (WDDY)	1964
Chuck Sweeney (WBCI)	1965
with Bob Gilmore, color, 1965	
Bob Gilmore (WBCI)	1966
Don Lloyd (WBCI)	1967–69
with Don Bentley, color, 1967–69	
David Nitz (WBCI)	1970–71
with Don Bentley, color, 1970–71	
Marty Brennaman (WMBG)	1972
with Buster O'Brien, color, 1972	

Play-by-Play, Station	Years
Dick Fraim (WMBG)	1973–977
with Don Bentley, color 1974–77	
Bob Rathbun (WMBG)	1978–82
with Don Bentley, color, 1978 & 1979	
with Mark Albin, color, 1980 & 1981	
with Jay Colley, color, 1982	
Jay Colley (WMBG then WXGM)	
	1983 to present
with Brent Bledsoe, color, 1983	
with Scott Hays, color, 1984	
with Bob Sheeran, color, since 1985	

(Three former William and Mary broadcasters went on to careers as play-by-play broadcasters for major league baseball teams: Dave Van Horn, Montreal Expos; Marty Brennaman, Cincinnati Reds; and Bob Rathbun, Detroit Tigers.)   (—WK)

Dixon, Jody	1989, 1990, 1991
Dixon, Mark	1980, 1981, 1982
Dodd, John	1972, 1973, 1974
Dodd, John	1992, 1993
Dodds, Mike	1971
Dodson, Danny	1986, 1987, 1988
Domescik, Eric	1989
Doolittle, Jeff	1970
Doss, Rob	1915, 1916
Dougherty, Steve	1992, 1993, 1994
Doughty, Todd	1992
Douglas, Otis	1929, 1930, 1931
Douglas, Robert	1938
Dovell, G.A.	1905, 1906, 1907
Dover, Tom	1974
Dowdy, Steve	1979, 1980, 1981
Dozier, Dick	1936
Dragon, Ted	1980
Drake, Mike	1986, 1987, 1988, 1989
Drewer, Alan	1976, 1977, 1978, 1979
Driscoil, Dan	1960, 1961, 1962
Driver, James	1908, 1909
Duckhart, Jim	1946
Duff, Junior	1954, 1955, 1956
Duffey, Tom	1968, 1969, 1970
Duffner, Mark	1972, 1973, 1974
Duke, Charles	1922
Dukes, John	1958
Duman, Ron	1973, 1974
Dunbar, Eddie	1943, 1944
Dunford, J.	1902
Dunn	1943
Durkin, Todd	1989, 1990, 1991, 1992, 1993
Dustin, John	1987, 1988, 1989, 1990

E

Early, K.	1915
Eason, S.B.	1925, 1926, 1927
Eastwood, Raymond	1907
Echevarri, Mike	1983, 1984, 1985
Eckerson	1943
Edel, Jon	1960
Edim, Etim	1994, 1995, 1996
Edmondson, Dan	1934, 1935
Edmunds, Dave	1956, 1957, 1958
Edwards, Vincent	1986, 1987, 1988, 1989
Edwards, Walter	1987, 1988, 1989, 1990
Egge, Mike	1985
Elim, Marc	1985, 1986, 1987
Elliott, Erick	1986, 1987, 1988
Elliott, Francis	1922, 1923, 1924, 1925
Elliott, William	1927

Ellis, Edward	1967, 1968, 1969
Ellis, J. Tyler	1906
Ellis, Munford	1916
Ellis, William J.	1926
Elliott, J.E.	1897, 1998
Elmassion, Phil	1971, 1972
Elzey, Bob	1952, 1953, 1954
Engel, Tim	1994, 1995, 1996
Englebert, E. Carroll	1929
Enslow, Keith	1992
Erdossy, Eric	1959, 1960, 1961
Erney, Douglas	1988, 1989, 1990, 1991
Evanovich, Bob	1957
Evans, Chip	1968
Evans, Mark	1985, 1986

F

Fagan, Sandy	1967
Fair, John	1943
Fakadej, Alex	1954
Falwell, Craig	1992
Farrell, James	1968
Farrell, John	1957, 1958, 1959
Feamster, Tom	1951
Fears, Ivan	1974, 1975
Fedison, Jimmy	1991, 1992, 1993
Feld, Lloyd	1957
Felder, T.J.	1996
Fentress, H.S.	1916, 1919
Feola, Tom	1963, 1964, 1965
Ferebee, Ryan	1985, 1986, 1987, 1988
Ferguson, George	1904, 1906
Ferguson, William	1912, 1913
Ferrall, William	1928, 1929, 1930
Ferris, Abe	1939, 1940, 1946
Feuerriegel, John	1968, 1969
Feurstein, William	1907
Field, Jno.	1900
Fields, Harold	1940, 1941, 1942
Fields, William	1927, 1928, 1929
File, Gerald	1958, 1959, 1960
Filer, Ted	1949, 1950, 1951
Fill, Steve	1994, 1995, 1996
Fimian, Keith	1975, 1976, 1977
Finch, Tom	1972, 1973
Finn, Bob	1947, 1948, 1949, 1950
Finn, Patrick	1996
Fishburne, Cary	1985
Fisher, George	1931
Fisher, Jordan	1996
Fitzgerald, Aubrey	1953, 1954, 1955
Fitzgerald, Derek	1991, 1992, 1993, 1994, 1995
Fitzpatrick, Bob	1970

Fitzpatrick, Dennis	1977, 1978, 1979, 1980
Fix, Jared	1995
Flanagan, John	1950, 1951, 1952
Flanders, G.E.	1921, 1922
Fletcher, Howell	1908, 1909
Fletcher, T.R.	1925
Fletcher, Tim	1979
Flickenger, Joe	1936
Flournoy, William	1900
Floyd, Ralph	1945, 1946, 1948, 1949
Flurie, Mike	1974, 1975
Flynn, David	1988, 1989, 1990, 1991
Fones, Larry	1949, 1950, 1951, 1954
Foran, Ryan	1991, 1992, 1993, 1994
Ford, Steve	1988, 1989, 1990, 1991, 1992
Forkovitch, Nick	1942, 1945
Forrester, Kevin	1985, 1986, 1987, 1988, 1989
Fortney, Alan	1985, 1986, 1987, 1988
Foster, Gary	1993, 1994, 1995, 1996
Foster, Jeff	1965, 1966
Foster, Malcolm	1919
Foussekis	1943
Fowler, C.E.	1904
Fowler, Vance	1937
Fox, Jim	1969, 1970, 1971
Franco, Tom	1977, 1978, 1979, 1980
Franklyn, Preacher	1933, 1934
Freaney, Greg	1971, 1972, 1973
Freeman, Earl	1951
Freeman, Jackie	1941, 1942, 1946
French	1945
French, Barry	1969
Frisina, Steve	1978, 1979, 1980
Frizzell, Emmett	1928
Fron, Joe	1968
Fuller, J.C.	1921, 1922
Fuller, Marty	1966, 1967
Fusco, Rudolph	1952

G

Gabeler, Bill	1967, 1968, 1969
Gadkowski, Bob	1965, 1966, 1967
Gaines, Clarence	1976, 1978, 1979
Galbreath, Warren	1943, 1946
Gale, Buck	1960, 1961
Gallagher, Brian	1993
Gallagher, Tim	1990
Garber, W.E.	1916, 1919, 1920
Gardner, Bill	1971, 1972, 1973
Gargano, John	1971, 1972
Garland, Peter	1900
Garlic, Alan	1987, 1988, 1989, 1990
Garrett, Clay	1995, 1996
Garrison	1943

Garrity, Chris 1979, 1980, 1981
Garrow, J.T. 1898
Gatti, Dave 1958, 1959, 1960
Gayle, S. 1913, 1914, 1915
Geczy, Paul 1970, 1971
Geddy, Vernon M. 1915
Gehlmann, Ted 1948, 1949, 1950
Geiger, William 1970
George, C.S. 1898
Gerdelman, John 1972, 1973, 1974
Gerek, Doug 1974, 1975, 1976
Gerhart, Doug 1972, 1973, 1974
Gertin, Chris 1986, 1987, 1988
Gessner, Chris 1985, 1986, 1987, 1988
Geyer, Ray 1993
Giamo, Brian 1993, 1994, 1995, 1996
Giannini, Jack 1939, 1940
Gibbs, George 1946, 1947, 1948
Gibbs, Jason 1987, 1988, 1989, 1990
Gibson, Merritt 1984, 1985, 1986
Giddens, Danny 1985, 1986, 1987, 1988
Gilden, Ron 1971, 1972, 1973
Giles, Andy 1968, 1969, 1970
Giles, J.E. 1932
Gilkeson, Andrew 1900
Gilley, James 1928
Gilliam, Randolph 1913
Gilliam, Ron 1983, 1984, 1985
Gillum, Scott 1993, 1994
Glasser, Greg 1983, 1984, 1985, 1986
Glazener, Charles 1970, 1971
Gleason, Chris 1981, 1982, 1983
Glenn, Lee 1982, 1983, 1984
Glesenkamp, Randy 1964, 1965, 1966
Gobble, Eric 1987
Gobble, John 1963
Goddell, Don 1969, 1970
Godwin, Jeff 1978, 1979
Goellnight, Bob 1935, 1936, 1937
Goetz, Andre 1925
Goiner, Ronnie 1949, 1950
Gold, Norman 1922
Goldberg, Aubrey 1962
Golden, Harrison 1959, 1960
Golden, Robert 1943
Goldman, Brent 1986, 1987, 1988, 1989
Gondak, Charles 1938, 1939, 1940
Goode, Allen 1975, 1976, 1977
Goode, Richard 1978, 1979
Gooden, Elmo 1941, 1942
Goodlow, Bill 1940, 1941
Goodlow, Ed 1939, 1940
Goodlow, Leon 1946, 1948, 1949, 1950
Goodman, Richard 1943

Goodrich, Scott 1974, 1975, 1976
Goodrich, Scott 1981, 1982, 1983
Goodwin, Edward 1909, 1911
Gordon, Armistead 1915
Goslee, A.H. 1915, 1916, 1919
Gottlund, John 1939
Govern, Frank 1960
Gowin, Ray 1964, 1965, 1966
Graham, Marvin 1942, 1946, 1947
Granger, Doug 1979, 1980, 1981
Grant, Denys 1955, 1956, 1957
Gravely, John 1960, 1961, 1962, 1963
Graves, F.E. 1910
Graves, J. S. 1908, 1910
Gray, Kerry 1985, 1986, 1987, 1988
Grazier, Dave 1972, 1973, 1974
Greaser, Raymond 1975
Green, G.P. 1915
Green, James 1967, 1968, 1969
Green, Jim 1960, 1961
Green, Preston 1975, 1976, 1977
Green, Robert 1988, 1989, 1990, 1991
Greene, John 1967
Greene, John 1979, 1980, 1981
Gregory, J.W. 1930
Grejda, Vince 1968, 1969
Grembowitz, Johnny 1941, 1942
Gremillot, Todd 1979
Grenadier 1943
Grider, Andy 1985
Grieco, Al 1952, 1953, 1954, 1955
Griffin, Chris 1978
Griffin, David 1984
Griffin, Melvin 1991, 1992, 1993, 1994, 1995
Griffin, Peter 1975, 1976, 1977, 1978
Griffith, Mark 1973, 1974
Grigg, Lane 1993
Groettum, Richard 1935
Groot, Mike 1985, 1986, 1987
Grove, George 1926
Grudi, Walt 1985
Guidice, Bill 1944
Gutowski, Steve 1976

H

Haas, Dave 1978, 1979
Hackett, Michael 1983, 1984, 1985, 1986
Hackett, Mims 1982, 1983, 1984
Hackley J. B. 1897
Hackley, W.M. 1898
Hadtke, Walter 1934, 1935, 1936
Haffner, Steve 1985
Haggerty, Pat 1946, 1947, 1948
Haglan, Dennis 1963, 1964, 1965

Hakel, Chris 1987, 1988, 1989, 1990, 1991
Hale, Roger 1959, 1960, 1961
Hall, Arthur 1919
Hall, J. Lesslie 1907, 1908
Hall, E.H. 1901, 1902
Hall, Harry 1937
Hall, Waverly 1943
Halligan, Thomas 1930, 1931, 1932
Hamilton, Tom 1951, 1952, 1953, 1954
Hammack, Bill 1954, 1955, 1956
Hammel, John 1919
Hammons, Terry 1991, 1993, 1994, 1995
Hamric, Jay 1992, 1993, 1994, 1995, 1996
Hankins, George 1904, 1905, 1906
Hankla, Kirk 1981
Hanna, Gordon 1937, 1938, 1939
Hansen, Dick 1968, 1969
Hanson, Bruce 1969, 1970, 1971
Hardage, Bob 1955, 1956, 1957
Harding, James 1951
Harding, Mike 1985
Hardy, Don 1959, 1960
Hardy, Isham 1921
Hardy, J. A. 1894
Hargrove, Booker 1970
Harkins, William 1930
Harper, George 1939, 1940
Harper, Oscar 1935
Harper, Roger 1939
Harrell, Larry 1964, 1965
Harrington, Craig 1975, 1976, 1977, 1978
Harris, Archie 1983, 1984, 1985, 1986
Harris, Bob 1957
Harris, Brian 1985, 1986, 1987
Harris, Earland R. 1927, 1928
Harris, Ed 1961
Harris, Tony 1994, 1995, 1996
Harrison, Billy 1948
Harrison, H.A. 1901
Harrison, Ron 1994, 1995, 1996
Hart, Brian 1995, 1996
Hartman, Scott 1984
Harville, Bill 1943
Harwood, W.S. 1921
Haselden, Brooks 1996
Haskell, Leo 1922
Hastings, Harvey 1920, 1921, 1923
Hatcher, Ray 1981
Havelka, Terry 1976, 1977, 1978
Hawkins, Eric 1989, 1990, 1991,92
Hayes, Thomas 1986, 1987
Haynes, Richard 1893
Haynie, Raymond Lee, Jr. 1938

Haynie, Russell	1935
Hays, Scott	1975, 1976, 1977
Head, Mike	1965, 1966, 1969
Healy, Joseph	1909
Hebditch, D.B.	1898
Hedgecock, Sam	1939, 1940
Hedrick, John	1913
Heflin, George	1943, 1946, 1948, 1949, 1950
Heineman, Scott	1983, 1984, 1985, 1986
Heitman, George	1985
Helies, Ed	1969, 1970, 1971
Helsander, Al	1940
Helsel, Brian	1993
Henderson, Aurelius	1988, 1989
Henderson, Bob	1931, 1932, 1933
Henderson, Pinky	1963, 1964
Hendrickson, Joe	1960, 1961, 1962
Hendrix, Ralph	1945, 1948
Henley, Doug	1952, 1953, 1954, 1955
Henley, R.E.	1904
Hennessey, Kevin	1969, 1970, 1971
Henning, Dan	1961, 1962, 1963
Henning, Frank	1988, 1989, 1990, 1991
Henning, Kyle	1994, 1995, 1996
Henning, Malcolm	1902
Henning, Vivian	1905
Hepburn, Lloyd P.	1893
Herb, Bob	1968, 1969, 1970
Herbert, Carrington	1969
Hermann, Walt	1952, 1953, 1954
Herring, Eddie	1965, 1966, 1967
Hertz, Mike	1993, 1994, 1995, 1996
Hetterman, Mark	1968
Heywood, Kenneth	1983, 1984
Hibbs, John	1969, 1970
Hickey, Jim	1939, 1940, 1941
Hickman, Dave	1985, 1986, 1987, 1988
Hickman, Jack	1948, 1949
Hicks, Lloyd	1954, 1955, 1956, 1957
Hicks, Robert	1986, 1987, 1988, 1989
Hill, Andrew	1996
Hilling, Harry	1948, 1949, 1950
Hillman, Earl	1930, 1931, 1932, 1933
Hindmarsh, Ross	1955, 1956, 1957
Hinds, Nigel	1988
Hines, A.P.	1898
Hines, Earl	1930
Hines, L.Q.	1951, 1952, 1953
Hines, Lloyd	1926
Hines, Mel	1951, 1952, 1953
Hinton, John	1906
Hodges, Craig	1989
Hodges, James	1978, 1979
Hodges, Reggie	1982, 1983

Hodnett, Reggie	1984, 1985, 1986, 1987
Hodson, Rich	1971, 1972, 1973
Hoehn, Pete	1985
Hoey, Jack	1944, 1945, 1946, 1947
Hoffmann, Paul	1978, 1979, 1980
Hogarth, Chris	1985, 1986, 1987, 1988, 1989
Hogg, Bill	1972, 1973, 1974
Hoitsma, Lou	1946, 1947, 1948
Hoitsma, Robert	1951, 1952
Holbrook, Carter	1938, 1939
Holland, David	1967, 1968, 1969
Holland, Joseph	1943
Hollingsworth, Howard	1939, 1940
Holloway, Drewery	1941, 1942, 1945
Holmes, Bob	1966
Holschuh, Edward	1941
Holt, Andy	1987
Holt, Donald	1991
Holwig, Brian	1996
Hood, Chuck	1967, 1968
Hook, Mike	1938
Hooker, Lester	1968, 1969, 1970
Hoover, Kent	1971
Hopkins, Andre	1980, 1981, 1982
Horne, J. Roy	1912, 1914
Horne, Paul	1989, 1990, 1991, 1992, 1993
Horner, Tom	1951, 1952
Hornsby, Robert	1951, 1952, 1954
Hornsby, Swanson	1951, 1952
Horovitz, Jon	1976, 1977, 1978
Hosmer, Jeff	1974, 1975, 1976
Hostetler, John	1971, 1972, 1973
House, Russell	1922, 1923, 1924, 1925
Housel, Chuck	1965, 1966, 1967
Hover, Dick	1957, 1958. 59
Howard, Jimmie	1939, 1940, 1941
Howard, Steve	1967, 1968, 1969
Howard, Walter	1908
Howell, Jerry	1971, 1972
Howren, Donald	1947, 1948, 1949, 1951
Hubard, "Buddy"	1942, 1946
Hubbard, Herman	1911, 1912
Huber, Tom	1974, 1975
Hubler, Vincent	1970
Huddleston, Phil	1971
Hug, Jeff	1988
Huge, Chris	1981, 1982, 1983
Huggins, Andy	1982, 1983, 1984
Hughes, Dave	1951, 1952
Hughes, George	1946, 1947, 1948, 1949
Hughes, Mark	1989, 1990
Hulse, Glenn	1948
Humphrey, Jon	1994, 1995

Humphreys, Harry Gass	1893
Humphries, Pat	1944
Hungerford, Dick	1947, 1948
Huntington, Charles	1905
Hurlburt, Richard	1985
Hurley, John	1969, 1970, 1971
Hurtt, W.M.	1898

I

Ingle, Ned	1962
Injaychock, Mike	1996
Irby, Bob	1960, 1961
Irving, Frank	1905
Irwin, Newell	1940, 1941, 1942, 1945
Irwin, Winston	1922, 1923, 1924, 1925
Isaacs, Garland	1940, 1941, 1946
Isle, Barry	1966
Ivanhoe, Dick	1951, 1952

J

Jackson, Charles	1966, 1967, 1968
Jackson, Darrell	1985, 1986
Jackson, Jess	1943
Jackson, Marques	1995, 1996
Jaggard, Steve	1966
Jasper, Keith	1985, 1986
Jean, Edwin	1960, 1961, 1962, 1963
Jenkins, Carlton	1922
Jennings, Clarence	1912, 1913
Jennings, Mike	1986
Jennings, William	1908
Jesse, Carl	1951
Jeter, Will	1987, 1988, 1989
Johns, Harry	1942
Johnson, Andrew	1993, 1994
Johnson, Benny	1957, 1958, 1959
Johnson, C.E.	1902
Johnson, C.E.	1904, 1905
Johnson, Dudley	1976, 1977, 1978
Johnson, Emil	1931, 1932, 1933
Johnson, Harvey	1940, 1941, 1942
Johnson, Kenneth	1970
Johnson, Matt	1989, 1990, 1991,92
Johnson, Milton	1991
Johnson, Tommy	1969, 1970, 1971
Johnson, Wilbur	1960, 1961, 1962
Johnston, Gordon	1958, 1959
Johnston, Lewis	1968, 1969, 1970
Johnston, Milton	1982, 1983
Jones, Arnold	1960, 1961, 1962
Jones, Eddie	1954
Jones, Gary	1993
Jones, Howard	1913
Jones, Jamal	1990

Lloyd, Mcpayne 1911
Locke, Mark 1984, 1985, 1986
Locke, Michael 1987, 1988,
1989, 1990, 1991
Lofrese, Jim 1963, 1964, 1965
Lohman, C.A. 1921
Longacre, Bob 1941, 1942, 1946
Looney, Kevin 1984, 1985
Lott, Bill 1963
Lovko, Ted 1987
Lowe, Otto 1919
Lowenstein, Eric 1992
Lubs, Dick 1948, 1949
Lucas, Al 1982, 1983, 1984
Lucas, Joe 1982
Lucas, Mike 1978, 1979
Lucas, Stephen 1983, 1984, 1985
Ludwig, Bob 1966
Ludwig, Corey 1989, 1990,
1991, 1992, 1993
Lum, Ben 1945
Lund, Jeff 1966, 1967, 1968
Lundvall, Richard 1978, 1979, 1980
Lunsford, Carl 1944
Lupo, Sam 1949, 1950, 1951
Lusardi, Vincent 1939
Lusk, Bob 1951, 1952, 1955
Lutz, Howard 1946
Lutz, Russell 1952, 1957
Luzar, Rex 1971
Lynd, John 1946
Lynn, Gray 1957, 1958, 1959
Lyons, Bill 1990, 1991, 1992
Lyons, Jeff 1992, 1993
Lysher, Peter 1974, 1975, 1976

M

Macarcyzk, John 1954, 1956, 1957
Macdonald, Stephen 1908
Mackiewicz, Chet 1944, 1945,
1946, 1948
Mackreth, Arthur 1900
Macmasters, Wayne 1980, 1981, 1982
Macon, E. Carlton 1926, 1927
Macpeak, Dave 1972, 1973, 1974
Macrae, Duncan 1908
Madden, Mike 1965, 1966, 1967
Maddox, Arthur 1915, 1916
Maddox, Moe 1951, 1952
Maddrey, Dennis 1961, 1962, 1963
Magdziak, Ed 1947, 1948, 1949, 1950
Magdziak, Stan 1944, 1945,
1946, 1947
Magner, Bill 1969, 1970
Mahnic, Bob 1967
Maier, Steve 1966, 1967, 1968, 1969
Maita, John 1956

Makriannis, Nick 1996
Malarkey, Bob 1961, 1962
Mallory, Jim 1985, 1986, 1987
Manarin, Aaron 1995, 1996
Manderfield, Joe 1975, 1976,
1977, 1978
Mann, Jeff 1968, 1969, 1970
Manning, Drew 1989, 1990
Marchant, Avalon 1900
Marcoccio, Frank 1991, 1992, 1993
Marczyk, Joe 1987, 1988, 1989, 1990
Marifzo, Bill 1952, 1953, 1954, 1955
Marino, Joe 1934, 1935, 1936
Mark, Joe 1947, 1948, 1949, 1950
Markland, John 1963
Marra, Alfred 1944
Marrazzo, Bernie 1980, 1981,
1982, 1983
Marrow, Edward 1910
Marrow, Harry 1909
Martin, B. 1953
Martin, Bill 1943
Martin, Bill 1946
Martin, Dave 1979, 1980
Martin, Ken 1980, 1981
Martin, Melvin 1976, 1977, 1978
Martin, Tommy 1949, 1950,
1952, 1953
Martin, Tommy 1956, 1957,
1958, 1959
Martin, William 1953, 1954
Martini, Doug 1979, 1980, 1981
Maskas, Jim 1972
Massey, Earl 1945, 1946, 1947, 1948
Masters, Hurlie 1939, 1940, 1941
Masters, Jerry 1965, 1966
Mastowski, Frank 1965
Matheny, J.C. 1935
Matheson, John 1981, 1982
Mathis, Gerald 1966
Matson, Dewey 1945
Matsu, Ichya "Art" 1923, 1924,
1925, 1926
Matthews, Waldo 1939, 1940
Mattox, Nathan 1914
Mattox, Richard 1943
Matze, William 1944
Maxey, Clarence 1929, 1930, 1931
May, Billy 1944, 1945
Mayberry, Jamie 1994, 1995
Maycon, Howard 1988, 1989,
1990, 1991, 1992
Mayer, Charles 1911
Mazefsky, Matthew 1996
McCain, Mark 1991, 1992,
1993, 1994, 1995
McCandlish, F. S. 1899
MCandlish, L. H. B. 1899
McCarron, Joe 1972

McCathern 1955
McClellan, Ryan 1995
McClester, Scott 1983
McComb, George 1937, 1939
McCormick, James 1946
McCurdy, Craig 1973, 1974, 1975
McCutcheon, Bruce 1972, 1973, 1974
McDermott, Sean 1993, 1994,
1995, 1996
McDonald, W Richard 1905,
1906, 1907
McDonald, W.E. 1901, 1902
McDowell, Dave 1982, 1983, 1984
McDowell, Jim 1946, 1947,
1948, 1949
McDuffie, Kevin 1981, 1982, 1983
McEntee, Larry 1982, 1983, 1984
McFarlin, Bruce 1976, 1977, 1978
McGarry, Brian 1991
McGee, R.P. 1902
McGinty, Cletus 1987, 1988,
1989, 1990
McGowan, Hugh 1935, 1937
McGowan, Michael 1992, 1993,
1994, 1995, 1996
McGuire, Donnie 1964, 1965, 1966
McGuire, Erin 1989, 1990,
1991, 1992, 1993
McHeffey, Jim 1982, 1983, 1984
McKinnon, Bill 1966, 1967, 1968
McLaughlin, Bob 1966, 1967, 1968
McLeod, Lou 1948
McNamara, Bob 1946, 1948,
1949, 1950
McNamee, Steve 1978, 1979, 1980
McReynolds, Arnold 1948
Meade, Edward 1930, 1931, 1932
Meade, Joseph 1904, 1905
Means, John 1985, 1986
Meell, Tim 1981, 1983
Meenan, Gary 1975, 1976
Meeteer, Wes 1968, 1969, 1970
Megale, Joe 1949, 1950, 1951
Mehlbrech, Fred 1995, 1996
Mehre, Harry 1985, 1986, 1987, 1988
Meister, Michael 1927
Meith, Bob 1954
Melrose, Bill 1975, 1976, 1977
Menke, John 1984, 1985, 1986, 1987
Meridith, Roy 1949
Messinger, Gary 1987
Metcalf, Wayne 1912
Metcalf, Will 1912
Meyer, Chris 1996
Meyer, Kevin 1982
Michaels, Albert 1934
Michaud, Peter 1990, 1991
Michelow, Dave 1983, 1984, 1985
Micher, Robert 1959

Pellack, John   1944, 1945, 1946, 1947
Pendleton, B.J.   1995
Pendleton, Ed   1985
Pendleton, Jason   1993, 1994,
                                    1995, 1996
Penkunas, Stan   1960, 1961, 1962
Pennington, W.A.   1929
Perkins, Scott   1985, 1986,
                                    1987, 1988
Person, Joe   1988, 1989, 1990,
                                    1991, 1992
Peters, S.C.   1921
Peterson, Johnny   1940, 1941
Petocz, Dennis   1970, 1971
Petralia, Ron   1964, 1965, 1966
Pfeffer, Peter   1978, 1979
Phillips, Ernie   1959, 1960, 1961
Phillips, Kevin   1981
Phillips, Lloyd   1938, 1939
Phillips, R. E.   1899
Phipps, John   1981, 1982, 1983
Picketts, Bernard   1946
Piefke, Bob   1944, 1945
Pierce, Ricky   1994
Pilch, Joe   1967, 1969, 1970
Pinch, Reginald   1934
Pirkle, Carl   1945, 1947
Pisano, David   1984, 1985, 1986
Pitsenberger, Todd   1991, 1992,
                                    1993, 1994
Place, Jack   1949, 1950,
                              1951, 1952, 1953
Plageman, Butch   1961, 1962
Plummer   1943
Plummer, Dan   1955, 1956,
                                    1957, 1958
Plummer, Jason   1994, 1995, 1996
Pocta, David   1984, 1985, 1986
Point, Wendell   1985
Poist, Joe   1958, 1959, 1960
Pokrywka, Stan   1957, 1958, 1959
Polhemus, Bryan   1987, 1988,
                              1989, 1990, 1991
Polhemus, Jon   1990, 1991
Polly, Andre   1971
Poms, Julius   1950, 1951, 1952
Pope, Daron   1996
Poplinger, Herb   1942, 1946, 1947
Porach, Jim   1958, 1959, 1960
Porch, Alvin   1993, 1994, 1995, 1996
Porch, Mike   1980
Porkorny, Mike   1958, 1959, 1960
Porter, Andrew   1908
Porter, Walter (Bud)   1958, 1960
Post, Bill   1946
Potts, Keith   1975, 1976, 1977
Powell, Jeff   1982
Powers, Leland   1926
Powers, Raymond C.   1927

Prickitt, Mason   1968
Pritchard, Bryan   1960, 1961
Prochilo, Frank   1972, 1973, 1974
Proctor, Bill   1984, 1985, 1986
Profitko, Bob   1966
Prosser, Bill   1981, 1982, 1983
Prosser, Reed   1991, 1992,
                              1993, 1994, 1995
Pryor, Jim   1954
Ptachick, Kevin   1984, 1985, 1986
Purtill, John   1937
Pushinsky, Mark   1995, 1996
Puskar, Chuck   1960, 1961, 1962
Pye, James   1935

Q

Qualls, Lee   1980, 1981, 1982
Quirk, Gerald   1931, 1932, 1933

R

Radeschi, Mike   1986, 1987, 1988
Ragazzo, Vito   1947, 1948,
                                    1949, 1950
Ragsdale, Duane   1979
Raimondi, Ben   1943
Ramsey, Clyde   1939, 1940
Ramsey, Garrard   1940, 1941, 1942
Ramsey, Knox   1944, 1945,
                                    1946, 1947
Rangely, Walter   1922
Ransone, Coleman   1909
Rash, Robert   1976, 1977, 1978
Ratamess, Scott   1985, 1986, 1988
Rausch, Harold   1963, 1964
Read, Ben   1939, 1940, 1941
Ream, Don   1941, 1942
Rearick, Duff   1969, 1970, 1971
Reeves, Pat   1949, 1950, 1951
Regan, Steve   1969, 1970, 1971
Regan, Terry   1972, 1973, 1974
Reid, Peter   1987, 1988,
                              1989, 1990, 1991
Reid, R. H.   1916
Reid, Scott   1992
Reid, Sean   1994, 1995, 1996
Reinerth, Bob   1946, 1948
Repke, Mike   1990
Reynolds, Paul   1943, 1944
Reynolds, Tom   1973
Rhodes, Dave   1956
Rice, Albert   1928
Rich, Adrian   1988, 1989,
                              1990, 1991,92
Richards, James   1910
Richards, Marc   1989, 1990,
                              1991,92, 1993

Richardson, Mike   1957
Ricigliano, Vince   1974
Ricketson, Elliott   1928
Ricketts, Bernard   1946
Riddle, Scott   1977, 1978, 1979
Riley, Bill   1952, 1953, 1954, 1955
Riley, Marty   1993
Riley, Stuart   1959, 1960, 1961
Rinker, Dick   1957, 1958, 1959
Risjord, John   1953
Risley, Jr., Tim Alan   1995
Roark, Warren   1991, 1992,
                              1993, 1994, 1995
Roback, Tom   1987
Roberson, Jim   1966
Roberts, Barrett   1930
Roberts, Lloyd   1902
Robertson, —   1893
Robertson, Don   1965
Robertson, Isaac   1914
Robinson, A.P.   1915, 1916
Robinson, Bob   1973, 1974, 1975
Robinson, Doug   1946, 1948
Robinson, Edward   1982, 1983, 1984
Roche, Edward   1928, 1930
Rodeers, Arthur G.   1927, 1928
Rodriguez, Mike   1989, 1990
Rogers, Kevin   1971, 1972, 1973
Rogers, Powell   1928
Rohaley, Scott   1986, 1987
Roper, L.J.   1902
Rosdol, Dave   1981, 1982
Rosenburger, Seth   1994
Rosier, Chris   1996
Ross, Hub   1957, 1958
Rosser, Jermaine   1991, 1992
Rossettini, Dan   1993, 1994,
                                    1995, 1996
Rothwell, Stuart   1914
Rousso, John   1968
Rovesti, Randy   1971, 1972, 1973
Rowe, Ben   1893
Rowling, Howard   1974, 1975, 1976
Rozantz, Tom   1975, 1976,
                                    1977, 1978
Rubal, Lennie   1955, 1956,
                                    1957, 1958
Ruckman, Andy   1989, 1990, 1991,
                                    1992, 1993
Rudacille, Matthew   1990, 1991,
                                    1992, 1993
Rule, Robby   1985
Rundio, Bill   1952
Rush, Bill   1954, 1955, 1956, 1957
Rusnock, Steve   1965
Russell, John   1969
Rutter, Patrick   1987
Ryan, Jim   1975, 1976, 1977, 1978
Ryan, Paul   1926, 1928, 1929

S

Saffele, Robert	1922	
Safko, Bill	1942, 1945, 1946, 1947	
Safko, Edmund	1951	
Saldutti, Greg	1983	
Salmon, Dick	1943	
Sanders, Jeff	1982, 1983, 1984	
Sandy, Jay	1991	
Sanger, Matt	1996	
Sanner, Jay	1955, 1956, 1957	
Sapinski, John	1961, 1962, 1963	
Saul, Bill	1972	
Savage, Don	1985, 1986, 1987	
Sawicki, Walter	1952	
Sayre, Clinton	1947	
Sazio, Jerry	1951, 1952, 1953, 1954	
Sazio, Ralph	1942, 1946, 1947	
Scanlon, Dave	1981, 1982, 1983	
Scarritt, Palmer	1989, 1990, 1991,92	
Scearce, Mike	1969	
Schaubach, Elliot	1954, 1955, 1957, 1958	
Scheff, Joseph	1929	
Schembri, Sean	1992	
Schenck, George	1909, 1910	
Scherer, Rip	1971, 1972, 1973	
Schiavone, Joe	1972, 1973, 1974	
Schiefelbein, Ed	1978, 1979, 1980	
Schlatzer, Bob	1954	
Schlossberg, Nathan	1907, 1908	
Schmalhofer, Bruno	1973, 1974, 1975, 1976	
Schmalz, Rick	1969, 1970, 1971	
Schmitt, Rodney	1963, 1964, 1966	
Schmollinger, Robert	1988, 1989, 1990, 1991	
Schnackel, Dale	1985, 1986, 1987	
Schools, Maxwell	1973, 1974	
Schug, Kevin	1994	
Schundler, Mike	1974	
Schutz, Henry	1941, 1942, 1946	
Schutz, Henry	1966	
Schwartzman, John	1948	
Scolaro, Paul	1970, 1971, 1972	
Scott, Bill	1976, 1977, 1978, 1979	
Scott, Ed	1963, 1964	
Scott, Sam	1952, 1953, 1954	
Scott, Walter	1959, 1960, 1961	
Scott, William	1927, 1928, 1929, 1930	
Scruggs, Frederick	1935	
Scruggs, Todd	1985, 1986, 1987	
Seamans, William	1938	
Secules, Phil	1954, 1955, 1956	
Secules, Tom	1955, 1956, 1957, 1958	
Sedlacek, Jarry	1965	
Shackelford, W.N.	1901, 1902	
Shade, Charlie	1932, 1933, 1934	

Shaffer, Mario	1981, 1982, 1983
Shallcross, Brian	1993, 1994, 1995, 1996
Shanafelt, Garrett	1995
Sharp, Drew	1981, 1982, 1983
Sharper, Darren	1993, 1994, 1995, 1996
Shatynski, Jim	1950, 1951, 1952
Shawen, Bill	1897
Shawen, F.	1894
Shawen, Harry	1900
Shay, Bob	1965, 1966, 1967
Shea, John	1965, 1966, 1967
Sheeran, Robert	1935
Shelhorse, James	1912
Shelton, Tyrone	1987, 1988, 1989, 1990
Shelton, Yonce	1992, 1993, 1994, 1995
Sherman, Al	1955, 1956, 1957
Sherman, Thomas	1989, 1990, 1991,92
Sherrill, Judson	1934
Sherry, Bob	1944, 1945, 1946
Shewmake, O. L.	1901, 1902
Shiffler, Matt	1985, 1986, 1987, 1988, 1989
Shipp, J.	1929
Shoemaker, John	1995
Shoemaker, Kurt	1978, 1979
Shook, Henry	1944, 1945
Short, Robert	1977, 1978, 1979, 1980
Showak	1946
Shuler, William	1959, 1960
Shull, Steve	1976, 1977, 1978, 1979
Shwiller, Seymour	1939
Sicari, Joe	1971, 1972
Sidwell, Charlie	1951, 1955, 1956, 1957
Sielski, Mark	1981
Sika, Paul	1950
Sikorski, Dick	1965, 1966, 1967
Silvestro, Jim	1969, 1970
Siminski, Theodore	1930
Simons, Bob	1984
Simpkins, Jim	1991, 1992, 1993, 1994, 1995
Simpson, Mervyn	1939
Simpson, Mickey	1954
Sims, Kirby	1966
Sizer, F.M.	1901
Skiba, Bernard	1945
Skinner, Todd	1989
Skultety, Al	1947
Slattery, Pat	1961, 1962, 1963
Slaughter, R.K.	1894
Slepokura, John	1968
Slifka, John	1960, 1962, 1963
Sloan, Jim	1946

Slotnick, Steve	1965, 1966, 1967
Slovensky, Joseph	1952
Sluss, James	1944
Smakosz, Mike	1987, 1988
Small, Raymond	1905
Smercznski, Jim	1954, 1955, 1956
Smith, Bill	1966
Smith, Chris	1991
Smith, Craig	1962, 1963, 1964
Smith, Dan	1990
Smith, Darryl	1985, 1986
Smith, Doug	1986
Smith, H.L.	1932, 1933, 1934
Smith, Jack	1934
Smith, Jim	1948, 1949, 1950, 1951
Smith, John W.	1893
Smith, Keion	1994, 1995
Smith, Kenny	1975, 1977
Smith, Larry	1968
Smith, Mark	1972, 1973, 1974
Smith, Todd	1984, 1985, 1986
Smith, Tom	1974, 1975, 1976
Smith, William	1928, 1929
Snoddy, Alan	1985, 1986
Snook, Robert	1970
Snyder, Dickie	1957, 1958, 1959
Sobus, Paul	1979, 1980, 1981
Solderitch, Robert	1983, 1984, 1985
Soleau, Bob	1960, 1962, 1963
Solomon, Justin	1995, 1996
Somers, Grover	1905, 1906
Somers, H.C.	1916
Somers, W.E.	1910, 1911, 1912, 1913
Sorenson, Chris	1932
Sorg, W.S.	1921
Sorrell, Brian	1993, 1994, 1995, 1996
Sottili, Dave	1968
Spack, Harry	1932, 1933, 1934
Sparrow, David	1972
Spear, Shawn	1991, 1992, 1993
Spencer, Blair	1910, 1911
Spencer, Bob	1970, 1971
Spencer, Gene	1972
Spencer, T.P.	1902
Spidle, G. B.	1894
Squires, Gerald	1960
Stanard, Ryan	1996
Stanchak, Sam	1987, 1988, 1989, 1990, 1991
Stanley, Isaac	1911
Staub, Craig	1989, 1990, 1991, 1992, 1993
Steckroth, Bob	1942, 1946, 1947
Steiner, Jason	1991, 1992, 1993, 1994, 1995
Stem, John	1990, 1991, 1992, 1993, 1994

Stephens, E.E.A.	1915, 1916
Stephenson, Jon	1958, 1959, 1960
Sterba, Brett	1996
Sterling, Brad	1960
Stevens, Craig	1986, 1987
Stevens, Frank	1939
Stevens, Robert	1945
Stevens, William	1949
Stewart, John	1979, 1980, 1981
Stewart, Mike	1972, 1973, 1974
Stewart, Waddy	1932, 1933, 1934
Stockey, William	1970, 1971, 1972, 1973
Stone, Patrick	1951
Stone, Webster	1913, 1914
Stotlemyer, Todd	1982
Stovall, Ivan	1970, 1971, 1973
Stoy, Bob	1957, 1958, 1959 60
Strong, Robert	1905, 1906
Stryker, H. M.	1915
Stull, Brian	1991
Sturgess, Bruce	1951, 1952
Sublett, Tommy	1966
Sullivan, George	1943
Sullivan, Robert	1986
Sullivan, Ron	1970
Summers, J.H.	1902
Sumner, Charlie	1951, 1952, 1953, 1954
Surface, Dan	1963
Suttle, Oscar	1928
Sutton, Mike	1981
Sutton, Mike	1983
Sutty, Eric	1990, 1991, 1992, 1993
Swan, Scott	1962, 1963, 1964
Swaney, John	1987
Swartz, Rowland	1952
Sweeney, Mark	1982, 1983, 1984, 1985
Swertfager, Bill	1979, 1980
Sydnor, Bill	1943
Sydnor, Tom	1954
Syer, Crawford	1929, 1930, 1931
Sykes, W.	1929
Szarko, Bart	1985
Szczypinski, Bob	1973, 1974, 1975
Szumigala, Abbers	1935
Szydlik, Dave	1984, 1985, 1986, 1987

T

Tadder, Tim	1990, 1991
Tafro, Al	1977, 1978, 1979
Taliaferro, E. C. S.	1894
Taliaferro, Tom	1994, 1995, 1996
Tanner, Arthur	1937
Tauber, Jim	1969, 1970, 1971
Taylor, E.C.	1901

Taylor, Horace P.	1927-28
Taylor, Lucius	1927, 1928
Taylor, P.P.	1913, 1914
Taylor, Stuart	1906, 1907, 1908
Templeton, Bob	1940
Tennis, William	1910
Texer, Toby	1986
Teza, John	1992, 1993, 1994, 1995, 1996
Thaxton, H.C.	1959, 1960, 1961
Theado, Walter	1971
Theokas, Andrew	1988, 1989, 1990, 1991
Thomas, Alvin	1910
Thomas, Bob	1955, 1956, 1957
Thomas, Jon	1983, 1984, 1985
Thomas, Julian	1944
Thomas, S.B.	1898
Thompson, Mark	1970
Thompson, Tommy	1944, 1946, 1947, 1948
Tillet, Brett	1993, 1994, 1995, 1996
Tilley, Thomas	1910, 1911, 1912, 1913
Timberg, Anders	1991, 1992, 1993, 1994
Tinnell, Jeffrey	1984, 1985
Tinsley, Barry	1961
Tinsley, Robert	1989, 1990, 1991,92
Tirelis, Alfred	1937
Tisinger, Andy	1969, 1970
Todd, Allen	1985
Todd, John	1921, 1922, 1923, 1924
Todd, John	1940
Todd, Lee	1923, 1924, 1925, 1926
Tofano, Scott	1981, 1983
Tomich, Tony	1989, 1990, 1991, 1992, 1993
Tomlin, Michael	1990, 1991, 1992, 1993, 1994
Tomlinson, Howard	1955, 1957, 1958
Torma, John	1940
Torrence, William	1946
Tracy, Alex	1985
Trainor, Bill	1985
Travers, Stumpy	1934
Trembley, Steve	1976
Trempus, John	1944
Tribelhorn, Karl	1965, 1966, 1967
Triplett, Roderick	1897
Triplett, Scott	1894
Trivers, Calvin	1983, 1984, 1985, 1986
Trotter, Elmer	1945
Troupe, Randy	1971, 1972
Trout, Valery	1951, 1952
Truehart, John	1934, 1935, 1936
Tucker, Charlie	1954
Tucker, Lemuel	1971, 1972, 1973
Tucker, Rudolph	1937, 1938, 1939

Tucker, William	1954
Tuohey, Mike	1981
Turner, Darwin	1993
Turner, Kevin	1991
Turville, William	1939
Tuthill, Jack	1929, 1930
Tuthill, Jim	1964, 1965, 1966
Twiddy, Clarence	1939
Tyler, Mark	1988, 1989, 1990, 1991, 1992
Tyner, Paul	1978, 1979, 1980
Tyson, Allan Campbell	1893

U

Uhl, Brad	1986, 1987, 1988, 1990
Unger, Raymond	1910
Upson, Irvin, J	1930, 1931, 1932, 1933
Utecht, Alexander	1989, 1990, 1991, 1992
Uzzell, Bill	1969, 1970, 1971

V

Vale, Wallace	1989, 1990, 1991, 1992, 1993
Van Wagoner, Chris	1972
Vanderbeek, Jeff	1975, 1976, 1977
Vandeweghe, Al	1940, 1941, 1942
Varacallo, Jerry	1972
Varney, Thomas	1928
Vaughan, Dick	1945, 1946
Victor, Stanley	1970, 1971, 1972, 1973
Vince, Bret	1990, 1991
Vozar, Andy	1956, 1957
Vujevich, Tony	1951, 1952

W

Wachter, Bruce	1970
Waddy, Jude	1993, 1994, 1995, 1996
Wade, Phil	1989
Waechter, Tom	1972, 1973, 1974
Wagner, Mike	1976, 1977, 1978
Waite, Burt	1966, 1967, 1968
Waitkus. Mark	1990, 1991, 1992, 1993
Waksmunski, Chet	1952, 1953, 1954, 1955
Walak, Andrew	1945
Waldruth, A.A.	1927
Walk, Larry	1962, 1963
Walker, Charles	1937

Y

Z

Appendix 6

Individual Records

Scoring

Most Points

Game:	36, Bill Palese vs. Bridgewater, 1931
Season:	114, Robert Green, 1990
Career:	279, Steve Christie (PK), 1985–89;
	270, Jack Cloud (RB), 1946–49

Most Touchdowns

Game:	6, Bill Palese vs. Bridgewater, 1931
Season:	19, Robert Green, 1991
Career:	45, Jack Cloud, 1946–49

Most Points after Touchdown

Game:	8, Terry Regan vs. Davidson, 1972
Season:	56, Chris Dawson, 1993
Career:	123, Chris Dawson, 1990–93
Consecutive:	42, Terry Regan, 1972–73

Most Field Goals

Game:	4, Chris Dawson vs. Lehigh, 1992
	4, Brian Shallcross vs. Villanova, 1995
Season:	21, Steve Christie, 1989
Career:	57, Steve Christie, 1986–89

Total Offense

Rushing

Most Yards

Game:	409, Dave Murphy vs. Marshall, 1983
Season:	3,466, Chris Hakel, 1990
Career:	8,168, Stan Yagiello, 1981–85

Rushing Attempts

Game:	37, Wes Meeteer vs. Davidson, 1969
	37, Troy Keen vs. Northeastern, 1994
	37, Derek Fitzgerald vs. Penn, 1995
Season:	272, Alvin Porch, 1996
Career:	720, Derek Fitzgerald, 1995

Rushing Yards

Game:	257, Phil Mosser vs. Ohio Wesleyan, 1970
Season:	1,408, Robert Green, 1990
Career:	3,744, Derek Fitzgerald, 1995

Passing

Passing Attempts

Game:	51, Dan Darragh vs. Virginia Tech, 1966
Season:	428, Stan Yagiello, 1984
Career:	1,246, Stan Yagiello, 1981–85

Passing Completions

Game:	35, Dave Murphy vs. Rutgers, 1983
Season:	261, Stan Yagiello, 1984
Career:	737, Stan Yagiello, 1981–85

Passing Yards

Game:	414, Stan Yagiello vs. Miami of Ohio, 1982
Season:	3,414, Chris Hakel, 1990
Career:	8,249, Stan Yagiello, 1981–85

Completion Percentage

Season: 69.4, Shawn Knight, 1993
Career: 65.5, Shawn Knight, 1991–94

Passing Efficiency

Season: *204.6, Shawn Knight, 1993
Career: *170.77, Shawn Knight, 1991–94
                 * NCAA Division I-AA records

Touchdown Passes

Game: 6, Shawn Knight vs. Maine, 1993
Season: 26, Mike Cook, 1996
Career: 51, Stan Yagiello, 1981–85

Receiving

Receptions

Game: 13, Glen Bodnar vs. Colgate, 1984
Season: 73, Michael Clemons, 1986
Career: 175, Jeff Sanders, 1981–84

Receiving Yards

Game: 232, Jeff Sanders vs. Miami, 1982
Season: 1,180, Mark Compher, 1990
Career: 2,748, Harry Mehre, 1985–88

Yards per Catch

Season (500 yd min): 25.5, Mike Tomlin, 1992
Career: 20.1, Mike Tomlin, 1991–94

Touchdown Receptions

Game: 4, Vito Ragazzo vs. Wake Forest, 1949
                 4, Corey Ludwig vs. Maine, 1993
Season: 15, Vito Ragazzo, 1949
Career: 22, Vito Ragazzo, 1948–50
Games in a Row: 11, Vito Ragazzo, 1949–50

Interceptions

Most Intercepted

Game: 4, Jack Bruce vs. Richmond, 1947
Season: 10, Jack Bruce, 1947
                 10, Darren Sharper, 1996
Career: 24, Darren Sharper, 1993–96

Individual Long Plays

Rush from Scrimmage

95 yards, John Truehart vs. Emory & Henry, 1934

Pass Completion

87 yards, Dan Henning to Tom Scott vs. Navy, 1961

Punt

77 yards Jack Freeman, 1942
77 yards, Russell Brown, 1972
77 yards, Joe Agee, 1975

Punt Return

101 yards, Dale Worrall vs. Bridgewater, 1932

Kickoff Return

100 yards, Dick Pawlewicz vs. U.Va., 1974

Run with Fumble

90 yards, Meb Davis vs. Columbia, 1926

Run with Interception

93 yards, Marvin Graham vs. Virginia Tech, 1946

Run with Intercepted Lateral

90 yards, Junie Smith vs. Georgetown, 1933

Field Goal

53 yards, Steve Christie vs. East Tennessee State, 1987
53 yards, Steve Christie vs. Virginia, 1988

Unusual—Shortest Kickoff

2 1/2 inches, Brown Oliver vs. West Virginia, 1956 (National Record)

Cumulative Records

Passing Yards

1. 3,414, Chris Hakel, 1990
2. 3,166, Mike Cook, 1996
3. 2,974, Chris Hakel, 1991
4. 2,962, Stan Yagiello, 1985
5. 2,801, Stan Yagiello, 1984
6. 2,609, Ken Lambiotte, 1986
7. 2,235, Shawn Knight, 1993
8. 2,093, Dave Murphy, 1983
9. 2,016, John Brosnahan, 1987
10. 1,966, Chris Garrity, 1981

Passes Attempted

1. 428, Stan Yagiello, 1984
2. 414, Chris Hakel, 1990
3. 413, Stan Yagiello, 1985
4. 385, Ken Lambiotte, 1986
5. 372, Mike Cook, 1996
6. 357, Chris Hakel, 1991
7. 315, Chris Garrity, 1981
8. 315, Chris Garrity, 1980
9. 313, Dave Murphy, 1983
10. 272, Craig Argo, 1989

Passes Completed

1. 261, Stan Yagiello, 1984
2. 245, Chris Hakel, 1990
3. 240, Stan Yagiello, 1985
4. 233, Ken Lambiotte, 1986
5. 232, Chris Hakel, 1991
6. 210, Mike Cook, 1996
7. 199, Dave Murphy, 1983
8. 186, Chris Garrity, 1981
9. 166, Stan Yagiello, 1982
10. 160, Craig Argo, 1989

Receiving Yards

1. 1180, Mark Compher, 1990
2. 1110, Ron Gillam, 1985
3. 1096, Josh Whipple, 1996
4. 950, Corey Ludwig, 1993
5. 930, Mike Sutton, 1983
6. 911, Kurt Wrigley, 1982
7. 871, Harry Mehre, 1986
8. 845, David Knight, 1971
9. 843, Dave Conklin, 1996
10. 834, Corey Ludwig, 1991

Receptions

1. 73, Michael Clemons, 1986
2. 70, Michael Clemons, 1985
3. 69, Ron Gillam, 1985
   69, Glen Bodnar, 1984
5. 67, Chuck Albertson, 1966
6. 66, Mike Sutton, 1983
7. 65, Josh Whipple, 1996
8. 64, Mark Compher, 1990
9. 61, George Pearce, 1965
10. 57, Jeff Sanders, 1982
    57, Alan Williams, 1991

Rushing Yards

1. 1,408, Robert Green, 1990
2. 1,286, Phil Mosser, 1970
3. 1,223, Derek Fitzgerald, 1995
4. 1,210, Alvin Porch, 1996
5. 1,175, Troy Keen, 1994
6. 1,164, Jim Kruis, 1976
7. 1,118, Michael Clemons, 1986
8. 1,101, Derek Fitzgerald, 1993
9. 1,082, Tyrone Shelton, 1990
10. 974, Bill Deery, 1974

Total Offense

1. 3,466, Chris Hakel, 1990
2. 3,159, Mike Cook, 1996
3. 3,013, Stan Yagiello, 1985
4. 2,950, Chris Hakel, 1991
5. 2,730, Stan Yagiello, 1984
6. 2,586, Ken Lambiotte, 1986
7. 2,546, Shawn Knight, 1993
8. 2,394, John Brosnahan, 1987
9. 2,134, Shawn Knight, 1992
10. 2,038, Dave Murphy, 1983

Scoring

1. 114, Robert Green, 1990
2. 108, Jack Cloud, 1947
3. 99, Red Maxey, 1930
4. 96, Michael Clemons, 1986
5. 90, Vito Ragazzo, 1949
   90, Steve Christie, 1989
7. 89, Dan Mueller, 1990
8. 84, Troy Keen, 1993
   84, Troy Keen, 1994
   84, Brian Shallcross, 1996

Touchdown Passes

1. 26, Mike Cook, 1996
2. 23, Stan Yagiello, 1985
   23, Kenny Lambiotte, 1986
4. 22, Chris Hakel, 1990
   22, Shawn Knight, 1993
6. 18, Buddy Lex, 1949
   18, Chris Hakel, 1991
8. 17, John Brosnahan, 1987
9. 16, Stan Yagiello, 1984
10. 14, Dan Darragh, 1966
    14, Dave Murphy, 1983

Completion Percentage

1. .694, Shawn Knight, 1993
2. .650, Chris Hakel, 1991
3. .644, Shawn Knight, 1994
4. .636, Dave Murphy, 1983
   .636, Shawn Knight, 1993
6. .610, Stan Yagiello, 1984
7. .605, Kenny Lambiotte, 1986
8. .592, Chris Hakel, 1990
   .592, John Brosnahan, 1987
10. .590, Chris Garrity, 1981

Punting Average

1. 42.8, Buddy Lex, 1947
   42.8, Russell Brown, 1971
3. 42.4, Steve Christie, 1988
4. 41.7, Dan Darragh, 1965
   41.7, Russell Brown, 1971
6. 41.6, Tommy Korczowski, 1948
7. 40.6, Steve Christie, 1986
8. 40.3, Bud Porter, 1960
9. 40.0, Steve Christie, 1989
10. 39.9, Dan Mueller, 1991
    39.9, Steve Fill, 1995
11. 39.6, Joe Agee, 1976
    39.6, Steve Christie, 1987
13. 39.5, David Cripe, 1970
14. 39.3, Buddy Lex, 1948

Punting

1. 77 yards. Jack Freeman, 1942
   77 yards, Russell Brown, 1972
   77 yards, Joe Agee, 1975
4. 75 yards, Art Matsu vs. Chattanooga, 1926
   75 yards, Fred Scruggs vs. Emory & Henry, 1935

Statistics—Eyes in the Sky

"**G**ive Fitzgerald 14 yards on that carry." Quickly the statistic was typed out. "Call it first down on the 28. No, make it the 27."

Quietly and with a precision the years made easy, Richard "Snake" Drake of Virginia Beach and Pete Babcock of Williamsburg, working together for thirty-seven years, compiled all the statistics that could possibly be needed about the William and Mary football games.

From their vantage point in the press box atop Zable Stadium at Cary Field, they recorded the play-by-play of the game and maintained and collected the team and individual statistics for the NCAA.

Richard Drake and Pete Babcock

Drake, a W&M alumnus, class of 1948, has been doing the job for nearly fifty years, excluding a brief hiatus in the late 1950s. Babcock, who attended the College briefly in 1953—"I always meant to come back, but never did"—began his W&M football statistical career in 1960. Their final football season together was 1996; Babcock died February 26, 1997, after a lengthy battle with cancer.

Drake first worked as a student assistant to sports public relations director John Cox in 1947. "I started during the glory years of the late '40s, had a break for a couple of years in the '50s, came back and have been here now for nearly forty years straight," he explained.

He acknowledged that his love for and knowledge of math has helped "more than a few times" in his statistical work.

But "Snake" Drake likes William and Mary and its football team. "If I weren't up here working, I'd be in the stands cheering," he added.

Drake's professional career was in public schools, initially as a teacher, later as a principal, and finally as a mathematics supervisor for the Portsmouth City School Division. He retired in 1992.

Babcock began his statistical career with W&M basketball "when Jeff Cohen was a freshman and Bill Chambers was coach."

I had first worked for Chambers during high school. At W&M I first worked as a clock operator in old Blow Gymnasium and handled the scorebook on the road trips and during the tournaments. About two years later, they needed some help with football, and I've been here ever since.

Babcock worked for many years with the Virginia Department of Transportation and regularly wrote in the sports section of the *Virginia Gazette*. He was best known in the Williamsburg area, however, for his efforts—for more than forty years—as director of the youth football and baseball programs of the Williamsburg–James City County and the Bruton District of York County.

The two W&M fans have known—by numbers and "stats"—several thousand W&M football players. They've also seen the stadium packed or virtually empty.

Their statistics drill was cut and dried by the years. Drake called out the ball carrier and the spot where the play ended. Babcock typed all the information, including tackler and length of play into the play-by-play account of the game. Drake also kept all the individual statistics—runs, passes, receptions, punts, etc.—that are forwarded to the NCAA.

The duo had the system down pat and, in recent years, augmented it by adding several assistants to keep related statistics, such as tackles and third-down conversations—run or pass.

Drake and Babcock easily remembered the days of the old press box—just below the current press facilities, under a canvas awning, where the college president's box is now situated. "We were open to all the elements," Babcock recalled. "The wind would blow everything away; the rain would come in. There were games when it was a constant fight."

Drake remembered the days when Cary Field had a six-lane cinder track with a white picket fence running along each sideline. There also were low bleachers—six or eight seats high—along the sides. "The end zones also had lower and less permanent seats than today," he said. "And water always collected in one area," Drake added, pointing across the field.

There was always a pond when it rained, but now the field is graded and drains very well. The surface is much improved with the green Bermuda grass. Years ago, we just had regular grass, I think, that tore up quickly.

In the early years, there were not as many requirements for statistics as now, Drake and Babcock agreed. "We never used to keep third-down conversions, time of possession, advanced fumbles, or blocked field goals," Drake said. "Now, I don't know of much we don't keep a record of."

Through all the years and all the players, certain games "definitely stand out," Babcock said. "I guess one of my favorites was the game against Virginia Tech in 1962. It was the first game of the season, and we won, 3-0, and Steve Bishop kicked a field goal. It's easier for me to recall games years ago, than recent ones," he confided.

Drake also remembered the 1949 W&M–University of North Carolina game. "UNC won, 20-14," he said, "and they had the great Charlie 'Choo-Choo' Justice. He returned a punt for a touchdown, and it was the only one he ever got against us, I believe." Drake also remembered the W&M victory over Duke at Cary Field in 1951.

Drake added that recent home games against the University of Delaware "have been very good and rivaled some of those games of years ago."

Naturally, these statisticians also started recalling other lists during their tenure: eight sports information directors, seven athletic directors, and five football coaches (for Babcock) and eight for Drake. Then they started listing the sports writers they remember who covered the team. Writers, then as now, nearly surround the statistics area in the press box.

"And don't forget, in your list," Drake said, "those 'Iron Indians'—the football team in 1953 that had only twenty-four or so players and finished with a 5-4-1 record." (—WK)

Tackles

1.   244, Dave Pocta, 1986
2.   190, Dave Pocta, 1985
3.   146, Jim McHeffey, 1984
4.   144, Owen Costello, 1981
5.   143, Kerry Gray, 1988
      143, Jeff Hosmer, 1976
7.   141, Mark Keslo, 1983
8.   139, Jim Ryan, 1976
9.   138, Brad Uhl, 1987
      138, Karl Wernecke, 1984

Punt Return Avg. Minimum 10 Returns)

1.   21.3, Jack Yohe, 1953
2.   19.2, Tommy Korczowki, 1948
3.   18.7, Chip Young, 1966
4.   13.5, Buddy Lex, 1947
5.   13.0, Charlie Sidwell,1955
6.   12.2, Palmer Scarritt, 1992
7.   11.75, Jack Bruce, 1947
8.   11.5, Mike Weaver, 1965
9.   11.3, Jack Bruce, 1948
10.   11.1, Dave Edmunds,1958
      11.1, Darren Sharper, 1995

Punt Return Yards

1.   500, Darren Sharper, 1996
2.   415, Palmer Scarritt, 1992
3.   333, Darren Sharper, 1995
4.   330, Michael Clemons, 1986
5.   317, Jack Bruce, 1947
6.   315, Chip Young, 1967
7.   277, Jack Yohe, 1954
8.   251, Tommy Korczowski, 1948
9.   219, Palmer Scarritt, 1990
10.   211, Dickie Lewis, 1949
11.   206 yards, Chip Young, 1966
12.   205 yards, Charlie Sidwell, 1956
13.   204, Daren Sharper, 1994
14.   200, Buddy Lex, 1947

Kickoff Return Avg.
Minimum 15 Returns)

1.   28.4, Dick Pawlewicz, 1974
2.   25.5, Michael Clemons, 1985
3.   24.6, James Blocker-Bodley, 1990
4.   24.3, Dick Pawlewicz, 1973
5.   24.2, Keith Best, 1979
6.   24.1, Mark McCain, 1995
7.   23.9, James Blocker-Bodley, 1992
8.   23.7, Phil Mosser, 1971
9.   23.4, Charlie Sidwell, 1956
10.   22.7, Chris Hogarth, 1987

Kickoff Return Yards

1.   617, Phil Mosser, 1971
2.   587, Dave Scanlon, 1982
3.   584, Dick Pawlewicz, 1973
4.   572, Eddie Davis, 1987
5.   509, Michael Clemons, 1985
6.   467, Charlie Sidwell, 1956
7.   460, Keith Best, 1979
8.   447, Phil Mosser, 1970
9.   426, Dick Pawlewicz, 1974
10.   343, Keith Best, 1978

Interceptions

1.   10, Jack Bruce, 1947
      10, Darren Sharper, 1996
3.   8, Dick Kern, 1963
      8, Steve McNamee, 1980
5.   7, Paul Scolaro, 1972
      7, Mark Kelso, 1983
      7, Daren Sharper, 1994
      7, Daren Sharper, 1995
9.   6, Chip Young, 1967
      6, Mark Kelso, 1981
      6, Jim DiNardo, 1980

Field Goals (Longest)

1.   53 yards, Steve Christie vs. East Tenn State, 1987
      53 yards, Steve Christie vs. Virginia, 1988
      53 yards, Steve Christie vs. Delaware, 1989
4.   51 yards, Chris Dawson vs. Brown, 1992
5.   49 yards, Brian Shallcross vs. New Hampshire, 1995
      49 yards, Chris Dawson vs. Boston U., 1992
      49 yards, Chris Dawson vs. Lehigh, 1992
8.   48 yards, Steve Christie vs. New Hampsire, 1988
      48 yards, Steve Christie vs. Harvard, 1986
10.   47 yards, S.L. Bertschley vs. Richmond, 1914 (drop kick)
      47 yards, Art Matsu vs. Chattanooga, 1926 (drop kick)
      47 yards, Steve Libassi vs. Richmond, 1977
      47 yards, Steve Libassi vs. Virginia Tech, 1978
      47 yards, Laszlo Mike-Mayer vs. Virginia Tech, 1980
      47 yards, Brian Shallcross vs. Villanova, 1995

Field Goals (Most)

1.   21, Steve Christie, 1989
2.   15, Steve Christie, 1988
3.   14, Dan Mueller, 1990
4.   14, Brian Shallcross, 1995
5.   13, Brian Shallcross, 1996
6.   12, Steve Christie, 1986
7.   10, Chris Dawson, 1992
8.   9, Brian Morris, 1985
      9, Steve Christie, 1987
10.   8, Brian Morris, 1982
      8, Brian Morris, 1984

Most Extra Points

1.   56 of 60, Chris Dawson, 1993
2.   47 of 50, Dan Meuller, 1990
3.   45 of 49, Brian Shallcross, 1996
4.   36 of 44, Stan Magdziak, 1947
      36 of 38, Steve Christie, 1986
      36 of 39, Chris Dawson, 1992
7.   33 of 34, Terry Regan, 1973
8.   32 of 34, Brian Shallcross, 1994
9.   31 of 35, Mike Dodds, 1971
      31 of 34, Brian Morris, 1985

Career Records

Rushing Yards

1. 3,744, Derek Fitzgerald, 1992–95
2. 3,543, Robert Green 1988–90
3. 2,949, Troy Keen, 1992–95
4. 2,534, Tyrone Shelton, 1987–90
5. 2,404, Jim Kruis, 1975–77
6. 2,401, Bill Deery, 1972–74
7. 2,171, Phil Mosser, 1970–71
8. 2,135, Michael Clemons, 1983–86
9. 2,056, Jack Cloud, 1946–49
10. 1,574, Todd Bushnell, 1970–72

Passing Yards

1. 8,249, Stan Yagiello, 1981–85
2. 7,025, Chris Hakel, 1988–91
3. 5,705, Shawn Knight, 1991–94
4. 4,536, Chris Garrity, 1979–81
5. 4,019, Tom Rozantz, 1975–78
6. 3,361, Dan Darragh, 1965–67
7. 3,197, Mike Cook, 1995–96
8. 3,087, Dave Murphy, 1980–83
9. 2,970, John Brosnahan, 1987–88
10. 2,777, Craig Argo, 1987–89

Total Offense

1. 8,168, Stan Yagiello, 1981–85
2. 7,058, Chris Hakel, 1988–91
3. 6,408, Shawn Knight, 1991–94
4. 5,385, Tom Rozantz, 1975–78
5. 4,589, Bill Deery, 1972–74
6. 4,320, Chris Garrity, 1979–81
7. 3,749, Derek Fitzgerald, 1992–95
8. 3,707, Dan Darragh, 1965–67
9. 3,561, John Brosnahan, 1987–88
10. 3,543, Robert Green, 1988–91

Passes Attempted

1. 1,246, Stan Yagiello, 1981–85
2. 913, Chris Garrity, 1979–81
3. 869, Chris Hakel, 1988–91
4. 696, Tom Rozantz, 1975–78
5. 580, Shawn Knight, 1991–94
6. 535, Dan Darragh, 1965–67
7. 481, Dave Murphy, 1980–83
8. 440, Craig Argo, 1987–89
9. 416, John Brosnahan, 1987–88
10. 392, Ken Lambiotte, 1985–86

Pass Completions

1. 737, Stan Yagiello, 1981–85
2. 523, Chris Hakel, 1988–91
3. 407, Chris Garrity, 1979–81
4. 380, Shawn Knight, 1991–94
5. 315, Tom Rozantz, 1975–78
6. 288, Dave Murphy, 1980–83
7. 268, Dan Darragh, 1965–67
8. 251, John Brosnahan, 1987–88
9. 241, Craig Argo, 1987–88
10. 237, Ken Lambiotte, 1985–86

Completion Percentage

1. 65.5, Shawn Knight, 1991–94
2. 60.5, Kenny Lambiotte, 1985–86
3. 60.3, John Brosnahan, 1987–88
4. 60.2, Chris Hakel, 1988–91
5. 59.9, Dave Murphy, 1980–83
6. 59.1, Stan Yagiello, 1981–85
7. 57.6, Mike Cook, 1995–96
8. 54.8, Craig Argo, 1987–88
9. 50.1, Dan Darragh, 1965–67
10. 48.7, Matt Byrne, 1993–95

Touchdown Passes

1. 51, Stan Yagiello, 1982–85
2. 46, Shawn Knight, 1991–94
3. 43, Chris Hakel, 1988–91
4. 36, Buddy Lex, 1946–49
5. 30, Dan Darragh, 1965–67
6. 27, Chris Garrity, 1979–81
7. 26, Mike Cook, 1995–96
8. 25, John Brosnahan, 1985–88
9. 23, Kenny Lambiotte, 1985–86
10. 22, Bill Deery, 1972–74

Receptions

1. 175, Jeff Sanders, 1981–84
2. 172, Michael Clemons, 1983–86
3. 161, Harry Mehre, 1985–88
4. 145, Glenn Bodnar, 1982–84
5. 141, Kurt Wrigley, 1980–82
6. 140, Corey Ludwig, 1990–93
    140, Terry Hammons, 1991, 1993–95
8. 131, Alan Williams, 1988–91
9. 125, Robert Green, 1988–91
10. 123, David Knight, 1970–72

Receiving Yards

1. 2,748, Harry Mehre, 1985–88
2. 2,352, Jeff Sanders, 1981–84
3. 2,349, Corey Ludwig, 1990–93
4. 2,134, Terry Hammons, 1991, 1993–95
5. 2,054, Mike Tomlin, 1991–94
6. 1,995, David Knight, 1970–72
7. 1,986, Kurt Wrigley, 1980–82
8. 1,895, Josh Whipple, 1994–96
9. 1,609, Mark Compher, 1988–90
10. 1,608, Ron Gillam, 1982–85

Kickoff Return Yards

1. 1,600, James Blocker–Bodley, 1990–93 (4 years)
2. 1,069, Keith Best, 1978–80 (3 years)
3. 1,064, Phil Mosser, 1970–71 (2 years)
4. 1,035, Mark McCain, 1992–95 (4 years)
5. 1,023, Dave Scanlon, 1981–83 (3 years)
6. 1,013, Michael Clemons, 1983–86 (3 years)
7. 1,010, Dick Pawlewicz, 1973–74 (2 years)
8. 867, Roger Hale, 1958–61 (4 years)
9. 863, Charlie Sidwell, 1955–57 (3 years)
10. 779, Chuck Albertson, 1964–66 (3 years)

Punt Return Yards

1. 1,027, Darren Sharper, 1993–96
2. 797, Palmer Scarritt, 1989–92
3. 521, Chip Young, 1965–67
4. 508, Jack Bruce, 1947–48
5. 495, Charlie Sidwell, 1955–57
6. 472, Dickie Lewis, 1949–50, unknown 1951

W&M Football on Television

The first William and Mary football game broadcast on television was the Delta Bowl on January 1, 1949. A local television station in Memphis, Tennessee, site of the bowl game provided the coverage.

On November 5, 1966, as a regional presentation of ABC Sports, the team made its first national television network appearance. The game between the Indians and Boston College was televised from Alumni Stadium in Chestnut Hills, Massachusetts. Through the years, various games have been broadcast on cable television either live or on a delayed basis. ESPN presented a national broadcast of the Epson Ivy Bowl between W&M and Nihon University from Tokyo Japan on a delayed basis in January 1993.

The *Jimmye Laycock Show* began on cable television in 1986 and completed its eleventh season in 1996. It was broadcast on the Home Team Sports (HTS) regional six-state cable network and in the greater Williamsburg area on Cox Cable in James City County and Williamsburg.

Jay Colley, the "Voice of the Tribe" was the host of the program, which featured game action highlights, narrated by Coach Laycock; a chalkboard illustrated "Play of the Week"; in-depth interviews with Tribe players and Olympic Sport athletes; and an evaluation of the upcoming opponent. Sports Information Director Jean Elliott was executive producer of the program.

As regional cable television increased, W&M has been able to make arrangements for Williamsburg-area cable services to pickup away games broadcast in other areas.   (—WK)

Career Extra Points

1. 123, Chris Dawson, 1990–93
2. 106, Steve Christie, 1986–89
3. 101, Brian Shallcross, 1994–96
4. 89, Bian Morris, 1982–85
5. 76, Terry Regan, 1971–74
6. 74, Stan Magdziak, 1945–47
7. 52, L.Q. Hines, 1951–52
    52, Steve Libassi, 1977–79
9. 50, Dan Mueller, 1990–91
10. 41, Buddy Lex, 1947–49

Career Total Field Goals

1. 57, Steve Christie, 1986–89
2. 33, Brian Shallcross, 1994–96
3. 31, Brian Morris, 1982–85
4. 22, Chris Dawson, 1991–93
5. 18, Steve Libassi, 1997–79
6. 14, Dan Mueller, 1990
7. 13, Laszlo Mike-Mayer, 1980–81

Single Game Records

Individual Passing Yards

1. 414, Stan Yagiello, vs. Miami, 1982
2. 405, Stan Yagiello, vs. James Madison, 1985
3. 401, Dave Murphy, vs. Marshall, 1983
4. 399, Chris Garrity, vs. North Carolina, 1981
5. 385, Greg Degennaro, vs. Bucknell, 1986
6. 381, Mike Cook, vs. UNI, 1996
7. 360, Dave Murphy, vs. Rutgers, 1983
8. 345, Chris Hakel, vs. Delaware, 1991

    345, Stan Yagiello, vs. Norfolk State, 1985
10. 339, Shawn Knight, vs. Maine, 1993

Most Receptions in a Game

1. 13, Glenn Bodnar, vs. Colgate, 1984
2. 12, Chuck Albertson, vs. Virginia Tech, 1966

    12, George Pearce, vs. Navy, 1965

    12, Jeff Sanders, vs. Miami, 1982
5. 11, Chuck Albertson, vs. Villanova, 1966

    11, Kurt Wringley, vs. Richmond, 1981

    11, Mike Sutton, vs. Marshall, 1983

    11, Dave Szydlik, vs. Bucknell, 1986

    11, Harry Mehre, vs. Lehigh, 1988
10. 10, Jim Cavanaugh, vs. Virginia Tech, 1967

    10, Jeff Powell, vs. East Carolina, 1981

    10, Harry Mehre, vs. Delaware, 1986

    10, Charlie Weaver, vs. Davidson, 1963

Individual Rushing Yards in a Game

1. 257, Phil Mosser, vs. Ohio Wesleyan, 1970
2. 219, Derek Fitzgerald, vs. Penn State, 1995
3. 189, D. Fitzgerald, vs. Villanova, 1993

    189, D. Fitzgerald, vs. Northeastern, 1995
5. 183, Alvin Porch, vs. Delaware, 1996
6. 181, Robert Green, vs. Navy, 1991
7. 180, Robert Green, vs. Citadel, 1990
8. 178, Tyrone Shelton, vs. Eastern Tennessee State University, 1989
9. 172, Bill Bowman, vs. Wake Forest, 1953
10. 170, Troy Keen, vs. Furman, 1994

Top Passing Games

1. 414 yards vs. Miami (Ohio), 1982
2. 412 yards vs. James Madison, 1985
3. 403 yards vs. East Carolina, 1981
4. 401 yards vs. Marshall, 1983
5. 397 yards vs. UNC, 1991
6. 385 yards vs. Bucknell, 1986
7. 374 yards vs. Norfolk State, 1985
8. 365 yards vs. Delaware, 1982
9. 360 yards vs. Rutgers, 1983
10. 358 yards vs. Princeton, 1985

Top Rushing Games

1. 453 yards vs. Ohio Wesleyan, 1970
2. 433 yards vs. Villanova, 1993
3. 419 yards vs. Davidson, 1973
4. 417 yards vs. Richmond, 1974
5. 413 yards vs. VMI, 1993
6. 408 yards vs. Virginia Tech, 1949
7. 392 yards vs. Davidson, 1972
8. 387 yards vs. VMI, 1970
9. 354 yards vs. West Virginia, 1972
10. 350 yards vs. The Citadel, 1962
(check 1996 records)

Best Total Offense (Passing & Rushing)

1. 681 yards vs. Richmond, 1991
2. 651 yards vs. VMI, 1993
3. 649 yards vs. Richmond, 1974
4. 635 yards vs. Virginia Tech, 1949
5. 618 yards vs. Brown, 1992
6. 602 yards vs. Villanova, 1994
7. 596 yards vs. VMI, 1990
8. 594 yards vs. Lehigh, 1989
9. 593 yards vs. Furman, 1990
10. 572 yards vs. Davidson, 1972

Best Defense against the Run (1960 to the Present)

1. -39 yards vs. Colgate, 1988

    -39 yards vs. Villanova, 1996
3. -11 yards vs. Quantico, 1967
4. -6 yards vs. Villanova, 1993
5. 3 yards vs. Bucknell, 1996
6. 26 yards vs. Lehigh, 1992
7. 28 yards vs. Virginia Tech, 1985
8. 33 yards vs. Colgate, 1987
9. 54 yards vs. VMI, 1987
10. 55 yards vs. Dartmouth, 1980

Best Defense against the Pass (1960 to the Present)

1. 9 yards vs. University of Massachusetts, 1995

    9 yards vs. Eastern Carolina University, 1980

    9 yards vs. Appalachian State, 1976
4. 11 yards vs. VMI, 1993
5. 15 yards vs. Southern Mississippi, 1965
5. 17 yards vs. The Citadel, 1970
6. 18 yards vs. VMI, 1979
7. 19 yards vs. Eastern Carolina University, 1981
8. 20 yards vs. Connecticut, 1978
9. 21 yards vs. VMI, 1964
10. 22 yards vs. James Madison, 1989

Records Still in "the Books"

National Collegiate Athletic Association

Division I-A Records

Kickoff, shortest

2 1/2 inches, Brown Oliver vs. West Virginia, 1956

Most Consecutive Games Catching a Touchdown Pass

12, Desmond Howard, Michigan, 1990-91
11, Vito Ragazzo, W&M, 1949-50

Division I-AA Records

Passing Efficiency

Season, 204.6, Shawn Knight, W&M, 1993
Career, 170.8, Shawn Knight, W&M, 1991-94

Longest Return of a Defensive Extra Point

100-yards, Rich Kinsman, W&M vs. Lehigh, 1992

Most Games with 200+ yards passing

Season, 11, Chris Hakel, W&M, 1991

Most Consecutive Games with 200+ yards passing

11, Chris Hakel, W&M, 1991

Yankee Conference

Passing Efficiency

Season, 204.6, Shawn Knight, W&M, 1993
Career, 170.8, Shawn Knight, W&M, 1991-94

Team Offense

Highest Passing Percentage, Season

69.4, W&M, 1993

Interceptions

Career, 24, Darren Sharper, W&M, 1996

Punt Return Yards

Season, 500, Darren Sharper, W&M, 1996
Career, 1,027, Darren Sharper, W&M, 1993-96

Southern Conference

Most Consecutive Games Catching a Touchdown Pass

12, Desmond Howard, Michigan, 1990-91
11, Vito Ragazzo, W&M, 1949-50

Longest Plays, Kickoff Return

100 yards, Dick Pawlewicz vs. Virginia, 1974

Interceptions

Game, 4, Jack Bruce vs. Richmond, 1947
Season, 10, Jack Bruce, 1947

Team Penalties

Game, 197 yards vs. Furman, 1962

Appendix 7

Individual Honors

All-America Players

1930
Hap Halligan, (Honorable Mention)

1933
Bill Palese, HB (All-American Board)

1942
Garrard "Buster" Ramsey, G (AP—First)

1946
Knox Ramsey, G (Deke Houlgate—First; UP-Second; AP-Third)

1946
Bob Steckroth, E (AP—Honorable Mention)

1946
Tommy Korczowski, TB (AP—Honorable Mention)

1946
"Flyin'" Jack Cloud, FB (AP—Honorable Mention)

1947
"Flyin'" Jack Cloud, FB (New York Sun—First)
Knox Ramsey, G (Deke Houlgate—First; UP—Second)
Harry Caughron, OT (AP—Honorable Mention)
Bob Steckroth, E (AP—Honorable Mention)
Tommy Thompson, C (AP—Honorable Mention)

National Football Foundation College Football Hall of Fame

Garrard "Buster" Ramsey, inducted in 1978
"Flyin'" Jack Cloud, inducted in 1990
Walter J. Zable, Gold Medal Recipient in 1980

1948
"Flyin'" Jack Cloud, FB (New York Sun—First)
Tommy Thompson, C (AP—Third)
Harry Caughron, OT (AP—Honorable Mention)
Lou Hoitsma, E (AP—Honorable Mention)
Jack McDowell, OL (AP—Honorable Mention)

1949
Vito Ragazzo, E (UP—Second)

1951
John Kreamcheck, T (AP—Honorable Mention)
Dickie Lewis, B (UP—Honorable Mention)
Sam Lupo, G (AP—Honorable Mention)
Ed Mioduszewski, B (AP—Honorable Mention)
George Parozzo, T (UP—Honorable Mention)
Sam Lupo, G (UP—Honorable Mention)

1952
Ed Mioduszewski, B (AP—Second)
Tom Keller, B (AP & UP—Honorable Mention)
Linwood Cox, G (AP—Honorable Mention)
John Kreamcheck (UP—Honorable Mention)

1953
Bill Bowman, FB (AP & UP—Honorable Mention)
John Bednarik (UP—Honorable Mention)

1955
Bob Lusk, T (Williamson System—Third)

1956
Walter Brodie, E (AP—Second; Williamson System—First)
Charlie Sidwell (AP—Honorable Mention)

1959
Mike Lashley, T (AP—Honorable Mention)

1962
Bob Soleau, G (AP & UPI—Honorable Mention)

1963

Bob Soleau, G (AP—Honorable Mention)

1965

George Pearce, E (AP—Second)

1970

Bob Herb, C (AP—Second)

1973

Joe Montgomery (Football News—Third)

1974

Dick Pawlewicz, TE (AP—Third; Recap—Second)

1976

Tom Rozantz, QB (AP—Honorable Mention)
Jim Kruis, TB (AP—Honorable Mention)

1977

Tom Rozantz, QB (AP—Honorable Mention)
Hank Zimmerman, C (AP—Honorable Mention)

1983

Mario Shaffer, OG (AP—First; Kodak—First)

1984

Mark Kelso, DB (AP—Honorable Mention)

1986

Michael Clemons, TB (Kodak—First)

1988

Scott Perkins, OL (AP—Second)
Steve Christie, PK (AP—Honorable Mention)
Harry Mehre, WR (AP—Honorable Mention)

1989

Steve Christie, P/PK (Kodak-First; Sports Network-Second; AP—Second)
Reggie White, OG (Sports Network—Second)

Sports Illustrated Silver Anniversary All-America Team

John W. Tuthill, E—1931
Dan Edmondson, HB—1936
Walter Zable, E—1937
Col. Seymour Schwiller, G—1940

"Teddy" Award NCAA's Highest Honor

(The Theodore Roosevelt Award is presented annually to a distinguished citizen of national reputation and outstanding accomplishment who has earned a varsity award in college.)

1987-Walter J. Zable '37

1990

Reggie White, OG (Sports Network—First; AP—First; Walter Camp—First; Kodak—First)
Robert Green, TB (AP—Third; Sports Network—Third)

1991

Peter Reid, OT (Sports Network—Honorable Mention)

1992

Tom Walters, OG (Sports Network—Honorable Mention)

1993

Craig Staub, DT (Sports Network—First; Walter Camp—First; Don Hansen's FB Gazette—First; AP—Second)
Tom Walters, OG (Sports Network—Second; AP—Second; Don Hansen's FB Gazette—Third)
Shawn Knight, QB (Sports Network—Honorable Mention)

1994

Darren Sharper, FS (Sports Network—Honorable Mention)
Greg Applewhite, LB (Sports Network—Honorable Mention)

1995

Darren Sharper, FS (Sports Network—First; Football Almanac—First)
Josh Beyer, OG (Sports Network—Third)

1996

Darren Sharper, FS (Sports Network—First; Football Gazette—First, American Football Coaches Association—First; AP—First; Walter Camp—First)
Josh Beyer, OG (Sports Network—First; Football Gazette—First; American Football Coaches Association—First; AP—First; Walter Camp—First)

Southern Conference

All-Southern First Team

1941
Garrard Ramsey, G
Harvey Johnson, B

1942
Garrard Ramsey, G
Marvin Bass, T
Glenn Knox, E
Harvey Johnson, B

1944
John Clowes, G

1945
Knox Ramsey, T

1946
Knox Ramsey, G
Jack Cloud, B

1947
Bob Steckroth, E
Knox Ramsey, G
Tommy Thompson, C
Jack Cloud, B
Harry Caughron, T
Ralph Sazio, T

1948
Tommy Thompson, C
Jack Cloud, B
Harry Caughron, T
Lou Hoitsma, E
Jack McDowell, G
Lou Creekmur, T

1949
Vito Ragazzo, E
George Hughes, G
Buddy Lex, B

1951
Ed Mioduszewski, B
Sam Lupo, G
Ted Filer, C
Jerry Sazio, LB

1952
Linwood Cox, G
Ed Mioduszewski, B

1953
George Parazzo, T
Bill Bowman, B

1954
Jerry Sazio, LB

1955
Walt Brodie, E
Bob Lusk, T

1956
Walt Brodie, E
Charlie Sidwell, B

1957
Elliott Schaubach, T
Bill Rush, C
Larry Peccatiello, E

1959
Mike Lashley, T

1961
Eric Erdossy, G

1962
John Sapinsky, T
Bob Soleau, G

1963
Bob Soleau, G

1964
Scot Swan, DB
George Pearce, DE
Craig Smith, OG
Jeff Craig, OT

1965
George Pearce, OE
Tom Feola, C
Tony Buccino, DT
Jim LoFrese, DHB
Bob Gadkowski, LB

1966
Chuck Albertson, E
Bob Gadkowski, DE
Adin Brown, LB
Joe Nielson, DT

1967
Bob Gadkowski, DE
Adin Brown, LB
Chip Young, DB
Brad Cashman, T
Jim Cavanaugh, E

1968
Bob Herb, C
Ralph Beatty, T
Terry Morton, HB
Jim Barton, S
Burt Waite

1969
Bob Herb, C
Tom Duffey, S

1970
Phil Mosser, FB
Paul Scolaro, S
Wally Ake, LB
Jackson Neal, G
Bob Herb, C

1971
Phil Mosser, FB
Paul Scolaro, S
David Knight, E
Jackson Neall, G

1972
Joe Montgomery, C
Terry Regan, K
Ron Chappell, DE
Stan Victor, OG
Paul Scolaro, S
David Knight, E

1973
Joe Montgomery,
Russell Brown, P
Dick Pawlewicz, TE

1974
Bill Deery, QB
Dick Pawlewicz, TE
Mike Stewart, SS

1976
Tom Rozantz, QB
Ken Cloud, TE
Jim Kruis, TB
Bruno Schmalhofer, DE

Player of the Year

1956:	Walt Brodie, E	**1962:**	Bob Soleau, G
1965:	George Pearce, E	**1970:**	Phil Mosser, FB

Athlete of the Year

1966:	Chuck Albertson (Football, Baseball)
1971:	Phil Mosser (Football)

Jacobs Blocking Trophy

1950:	Lou Creekmur, T	**1962:**	Bob Soleau, G
1963:	Bob Soleau, G	**1970:**	Bob Herb, C
	1971:	Jackson Neall, G	

Yankee Conference

Defensive Player of the Year

1993:   Craig Staub, DT
1995:   Jason Miller, LB
1996:   Darren Sharper, FS

Rookie of the Year

1996:   David Conklin, WR,

All-Yankee Conference

1993

Craig Staub, DT - 1st
Wally Vale, OT - 1st
Tom Walters, OG - 1st
Chris Dawson, P - 1st
Greg Applewhite, LB - 2nd
Derek Fitzgerald, TB - 2nd
Shawn Knight, QB - 2nd
Corey Ludwig, WR - 2nd
Tony Tomich, C - 3rd
Mike Bertoni, DE - 3rd
Eric Lambert, LB - 3rd

1994

Darren Sharper, FS - 1st
Shawn Knight, QB - 2nd
Greg Applewhite, LB - 2nd
Mike Tomlin, WR - 2nd
Troy Keen, TB - 2nd
Josh Beyer, G - 2nd
Jude Waddy, LB - 3rd

1995

Derek Fitzgerlad, TB - 1st
Jason Miller, LB - 1st
Josh Beyer, OG - 1st
Darren Sharper, FS - 1st
Jim Simpkins, DT - 2nd
Charlie White, C - 2nd
Stefon Moody, LB - 2nd
Troy Keen, TB - 3rd
Pete Coyne, DT - 3rd
Mark McCain, KR - 3rd
Brian Shallcross - 3rd
Jude Waddy, LB - 3rd
Terry Hammons, WR - 3rd

1996

Darren Sharper, FS - 1st
Josh Beyer, OG - 1st
Mike Bertoni, DE - 1st
Luke Cullinane, DE - 1st
Alvin Porch, RD - 1st
Mike Cook, QB - 1st
Brian Giamo, DT - 2nd
Mike McGowan, LB - 2nd
Stefon Moody, LB - 2nd
Jude Waddy, LB - 2nd
Dan Rossettini, OG - 2nd
Peter Coyne, DT - 3rd

All–Eastern College Athletic Conference

1973
Joe Montgomery, C

1976
Jim Kruis, TB
Hank Zimmerman, C

1977
Joe Manderfield, WR

1980
Steve McNamee, FS
Kurt Wrigley, WR (Rookie of the Year)

1985
Stan Yagiello, QB
Michael Clemons, TB
Archie Harris, OT
Bob Solderitch, TE

1986
Michael Clemons, TB
Ken Lambiotte, QB
Archie Harris, OT
Dave Pocta, LB

1987
Steve Christie, PK
John Menke, OL

1988
Steve Christie, PK
Scott Perkins, OL
Harry Mehre, WR

1989
Steve Christie, PK and P
Reggie White, OG
Alan Garlic, DE

1990
Reggie White, OG
Tyrone Shelton, RB
Alan Garlic, DE

1991
Greg Kalinyak, OC
Mark Tyler, DT

1992
Tom Walters, OG
Palmer Scarritt, CB
Derek Fitzgerald, TB (Rookie of the Year)

1993
Craig Staub, DT
Wally Vale, OT
Shawn Knight, QB
Tom Walters, OG
Eric Lambert, LB
Marc Richards, CB

1994
Darren Sharper, FS
Shawn Knight, QB
Greg Applewhite, LB

1995
Josh Beyer, OG
Jason Miller, MLB
Darren Sharper, FS
Jim Simpkins, DT

1996
Darren Sharper, FS
Josh Beyer, OG
Mike Cook, QB
Luke Cullinane, DE
Brian Giamo, DT
Mike McGowan, LB
Alvin Porch, RB

All-Southern Scholastic Team

1955
Denys Grant, G

1956
Denys Grant, G
Charlie Sidwell, HB

1957
Denys Grant, G
Bill Rush, C

1959
Ben Johnson, E
Laurent Kardatzke, FB

1960
Bob Stoy, QB
Loye Bechtold, T
Joe Poist, E

1962
Dennis O'Toole, E

1963
Bill Corley, E

Postgraduate Scholarship Winners

1978
Kenneth Smith (NCAA)

1980
Clarence E. Gaines (NCAA)

1985
Mark Kelso (NCAA)

1986
Ken Lambiotte (NFF)

1988
Chris Gessner (NFF)

1990
Reggie White (NFF)

1993
Craig Staub (NFF)
NFF=National Football Foundation

Academic All-America

1974
John Gerdelman, FB (1st team)

1975
Ken Smith, DB (1st team)

1976
Ken Smith, DB (1st team)

1977
Ken Smith, DB (1st team)

1978
Rob Muscalus, TE (1st team)

1979
Clarence Gains, TB (2nd team)

1981
Steve Dowdy, LB (2nd team)

1983
Mark Kelso, FS (1st team)

1984
Mark Kelso, FS (1st team)

1986
Ken Lambiotte, QB (2nd team)

1988
Chris Gessner, CB (1st team)

1990
Jeff Nielsen, LB (1st Team)
Greg Kalinyak, C (2nd Team)

1991
Jeff Nielsen , LB (2nd Team)

1992
Craig Staub, DT (2nd Team)

1993
Craig Staub, DT (1st Team)

All-South—First Team

1980
Doug Martini, OG

1981
Steve Dowdy, LB
Doug Martini, OG
Jerome Watters , DB

1982
Steve Zeuli, DT

Virginia Sports Hall of Fame

1974 Gerrard S. Ramsey	**1979** Otis W. Douglas	**1983** H. Lester Hooker, Jr. George S. Hughes	**1989** Lou Creekmur
1975 Tommy Thompson	**1981** Marvin Bass	**1984** Jack Cloud Meb Davis	**1990** Suey Eason
1978 Eric Tipton Dr. John B. Todd	**1982** Glenn Knox	**1986** Buddy Lex William "Pappy" Gooch	**1993** Vito Ragazzo

Players in Postseason Honor Games

Blue-Gray All-Star Football Classic

(Montgomery, Alabama)

1942
Harvey Johnson, B
Garrard Ramsey, G

1945
Doc Holloway, G

1946
Mel Wright, T

1949
George Hughes, G
Jack Cloud, FB
Buddy Lex, B
Lou Creekmur, T

1952
Ed Mioduszewski, B

1974
Dick Pawlewicz, TE

1978
Tom Rozantz, QB

1986
Archie Harris, T

1991
Chris Hakel, QB

College-NFL All-Star Game

(Chicago, Illinois - Discontinued in 1976)

1943
Garrard Ramsey, G
Harvey Johnson, HB

1946
Garrard Ramsey, G

1948
Knox Ramsey, G

1949
Tommy Thompson, C

1950
Lou Creekmur, T
George Hughes, G

Shrine Game North-South

1951
Ed Weber, HB

1953
Bill Bowman, FB

1965
George Pearce, E

1972
David Knight, FL

1973
Joe Montgomery, C

Shrine Game North-South

1951
Vito Ragazzo, E

1964
Bob Soleau, G

1991
Chris Hakel, QB

All-American Bowl

(Discontinued in 1992)

1990
Reggie White

East-West Senior Bowl

(San Francisco, California)

1950
Jack Cloud, FB
Lou Creekmur, T

1951
Vito Ragazzo, E

1953
Ed Mioduszewski, B

1964
TW Alley, T

1990
Steve Christie, PK

Appendix 8

Players in Professional Football

Former W&M Athlete	Pro Team	Years	Position
Bill Bowman	Detroit Lions	1954, 1956	Back
	Pittsburgh Steelers	1957	Back
Tom Brown	Pittsburgh Steelers	1942	End
Dennis Cambal	New York Jets	1973	Tight End
John Cannon	Tampa Bay Buccaneers	1983-1989	Defensive End
Winston H. Charles	Dayton	1928	
Steve Christie	Tampa Bay Buccaneers	1990-1991	Placekicker
	Buffalo Bills	1992-present	Placekicker
Michael Clemons	Kansas City Chiefs	1987	Back
	Tampa Bay Buccaneers	1988	Back
	Toronto Argonauts	1989-present	Back
"Flyin'" Jack Cloud	Green Bay Packers	1950-1951	Back
	Washington Redskins	1952-1953	Back
John Clowes	Detroit Lions	1951	Tackle
Louis Creekmur	Detroit Lions	1950-1959	Tackle
Dan Darragh	Buffalo Bills	1968-1970	Quarterback
Otis Douglas	Philadelphia Eagles	1946-1949	Tackle
Nick Forkovitch	Brooklyn Dodgers	1946	Halfback
Robert Green	Washington Redskins	1992	Halfback
	Chicago Bears	1993-1996	Halfback
	Minnesota Vikings	1997	Halfback
Chris Hakel	Washington Redskins	1992	Quarterback
	K.C. Chiefs, Atlanta Falcons	1993	Quarterback
Isham Hardy	Akron	1923 & 1926	
Chris Garrity	Washington Federals	1982	Quarterback
Dan Henning	San Diego Chargers	1966	Quarterback
George Hughes	Pittsburgh Steelers	1950-1954	Guard
Harvey Johnson	New York Yankees	1947-1948	Placekicker
Mark Kelso	Buffalo Bills	1986-1993	Safety
David Knight	New York Jets	1973-1977	Wide Receiver
Shawn Knight	Toronto Argonauts	1994-1995	Quarterback
John Kreamcheck	Chicago Bears	1953-1955	Tackle
Kenny Lambiotte	Philadelphia Eagles	1987	Quarterback
Corey Ludwig	Calgary Stampede	1995	Wide Receiver
Buddy Lex	Hamilton Tiger Cats	1954	Quarterback
Bob Lusk	Detroit Lions	1956	Center
Art Matsu	Dayton Triangles	1928	Halfback
Melvin Martin	Saskatchewan Roughriders	1979	Linebacker
Joe Montgomery	Charlotte Hornets	1975	Center

Professional Football Honor Roll

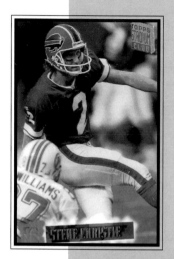

Steve Christie

Tied Tampa Bay Buccaneer record with forty-nineconsecutive PATs.

Michael Clemons

Canadian Football League, Most Valuable Player, 1990
Canadian Football League, Tom Pate Memorial Award, 1994

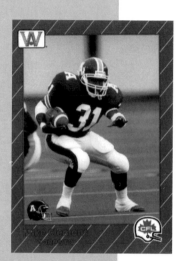

Lou Creekmur

National Football League, Pro Bowl, 1951–58

George Hughes

National Football League, Pro Bowl, 1952 & 1954

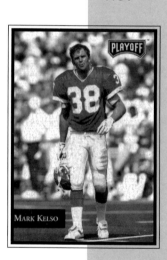

Mark Kelso

Sports Illustrated, All-Pro, 1988

Garrard "Buster" Ramsey

National Football League, All-Pro, 1947–49

Tommy Thompson

UP, All-National Football League, 1953

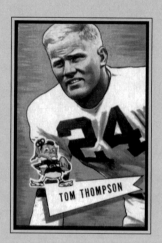

Pro Football Hall of Fame

Lou Creekmur, Detroit Lions (1950–59), inducted in 1996.

Former W&M Athlete	Pro Team	Years	Position
Vito Ragazzo	Hamilton Tiger Cats	1953-1954	End
Garrard "Buster" Ramsey	Chicago Cards	1947-1949	Guard
Knox Ramsey	Los Angeles Dons	1946-1949	Guard
	Chicago Cardinals	1950-1951	Guard
	Philadelphia Eagles	1952	Guard
	Washington Redskins	1953	Guard
Tom Rozantz	Saskatchewan Roughriders	1979	Quarterback
	Hamilton Tigers Cats	1980	Quarterback
	Toronto Argonauts	1981-1982	Quarterback
	Chicago Blitz	1983	Quarterback
	Pittsburgh Maulers	1984	Quarterback
	Birmingham Stallions	1985	Quarterback
Jim Ryan	Denver Broncos	1979-1988	Linebacker
John Sapinsky	Oakland Raiders	1964	Off. Tackle
Jerry Sazio	Hamilton Tiger Cats	1955	Linebacker
Ralph Sazio	Brooklyn Dodgers	1948	Tackle
	Hamilton Tiger Cats	1950-1953	Tackle
Darren Sharper	Green Bay Packers	1997	Safety
Steve Shull	Miami Dolphins	1980-1983	Linebacker
Bob Soleau	Pittsburgh Steelers	1964	Linebacker
Charlie Sumner	Chicago Bears	1955-1959	Halfback
	Minnesota Vikings	1961-1952	Def. Back
Tommy Thompson	Cleveland Browns	1949-1953	Center
"Tex" Warrington	Brooklyn Dodgers	1946-1947	Tackle
Ed Weber	Los Angeles Rams	1952	Fullback
Al Vandeweghe	Buffalo Bisons	1946	End
Stan Yagiello	Pittsburgh Gladiators	1987	Quarterback
	New York Knights	1988	Quarterback

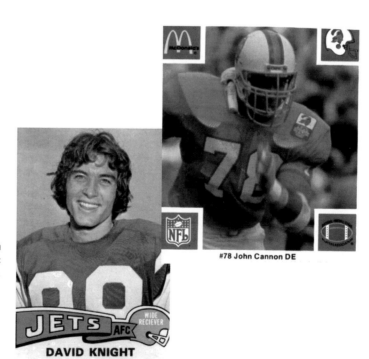

Professional football cards on these pages come from the collection of Bob Sheeran.

#78 John Cannon DE

DAVID KNIGHT

All-Time All-Star Teams

By George Trevor of the *New York Sun*, published in 1940

First Team		Second Team
John Todd '25	Center	Joseph Bridgers '34
Crawford Syers '31	Guard	Russell House '26
Otis Douglas '32	Guard	Otto Lowe '22
Flit Neblett '10	Tackle	Francis Elliott '26
Bob Wallace '20	Tackle	Stan Weber '28
Lee Todd '26	End	Suey Eason '28
Happy Halligan '31	End	Meb Davis '27
Stanton Bertschey '19	Quarterback	Art Matsu '27
Leslie Hall '11	Back	James Driver '10
Billy Palese '33	Back	Bill Scott '31
Clarence Maxey '31	Back	Melville Bryant '36

With a history so notable, is it any wonder that the football teams of William and Mary have covered themselves with glory? The Green, Gold and Silver warriors journeyed to the Harvard Stadium in 1930 and there astounded the Crimson by holding them to a 13-13 tie. Some called it an upset, but in 1932 William and Mary again amazed the football world with a 6-0 victory over Navy.

The William and Mary All-Time team consists mainly of players from the last decade, since that was the period of greatest development. John Todd, because of his great all-round ability, gets the center post by a nod over Joe Bridgers, a 60-minute man who captained the 1934 Indian eleven. Syers was a huge but surprisingly shifty guard who, on the 1931 team, had for his running mate Otis Douglas, one of the most outstanding athletes of that period. Douglas, who coached at William and Mary for seven years, is now assistnat coach at Akron University in Akron, Ohio.

Bob Wallace, gigantic captain of the '20 team would have paired nicely with "Flit" Neblett, who used his brains more often than his brawn. Both were smart, aggressive tackles. Lee Todd, an end, followed his brother John on the path to William and Mary gridiron fame. Lee had a unique style of end play that had enemy quarterbacks constantly puzzled. At the other flank position would be Happy Halligan, six feet three inches of sinewy muscle, a giant on defense and one of the South's finest punters.

Stanton Bertschey was the gambling type of field general with an uncanny instinct for selecting the proper play. Ace of the Indian backfield in 1919, Bertschey later went to V.M.I where he co-starrred in football with the Keydets immortal Billy Leech. Art Matsu, the diminutive Japanese, could pass and kick with the best of them and the combination of Matsu to Davis is now William and Mary legend. Leslie Hall, of the old era, was a reliable ground gainer and also a bulwark on the defense. Bill Palese, known as the 'Camden Flash' or the 'Camden Express', excelled in broken-field running.

Bill Scott, fastest of all William and Mary runners, also could kick and pass. Bryant, captain of the 1935 team, was one of the finest kickers in the South and also a good ball-carrier. Jimmy Driver, '11 was one of William and Mary's greatest ball-toters and an excellent all-around athlete.

One of the most colorful of William and Mary gridders was Clarence "Red" Maxey, who ran, passed and kicked his way to All-American backfield mention in 1931.

Richmond Times-Dispatch, 1950

In 1946, the *Richmond Times-Dispatch* conducted a poll to select the top William and Mary All-Time, All-Star team. Members on the squad came from teams from 1921 to 1944

Among the selections were six members of the 1942 W&M team, considered by many old-time observers of the Virginia football scene "the greatest aggregation of football players ever to perform in the Old Dominion," according to Chauncey Durden, *Times-Dispatch* Sports Editor.

The top vote getter was Gerrard "Buster" Ramsey, the All-American guard. Following one-vote behind was Harvey Johnson, the big fullback who did the heavy backfield work for Ramsey's team.

The All-Stars were:

First Team	Positions	Second Team	Third Team
Glen Knox '43	end	"Happy" Halligan '32	Lee B. Todd '27
Marvin Bass '43	tackle	Waddill Stewart '35	David Stanley Weber '28
"Buster" Ramsey '43	guard	Crawford Fryer '32	Edwin R. House '26
"Tex" Warrington '44	center	John Todd '26	Joseph M. Bridgers '35
Otis Douglas '32	guard	Otto Lowe '23	Drewery H. Holloway '44
"Pappy" Fields '43	tackle	Bob Wallace '21	Gerald Leo Quirk, '34
Meb Davis '28	end	Al Vandeweghe '43	Charles Gondak '41
Art Matsu '27	back	Billy Palese '33	Stanton L. Bertschey '17
Billy Scott '31	back	Harlie Masters '42	James G. Driver '09
Clarence Maxey '32	back	Mel Bryant '42	John Joseph Freeman '43
"Stud" Johnson '43	back	Nick Forkovitch '46	James E. Howard '43

Durden said several Indians of all-time stature were overlooked by the public voters. "Flit Neblett, a mighty tackle on the 1910 team; Frances Elliott '26, another great tackle; Suey Eason, crack end of the 1928 team; and Leslie Hall, backfield star of the 1911 season who had been picked on other all-time W&M elevens, were almost completely passed up by the readers," the sports editor explained. "Buster" Ramsey received the largest number of votes with 528, followed, one vote behind, by Harvey Johnson.

In 1951 another *Times-Dispatch* ballot resulted in the addition of the following players to William and Mary's All-Time squad: "Flyin'" Jack Cloud '50, back; Tommy Thompson '49, center; Lou Creekmur '50, tackle; and Knox Ramsey '48 , guard

Richmond Times-Dispatch—Virginia's All-Star Team, 1950

In 1950 the *Richmond Times-Dispatch* selected an all-time Virginia eleven, again by a vote of its readers. The Indians placed seven on the first team and many others on the reserve list.

Making the first-team eleven were: "Flyin'" Jack Cloud '50, fullback; Vito Ragazzo '49, end; Glenn Knox '43, end; Marvin Bass '43, tackle; Garrard "Buster" Ramsey '43, guard; Knox Ramsey '49, guard; and Tommy Thompson '49, center

Backs Bill Dudley of Virginia, Bosh Pritchard and Joe Muha of VMI and tackle Malachi Mills of VMI rounded out Virginia's Modern All-Time football team.

Otis Douglas '34 was voted second team tackle, while Lou Hoitsma '48 and Harvey Johnson '43 were voted third team end and back respectively.

William and Mary's All-Star Team

As part of the festivities to commemorate the 100th meeting between W&M and the University of Richmond on Nov. 17, 1990, an All-Time W&M team was selected. The players named were:

Quarterbacks

Buddy Lex '50 and Stan Yagiello '86.

Running Backs:

Michael Clemons '87, Jack Cloud '50, Tommy Korezowski '50 and Phil Mosser '72.

Receivers:

Harry Mehre '89, David Knight '73, Vito Ragazzo '51 and Walter Zable '37.

Linemen:

Marvin Bass '45, John Cannon '82, Lou Creekmur '50, George Hughes '50, Joe Monaco '88, Joe Montgomery '73, Buster Ramsey '43, Knox Ramsey '48, Ralph Sazio, Bob Soleau '64, and Tommy Thompson.

Linebacker:

Bob Gadkowski '66, Dave Pocta '87, Jim Ryan '79, Steve Shull '80,

Defensive backs:

Jack Bruce '49, Mark Kelso '85, Paul Scolaro '73 and Charlie Sumner '55.

Punter/Placekicker:

Steve Christie '90.

Punt/Kickoff Returns:

Mark Kelso '85 and Michael Clemons '87.

The 100th game between W&M and Richmond was the venue for selecting the "All-Time" teams of each school. Returning for W&M were: (first row, left to right) Tom Mikula accepting for Jack Cloud, Stan Yagiello, Buddy Lex, Phil Mosser, Tommy Korczowski, Joe Monaco, and Jack Bruce; (second row) Harry Mehre II accepting for Henry Mehre III, Dave Pocta, Lou Creekmur, Vito Ragazzo, David Knight, George Hughes, Joe Montgomery, Knox Ramsey, Bob Gadkowski, and Bob Soleau. Courtesy of the W&M Sports Information Department.

Bibliography

Primary Sources

College Papers

Faculty Minutes (1890–52), Special Collections Division, University Archives, Earl Gregg Swem Library, College of William and Mary.

Minutes of the Board of Visitors (1890–90), Special Collections Division, University Archives, Earl Gregg Swem Library, College of William and Mary.

The *William and Mary College Monthly* (1890–12), Special Collections Division, University Archives, Earl Gregg Swem Library, College of William and Mary.

Alumni Gazette, Society of the Alumni (1934 to present).

Colonial Echo, the student yearbook, College of William and Mary (1899 to present).

Flat Hat, the student newspaper, College of William and Mary (1911 to present).

Newspapers

Daily Press (Newport News, Virginia)

Norfolk *Pilot* (Norfolk, Virginia)

Richmond Dispatch (Richmond, Virginia)

Richmond Times (Richmond, Virginia)

Richmond Times-Dispatch (Richmond, Virginia)

Virginia Gazette (Williamsburg, Virginia)

Norfolk *Virginian-Pilot* (Norfolk, Virginia)

Books

Bowman, John S., ed. *Ivy League Football.* Crescent, 1988.

Goldblatt, Abe, and Wentz, Robert W., Jr. *The Great and the Near Great, A Century of Sports in Virginia.* The Donning Company/Publishers, 1976.

Kale, Wilford. *Hark upon the Gale: An Illustrated History of William and Mary.* The Donning Company/Publishers, 1985.

Larson, Melissa. *The Pictoral History of College Football.* Gallery Books, 1989.

McCallum, John D., and Pearson, Charles H. *College Football, USA, 1869-1973.* Hall of Fame Publishing, Inc., 1973.

Newcombe, Jack, ed. *The Fireside Book of Football.* Simon and Schuster, 1964.

Whittingham, Richard. *Saturday Afternoon: College Football and the Men who Made the Day.* Workman Publishing, 1985.

Index

The Authors

Wilford Kale has spent 65 percent of his life in and around the College of William and Mary and its campus. He is a William and Mary alumnus and recipient of the Alumni Medallion for Service and Loyalty presented by the Society of the Alumni. A graduate of Park College in Parkville, Missouri, with a B.A. degree in history, he began his professional newspaper career in the sports department of the *Charlotte Observer*. He later served for twenty-five years on the staff of the *Richmond Times-Dispatch*, working for twenty-one years as Williamsburg bureau chief.

A native of Charlotte, North Carolina, Kale is currently senior staff adviser at the Virginia Marine Resources Commission in Newport News, Virginia. He has been active in many professional journalism programs, serving for five years (1985–90) as Region 2 Director (for Virginia, North Carolina, Maryland, and the District of Columbia) on the national board of the Society of Professional Journalists. He also served as president of the Richmond Professional Chapter, SPJ, and currently is president of the board of trustees of the Richmond SPJ/SDX Educational Foundation, which raises scholarship money for college students interested in journalism as a career. He also served eight years on the board of the Society for Collegiate Journalists (1977–85) and was national president of the student journalism group from 1979 to 1981.

Kale has written several other books on William and Mary, including *Hark Upon the Gale, an Illustrated History of the College of William and Mary*. Kale also has won regional and national awards for his reportorial and book projects.

And, he has missed only a handful of William and Mary home football games in the past thirty-five years.

Bob Moskowitz is a retired sports writer. A graduate of Miami University of Ohio, he came to Virginia's Peninsula to work for a year or so in the sports department of the Newport News *Daily Press* and stayed with the paper for a career from 1957 until his retirement in 1991. He covered William and Mary intercollegiate sports teams, including its football program, and wrote columns from 1958 until 1987. He also was president of the Virginia Sports Writers and Sportscasters Association in the 1970s.

Moskowitz grew up in Mount Vernon, New York. He received a master's degree in journalism from the University of Missouri. Prior to coming to Virginia, he worked on newspapers in St. Joseph, Missouri; Terryville, Connecticut; and Shreveport, Louisiana. After retiring from the *Daily Press*, he has worked for the *Yorktown Crier*, where he has won several significant writing awards.

He has also worked as part-time sports information director at Christopher Newport University and the Newport News Apprentice School. He has been official scorer for the Norfolk Tides, Class AAA International League, since 1993.

Charles M. Holloway was director of university communications for the College of William and Mary from 1982 until 1985. During the 1960s and 1970s, he served as director of information and corporate communications for the College Board in New York. Prior to that, he worked in Washington, D.C., for the National Education Association and then became special assistant to the U.S. Commissioner (now Secretary) of Education.

After retiring from William and Mary, he established his own writing and consulting firm and has written for a variety of national and state publications. In 1987, he completed a book, *Profiles in Achievement: Eight Outstanding People Who Made Education Their Springboard to Success*, which was published by Macmillan and the College Board.

Holloway holds degrees from the University of California at Berkeley and Washington State University and has studied at Columbia University and in France.

The Production Staff

S. Dean Olson, production director, has been director of University Publications and University Editor at the College of William and Mary since 1974. A member of the William and Mary administration since 1967, he has served as news director, assistant to Presidents Davis Y. Paschall and Thomas Graves, Sr., and as editor of the *Alumni Gazette* and *William and Mary Magazine.* During the College's tercentenary celebration in 1993, he oversaw the production of several prize-winning publications, including *Traditions, Myths and Memories* and the *William and Mary Cookbook.*

Mary Ann F. Williamson, designer and copy editor, is a graduate of Walsh College (now University) in North Canton, Ohio. She began working in the publications office at William and Mary in November 1984 as a copy editor and proofreader and has combined those skills with a talent for design to become a desktop publishing specialist, working on projects ranging from brochures to catalogs and books. In 1996, she designed the promotional materials for the Greater Williamsburg United Way campaign.

C. James Gleason, copy photographer, is a free-lance photographer, who has taken pictures for William and Mary for more than ten years. Before moving to Virginia, he was a professor of photgraphy at Rochester Institute of Technology, where he taught four future Pulitzer Prize–winning photographers.